JIM
The Life of E.W. Swanton

JIM
The Life of E.W. Swanton

DAVID RAYVERN ALLEN

First published in Great Britain
2004 by Aurum Press Ltd
25 Bedford Avenue, London WC1B 3AT

A catalogue record for this book is available
from the British Library.

ISBN 1 85410 900 6
1 3 5 7 9 10 8 6 4 2
2004 2006 2008 2007 2005

Designed and typeset in 11/13 pt Sabon by M Rules
Printed by MPG Books, Bodmin, Cornwall

Dedicated
to those
remarkable
women who have helped
maintain
both health and sanity:

Annie
Francesca
Joanna
Lindsey
Lindsay
Briony
and
ROSEMARY

Contents

JIM
The Life of E.W. Swanton

Chapter 1

Who is Swanton, what is he?

Why write a book about someone who has written so much about himself? I had asked the question of myself even though I knew the answer. The need to do so reflected the size of the undertaking. For everything about E.W. Swanton, or 'Jim' as he was universally known, was on the large scale.

His life, the majority of which ran along conventional lines, was extraordinary. Mostly because of who and what he was and the influence he had on cricket over so many years. But just who and what was he? Where did he come from? What shaped Swanton? The desire to find out could not be stifled easily.

I cannot be sure when I first met Jim. Somehow he had always been there. An abiding image is of him ensconced magisterially in the Judgement Seat above the action. When any issue or proposed development in the cricket world needed to be resolved he would condescend from on high to deliver his opinion. The figment was not far from reality. Before we ever established personal contact I was aware of faintly disapproving looks when in his vicinity at social gatherings. As if a semi-luxuriant hirsute appendage (before the days of designer stubble) could only have been worn by an alien being. Or had I undergone some sort of transmogrification from one of the ancient archons depicted on the walls of the Long Room at Lord's? If so, surely he should have felt at ease. After all, Swanton was with cricket for a large part of the twentieth century, and he it was who had spoken first-hand to those who were involved with it in the last part of the nineteenth. As a babe in a pram, apparently, he was on the same field as 'W.G.' And certainly few beards could match that of the legendary Grace.

For a long time, even when I began to know Jim better, I did not like him. Too often there would be an abrupt departure in the middle of a conversation if somebody whom he felt was more important came into view. The averted glance over the shoulder is a common phenomenon, but Jim cultivated it beyond acceptable bounds. I was not alone in experiencing this off-putting manoeuvre. The social climbing was overt as too was his extreme snobbishness. The airs and graces accompanying his lordly manner were not calculated to endear. And yet . . . there was something about him that was compelling. At that stage I was not sure what it was. Could it have been his own inner compulsion?

We worked together several times. He invited me to contribute to his monumental *The World of Cricket*; I engaged him for broadcasts on BBC Radio. We then had a minor discord on an Award Committee. A book that should have been in strong contention for the prize had not even been read by the rest of the panel including Swanton. He as paterfamilias had more or less chosen the book he thought should be the rightful winner and presumably had persuaded the others to accept that view. I, as an unabashed newcomer, had the temerity to insist that, before a decision was reached, the unread book should at least be studied. After much fidgety debate this was agreed – reluctantly. 'I am bound to admit that I am somewhat embarrassed,' came Jim's voice from a cavernous depth. Three days later, the motions were reckoned to have been gone through. The verdict, of course, remained unaltered.

Strangely, soon after that episode I started to like Jim, and also, quite unwittingly, with him I think I had made a mark. We continued occasionally to share projects. I became aware that beneath the outward blemishes was a warmth and humanity that I had previously failed to detect; and of great kindnesses shown to those who were in trouble.

Eventually there came an opportunity to write this biography. The magnitude of the task – partly self-set, I had to admit – was almost overpowering. Here was somebody whose life symbolised practically the whole of the twentieth century. He had touched it at so many levels from a position that he had sought to attain. Along the way, perforce, he had become an icon.

Principally known as the doyen of cricket correspondents, reporting for the *Daily Telegraph*, editorial director of *The Cricketer* magazine, summarising the day's play on both radio and television, the mellifluous bass-baritone with its treacly coating reminded me of a favourite great-uncle with a partiality for Brown Windsor and Gentleman's Relish.

Cricket historian David Frith captured it succinctly when he described the Swanton voice as 'sealskin'. But the voice was only a part of the impression. There was also the manner and the content. When speaking in public, Jim would strike an imposing figure. The speech would be long on gravitas but not necessarily short on laughs. When making a sly dig he would notify his audience that he was deliberately verging on the indelicate by pursing his mouth into a sort of moue; half curl of the lip, half tongue-in-cheek. And also he would stand with his left leg half-turned inwards in a slightly affected way that did nothing towards dispelling rumours of a latent sexual ambivalence.

But ambiguity did not enter any Swanton speech or article; usually they were utterly uncurious. He was not the person to compose a symphony in grey, because he did not perform with nuance. He had made up his mind. He knew what he wanted to say. And if he projected elitism, from his pedestal he also embraced a common welfare for cricket.

All these aspects chased one another across my mind as I contemplated a journey round Swanton. It was unthinkable just to present a rehash of known facts. It had to be a voyage of discovery, an investigation of those areas which, for whatever reasons, he forbore to write about himself. Certainly one would want to present Jim's convictions, where known, in spoken or written form, in order to complement the comments of those who knew him. In that way a biography becomes a two-way mirror and gives the reader the opportunity to be a one-person jury. The term 'jury' in itself is revealing for throughout his life Jim could not help but create contention. But it had to be a balanced and rounded portrait, if also one with a view. Above all, there were questions which needed answering.

Here was a man whose style of writing was the same at the age of thirty as at ninety. So, even in his own time, why was he not an anachronism?

Here was a man apparently without doubts or uncertainties, or without any nervousness in social situations. So, what was the foundation of his huge self-confidence? Were there hidden insecurities? Even, incredibly perhaps, the insecurity of his security?

Here was a man apparently without any real private life until the age of fifty. And from then on, a seemingly blissful marriage for forty years. Where was the private person? Was the interior existence indistinguishable from the all-but-impenetrable public exterior? What was his emotional being?

Here was a man, of great convention, of insistent formality and immaculate dress, and with a love of grandeur, who spent three and a half years amidst the squalor and degradation of POW camps on the notorious Thailand–Burma 'Death' Railway. How on earth did he cope? What did he do? How was he affected by the awful experience, and what was the effect on his life?

Here was a man, a stereotypical Establishment figure – MCC, Lord's, the *Daily Telegraph,* High Church Christianity – who relished hobnobbing with royalty, prime ministers, governors-general and the great and good, and who enjoyed an archetypal snobbery. What would his response today have been to the lack of deference shown to those in authority? And indeed, to Islam arguably becoming a more vibrant religion than Christianity? Where was the small child inside the big man?

Here was a man, who planned, choreographed and directed practically everything with which he was involved from tours with cricket teams to his own funeral. What drove him to do so? Why should he want to?

Faced with these factors the previous two biographies I had written seemed, in retrospect, remarkably uncomplicated. I had never met Sir Aubrey Smith, who died in 1948, and therefore much of the information about him had been gleaned through documentary evidence, interviews with the few remaining survivors from his heyday and in particular long conversations with his daughter, Honor Cobb, who, at the moment of writing, is only a few weeks away from her one hundred and second birthday.

With the legendary John Arlott, I was a close friend. I knew all about John and had worked and socialised with him continually over twenty years. He was just what he was. The liberalism, the defiant opposition of apartheid, the effect of the deaths of James his eldest son and Valerie his second wife leading to lugubriosity, the bibulousness, wisdom, warm-heartedness and unforgettable generosity – that was the man. His strengths, weaknesses and foibles were as evident to him as to anyone else. You did not need microscopic surgery to reveal Arlott's heart. It was forever open . . .

But with Swanton essentially there was something hidden. And it was not just the hooded look countenanced in a few odd snapshots that are rather reminiscent of Marlon Brando's portrayal of Mario Puzo's Godfather, Don Corleone. Rather it was what the look might represent. Could there be something behind the front? What was it that sustained him? What did he think about when he awoke at four in the morning and found himself staring at a blank wall? Was he always so ineffaceable?

With most people, *life*, or the accident of their birth, makes them do things; their parents, their upbringing, their friends, their relationships, their random circumstances. With Swanton, did *anything* during his ninety-plus years ever really trip him up? Did he ever land flat on his face and find himself forced to start again?

I cannot pretend that what follows necessarily will be the whole Swanton, even though the parameters of his life are generally known. To try to record every encounter and incidental happening over ninety-two summers would lead to a tome of encyclopaedic proportions and, more importantly, would endanger the object of this exercise, which is to search for the real man. As has been said, in terms of whom Jim met and what he did, he himself has written voluminously. (And yet, for those who believe they are aware of the complete story already, we would urge them to read on.) Therefore, the intention is to set off along a broad chronological avenue, only stopping to retrace our steps in order to explore another part of Jim's considerable corpus. In the main, I will attempt to let the events of his life lead us to our own conclusions. That is not to say that an opinion will not be given along the way. Or that some of those opinions are not likely to be disagreed with by those whose thoughts have been culled and conjoined through their association with big 'Jim'. With a man who made such an individual impact that is inevitable.

Every author knows only too well the excuses that can be engaged to avoid beginning a book. And I suppose this introduction basically is just one more plea for exemption. Oh, dear! Really, there is no reason now not to start . . .

Chapter 2

Preparation for Life

When asked about his early life Jim was always a touch impatient. And furrowed brows accompanied the impatient touch when questions revolved around family rather than career. 'I stick to my contention that in most cases the interval between the cradle and adolescence is best taken as read unless it has been in any important respect extraordinary', he wrote in *Follow On*. Was that defensiveness simply a matter of regarding his childhood as unimportant – 'of scant interest', as he once put it to me – or was it something more? Could it have been an embarrassment about the circumstances of his background? Were the juvenile images locked away so removed from the position he eventually attained and indeed the way he liked to think of himself, that he much preferred to airbrush them out of existence? As if these memories actually belonged to somebody else and that somebody was a person he did not care to recognise. If so, he would not be the first to have felt that way. The changes wrought in the twentieth century, technological, economic and particularly sociological, were so great that almost anybody who lived through virtually its entirety could experience a disrupted sense of quiddity.

And yet, staring out from many of his childhood photographs there is a hint of the haughty look we came to know so well, prompting the thought that already he had taken cognisance of who he was and what he wanted to be.

Jim, or, to follow the letter of the birth certificate, Ernest William Swanton, was born on 11 February 1907 at 64 Vancouver Road, just off Catford Hill. In later life Jim would always give his birthplace as Forest Hill and while technically that might be correct, the boundary division between the districts at that point is a matter of only a few yards and one can imagine that the name Catford sounded a bit too 'sarf Lunnon' for Jim's finer sensibilities. To be fair, he was brought up just on the right side of the line and many with strong county allegiances preferred to think of that part of south-east London as a north-western extremity of metropolitan Kent, notwithstanding its unremarkable suburban landscape of moderately sized Victorian villas and green parks. Essentially, at that time Forest Hill was quiet, respectable and unpretentious with inhabitants who tended to be unpretentious, respectable and quiet and neither appeared the sort to be exactly waiting to help the police with their inquiries.

The Swantons had lived thereabouts for some time. Jim's father William was denoted as a clerk on the marriage register at his betrothal to Lillian (sometimes Lilian) Emily Wolters on 28 April 1906 at the parish church of St George's, Perry Hill and she was put down simply as spinster. And it was in a semi-detached residence at 19 Perry Hill – a long throw away from the church – that the young couple were to start to bring up their family. At the time of their marriage both were twenty-seven, Lillian, who was always called Lill, being fifteen days the elder. Her father and his forebears were German, from the industrial city of Dortmund in the Ruhr Valley. Papa, namely Heinrich Lucian Wolters, described as a merchant, was the eldest of nine children of a head teacher, choirmaster and precentor at the cathedral of St Reinold, whose spire is the symbol of the city. Wolters had moved to England, married an English girl, Eliza Sarah Burrage, and was naturalised in 1882. Their five children, including Lillian, who was the youngest and the only daughter, were born in England and were British subjects.

On the paternal side Jim's great-grandfather, grandfather and, as has been seen, father, were all called William, their professions being respectively Chief Officer of the London Salvage Corps; commercial clerk/brush manufacturer/cashier; and, eventually, stockbroker. Grandfather William had married Elizabeth Ann Westover, the daughter of a grocer, Friend 'Wendy' Westover, in 1875 and at the time of the birth of their son (Jim's father) four years later, were living at 15 Brookbank Road, Lewisham, very near to a cricket ground which, as can be surmised, perhaps was not insignificant to future events.

The Westovers had Irish/American connections; as did the Swantons, who possessed one branch line which, in the first part of the twentieth century, delivered a somewhat eccentric character called 'Holy' Swanton. 'Holy', obviously called thus because of his fervent religious leaning, farmed on the north bank of Cork harbour where he kept an astonishingly large collection of Alvis cars corralled within a stockade of bamboo sticks. As for the Westover side, Elizabeth (Jim's grandmother), by faith a Quaker, was described by her great-grandson Martin Nelson as 'a fine old lady, impressively built, big-boned and not dissimilar in size to her grandson'.

Jim became 'Jim' at a very early age. His mother, perhaps hoping that her young son would not reflect the conventional Atticism of 'Ernest by name, earnest by nature' – she was after all, a local secretary of the National Society for the Prevention of Cruelty to Children – dispensed with his Christian names altogether and dubbed him 'Jim'. The subject himself always maintained he was so called after a favourite uncle. Informed family opinion offers a different provenance. Apparently his sunny disposition in childhood was likened to the character striding out in black, red and white garb with top hat and ponytail that adorns Force Wheatflakes: *High o'er the fence leaps Sunny Jim, Force is the food that raises him.* One has to say, this account does sound more likely.

In a rare and bland revelation of his early years, Jim would acknowledge that he was always comfortably and affectionately surrounded and grew up with few limits on his behaviour other than to mind his manners, work hard at his books and wash behind his ears. His parents were dissimilar in temperament – his mother an outgoing friendly soul, warm and hospitable, his father a gentlemanly quiet man, comparatively shy and slow to anger. William, known as 'Billy' for easy identification from the previous two generations, became a fully fledged member of the Stock Exchange in 1919 as a partner with William Norton & Co. in the City and worked for that one small and rather old-fashioned firm throughout his life. He was a somewhat untypical stockbroker who seemed not always to believe in his hunches when it came to his own investments; his wife Lill would remark with some asperity, 'You seem to make money for other people but not for us.' They had met when she was working as a barmaid and were totally devoted to each other. Throughout their marriage Billy would look on in some bemusement at Lill, who was always busy organising one thing or another and espousing good causes in a practical way.

In time, the household was augmented by the arrival of two sisters for Jim: Lilian Ruth Winifred, known as 'Ruth', born in 1909, and Christine Mary, known as 'Tina', born in 1913. Ruth, the more academically inclined of the two, eventually worked as a schoolteacher and as a volunteer at a settlement in Bermondsey. As a part-time student at Goldsmiths Art School – an adjunct of the University of London – she met and later married Edmund Nelson, the highly regarded portrait painter.

Tina, having left school at sixteen and despite parental opposition, finally managed to get to the Guildhall School of Music and Drama to study acting and singing. It took her eight years to achieve that ambition, during which time she worked as a kennel maid, a nursemaid, a waitress, as an assistant in a herbalist shop and in helping to run a dress agency near Harrods in Knightsbridge. At the Guildhall she was a contemporary of Diana Churchill and often competed for the same roles. Subsequently she worked in repertory at Penge, Birmingham, Nottingham, Leeds, Sheffield and at the Everyman, Hampstead, and acted with Mona Washbourne, Basil Dignam, Noele Gordon and BBC Radio's PC49, Brian Reece. A young curate called Bill Langdon (later to become a canon) used to take his Youth Club from the local St Bartholomew's Church to the Penge Empire and wait at the stage door. Very soon Tina and he were married. But all this is skipping way ahead with the story.

Back in the blessed days of childhood the budding spirits of the siblings interacted most of the time in more or less perfect harmony. Tina, now in her ninetieth year, remembers frequently falling out of her pram when being pushed around the garden in cavalier fashion by Jim: 'He always picked me up afterwards. I don't know if you'd call that loyal. We got on very well.' There were also games of cricket in the back garden, 'I was rather fierce when batting to Jim's bowling. Invariably, I nearly knocked out the hens which were in the firing line and which I loved.' In order to save the chickens from this onslaught and maintain a supply of eggs on the breakfast table, they would sometimes scramble through the hedge and practise cricket on the adjoining Cuaco (Commercial Union) ground. Jim, in particular, had inherited his father's love of games which he in turn had inherited from his father and through their watching of cricket together on the ground at Lewisham.

At the age of five, Jim was sent to a kindergarten school in Vancouver Road close to his birthplace, run by a Miss Whatmough. Having been provided with a slate with his name and the date, May 1912, inscribed on the wooden frame, he was ushered into his first assembly: 'I remember the hymn we sang – No. 4 in the *Ancient and Modern*, 'New Every Morning is the Love', observed Jim, 'And standing next to me was a friend who didn't sing a note, one Alec

Edwards who afterwards succeeded his father as my parents' family doctor. He didn't sing because he was a Roman Catholic!'

Jim never forgot this embryonic evidence of the divide between Rome and Canterbury in 1912, and the mental pabulum was to remain with him for the rest of his days. Sixty-five years later when gathering together his reminiscences in mature reflection, he was to return to the theme:

> One may deplore the centuries old anti-Catholic prejudice and antipathy in Great Britain, in these more ecumenically-minded days mercifully growing less, but surely nothing could have been better designed to fan the flames thereof than to tell a little boy that he must not sing a hymn with fellow Christians. Isn't it significant that this tiny cause of discord – repeated, no doubt, in schools everywhere – has stuck in my mind for 60 years and more? Thank God things are better now.

The Swanton family were regular churchgoers. Whereas the three girls and their father would happily spread their favours around several of the local churches regardless of denomination, Jim and his mother would feel uncomfortable with any service other than that of the Church of England and as far as Jim was concerned, preferably high C. of E. 'He would go some distance to a higher service. It may not have been convenient, but he'd always try and go,' remarked Tina. 'It would worry him terribly if he hadn't gone to a service on a Sunday . . . I felt that if he'd had the opportunity he might have gone into the Church.' The chance to do so came, if not before, at the end of the Second World War, but by then, as we shall see, other factors held sway. Several times Jim persuaded Tina – and, in later years, her son David – to accompany him to a high church service at All Saints, Margaret Street in London: with his nephew he would take great trouble to explain the liturgy and rituals of the service.

Back during the days of the First World War, a Lutheran church was the focal point of a noticeable German community in Forest Hill and they experienced some overt hostility. Considering the terrible toll exacted on foreign shores, it was not surprising that in some quarters there was considerable intolerance, not to say persecution, of those who did not quite fit into the accepted pattern of British life.

A neighbour of the Swantons was one who was vulnerable. His name was Streit and, to ward off potential problems, he quickly had it adapted to Street. Shortly before war was declared, Lill, Jim's mother, was in the garden one evening, transfixed by a blood-red sunset. It seemed an omen. Turning to Mr Streit over the wall she said, 'This is a terrible foreboding, it must be war.'

When relating this incident Jim did not feel it necessary to disclose that he too was a scion of part-Teutonic ancestry and that years before, his maternal grandfather had likewise conveniently altered Wolters to Walters. What her feelings were cannot be imagined, but Lill Swanton must also have felt vulnerable at this time and perhaps some small trepidation found its way into the soul of her son.

She had hustled him up to bed on hearing the big munitions explosion at Silvertown near Woolwich and this had made a lasting impression on his young mind, as had the memories of the glow over north London when the Zeppelin was brought down over Cuffley and the newspaper placard in purple type announcing the 'Death of Kitchener in 1916 on the corner of Catford Hill'. There was, as well, the remembrance of indignation felt when Mr Wallace, the proprietor of a local ironmongers, enquired brusquely why his father was not away fighting in the war. Did the man not know that his beloved parent was a special constable, having been turned down for military service because of seriously deficient vision?

Billy's poor eyesight seriously limited his enthusiastic playing of cricket. He was, for many years, treasurer of Forest Hill Cricket Club and captain of their Fourth XI before being promoted to skipper the Third. His younger brother Ernest George Swanton also played for the club. 'Dick', as he was known, worked in both the motor and aircraft industry and travelled widely. He knew many motoring pioneers: Lord Nuffield, Sir William Lyons, Messieurs Renault and Lancier, and later on helped to ship the first aeroplanes to start the Australian air services.

When it came to the alfresco smoking concerts which were the highlight of the Forest Hill Club's social calendar and held in the pavilion which was specially decked out with hundreds of coloured lights, both Billy and Dick's resonant baritone voices could be heard rendering the popular ballads of the day. The local press would often name Mr W. Swanton as musical director and after the concerts there would usually be dancing on the lawn.

At the matches Lill would help with the teas. So too on occasions did Tina and a somewhat reluctant Ruth, who tended to become bored with the game. She was a pacifist and of a studious nature, whereas Tina was more extrovert and adventurous. It was during a game at Forest Hill between the club and London County in 1907 that

Jim – so he was later told – was just beyond the boundary being rocked in his pram when the great W.G. Grace made 140. Only a few months old at the time, he had no memory of the event.

After kindergarten Jim spent a few terms at St Dunstan's College, close to his home, before continuing his schooling at Brightlands College, on the corner of Dulwich Common, which is now the preparatory school for Dulwich College. Jim was a weekly boarder and remembered being released on a Saturday in May 1919, walking up the Common to the buses and trams which went to Kennington and arriving at the Oval just in time to see the Surrey side coming off the field, having been beaten by Hampshire inside two days. That briefest of brief encounters with the first-class game was not enough to dissuade him from returning to the Oval in August of the same year. Surrey were playing Yorkshire and the names of both sides were indelibly imprinted on his memory as if carved in tablets of stone. Coincidentally another doyen-to-be of the cricketing world, the now recently departed Geoffrey Howard, sometime Secretary of Surrey and Lancashire and Manager of MCC tours, made his very first visit to the Oval to see the same match. Two years later, in 1921, Jim was elected a junior member of Surrey having been proposed by a friend of his father, N.A. Knox, the famous Surrey fast bowler. He soon found himself attending schoolboy nets under the supervision of Harry Baldwin, later renowned as an umpire, and the young lad was thrilled, not only to tread the famous turf, but to be in such close proximity to some of the great players of the time, notably Jack Hobbs.

At Brightlands Jim was prominent at sport. On the cricket field he pursued the lost art of lob bowling and in a game against Clare House managed to take six wickets in an innings. Capturing the remaining four at the other end 'by varying his pace cleverly' was the best bowler at the school, K.S. Dilawarsinhji, a cousin of Duleep. A review of the season in *Brightlands Chronicle*, 1920, reports that 'Swanton the lob bowler was also quite successful at times', which appears to be rather a grudging recognition for getting overall thirteen wickets in 34.4 overs at a cost of 117 runs. As a batsman he jumped up and down the order from opener to No. 10. His top score was 17 against the Police and in thirteen innings he accumulated only 71 runs. In noting the 'characters of the XI', the *Chronicle* reporter felt that he had 'improved during the season' and was 'a fair field'.

At soccer Jim played both in the forward line and in goal. He enjoyed somewhat mixed fortunes. We read that 'Clare House pressed and from a miskick by Swanton were able to score again' and 'Swanton punched the ball away, but it rebounded off the forward into goal'. Then against Homefield 'Parker tricked the backs and scored and then with a good pass Swanton enabled him to add another!' When playing Bickley Hall 'this was rather an anxious time for Brightlands, but Swanton was brilliant in goal'. Oh well, that is all right then. With Jim in goal, the reporter never had to search for an adjective: in a match against Stratheden 'from a corner Swanton saved *brilliantly*' and then, 'Swanton in goal deserves special mention'. The review of the season reported that, 'E.W. Swanton had started the season in goal where he showed much promise. Afterwards he played forward with some success.' For Brightlands the season had been a *complete* success for they won every game.

Brightlands led to Cranleigh – eventually. First though, rather than seek entry to the nearby Dulwich College, and in order to help the family exchequer, Jim tried for an exhibition to Eastbourne College. This he just missed and so arrived by normal acceptance, although abnormally a year late, at Cranleigh in the summer term of 1921 when he was aged fourteen.

Cranleigh was one of a number of public school foundations during Queen Victoria's reign to be based on the principles of Arnold's Rugby. The idea was to cater for the rapidly expanding middle class with adequate, if not excellent, schooling. Nestling below the North Downs in Surrey, it was reached by single-track non-electrified railway. Catching the train at Waterloo Jim would have been among a milling crowd of boys, wearing his new bowler hat and a neck-chafing Eton collar with a blue serge suit. In an evocative chapter on the life of a schoolboy in his excellent history of the school, Alan J. Megahey reveals how the new arrival might find he knew nobody on the train or at the station and with sinking stomach faced a solitary walk up Pitch Hill to the school. There he would be introduced to the rites of initiation such as BRA, or 'Boot Room Afterwards', entailing an uncomfortable session in the boot room being smeared with polish and knocked about, or having to stand on a stool in the dormitory and sing a song while being pelted with fruit or anything else that came to hand.

Already he would have been allocated a house – in Jim's case, East – the geographical location giving the name to what, in effect, was a hostel. East had a reputation as the rough house, because it contained an unequal mix of day boys and boarders with the ever-present likelihood of partisan conflict. New boys had to be out of bed and with ablutions completed by 6.55 a.m. and once down in the house room they faced the invariable routines, customs and rules of every day. Cranleigh was no different in this respect to any other public school in the 1920s and what now seems a draconian existence was accepted then as the norm: one-and-a-half-hour preps during which it was forbidden to look up; half-hour drills imposed as punishments for maybe minor misdemeanours during which the culprits were required to run round the quad with arms upraised; beatings for bad work administered by either the headmaster, one Herbert Alexander Rhodes, a reverend gentleman who was short but not sweet and who had large blue and protuberant eyes, or more often by a senior prefect or house captain; and fagging, which involved running errands, brushing clothes and cleaning shoes for prefects. Jim fagged during his first term. On one occasion he apparently did not take sufficient care with his task, for which he received a caning – or bimming, to use the argot of the school.

Bullying was endemic; so were adolescent 'love affairs' between older and younger boys, which in such an exclusively male community was entirely to be expected. On one memorable day a preacher in chapel enlarged on the text 'See that you love one another', which apparently caused considerable alarm and despondency amongst the masters present who had expended a lot of time and energy trying to ensure that no such thing ever happened.

Respect, responsibility, hierarchical privilege and the minutiae of regulation and prescription governed most aspects of daily existence. Treats for the few – short cuts to the baths, jacket buttons to be undone and cravats to be discarded – were, despite their apparent triviality, highly prized; whereas the convention which, for instance, demanded chits for telephone calls by so-called 'plebs' or 'scrubs' was taken for granted. As for the ceremony at mealtimes, this had endless comedic possibilities. Megahey tells how 'The master of the week, the prefect of the week, the beakies or jims (servants) and the head jim [*our boy would have had a tough time here with his moniker, which was perhaps why throughout his time at Cranleigh he was known by friend and foe as Swanton*] all had their part to play: the ritual slamming of the door, all standing at their house tables, no talking, the saying of grace, the sitting down by order of seniority.' When the food finally arrived on the plate, it obviously did not deserve such a fanfare – tea and toke (bread), dead man's leg, cat pie, burst boil – none of which, even allowing an imaginative schoolboy licence, sounds in any way edible, even if organic. Recently snared rabbit could on occasions supplement the meagre ration, that is, if the cook could be prevailed upon to be accommodating.

Having somehow survived all this and reached bedtime, with every boy seeking his own escape route to the land of nod, whereby the three gas mantles, which cast a flickering light down the long dormitory, were extinguished with ostentatious solemnity and in total silence by a rather spooky servant called 'Dirts'.

Into this spartan compound had come Jim, unabashed, it would seem, by the prospect and the result. 'I got by at Cranleigh,' he said. 'I was not very good at anything. But I had a very good English and Latin master called G.L.N. Antrobus, a figure of formal dress and awesome dignity. He induced in me an appreciation of the derivation of the one language from the other and he it was who impressed in my lazy head the proper construction of a sentence. He gave me a respect for good English and some sort of a critical standard.'

Antrobus would appear to have been one of the few top-class teachers at Cranleigh. In 1921, Education Inspectors had reached the conclusion that while the staff were keen and 'much involved in all aspects of school life . . . they were not intellectually distinguished and their teaching methods were frankly old-fashioned'. The inspectors had also noted that the quality of the boys they taught was not high either. In order to fill the places available, the headmaster had accepted many boys of low academic attainment, which was made possible by the lack of entrance scholarships and leaving exhibitions.

Despite these handicaps, Jim passed the School Certificate in the fourth form and soon afterwards the London Matriculation as well. During his three years at Cranleigh most of the staff had remained stable – in body, if not all in mind. At least they were not short of character. Alongside the polymath 'Tum' Purvis who eventually became Canon of York, there was the archaeologist Max Machin, and 'Stinker' Hayter who called every boy by the nickname that inevitably he himself was to acquire. And then there was 'Dick' Harris, who had tried to teach young Swanton music but had found, along with many others subsequently, that sadly there were too many imperfect cadences to achieve perfect harmony. Inevitably too, there were the figures of fun, who got no more than they deserved when it came to ragging. In one commotion, Jim was a not unwilling participant.

Mr Clinton was always in difficulty getting his forms started because boys straggled in with one impertinent excuse after another. One day for a long time no boys came at all, and when they all cascaded in together, each with an excessive number of books, and plumped themselves down at their long desks, these all forthwith collapsed, so that boys and books and benches, ink, pens and the whole paraphernalia of learning subsided in an unholy tangle on the floor.

Above the chaos bleating cries arose. 'Sir' came in for a multitude of injured complaints. It was a bit thick, Sir, someone must have taken all the screws out of the desks. A joke's a joke, Sir, but this was a bit much. The clear implication was that the whole affair was Sir's own fault. No doubt at the height of the hubbub Sir's long-suffering colleague teaching next door looked in to discover what the uproar was about, and hurriedly departed, a witness to his shame, and to a story that would lose nothing in its telling in the Common Room.

How many perpetrators were there, I wonder, of this particular rag? How many screwdrivers did the job? Did anyone 'own up'? Who did the repairs? Perhaps the missing screws were 'discovered' by someone, planted in the wretched fellow's own desk. That would have been a subtle touch.

Herbert by contrast was not raggable, it was just that the sight of him 'rendering' a particular chapel solo was somehow inexpressibly funny. His lines told us how at the last day the eyes of the blind shall be opened, and the ears of the deaf shall be unstopped, and the mouths of the dumb shall sing. Little Herbert managed to convey that he himself had been suddenly released from all these dire handicaps, and that he was making the very most of the three faculties having been restored. The wide eyes and the fully opened mouth, to say nothing of the quivering beard, let themselves go in such an ecstasy of feeling that by the time he reached the next bit about the lame man leaping as an hart the congregation was reduced to helpless, silent mirth. In the end the anthem had to be tactfully dropped from the chapel calendar.

At sport Jim was in his element, if not always excelling. The school took great pride in its rugby. In 1923, on St Andrew's Field in the Michaelmas term, the tall, slender and spindly-legged Swanton would turn out for the Second XV and bury his head deep in the scrum, hoping not to be noticed by the unkempt Welsh rugby coach, Charles Gower. In the classroom Gower's scholastic attainments were not immediately obvious, nor at all times was his couth – accompanying his habit of activating the olfactory systems of the entire class with an accusation that some poor unsuspecting youngster had 'broken wind', he also had difficulties in differentiating between rotation and revolution when describing the movement of the earth – but on the rugby field he displayed nothing but skill and enthusiasm. 'I was never any good at rugger,' admitted Jim. 'I was a little bit light. I wasn't a scrummaging forward and I wasn't really very fast.'

Jim was, however, good at cricket (step forward J.G. Fawcus, founder of Cryptics Cricket Club, Frank Winsloe and E.A. Clare who all had a hand in that), although he never quite gained a place in the First XI. At that time Cranleigh had a powerful side skippered by Maurice McCanlis, who went on to captain Oxford, and the last vacancy was filled (to Jim's chagrin) by an Italian called Parlato. Young Swanton's sole appearance for the XI was against the Masters in 1924 in which he scored 33, although during that year for the Second XI in matches with Highgate School and Christ's Hospital he had made notable contributions. Four years later he made up lost ground by scoring his first hundred – 144 not out – for Old Cranleighans against Old Rossallians in a two-day match on the latter's southern tour.

During his first vacation at Cranleigh Jim had attended his first Test match – England v. Australia at the Oval. In a drawn game Phil Mead shared a big stand with Lionel Tennyson, Mead remaining undefeated with 182 not out. The match remains in posterity for one incident. Warwick Armstrong became bored with proceedings and at the fall of one wicket lay down on the outfield reading the evening paper. When reproached later by Arthur Mailey, he retorted: 'I wanted to see who we were *plying!*'

Jim enjoyed his time at Cranleigh – at least, fifty years later he said he did. Retrospective views cannot always be trusted because memory is selective. However, as an overview it was probably mostly true. If today we tend to shudder with distaste at the upbringing of our ancestors, we should not forget either that a boy at that time would have no experience by which to make a comparison or indeed any expectation that things would or could be different. Therefore, he was not disappointed.

Dispensing with these speculations on Jim's mindset, we should instead focus on his leaving of Cranleigh. A glance at the bald details of the *valete* in the School Magazine of 1924 reveals that he was a house prefect and a sergeant in the OTC – no doubt enjoying lording it over the new recruits with regimental left, right and about turns. By his own account, he spent a restful final year in the Upper Sixth reading and writing with *John O'London's Weekly* and Gardiner's *Prophets, Priests and Kings* providing stimulus. Already his thoughts had strayed to a career in journalism. University was out of the question. The cost factor was prohibitive. And anyway few from Cranleigh trod along that path. At that time most left at the age of sixteen for a career in business and a lesser number went to medical school or into the army. How Jim would come to regret deeply not having the social cachet that, in his view, university would have given. Whilst at Cranleigh, his interest in sport generally and cricket in particular had sustained him. Whether or not it would continue to do so remained to be seen.

Chapter 3

Setting out his stall

The progress from one stage to another in life can be painful – particularly when young. Security and certainty disappear, to be replaced by apprehension. The fear of saying the wrong thing, of being noticed doing something differently to the accepted norm and of inadvertently making a fool of oneself in front of strangers is unsettling for most. And yet it is difficult to envisage the teenage Jim harbouring these sensations on his first day in gainful employment.

He had arrived at Fleetway House courtesy of Daddy. Throughout his life Jim rather quaintly referred to his parents as 'Mummy and Daddy' or 'Mama and Papa'. Daddy – let us revert at once to the formality of father – shared a railway carriage not on the 8.07 to Victorloo (the term adopted by composer Sidney Torch in his London Transport Suite to embrace both South London termini) but in his case to London Bridge, with a director of the Amalgamated Press. An approach was made. 'Does the boy write at all?' enquired Tod Anderson. 'Yes,' replied 'Billy' Swanton, 'he writes a decentish sort of essay, I suppose.' Game on.

Fleetway House was the headquarters of the Amalgamated Press in Farringdon Street in the City and it was there that Jim was to spend the first three years of his working life. As general dogsbody he was expected to make the tea, teach himself to type and do the odd jobs around the office – for twenty-five bob a week. It was to be a little while, however, before he was allowed to embark on that 'decentish sort of essay'. First, he was grateful to be allocated work on a paper aimed at those who liked their reading to be middle-brow and light, *All Sports Weekly,* thus avoiding less welcome stints with

Harmsworth's Encyclopedias or *Comic Cuts* which were at opposite ends of a variety of material printed from the House.

All Sports Weekly was an ideal training ground for Jim in the fundamentals of journalism. The paper lived up to its name by being informative and conversible over a wide range of activity. For two-penn'orth every Thursday readers could generally find something in the twenty or more pages that interested them on their own favourite sport. For instance, cricket-lovers might learn of J.W. Hearne's thoughts on 'Modern Bowlers' or Surrey's Pressing Problem – can Peach fill the need? or read Arthur Mailey on the googly, which he called 'Cricket's Ugly Duckling'. In those pre-sexism days, there were also series for female readers: 'The Dancing Girl, a Tale of Test Match Cricket, being the story of Rita the Girl who saved England. A Woman's influence on the Destiny of England in Test Match Cricket.' What did our lad make of all this, I wonder?

Apart from looking after the tea cosy, Jim was soon inducted into the intricacies of sub-editing and within a few months was subbing none other than J.A.H. Catton who, under the nom de plume 'Tityrus', edited the *Athletic News Cricket Annual* either side of the First World War. Jimmy Catton's knowledge of cricket was in inverse proportion to his diminutive stature, as is evidenced in his compilation of a thirteen-volume manuscript *Dictionary of Cricketers* which now resides in the library at Lords. He was an ideal person to pass on tips of the trade and information to a young man finding his way. Not that Jim was necessarily very receptive. During the summer of 1925, Catton was providing voluminous profiles of 'Cricket Favourites' for *All Sports Weekly,* including the likes of Charlie Hallows of Lancashire and Fred Root of Worcestershire. Catton would never use one adjective when three were available; he gave the accurate impression of being paid by the word. After sending off Catton's cheque, based on the number of words ordered and received, Jim proceeded with youthful self-assurance, not to say arrogance, to cut his copy to the bone.

While with the paper, Jim was given the chance to do a couple of interviews. One was with Frank Woolley at Blackheath, the path to the great man having been cleared by a stockbroking friend of his father's, George Wood, the Kent wicket-keeper who had played for England in 1924. The other was with a figure yet to become a legend, Wally Hammond, at the Gloucestershire team's hotel in London.

Woolley was one of Jim's lifelong heroes, and having interviewed him he could at last make his very first venture into print in July 1926

at the tender age of nineteen. Written under his Christian name –
Ernest Swanton looks strange to eyes accustomed to his usual prefix
E.W. – the piece contained an error regarding the location of Lionel
Tennyson's historic 'one hundred' innings – it was at Headingley, not
Lord's. Otherwise the article was certainly 'decentish' and more than
a hint of the Swanton to come. Boldly, Jim began with verse:

> *It's good to be born*
> *At Tonbridge in May*
> *You'll say, I'll be sworn*
> *It's good to be born,*
> *For Life's at the morn,*
> *And the umpire calls 'Play'*
> *It's good to be born*
> *At Tonbridge in May.*

Perhaps it was as well that the poetic muse was not pursued . . .

By 1927 Jim was looking to feather his nest, if not fly it altogether.
Already he had been contributing articles to the *Evening Standard*,
under his own name for club cricket and under the Latin tag 'Juventus'
for pieces on schools' sport. He had discovered that, to use his own
words, 'entry to the sporting world of Fleet Street in the 'twenties lay
through a number of doors marked Saloon Bar: also up the stairs,
flanked by innumerable Spy cartoons, of the Press Club off Salisbury
Square. Then there was Anderton's Hotel – and, a little later, the
Temple Bar Restaurant where the clientele was to me of dazzling
distinction.'

By using these watering holes Jim began to make contacts. His
networking brought results. An introduction to 'Beau' Vincent and
Jack Board, both of *The Times* golfing fraternity, over a tankard of
beer in The Baynard Castle just off Printing House Square, led to an
unsigned 800 words for the paper on Old Merchant Taylors v.
Cambridge. Just by listening to him talk, *The Times*'s Sports Editor
Captain Bob Lyle knew that Swanton would not be short of a
sentence. He was, after all, of the persuasion that public school vowels
translated to the printed page with a minimum of subbing.

Emboldened – not that he needed to be – by the acceptance of more
offerings to several newspapers, mostly by way of Diary paragraphs,
Jim decided to set out his stall. With his *Evening Standard* freelance
earnings in the region of £10 a week, he wrote to them pointing
out that for a mere £13 they could command his valuable services

full-time. There would appear to be no answer to that. Fortunately for Jim there was. It came from one Stanley Tiquet who broadly welcomed the proposal 'though regretting the maximum remuneration would be £11'. And so on 1 September 1927, Jim literally went up the road from Fleetway House in Farringdon Street to 47 Shoe Lane to join the *Evening Standard* as 'rugger' correspondent. The word 'rugby' was not in vogue then and always passed Jim's lips with difficulty as he thought it rather infra dig.

Feeling flush with a salary exceeding £500 a year Jim immediately lavished over twenty per cent of it on a royal blue AC Tourer. Not yet twenty-one and still living at home, he rather fancied he was cutting quite a dash, which no doubt he was – in some quarters.

Never averse to mixing with distinguished company, he enjoyed rubbing shoulders in the press box with the 'name' correspondents of the day: the fatherly Stewart Caine and the acutely deaf Hubert Preston with his expanding ear trumpet, both of them, in turn, editors of *Wisden Cricketers' Almanack*; Harry Carson of the *Evening News*, who had impeccable manners; 'Bertie' Henley of the *Daily Mail*, who, as well as bringing a theatrical flavour and a lame leg to matches, persisted in calling Jim 'Jimmy', rather to the irritation of the recipient who, already busy establishing his position, felt it was a touch *lèse-majesté*, especially when he was spending quality time with the big boys; the inimitable Neville Cardus of the *Manchester Guardian*; Colonel Philip Trevor CBE – always CBE – of the *Telegraph*, mocked for his regular rider 'Good too, was so and so', but who, with his ever-present daughter, befriended Jim and helped bring him into the group; and Archie MacLaren, the old England captain, surrounded by pundits and who had an unbearably condescending manner when handing over his copy for young Swanton to pass on to the telephonist.

There was too, 'the rough diamond' Sidney Southerton, son of James who had played for England in the first of all Test Matches at Melbourne in 1876–77; and the extraordinarily prolific C.B. Fry, never shy of voicing an opinion and invariably accompanied by his butler Brooks who readily dispensed vintage champagne to invigorate his master's creative juices. Venturing to metropolitan grounds occasionally would be 'Old Ebor', A.W. Pullin, the swarthy, bearded sports columnist of the *Yorkshire Evening Post*, who once memorably failed to notice that Herbert Sutcliffe's opening partner was not as usual the right-handed Percy Holmes but Maurice Leyland who, of course, was a left-hander. Pullin's copy on that occasion failed to amuse his editor in much the same way as his hirsute appendage failed to hide a hot flush and an awareness of his colleagues' chuckles.

The Press corps – not that they were called that then – was demonstrably strong on personality, and to be one of them was a heady experience for the young tyro. In conversation nearly seventy years later Jim took the view that his appointment was ridiculous; there he was, not yet twenty-one, with only his Cranleigh background in rugby football, reporting on International and England Trials and commenting critically on aspirants and veterans. Admittedly there was a weekly article from W.J.A. Davies, an England stand-off half of distinction, and contributions from Norman Hillson, an Old Rugbeian who was essentially a foreign correspondent, but there is no doubt that the engagement of Jim seems to have been made without a great deal of forethought or care. The pervading sense of cavalier amateurism ruling all areas of sport and its coverage in those days which are now nearly out of living memory is not without its attraction. It did not mean the results were not professional. In this era of specialisation the mere thought that any one man – say, Howard Marshall, the distinguished broadcaster, who was shortly to be within Jim's orbit – could speak and write with authority on areas as diverse as cricket, rugby, boxing, athletics, angling, slum housing, religion and state occasion is totally untenable. And yet Marshall and others with equally wide interests thought nothing of doing so, nor did their listeners and readers think it strange. The media – another term not then in use – was more cottage than industry and perhaps none the worse for that.

Trying to discover a cohesive pattern to Jim's life in the late 1920s and 1930s is difficult if only because, in retrospect, it seems to have consisted of constant restless activity. Hearing his thoughts in person, marvelling at his memory of events in detail, reading his observations on people, place and occurrence is to have the flavour of an era tasted by proxy. This, it can be seen, was the time that fashioned Swanton, that honed his views and cultivated his responses. But we should not expect that by attempting to disentangle the complicated mosaic of his existence during these years there will be revealed a sense of direction; because in the logical sense there was not one. Dabbling in this, trying that and testing something else, obviously here was a young man on the move. But his path strayed down several cul-de-sacs before reaching the junction of the Second World War. The common factor in all that he did was a driving ambition (which he tried to disguise) and a thirst for all kinds of experience; a cultivation of acquaintance, of what might be called 'non-friends'; and a taste for the good things on offer with a determination to enjoy the freedoms that many of the leisured classes had in those days, even if he was not one of them. In other words he adopted a style, 'the grand manner', part an unconscious component of his make-up since childhood and part acquired consciously as a means to being somebody. It was, perhaps, no more than could be expected.

We left Jim in the company of the established games reporters of the day. Some of that company and others in the journalistic firmament were to prove useful in furthering the career of young Swanton. As time went on, Jim became something of a social centipede and astutely managed to combine work and pleasure in a way that made them indistinguishable. On one day he might be one of the coterie surrounding the eminent literary critic and poet Jack Squire at the 'Temple Bar Restaurant' before shortly being found on the football field letting in far too many goals for 'The Invalids' despite having the capable defensive assistance of J.B. Priestley at right-back. A request for an article from Squire in his editorial role at *London Mercury* was then likely to be forthcoming – that is, assuming that he had forgotten that Swanton was responsible for his side's defeat. (An unserious observation because Squire was the most benevolent and charitable of men.)

And then on another day, having left home, Jim might be found putting together his pieces in a room he had rented above a public house in Dorking, before undertaking an afternoon game of hockey for Dulwich (it was, according to his close friend and fellow Cranleighan, Vivian Cox, a sport he had looked down on at school) to be followed by an energetic three-setter of real tennis at Hampton Court in the evening. Coverage of the hockey match would then be incorporated into a sporting column for an appropriate magazine or paper which just might have been under the stewardship of the man with whom he had played *jeu de paume*. There was nothing really wrong with all of this – networking is the world's second oldest profession – but it did repel some who disliked the manoeuvring being so overt. Having said that, in Jim's mind it was the only way to climb as many ladders as possible at the same time – social and vocational acclivity Swanton-style. In time, he was to make it into virtually an art form.

But to balance the pendulum, it is only fair to add that Jim was not too overcome by his sense of self-awareness to indulge in moments of levity. J.B. Morton, 'Beachcomber' of the *Daily Express*, whose columns on the exploits of Captain Foulenough and Doctors Strabismus and Smart-Alick entertained his thousands of readers, was wont to enjoy liquid luncheons. On one afternoon as he made a dilatory return to his office he was accompanied by Jim: 'I bowled some sort of improvised ball at Johnny, who was guarding with a walking-stick the lamp post at the junction of Fleet Street and Chancery Lane,' wrote Jim. 'When the policeman on point duty strode solemnly over to move us on Johnny said: "What's the matter, officer, isn't my bat straight?"'

In the summer of 1928 Jim took another step forward. He began reporting on cricket for the *Evening Standard*, as second string to his erstwhile provider at Amalgamated Press, J.A.H. Catton. (One wonders whether Catton was mischievous enough to practise a touch of role-reversal and occasionally supervise Jim's copy – to have done so, no doubt, would have caused a few splutters in the cornflakes.) The addition to his duties meant that Jim could now justify a more regular attendance at prime fixtures. His first clear memory of Test cricket had been at the historic Oval Test of 1926 when he had sneaked away from work to see Hobbs and Sutcliffe help win back the Ashes – he had arrived a few moments before Hobbs was bowled for 100, but if modern technology had then been available he would have not seen him at all as slo-mo treatment of archive footage shows that Hobbs had failed by inches to make his ground earlier in the innings.

Memory is selective and it is no surprise that Jim with his particular sense of priorities would juxtapose chronologically the Eton and Harrow game at Lord's in 1928 with the feats of Don Bradman on his first tour of Britain in 1930. The first event was primarily a social occasion, albeit the result mattered to those involved. The perambulation of the ground with, over the two days, 40,000 people *en grande tenue*, men and boys peacocking in morning dress and every woman and girl displaying her plumes, was an extraordinary sight. Essentially it was all about the toffs demonstrating their tribal loyalties. The second event was a strictly professional and hard-nosed run-getting crusade in which any fripperies and sideshows were ignored by the central character.

In 1930 Jim was elevated to the ranks of Test reporters. He missed the first Test Match against the Australians at Trent Bridge by being deputed to sub in the office. The second Test at Lord's was the first he ever wrote about and was considered by him to be one of the best he ever witnessed. Seated in the press annexe at ground level among the public seats under the balcony of the Grand Stand, he went through

an emotional gamut, enthusing, suffering and hoping, during an epic
encounter which eventually went Australia's way by seven wickets. To
the end of his life Jim could recall cameos of the game:

> I can readily summon the sights and scenes of those four days in the
> sun: the peerless stroke past cover-point with which Woolley despatched
> his first ball for four: 'Tim' [Tom] Wall's catch right down on his boots,
> standing nominally in the gully but actually halfway to third man, that
> brought Frank's marvellous 41 to an unlucky close: 'Duleep' cutting
> and glancing on that first day; the little old King, with grey bowler, big
> button-hole and high walking-stick, shaking hands with the players in
> front of the pavilion; Hammond pouching a slip catch off the very first
> ball afterwards; the Don's unhurried entry into the sunlight; his swift
> advance down the wicket to hit the next one, from White, full pitch up
> to the Nursery Clock-tower; the board at close of play showing
> Australia 404 for two, last man (Woodfull) 155, number 3 155 not out;
> Bradman's further relentless plunder on the Monday; the wry joke of an
> improvised '7' having to be found for the Tavern scoreboard before the
> declaration at 729 for six; Hobbs being bowled out of the rough round
> his legs by Grimmett; Woolley smacking him for four, only to find that
> he had brushed the stumps with the back of his pad; Chapman
> apparently 'farming' Grimmett during his partnership with Allen and
> carting him lustily every so often into the Mound Stand; the excitement
> when Robins' spin on the dusty fourth afternoon for about half-an-
> hour raised feverish expectations; the splendour of the Maharajah Jam
> Sahib of Nawanagar, otherwise 'Ranji', in full Eastern dress, jewels
> flashing from his tunic and turban, holding a sort of levée behind the
> pavilion.

Over sixty years later Jim was sitting with John Major at Lord's and
astounded the Prime Minister with his retention of the individual shots
of Bradman's assault on the England bowling.

> I put it down to the fact that he concentrated fiercely at cricket, noting
> individual actions, in order to write accurately about the game in the
> following day's newspapers; later he incorporated the same stories in
> his lectures, and in his books, as well as in subsequent conversations.
> I concluded that the reiteration of these vignettes fixed them firmly in
> his memory, which was why talking to him about cricket was like
> entering an Aladdin's cave of history.

In correspondence between Bradman and Swanton years afterwards and in answer to a question from Jim as to whether the 254 was his greatest innings, the Don replied, 'I don't think it is possible to say without qualification that it was my greatest innings. On a purely technical level I suppose so, but in value to the side . . .'

In his mid-twenties, Jim was now the accepted cricket and rugby correspondent of the *Evening Standard*, writing on the New Zealand tour during the cheerless wet summer of 1931 and the Indian visit of the following year under the nominal leadership of the Maharajah of Porbander with his fleet of white Rolls-Royces in tow. In May of that year Jim had been told by his sports editor that he would be going to Australia in the winter to cover the MCC tour. But that was before the well-documented and unfortunate episode at Leyton. In mid-June after watching Holmes and Sutcliffe accumulate run after run for Yorkshire against Essex until they finally reached the new record first-wicket stand of 555, Jim was last in the queue for the one public telephone. The Press Association and the other two London 'evenings', the *News* and *Star*, were ahead of him and for once Jim's renowned pushiness was to no avail. He missed the edition. The humiliating result was that the *Standard* decided to send S. Bruce Harris, the lawn tennis correspondent, to Australia instead. For Jim it was heartbreaking. 'I had lost the chance to become the first journalist ever to have been sent on an overseas tour by an individual newspaper', he wrote.

In retrospect the decision seems harsh. Admittedly the *Standard* might have felt that Jim's relative inexperience would prove too great a handicap, on the basis that 'If he can't get us a story from a few miles away, what will he do at the other end of the world?' But to send somebody who knew little about cricket even if he did have greater news savvy smacks of desperation.

Were there other factors at work? When speaking to the author, the late Geoffrey Howard, one-time secretary of both Surrey and Lancashire who managed an MCC tour to Australia in 1954–55 and who played with and against Jim in club cricket in the 1930s, remarked, 'He wasn't the most liked young man.' Which, given Geoffrey's perpetual benignity, is revealing.

Allowing a youthful brashness the *Standard* simply could have decided that young Swanton's imperious manner would not be their most diplomatic tool. They also needed him at home as the rugby correspondent. End of story.

But, of course, it was not the end of the story, more the start of a saga. And, unfortunately, one with which Jim was not directly involved. With

Harris becoming England captain Douglas Jardine's virtual mouthpiece during the furore over 'Bodyline' and no really independent English voice, and with only criticism from Warwick Armstrong in the *Evening News* and factual description from Reuter's Gilbert Mant, another Australian, and the *Star*'s Jack Hobbs (ghosted by Jack Ingham), Jim forever wondered whether he could have influenced events. Which on the face of it seems a preposterous thought.

Certainly anti-Bodyline comment in the *Standard* might have led to an earlier change of climate in England and possibly have encouraged MCC to tone down their initial response by cable. If Jim had been writing on the spot, conceivably he could have claimed an influence if that had happened. But to suggest, as he did more than once in conversation, that a quiet word in Jardine's ear might have persuaded him to alter his tactics is surely to enter the realms of fantasy. Why on earth would the ruthless and inflexible MCC skipper entertain for a moment the opinions of someone he would probably privately view at that time as a couple of stages further on from cub reporter? And yet Jim, who was on first-name terms with many of the county captains who were of a similar age, and who, as we shall see, was not slow in giving his opinions on tactics and policy to future England captains, believed possibly he could have persuaded him to do so. It all sounds extremely unlikely and, of course, we shall never know. We do know of Jim's understandable pique at not having had the chance to change cricket history.

In August 1933 Jim embarked – as a player – on the *Empress of Britain* for a seven-week tour of Canada, the USA (in effect, Chicago and New York) and Bermuda with furniture magnate Sir Julien Cahn's side. Although an indifferent player himself, Cahn was a great patron of country house cricket. On his beautifully kept grounds at West Bridgford, Nottingham and at Stanford Hall at Loughborough where he lived, he would entertain touring sides of both international and local level. Cahn had his eccentricities. With the visiting team accommodated in the 'Cricketers Wing' of his mansion, he would sometimes practise on the Wurlitzer organ in the 350-seat theatre below at unearthly hours of the night, which ensured that his opponents would not be seeing the ball too clearly on the following day. He also had a predilection for practical jokes. At the dinner table a strategically placed 'whoopee cushion' would often discomfit unsuspecting guests. As a prey to his own superstitions he was known to turn around three times before passing through a doorway and always put on his right inflatable pad first when preparing to bat. At times when a wicket had fallen unexpectedly these operations took place virtually simultaneously. An onlooker once likened the performance to 'an ostrich doing a courtship dance'.

The pneumatic pads had been blown up by his butler, but although cumbersome they were a definite asset when it came to getting leg-byes. Most of these runs off Sir Julien's pads were added to his score, as the umpires suffered from a convenient touch of temporary myopia. After all, it was but a small return for his hospitality.

In some games on this North American tour Cahn's side played teams with greater numbers; nevertheless they won sixteen of the twenty matches and drew the rest. The tourists included four Test cricketers and one eventually to become so – Denijs Morkel of South Africa; Roger Blunt of New Zealand; Walter Robins, Ian Peebles and Paul Gibb of England. On a personal level, Jim scored fifties in Ottawa, Chicago and New York.

Jim had met Cahn initially through Peebles who played for the millionaire's side irregularly. (Cahn had soon become aware of the potential publicity to be gained by having Jim as one of his team.) And Jim had met Peebles several years earlier through being sent by the *Evening Standard* to get his acquiescence to a series of articles for the paper. At the time Peebles was acting as secretary and coach at the Aubrey Faulkner School of Cricket at Walham Green in West London. His Test career was soon to finish – he played in thirteen Test Matches for England – but his smooth rhythmical run-up, zippy leg-break and dip at the end of the flight was still in evidence for Middlesex.

It did not take long for Ian – a son of the manse in Elgin, Scotland – and Jim to become bosom buddies. They began to share rooms at 3 Grosvenor Cottages just off Sloane Square in London, although the stay was not protracted. On a cold day the walls were streaming with damp and to their dismay they discovered the abode had been built over a plague pit.

At 8 King's Bench Walk, in the Temple, there was no such problem and they were to remain there with intermissions until the outbreak of war in 1939. Despite their Temple residence being 'un-plagued', it was not devoid of peculiarity. An exquisite exterior was matched with an antiquated interior. A conspicuous daily reminder of the longevity of some of the fixtures and fittings was seeing the hot water being directed by an ancient piece of garden hose from an even more ancient gas geyser into a copper-stained bath. Sharing these amenities in the Temple with Swanton and Peebles was an eventually-to-be-renowned figure in the golfing world, Henry Longhurst. Longhurst was another who was born to travel first-class but lacked the price of a ticket. A golfing Blue at Cambridge led to celebrated scribing in the *Sunday Times*, a period in the army as, in his own words, 'Learner-Gunner 1737288 Temporary Acting Unpaid Supernumerary Lance-Bombardier, running about Blackpool sands in little knickers waving a great bamboo pole', followed by a seat in the House of Commons as the Hon. and Gallant Conservative Member for Acton, then much gap-filling adventure as a globe-trotting writer and finally coming up the home fairway as a legendary golf commentator. In a strange way, he could be thought of as Swanton's equivalent with the little white ball. But most of this, of course, was yet to come.

At King's Bench Walk the three musketeers were mothered to perfection by Mrs Mabel Smallbone whose size was suited perfectly to her surname. Every day she would journey from her home at 11 Rossetti Gardens, Battersea, 'to go and do my young men'. The warmth she generated was reciprocated many years later in the 1970s when Jim somehow rediscovered her, now aged seventy-five and living with her husband in a Chelsea backwater, and on behalf of her erstwhile charges presented her with a suitably inscribed clock as a rather belated memento.

The landlord of their Temple lodgings was a retired barrister with mutton-chop sideboards called W.H.S. Truell. Truell was a Dickensian character whose florid handwriting was to be seen in idiosyncratic letters enquiring about his fifteen guineas a month. The letters always started: 'Dear Mr Swanton, In re the rental . . .' which became a pet phrase that always guaranteed a laugh.

Whenever cash flow became strained they would sub-let the rooms to rich Americans and move in with friends. During the 1930s Jim led a somewhat peripatetic existence. He rented for one winter No. 5 Holywell, Oxford, and then the next, Palace Yard at Sonning-on-Thames in the Berkshire countryside. He also for a time moved into King Street, St James's, SW1, as paying guest to the editor of the *Illustrated Sporting and Dramatic News,* James Wentworth-Day. Wentworth-Day incidentally was married to Nerina Shute, a film journalist, who, after their divorce, became Mrs Howard Marshall. A pioneering figure in many branches of broadcasting, Marshall, of course, was a colleague of Jim's in the cricket commentary box. Eventually Marshall's marriage to Nerina fell apart after she admitted an attachment to the home help, a young French girl, and acknowledged her own bisexuality. All very confusing, if you are not paying attention.

As well as his regular output for the *Standard* Jim was, by the early 1930s, a contributor to the *I.S. and D.N.* He wrote three series for the magazine which made considerable impact: 'Great Schools in Sport', 'Pavilion Parade', and 'County Cricket Club Histories'. Wentworth-Day was kindly but quite specific in his requirements:

> My dear James, Forgive me if I seem a little exacting in my criticisms of copy but I have to watch the printer's bill for corrections pretty closely, so if you could see that all copy before being sent out is well and truly punctuated and that all the esquires, unless they merit it, are turned into Mr's and other small points, I would be glad. It really does make a difference of so many pence per line.

Besides taking Swanton mildly to task, Wentworth-Day did enjoy fun at his expense too. Here is his editorial introduction to 'Pavilion Parade' in April, 1937:

> That literary fay of the cricket and rugby fields, Mr E.W. Swanton, here gambols into print in a new and spring-like guise. During the course of an ill-spent youth, this pillar of the Old School Tie has contrived to build up not only an extensive and peculiar knowledge of the public schools of England, but a not inconsiderable reputation as an almost first-class cricketer. As a presumably paid agent wrote of him not long ago: 'He puts precept most charmingly into practice and shows an ease of footwork that belies his contour.' Mr Swanton's notes and comments on the games of the week and the moving matters of public schools sport will, we trust, introduce a new, more personal, and hitherto lacking, feature into this newspaper. Readers who wish to earn immortality should address notes, comments, criticisms and contributions to him – or about him – at this office, 32 St. Bride Street, E.C.4.

Jim's series on 'Great Schools in Sport' ran for three years and included nearly a hundred well illustrated articles covering seventy-odd schools. 'I visited many, but not by any means all of them, finding Headmasters and their sporting assistant-masters extremely co-operative,' wrote Jim. Not surprisingly, they were particularly cooperative in the smaller, less illustrious schools where they needed the oxygen of publicity. Considerable research was involved in the project and not all of it was undertaken by the schools themselves. Jim's vast knowledge of social and sporting distinction through alma mater to 'varsity and beyond was of inestimable value. Here was the oracle whose remembrance repertoire interrelated place, person and achievement – knowing instantly who had gone where, their kith and kin and what they had done. His ability to write easily and quickly, marshalling facts into his own conversational prose, was a major factor in the series' success.

Some have speculated whether Jim received some kind of homoerotic charge from all this time spent watching young manhood in athletic activity. The aesthetic beauty of white flannel on green sward no doubt had its attractions in the pursuit of what is known as the Corinthian ideal; handsome youth seeking the well-being of the whole body through pure thought, noble spirit and princely deed as they assumed the *toga virilis*. Well, that principle of perpetuating the subliminal self sounds fine until one remembers that not all followers of St Paul practised the celibate state. Nevertheless in the 1930s there was a certain sort of bond and brotherhood on the playing fields that was entirely innocent and is very difficult to define. Much of it emanated from behavioural observances – manners, courtesy and respect from one to another. Sadly, it seems to have vanished today.

Meanwhile, back in the homestead Henry Longhurst was perhaps ruminating on a book of philosophical reminiscence. A chapter entitled 'The Old School Tie' in *It was Good While it Lasted*, which was published in 1941, addresses the subject which then dared not speak its name.

> A boy learns at least as much of his education from the close company of other boys as he does from those employed to instruct him. Incidentally I believe that no friendship between man and woman ever began to approach the intensity of the fellow feeling which boys may develop for one another. Which brings us automatically to that dark subject without which no discussion on school life is complete, a subject of which none of your professional 'educationalists' can bring themselves to face the existence. Yet the problem prevails, and should be faced, in schools, in prisons, in the Army, in the Navy – in fact, in any congregation of males habitually denied the pleasures of female companionship.
>
> This, I hope you will agree, is a topic on which a person may legitimately write without personal experience. For myself I have not strayed from the normal path for the good reason that I have never been tempted or inclined to do so. I had the good luck to be born with no 'queer' streak in my make-up. Others, through no fault of their own, were not so fortunate.

It was Longhurst, in one of his books, who commented that the *Daily Express* was a newspaper that hated public schools. Whether that was a factor in Jim's invention of a nom de plume in 1935 when, for that year only, he reported Tests for their sister paper the *Sunday Express* is unlikely to be uncovered. He could not remember himself why he chose the name Michael James. Possibly it was in order not to be seen too obviously putting an excess of eggs into a couple of baskets.

Apart from the *Evening Standard* and *Illustrated Sporting and Dramatic News*, Jim provided material for *The Field* and *The Cricketer* magazines and was broadcasting on rugby and cricket for the BBC (his experiences in the world of the wireless are dealt with in the next chapter). All this burgeoning activity had, however, not gone down well with the Sports Editor of the *Standard*, a forthright Yorkshireman called Clucas. For some time he and Jim had not seen eye to eye and after another positive exchange of views in 1938 Jim's contract was severed. Not that it mattered too much, because he continued to work for the paper on a freelance basis and at around the same time came an invitation from a hugely respected figure in the cricket world, Harry Altham, to assist in the updating of the definitive *A History of Cricket*. This was an unexpected accolade – Jim had first met Altham some years before when playing for Eastbourne at the Saffrons – and he was quick to reply in the affirmative to the following dispatch:

Chernocke House
Winchester
Hants
14th February, 1938

My dear Jim,

I don't know what you will say to the following proposal, but at least it can do no harm to make it.

Allen and Unwin, who published my 'History', have been at me for a year past to bring it up to date. The old edition is completely sold out, and it is, I believe, almost impossible to obtain a copy second-hand. They seem pretty confident that a new edition at a lower price should enjoy a steady sale for some years to come.

Now I simply do not see how I am going to effect this revision myself, or rather the writing of the new chapters necessary to bring the book up to date, for of actual revision work there would, I think, be little necessary. I cannot possibly do it in term time, and I cannot in justice to my family bury myself for a fortnight or so in the holidays. In my last letter to the publishers I asked them whether they would consider me offering you the work involved. They wrote today welcoming the suggestion, and asking me to get in touch with you. The whole question of payment involved would, of course, have to be discussed between us, but there is first the question as to whether you find the idea palatable at all. You know the book yourself, and my idea would be to bring it up to date on the lines that I have followed throughout, i.e. by dealing separately with (1) International cricket; (2) County cricket; (3) Gentlemen players from the Varsity; (4) Public Schools. I don't think that we could work on the same scale as I did in 1900–14. There has been so much cricket, especially international, that the edition would be unwieldy.

I should like to have the last say in any general verdict on major issues, e.g. body line, and the policy of the MCC, but I don't think that we should often be at variance.

If you would entertain this proposal, would you come down and spend a night with me, and we can go into details together. The publishers are anxious to produce the book by the early summer, as they seem confident that there would be a considerable sale for it straight away.

All good wishes
Yrs ever
Harry Altham

The result of a productive collaboration was available to the public later that same year.

Much of Jim's writing, of course, centred on rugby and there were very few important games in London and the south-east that he had not seen during his job with the *Standard*. Two of the most thrilling occasions occurred during the Third All Blacks tour of 1935–36 when both England and Wales won memorable victories. Obolensky's try at Twickenham and the epic win by a single point at Cardiff Arms Park became indelible memories. Writing of the Welsh triumph, 'Such a release of pent-up emotion I have never known. One seemed afterwards not to be walking from the ground to the sanctuary of the Angel Hotel so much as transported there on the uplifted spirits of the crowd'. In the Welsh XV on that day was Vivian Jenkins at full back, who was also an Oxford Cricket Blue, then soon to be Jim's colleague in the Press posse. As the team celebrated by getting uproariously drunk back at the hotel and with the manager out of sight, Jenkins was one of several whose broad shoulders were supposed to have helped a grand piano make an unexpected clanging, fortissimo descent of a spiral staircase. Aged ninety-two, he remembered attending an International match at Murrayfield in the 1950s on behalf of the *Sunday Times* when fog completely obscured the press-box eyrie at the top of the stand. 'It was Jim who managed to persuade a Scottish Rugby Union official to shift us into a couple of ring-side seats, so that we could see the match. All highly irregular like, but he was the No. 1 man.'

As if he had not enough to do, throughout this period Jim had been match secretary to the Old Cranleighans RFC. Playing for OCs was his old friend – in terms of age differential, perhaps it should be young friend – Vivian Cox. A brilliantly individual scrum-half with English Schoolboys, Cox had international potential, but instead turned to hockey, won a Blue while at Jesus, Cambridge, and then played four times for England in the same season.

He was to go on and have an eventful war. From being a member of a trawler mine-sweeping crew he rose meteorically to man the Admiralty War Rooms and then, after Pearl Harbor, sailed with Churchill to Washington. When in the White House map room, Roosevelt was not slow to recognise his expertise after he quickly identified a few specks on the atlas as the Marianas, an island group in the Western Pacific which were to be seized by American forces in 1944. Roosevelt then craftily managed to negotiate Cox's transfer as a naval attaché. Churchill was not best pleased. 'I suppose you've taken this job to get away from me!' was his testy response. But Cox's war was not finished. Another transfer to Admiral Fraser's staff entailed flagship duty on Malta and Arctic convoys and then being part of Pacific operations in the Philippines and at Okinawa.

After the war, Cox was to become a sought-after film producer with *Father Brown*, *The Prisoner* and *Bachelor of Hearts* among his credits. But ultimately he became disillusioned with the film industry and returned to Cranleigh – only this time as a member of the staff.

Vivian had first met Jim in 1927. As a twelve-year-old in the preparatory school he had painfully chiselled out the runs on an old-fashioned scoring block during two long innings in a match on the Jubilee ground between Gentlemen of Essex and E.W. Swanton's XI. Apparently the scorebook had gone missing. For his endeavour Jim tipped him five shillings – a substantial sum for a schoolboy in those days. The money did not last – the tuck shop was not far away – but their friendship did.

Having left school Vivian would call on Jim and Ian at King's Bench Walk and the three, sometimes joined by Henry Longhurst, would go out on the town. As premonitions of war spread wider, one of the most comical productions ever to be mounted on the London stage became an irresistible attraction. A play called *Young England* by an octogenarian author named Walter Reynolds was a reincarnation of the style and language of the most lurid Victorian melodrama. As Jim remarked, 'it was far too bad to be missed'.

Longhurst picks up the story:

It was all about Boy Scouts and Girl Guides and the wicked Scoutmaster robbing the safe in the Scouts' Hut and the even more wicked Mayor evicting the widow, and somehow the Duchess came into it too. What the presumably sophisticated first-night audience must have thought of it I do not know but the play could hardly have survived half a dozen performances if some unknown wag had not called out some ribald comment on the second night. Others followed, and by next day it had got round the clubs of London that there was going on at the Victoria Palace something that must be instantly seen before they took it off. Peebles was in, I think, on the third night and in the end became so word-perfect that he could conduct a whole conversation exclusively in quotations from the play. The plot was melodramatic rubbish of a high order but its success – it ran for months – was due to the splendid way in which the principals, John Oxford as Jabez Hawke the wicked Mayor, Guy Middleton as the scoutmaster, and the beautiful Sylvia Allen as the Girl Guide mistress, night after night played it 'straight'. Having robbed the safe in the Scout's Hut, Guy Middleton had to come back, take out his handkerchief and wipe the handle against fingerprints. On the second or third night as he was preparing to slink away someone cried, 'Wipe the handle!' and later on, when the original wit had been exhausted and the rugger types had taken over, the noise of 'Wipe the handle!' would be almost like that of a football crowd. At first, however, the wit was extremely subtle and often one would think of some line one night, too late to get it in, and return on the following night for the sole purpose of trying it on. If it succeeded, it would probably go into the saga and be picked up by someone or other night after night. Often the aged author would himself attend, striving vainly to keep order from his box. 'Order, order!' he cried one night. 'Large whisky and soda,' was the instant reply from the back. Some people picked up lines which particularly pleased them and would utter them just before the player did so, and really it could be very comical. If, for instance, as the mayor discovered the footprints of the fleeing widow, you heard a voice from the auditorium saying in deep, theatrical tones, 'Footprints on the soggy ground,' you could be sure that Swanton was in the house. 'Ha!' John Oxford would say, without turning a hair. 'Footprints on the soggy ground.'

Apparently the play had been written in all seriousness in a mood of fervent patriotism. Presumably the author was not too dismayed after he had seen the box-office takings. During 1938–39 the play wound its way round several theatres, from the Victoria Palace to the Kingsway, to the Piccadilly, to Daly's and back to the Kingsway. Mind you, a few people were not amused: 'Don't you *want* to hear the play?' exploded an angry lady one night. 'Good God, no, madam! Do you?' retorted the man beside her.

A look through the revolving optical tube of Jim's personal kaleidoscope during the 1930s is dizzy-making; endless communication with people of note, attendance at social functions, and a continuing quota of cricket and rugby club events – in the majority of the former of which he was playing.

Having abandoned schoolboy lob-bowling Jim had been busy developing what he liked to think was challenging leg-spin that kept a length and turned a little – eventually to be dubbed by unkind team-mates his 'holy rollers'. As a batsman he preferred to go in first as he was uneasy facing spinners. Perhaps it was that fact, and being in close company with master leg-spinner Ian Peebles, that persuaded him to try and unravel the mysteries of the art.

According to one report it would appear he had done so. In a game for Beckenham against Blackheath (just after the war) the local newspaper headline reads: 'Swanton proved unplayable'. The narrative tells us more: 'Swanton was in devastating form with the ball and took five of the later Blackheath wickets for seven runs. His last three came with five balls. He had previously opened the Beckenham innings with Collingwood and knocked up a useful 57.'

And it was as a batsman that Jim achieved a fair measure of success. As has been mentioned, back in 1928 and playing for Old Cranleighans against Old Rossallians in a two-day match, he had hit 144 not out in a winning second innings total of 309 for 5. It was his first hundred and highest score, and yet he was to reach three figures on a number of occasions.

During the 1930s Jim somehow managed to find the time (as John Woodcock has pointed out in *The Cricketer* of April 1987) to 'play enough cricket himself to score 1000 runs a season (except in 1933) and 2000 in 1936, most of them for MCC, Wimbledon, Incogniti, the Romany, Eastbourne and the Cryptics': on average about thirty games a season. He also turned out for a Sunday wandering club called the Musketeers. More often than not Jim would open the innings. For Eastbourne against Old Eastbournians at the Saffrons in 1931, he was the foundation of the side's score of 294 for 9 declared with a solid 89. Five years later, again he was in the runs. In a two-day game against Bradfield Waifs and facing a total of 412, Jim made 90 including ten fours as part of a first-wicket partnership of 145. When Eastbourne were asked to follow-on, 107 runs behind, he responded once more with a 112 in which he hit three sixes and fifteen fours. The home side then declared with five wickets down and set the Waifs a target of 103 for victory. There was nearly an unexpected reversal of fortune as they lost seven wickets in making 57 before stumps were drawn. 'At the Saffrons, I recall a very agreeable outlook,' remarked Jim, 'not only towards Beachy Head, but from the pavilion to the Town Hall which is quite a nice building. There were always red geraniums in front of the pavilion and Larkins Field was full of buttercups. The great joy of playing at Eastbourne in those days was that one could play two-day cricket during the whole of August. I loved two-day cricket. It's got so much that you can't get in a one-day match – the fellowship of it and the dining afterwards. Visiting teams used to stay at the Grand Hotel. Dick Beattie at the Grand, who was the father-in-law of Hubert Doggart, the Cambridge, Sussex and England cricketer, used to give special terms to touring sides.'

Being Jim, naturally he could not resist the opportunity to make a professional penny out of his leisure activity. *The World News Weekly: Everyman Cricket Supplement* in 1934, edited by Viscountess Dunedin – how Jim would have appreciated that – contains his views on how the game should be approached:

The Spirit of Club Cricket

by E.W. Swanton

There is a deal of tiresome, high-falutin' stuff talked and written about the 'spirit' of cricket, and I expect most players share with me that uncomfortable, prickly sensation when the local big-wig, doubtless with the best of intentions, bursts upon the pleasant intimacy of a club dinner with a pious homily in which he philosophizes on the Game of

Life in a series of more or less muddled metaphors from the cricket field. 'Cricket's manly toil,' like other forms of honest endeavour, must play its part in the development of character, but we play the game for no more laudable reason than because we love playing it, certainly not for the good of our souls.

However, there is compensation for the extravagances of the sentimentalists in the satire of 'Beachcomber', who has given some immortal advice on the playing of Life's Googlies. 'Straight be thy bat, aye, straighter year by year . . .' For the rest of this article, therefore, let it be taken for granted that the club cricketer plays the game for its own sake, plays for his side and not for himself, is not unduly elated in victory nor cast down in defeat, accepts all decisions of the umpire without question or dispute, and in fact conforms fairly well to the ordinary criterions [sic] of civilized society.

I would ask the club cricketer one question: Does he extract from the game the very maximum amount of fun? No two people can approach cricket in precisely the same way, for all depends upon the degree of skill of the individual and the conditions in which he is able to play. There are, however, if I may say so, two faults common to all sorts and conditions of club cricketers, from the greatest to 'the illustrious obscure'. There are those who betray their keenness too blatantly, and there are those who palpably have too little keenness to betray. Both are types which cannot fail to irritate those who flatter themselves their deportment is what it should be, and of the two I have infinitely more sympathy with the ultra-enthusiastic, although he is likely to be the less popular. Often in fact the casual performer casts his spell over the remainder of his side. He preaches the doctrine of 'What does it matter who wins so long as we enjoy ourselves?' The answer to such a question is so nearly that it doesn't matter at all that some are liable to be deluded by it.

The environment of cricket and the friends one makes are, of course, a great deal of the joy of playing, but both may be relished all the more in their proper perspective. For it is the game itself which should take first place. In truth it is not always easy. A green field and a deck chair on a drowsy June day are conducive to a state of mental as well as physical inertia which encourages a casual attitude. But there is no happiness like that to be derived from a contest fought to the last inch by two sides well led and inspired by a single purpose. Then indeed it does not matter who wins.

Everyone, at one time or another, ought to be given a good dose of active management, either running a side or acting as its captain. For it is almost impossible to take an intimate interest in affairs such as an official position demands without adopting a sort of outlook from which the most complete enjoyment of cricket is to be extracted.

I often feel the club cricketer has much to learn as regards his attitude towards the game from the first-class player. This, I know, will not be a popular observation, but then many club cricketers express a contempt for the first-class player which, whether it be forced or genuine, is singularly out of place. The county batsman may be slow and unenterprising, but he does apply his mind to what he is doing. He does not fail from lack of concentration. How largely, after all, once one has reached a certain standard, is cricket a matter of concentration? A famous professional, who would not be generally suspected of any great profundity, has described the difference between the two classes of players as depending first and foremost on this question of concentration. It is not difficult to think of many who by intelligent endeavour have triumphed over their physical limitations and made good players. Cricket is after all worth giving your whole heart and mind to while you are playing it.

The chance to put these precepts into practice came in 1935. He started his own wandering club. The birth of the Arabs happened, in effect, because of an abortion.

The success of Cahn's tour in 1933 had led to an invitation to Jim to take a side to Bermuda in 1935. The offer had come from the ADC to the governor, Lord Carew. However, the funding of the visit by the hosts fell through (they had spent the money on a tour of Canada) and so Jim was left with an expectant team but nowhere to go. He soon found somewhere – the Channel Islands – and so on Sunday, 8 September 1935 our intrepid leader and his gallant men took off from Heston on their way to Jersey in what is believed to be the first air journey by a touring cricket side: it was certainly Jim's first flight. But the life and times of the Arabs deserves a chapter in itself and there shall be one.

Earlier in the same year Jim had played his first game at Lord's for MCC against Indian Gymkhana – Bill Edrich had got 60 and E.W.S. was lbw b. Amar Singh for 7. He then scored 120 for Romany against the National Provincial Bank and 119 for MCC v. Henley and, to recuperate from his exertions, took a river holiday from Wargrave (in Berkshire) with Henry Longhurst and two female companions. Jim made a lot of runs when playing qualifying matches for MCC. In 1934 he got 102 and 61 retired hurt in a two-day match against Eastbourne: 'I was going for a hundred in each innings, but a chap called

Matthews was bowling slow off-breaks for Eastbourne and I tried a sweep shot. It ran up the outside edge and hit me on the ear lobe and I started to bleed so I had to go off. My mother was there, she didn't watch much cricket, but was terribly concerned about this and had to be restrained from coming out to see what was the matter! I had some stitches in it – but we won the match. It was an interesting MCC side of extremes in strength and ordinariness and was managed by H.D. Swan who was the worst cricketer I ever saw in my life. He went in last and was bowled for 3, which was about his average. He was a nice avuncular chap who went on playing much longer than he should have done. His wife was a much more masterful character than him and was the Mayor of Eastbourne. We used to call him "Swanny", or the "Mayoress of Eastbourne".' Playing in that match was Major The Hon. E.G.F. French, a one time minor county cricketer for Devon and a noted member of I. Zingari for over sixty years. Two years later, in 1936, when Jim was elected to membership of MCC, French was the proposer. Seconding the application was former England and Surrey opening batsman, D.J. Knight.

In 1936 came the chance to go up a further stage when Middlesex captain Walter Robins invited Jim to make his county debut for the Second XI in the Minor Counties Championship. He went in first, against Kent at Folkestone, and 'with the score about 20 for four was joined by this eighteen-year-old with the loose-jointed, slightly wayward walk which was soon to become so familiar.' In fact, Jim's memory was slightly awry: the fourth wicket went down when the score was 54. The loose-jointed eighteen-year-old who had joined him was, of course, Denis Compton and together they made a stand of 67 before Jim was dismissed for 49. Nine days later at the Oval, again he fell just short of a half-century, with 46 against Surrey II. In all, in seven innings for the Seconds in that year he made 194 runs at an average of 27.71.

In the next two years Jim played against Oxford University twice and Cambridge University once for the First XI. He almost seemed to have a foothold in county cricket. But it was not to be. At the Parks in May 1937 after a delayed start on a saturated turf and with the ball lifting and turning he was bowled for 1. There was no further chance to impress as the weather intervened. At Fenner's, ten days later, Jim did a little better. A first innings score of 12 before putting his leg in front of a straight ball from Rought-Rought and a catch in Cambridge's first innings to dismiss the future England wicket-keeper, Paul Gibb, was encouraging. And then in Middlesex's second innings,

Jim at last made a fairly reasonable score. Opening the batting with another future England player, this one a captain, George Mann, he made 26 in a stand of 73. In an interview shortly before he died, Mann remembered that when he had 'mischievously made him gallop extra fast for a third run, taking on a throw from the deep field, he came walking back up the wicket towards me before the next ball could be bowled and panted, "Now, look here, young fella, we've got to play the game properly."'

It is perhaps worth remembering that Jim conceivably could have pursued a cricketing career with Middlesex's rivals south of the Thames, as back in 1926 he had turned out at the Oval for Surrey Club and Ground against Public Schools of South London. On that occasion he had made 25 before being stumped by R.F. Tobitt, a wicket-keeper from his previous *palaestra,* St Dunstan's.

As we prepare to take an adjournment from this madcap romp through what Jim called 'The Gay 30s', it is illustrative to take a random skim through his Badminton diaries (equine sports were about the only thing in which he appeared not to take an interest).

1934
Jan.

21	Sun	Oxford
22	Mon	R. (Friend) luncheon
		O.C. May [*no doubt an article for the Old Cranleighans magazine*]
23	Tues	John H. Luncheon
		Pat D. Squash
24	Wed	Snooker final
25	Thurs	John Mahaffy – Carson's Life [*Mahaffy was an Oxford sportsman who lodged at King's Bench Walk after Longhurst left to get married*]
	Pat	Cricket
26	Fri	Squash – Alan
27	Sat	Wasps v. OM
		Rosslyn Park dinner
		OC v. Rugby
28	Septuagesima Sun.	Golf

Feb.

2	Fri	Saturday's Children with Patrick
3	Sat	Richmond v. Oxford
		OL v. OM

4	Sexagesima Sun.		Henry, Pat & John, Golf: Tyrrell's Wood
5	Mon	OC Committee	
6	Tues	12.00	BBC. de Lotbinière
		7.30	Songs
		8.30	Show

And so it continued. On other dates and times the entries included:

Seven-a-side finals at Twickenham
U.C.H. v. Thomas's on Shrove Tuesday
Dogs – Henry, Margaret & John
Ireland v. England – Dublin
Write Haileybury article
Sheila's lunch
Golf: Crusoe and Henry L.
Harlequin Ball – [2 *guineas for supper and breakfast at the Dorchester*]
Blackheath Party
Guy's v. London
Bart v. OC
Wasps Dance
Standard article
Cambridge Freshmen
P.S. Championships – Stamford Bridge
Cryptics v. Magdalen
Lancing OB Cricketers' Dinner
Sportsman's Club Lunch
Jesters CC Dinner
Musketeers v. B of B
Eastbourne v. Yellowhammers
Incogniti AGM at Victoria
Jesters v. Cross Arrows at Lord's
Australians arrive) on Gallipoli and
Australian practice) Anzac Day
MCC v. Wisbech Town
Flat redecorated
Nora Bonsey – Queen's Gate
Young Blackshaw birthday [*the son of Charles Blackshaw, schoolmaster, Cranleigh Junior school*]
Frank Woolley – Surrey
Surrey v. Sussex

Margaret back – hamper & dance
Joanna Findlay
Fitzgerald – Field
Yglesias
Marion Howard
Mr Chips – Passion Sunday
Cicely Brown
Julie Nicholls' birthday !!! [*The daughter of a family who lived next door to Swanton's parents in Sydenham*]
Income Tax
new driving licence

and on the next day

lending Roy my ear because I promised I would . . .

The diaries also contain details of bets placed on the results of matches – mostly in the region of fifteen shillings or £1:

Crusoe owes £1 [*Pen-name for Robertson-Glasgow*]
Terry Rattigan owes £1 [*The playwright obviously fancied a flutter*]

This is a lengthy list, but in fact it is only a small portion of the whole and is indicative of the range of Jim's interests. Many of the dances he attended were as one of a group which included his sister, Tina, and also Rosalind Edwards, who in turn was the sister of his childhood chum at kindergarten. On occasions they might go to the Savoy or the Monseigneur in London's West End where the bands of Lew Stone and Roy Fox could be heard, or more locally, as far as the family home was concerned, to the Crystal Palace before it burned to the ground.

Jim's parents moved house a number of times in the decade before the war, mostly living in rented property in Beckenham and Sydenham. His father 'Billy' had suffered a nervous breakdown at the time of the financial crash in the City, but recovered sufficiently to win an arithmetic competition in Catford. When, though, his elder daughter Ruth brought her fiancé Edmund Nelson to the family home at 'Chalvadune', in Lawrie Park Gardens in Sydenham, the prospective son-in-law thought his in-laws to be 'immensely hospitable', confident and comfortably off. As has been mentioned, Ruth and Edmund had met while she was studying art at Goldsmiths College and, of course, in time Nelson was to make his name as a notable portrait painter. 'Jim had a lot to say,' recalls Nelson, now in his ninety-fifth year, 'and a confident manner of saying it. I think largely the confidence came because of his size and his voice. There was nothing of the scholar about Jim although he was decidedly public school and upper strata and I thought he was a frightful snob, but I grew to like him and we got on well.

'I remember one day when Ruth picked up a critique of Jim's work which described him as a great writer. "You're not a great writer," she snorted, "you're a sporting journalist." Jim chuckled, "Oh well, that's salutary!" He was very good when she was sick with breast cancer. I was nursing her and he came and spent time with her and helped with the cost of the nursing home.'

Of Jim's parents, Nelson thought his mother 'an incredibly warm woman – there was always an enormous crowd of friends coming and going' – and his father 'a very nice man, gentlemanly, quiet, comparatively shy and slow to anger. He was nobody's idea of a stockbroker who you would think of as normally somebody a bit louder.'

For Jim the era had been a remarkable one. On his march to be successful at whatever he was doing, he had passed some and been left behind by others; nobody though could deny his progress. Although he perhaps did not feel it, he was now an established figure in print and, as we shall see shortly, also on air. Another broadcaster of practically the same generation, and who had started a career behind the microphone at more or less the same time, was actor Hubert Gregg, composer of the song 'Maybe it's because I'm a Londoner' and much else. Gregg once memorably summed up the 1930s as a time when

> young men and women were high on life and didn't need drink or drugs to make them so. It seemed not to matter if you had no money, although it was nice if you had it. There was an innocence and lack of distrust. Creativity was happening everywhere – not only in the theatre, but other places as well. There was a pleasant discipline going on – gentlemen wore their best suits when out and ladies dressed for the occasion – it was an expected part of life. The phrase everybody used for moving from one location to another was 'Shall we go on?'

Chapter 4

He shall speak his piece
unto the Nation

Before installing Jim behind the microphone for the first time in 1934, we should take a brief look at the business he was getting into. By the early 1930s 'Auntie Beeb' had expanded enough as a body to have acquired a Corporation. Having dispensed with Company status, it had at last plucked up sufficient courage to be more venturesome with some of its programmes. This was particularly true with the coverage of sport.

It was in 1927, five years after the BBC's formation, that the new charter gave the right to send reporters out into the field to give on-the-spot accounts. The great Outside Broadcasts pioneer Lance Sieveking had then quickly seized the chance to send ex-Harlequin H.B.T. 'Teddy' Wakelam to Twickenham to commentate on the England v. Wales Rugby international. Allowing a dummy run two days before for an inter-schools match at the Old Deer Park, Richmond, it was the first ever English sports commentary over the air.

The only actual instructions Wakelam had been given was spelled out in large red letters on a piece of cardboard propped in front of him: 'Don't swear!' But Sieveking had provided his protégé with a reinforcement of far greater value. He seated a blind man from St Dunstan's just in front of the broadcasting box and suggested to Wakelam that he concentrate on describing to this one individual exactly what was happening. Thereafter that thought-process became almost a tenet of the art of commentary.

When it came to BBC commentary on cricket – the first attempt took place in that same year, 1927 – there was a much more tentative start. Despite successful ventures in Australia from L.G. Watt and H.P.

Williams and remarkably compelling synthetic commentary from New South Wales all-rounder Alan Fairfax while seated in commercial station Poste Parisien's studio in the Eiffel Tower during the 'Bodyline' tour of 1932–33 (he was being fed information by cable and used his experience as a player to give an imaginative interpretation of what had just happened), there was considerable opposition to such a development at home. Both the press and the cricket authorities were alarmed at the thought of readers and spectators respectively being enticed away from their newspapers and grounds. And for a long time the BBC itself was wary, if only of the *longueurs* between the interplay of bat and ball being left unfilled. Especially so after the Essex cricketing parson Frank Gillingham, later to become a canon and chaplain to King George VI (an appreciative snort here from Jim), had given, in effect, a free commercial by describing in some detail the advertisement hoardings around the ground during a break for rain (certain to have stirred the ire of Director-General John Reith).

Their caution was not reduced when 'Teddy' Wakelam himself, whose affinity to cricket was not as close as that to rugby, had been dismissive of its long-term feasibility after commentating on a rather turgid day's play of a match between Surrey and Middlesex at the Oval. But by the time the magisterial Howard Marshall got under way in the 1930s, first under the watchful eye of the Director of Outside Broadcasts Gerald Cock and then eventually under the towering figure of Seymour Joli de Lotbinière (literally towering – he was six foot eight and a quarter inches and still growing at the end of his schooldays), cricket commentary was beginning to enjoy a sunnier clime. Marshall was a masterful broadcaster and as Christopher Martin-Jenkins has observed in his informative book on the story of cricket broadcasting, *Ball By Ball*, 'he had a rich store of knowledge, both of cricket and of life, an innate sense of when to use facts, "associative material" as de Lotbinière called it in his guidelines, wit in both the sense of ready humour and alertness of mind; and the observational qualities of a journalist and artist.' As for Jim, he remembered Marshall having 'a balance in both his estimations and the language in which he conveyed them'. Heady praise, yet, with a hatful of achievements in many other fields as well, Marshall was the most modest of men.

Jim's initial contact with the BBC came when he was still nursing his wounds after being offloaded from the 'Bodyline' tour by the *Standard*. Looking to maximise the pecuniary potential of all his ventures – as was his habit, and who could blame an ambitious young man for doing just that – he had proposed a topical talk on Sir Julian

Cahn's North American tour of which, of course, he was a member. Unfortunately, in the latter part of 1933 the BBC did not think it was very topical. Undeterred, a few months later, Jim then managed to talk his way into an appointment with the aforementioned de Lotbinière – 'Lobby' to one and all – soon to become Head of Outside Broadcasts.

'Swanton, the *Evening Standard* cricket and rugby football correspondent, came to see me this afternoon' wrote 'Lobby' to the Head of Topical Talks.

> I gave him a voice test and got him to describe to me some of his experiences as a member of Sir Julian Cahn's team who toured the West Indies [sic] this summer. He struck me as having rather the Howard Marshall manner. I told him that we would bear his name in mind, but that we were well satisfied with Howard Marshall. However, he might be useful to you if you wanted him suddenly to do some match for a 9.10 topical talk – say, the first match which the Australians play against Worcester some time in mid-April or early May.
>
> I rather think that you may have seen him when he came here in the summer. If you didn't, Madden did. He has not a very attractive personality, but I think he might do the job reasonably well . . .

The Madden mentioned by 'Lobby' was Cecil Madden, then a Talks Assistant (in effect, a producer), who later became a big wheel in television. Luckily for Jim, Madden had taken a much more positive view than de Lotbinière, noting in his report that Swanton had 'a good voice and a strong personality'. (Whether or not he thought it attractive is not revealed.) Very soon he was writing to Jim with details of an engagement:

> 20th November, 1934
>
> Dear Mr. Swanton,
>
> Thank you for coming to see me today. This is to confirm that we have fixed up for you to give a five minute (five hundred word) summary of the week's Rugger next Sunday (25th) at approximately 9.45 am.
>
> I hope this will be only the beginning and that you will do many more talks for us.
>
> Will you please remember to speak slowly and with plenty of emphasis as rehearsed?
>
> Yours sincerely
>
> C.M.

The letter was addressed to *B.W.* Swanton, Esq. at 8 King's Bench Walk, Temple, EC4. Not that that in any way would have affected Jim's confidence. Whenever recalling his first broadcast Jim would say that he was attending the Blackheath Football Club's Annual Dinner at the Café Royal and that, while still wearing his black tie and dinner jacket, he slipped away, took a cab up Regent Street to Broadcasting House and – relaxed by the dinner and the company – said his piece and returned to the party. And that he never remembered 'being nervous of the microphone since'. What he did not say was that his five-minute summary on the Empire Service was of course being recorded on to disc that Saturday evening for transmission on the Sunday morning. Apart from convenience and possible studio availability, it was a sensible precaution to take and allowed the BBC the chance of correcting any blunders that an inexperienced broadcaster might make.

After the broadcast, however, Jim was his own harshest critic:

Dear Mr. Madden,
    I enclose the script of my talk yesterday, as requested. Frankly, I was not altogether pleased with it, because, though it seemed to read well enough, when spoken it seemed somewhat stiff and disjointed. On another occasion this should be remedied quite easily.

Madden, though, thought it most effective and Jim must have come through his probationary period with flying colours, for by the following February both Madden and 'Lobby' were extolling his virtues in other quarters of the Corporation.

You might be interested in E.W. Swanton [by now, they knew his first initial] who does Rugger summaries for us in Empire programmes. He gives a 'Summary of the Week's Rugger' once a fortnight and his talks are excellent. We think he might be interesting for Home Programmes as he is very good on his subject and his manner and matter are also good. He is rugger and cricket correspondent of the *Evening Standard*.'

Even with this encomium, there was no question yet of letting Jim try his hand at running commentary. In spite of Howard Marshall having carved a small niche for himself commentating on cricket from a small room above the Tavern at Lord's, there were still many doubters at the BBC over the efficacy of broadcasting the game with commentary rather than report.

The year before, Marshall had won countless admirers when describing England's historic innings victory over Australia at cricket's headquarters. As the Yorkshire left-arm spinner Hedley Verity took fourteen wickets during the third day, Marshall, from his unsatisfactory side-on-to-play position, went on for hour after hour in that languid, almost hypnotic voice. 'Over goes the arm' became his catchphrase. Apart from hurried intermissions, there was no one to relieve him either in person or in body. 'The engineers were very helpful', he said later. 'They were always ready to fetch me a glass of beer or a cup of tea, or get the bowling figures from the scorers. They couldn't widdle for me, though.'

At least Marshall would have been pleased that he was now allowed to broadcast from inside the hallowed precincts instead of being obliged to go around the corner to a house in Grove End Road which was owned by the legendary teacher and accompanist Harold Craxton. On one occasion there he had had to contend with the intrusion of a girl practising her scales on the piano while he was trying to give an account of the day's play; the sound was so fortissimo Marshall felt that he was the one who was providing the accompaniment.

But for Jim all the trills and tremolos of running commentary lay in the future. And to judge from the wealth of nimious comment that accompanied his broadcasts over the next couple of years he was lucky there was a future. With the praise for his early efforts fast forgotten, adverse criticism took over. Criticism, one should add, that came from within the Corporation rather than without; listeners, as far as one can tell, seemed, on the whole, to like what they heard of E.W.S. Some of the quibbles could be thought to range from the extremely nit-picking to the ludicrous, indeed hilarious, when compared to the profanity-strewn airwaves of the twenty-first century. Other upbraidings from the overly safety-conscious programme executives and editors – who, we must remember, were operating under the easily incurred disapprobation of the Calvinistic Reith and in a very sheltered and shockable Britain – suggest that with his many activities, Jim was trying to do too much in too little time and was taking a few of life's responsibilities rather too lightly. His disordered existence, 'I am out of one flat and not yet in another and my affairs are rather chaotic,' is surprising for those who knew of his predilection for organisation and method in later years. But an anarchic, dislocated way of life is, of course, a young man's prerogative, if not always recognised.

19th March 1935

Dear Mr. Swanton,

[It was] noticed that at the end of your talk last Sunday you mentioned that you would be speaking again 'next Sunday'. This is perhaps just a typing error which you corrected in actually speaking, but [I have been] asked to let you know that we hope you will be able to give your 'Summary of the Season' on Sunday, the 31st March, that is, Sunday week.

29th March 1935

E.W.S.: I am afraid I did slip up in giving notice of the next Rugby talk. I did say next Sunday, and of course we arranged Sunday week. I am so sorry.

14th May 1935

Dear Swanton,

There is one point in the manuscript of last Sunday's Talk which I think I ought to mention. You spoke of a man taking three-to-one against Middlesex's chance of winning the Championship. We feel that it was perhaps a pity to give even the slightest impression that cricket in this country is becoming a subject of betting. [*The writer was obviously unaware of how the game achieved prominence in England during the eighteenth century, or indeed that Jim was not averse to a flutter himself.*] Obviously, this was simply a small private bet, but listeners are not always very careful in the inferences they draw from what they hear, and such a remark might easily give a wrong impression.

What you might have said is 'People are saying the chances are as much as two-to-one in favour of Middlesex winning the Championship', or something like that.

You may perhaps feel that this is rather a quibbling point, but I can assure you we do have to be astoundingly careful.

E.W.S: from The Trout Inn, Godstow, Oxford May 17th

I note the contents of your letter and will endeavour not to offend again. Clearly you do have to be most careful, and, in retrospect, the remark was certainly better omitted.

6th August 1935

Dear Swanton,

There is one question of delivery that I want to mention. We have recently come to the conclusion that a good deal of our Empire broadcasting is being done at too high a speed for consistently good reception. The announcers are, therefore, being encouraged to slow up considerably in the reading of News Bulletins; and we are trying to get speakers to do the same. Perhaps you would kindly note this, and try a rather slower delivery. Incidentally, this means, of course, a shorter script. (Last Sunday's was distinctly too long, even at the higher rate of speed.)

Another point which is noticeable is that you are tending nowadays to slur your words a little and drop your voice at the end of sentences. I know you would be perfectly intelligible under home broadcasting conditions; but distant reception of short waves is a good deal trickier, and we have to ask for definitely more careful delivery. It is rather an art to achieve an appearance of naturalness in those circumstances, but I am sure you can adapt your style to what is wanted.

E.W.S.:
. . . Your points about delivery are noted, and I will shorten my script in order to accommodate slower delivery.

A few days later Jim walked into a studio while an announcer was delivering a news bulletin, but on this occasion he was adjudged not to have sinned as he had been given misleading information. Some months later though, there was more internal angst.

13th January, 1936
Swanton's delivery yesterday was extremely hesitant, and suggested, in some places, that he had no notes of what he wanted to say, far less a script. Moreover, he seems to have over-run his time . . .

When it came to admonishing Jim, the tone was a model of circumspection.

17th January, 1936
Dear Mr. Swanton,
We have received reports on your Sports Talk last Sunday, which suggest that it must have sounded unusually hesitant to the listener. I have no doubt that this arose from your desire to sound natural and to avoid anything like a set speech. This, of course, is obviously the right effect to aim at, and I am sure that you will be able to avoid any appearance of excessive hesitancy in the future, perhaps by the use of fuller notes.

I also see from the log that your last talk ran to nearly ten minutes. We are particularly anxious to keep the Newsletter and Sports Summary to their correct timing as they are often followed by important programmes, and there is no room for any elasticity once your talks have been recorded. So can you try to keep your talks down to seven minutes, or at any rate to let us know if you are likely to over-run when there are a special lot of important things to record?

Please believe me when I say that these suggestions are made only in the friendliest spirit.

E.W.S.:   20th January, 1936

Thank you for your suggestions, received, I assure you, in the spirit in which they were sent

I have been experimenting with fewer notes because, as you say, they tend towards a more natural effect. It so happened that I went in on Sunday and listened to my talk, and realised that it was unusually hesitant. I am inclined to trace this more to a dose of catarrh, and an accompanying mental congestion, than to the absence of a set talk! Your note about the time limit will be duly observed.

But still the complaints continued.

                                                        27th February, 1936

His speech was much too fast (with a general unevenness of pace), and punctuated with er er's.

I think Swanton has been rather better lately, since the very bad one on which we pulled him up. On the other hand, he does sometimes give the impression of being slightly sloppy in his style; and this question of pace is important. Will you see what you can do?

                                                        13th March, 1936

I had Mr Swanton in today to listen to the tape of his last Sunday's talk. He was rather surprised, and quite shocked, to find how jerky his delivery had become. I improved the shining hour by arranging with him that, for the time being, at any rate, he could work from a full script. This will also meet the Announcer's point.

I made it clear that we did not want any alteration in the actual style or wording of his talk – which are admirable – but only in the tempo.

And then, suddenly, a shaft of light parted the clouds.

24th March, 1936

Dear Swanton,
    I have just been listening to the recording of your sports talk of last
Saturday. There seemed to me to be a great improvement in the flow
and smoothness of the talk, with no loss of spontaneity. So I hope you
will be able to keep on in this same style . . .

The brighter aspect, however, was not to last. Jim transgressed thrice
more – first by forgetting to leave his script behind . . .

Once again, no manuscript of Swanton's talk was available. Would you
kindly see what happened to it?

Dear Mr Swanton,
    The object of the talk being written out is twofold: firstly, so that if
anything goes wrong with the recording the Announcer can read the
talk from the script; and secondly, in order that the Sub-Editor on duty,
who is personally responsible for the policy, as opposed to the actual
matter of the talk, may have an opportunity of reading it before it is
given, and ensuring that there is nothing objectionable in it.
    Although the second of these reasons, in your case, is of course a
pure formality . . .

Ah, but was it? Soon we shall see. Meanwhile, Jim having remembered
to leave his script behind, it was found to be illegible . . .

May I take this opportunity to ask whether it would not be possible for
you to have the script of your Sunday talks typed before they are
given? . . . I think you will agree with me that your scripts hardly lend
themselves to being read by an Announcer should the works go
wrong . . .

'I will indeed endeavour to co-operate with you as regards the
condition of my script,' replied a harassed Jim;

Circumstances, as you may have guessed, are however rather tiresome. I
return to London on a Saturday evening from a match – very often with
not a great deal of time to spare. To type my notes would involve
carrying a typewriter around London all day; which, frankly, would be
rather a bore . . . [However,] I will undertake to improve the legibility of
my handwriting and I hope that that will meet the case.

The third transgression occurred when Jim arrived late for his Talk and once more walked into a studio with seconds to spare, thereby distracting an announcer who was reading the News.

E.W.S.:
I must apologise. I am afraid you must think me rather a nuisance . . .

Well, yes, – I'm sure they did. But they didn't say so – in print, at least.

In some ways this learning curve in the art of broadcasting had probably attracted not many more strictures than for anyone else coming to terms with the unforgiving microphone. But reading between the lines of the correspondence and internal circulating memorandums, one is left with an overriding impression that Jim's youthful arrogance and imperious manner had not helped his cause when it came to dealing with those who mattered. He had already achieved a lot in several fields – a début for Middlesex, captaining his own team the Arabs, where he enjoyed a dictatorial role; writing for the national press and for other magazines; broadcasting, socialising and networking with his name now known in influential circles – and yet, he was still constantly striving to achieve more. It left little time or inclination to nurture the goodwill of those who were the cogs that made the wheels turn round – those, he perhaps felt, who were less important. With so much happening in his life, he was in danger of overreaching himself. These factors, compounded by tiredness and an admitted short fuse, meant that sooner or later some sort of explosion was inevitable. A few days before Christmas in 1937, it happened.

The game had been the Second International Rugby trial between the Probables and Possibles at Portman Road, Ipswich, on the Town football club's ground. The football ground had been used because there was no rugby ground capable of accommodating the large crowd that was expected. Having spent what he described as 'a pleasant afternoon' watching the Probables triumph 18–11, Jim returned to London for his 'Weekly Sports Summary' for the Empire Service. In the studio that Saturday evening was, as usual, a sub-editor whose duty it was to make sure that any script contained nothing libellous or likely to give offence. Normally, if the script had been fully legible and complete (as it nearly always was when Howard Marshall or Charles Eade, Sports Editor of the *Sunday Express*, were giving their talks), he would have been able to leave the studio having checked the script.

But Jim's scripts, as we know, were not often legible nor always complete. On this occasion, the sub-editor stayed and eventually reported on what had transpired.

20th December, 1937

. . . He began with an account of the match between the 'Possibles' and the 'Probables', and went on to criticise the individual players. After he had criticised a number of them, he mentioned that he had marked the players on his card as 'A' and 'B', adding, 'and so-and-so is "B"'. This sentence was so constructed and spoken in such a way that although the words were innocent, the effect was that 'so-and-so is "b——"' ('bloody'). I waited for well over a minute, expecting to hear that other players were 'A' and 'B', but apparently the 'A B' system was only applied to one player – and he was 'b'. Had Mr. Swanton applied his 'A B' categories to a number of players (as he elected to do in the second and final version of his talk) it might have dissipated the immediate impression I received, that so-and-so was being referred to as 'b——'. (I do not recall the name, nor does it matter.) But when he went on with his criticisms of individual players without again referring to his 'A B' system, the immediate impression was strengthened – I was sure that some listeners would feel that the 'A B' system had been dragged in simply to make the point that 'so-and-so was b——'.

This seemed to me clearly objectionable, and I had no option but to stop Mr. Swanton, and to tell him that the remark 'so-and-so is B' was capable of being misinterpreted and might give offence, and that I could not pass it over. At first he professed ignorance, and had to be told that 'b' is sometimes used as an abbreviation of 'bloody'. I put my objection with some nervousness, for the mantle of censor is not my chosen garb. But my placatory demeanour was wasted, for Mr. Swanton flew into a violent rage. He kept repeating that my objection was 'fantastic', and that it would occur to 'nobody outside a madhouse'. I told him that it had occurred to me, and that other listeners might hear the remark as I had heard it. I pointed out that the objection could be easily overcome by using 'first-class – second-class' or 'alpha-beta' instead of 'A and B'. He replied that listeners didn't understand Greek, that it was 'his talk', and that he would say what he jolly well liked. I then reminded him that if offence were given in the talk, I was responsible for the consequences. He became so unmanageable, in spite of being told that the circuit was still alive and that others could hear, that I invited him to come with me to ring up E.N.E. [Empire News Editor] to discuss the matter with him. I repeated this invitation several times, and held open the studio door for him to come. But the invitation was not accepted, though Mr. Topping also tried to persuade him to phone E.N.E. Mr. Swanton continued to pour contempt on the point I had made. His discourtesies received no reply, but when he again repeated that my idea 'could occur to nobody outside a madhouse', I told him that I resented the remark as insulting, and withdrew from the studio.

Shortly afterwards, Mr. Swanton sat down at the microphone to begin again, apparently under the impression that his bluster had swamped my objection. I therefore asked him whether it was his intention to modify the remark in his talk, to which I had objected. I was not given the courtesy of a reply, so I retired to the listening-room, where I listened to his second talk on the earphones. In this revised version (which was the one used on Sunday), Mr. Swanton spoke of alpha, beta, and even gamma, and – a point of some interest – applied the system to a number of players, not to one only. The second version differed from the first in other particulars, not directly concerned with the single objection I had raised. It also ran to 8½ minutes, instead of 7 minutes, and the end part (a number of football scores) had to be cut. Mr. Swanton wrote out these scores, which were added to football results for announcers to read.

My chief regret is that Mr. Swanton's first version of his talk, and his conversation with me, are not available as a recording (tape-room washed off the first version immediately it was interrupted). But Mr. Topping, and possibly the tape-room and control-room engineers, heard what happened, and I feel sure that these witnesses will agree that Mr. Swanton gave a display of temper that was quite uncalled-for. Whether their 'technical ears' also caught the possible hearing of the 'so-and-so is b' remark it would be interesting to know. They can at any rate confirm that my objection was put forward in the form that 'some listeners might misinterpret the remark', and that at no time did I suggest or imply that Mr. Swanton had meant to say something offensive. Mr. Swanton is the sole judge of what he meant to say, but I take it that I have the right, and the duty, to point out how his remarks may strike others. The point I took up was a perfectly clear one, and one easily covered (as it eventually was) by a change of phrase.

There is, in fact, no excuse for Mr. Swanton's behaviour, and in my considered opinion, his rage is inexplicable except as that of a man who realises that he has been detected in a childish manoeuvre of 'putting something over on the BBC'. It was psychologically illuminating, but personally insulting, and to me the episode was extremely distasteful. Mr. Swanton owes me an apology, but whether he apologises or not, I want nothing more to do with him, and I therefore ask that if he should be admitted to give another talk, some person other than myself be deputed to soothe his tantrums.

By modern standards, it would all seem to be rather a squall in a saucer. The initial response to Jim's choice of expression would appear, on paper at least, to be heavy-handed, but given his sonorous emphasis to certain consonants and syllables when speaking, one can imagine the effect producing a different perception in the close proximity of a studio. Obviously, the strain of creating a programme against the clock and with very little time for preparation can easily cause a flare-up, but here again one senses contributory factors to the altercation other than those that are seen to have lit the fuse. The vexation the sub-editor would have felt on arrival at being presented with an incomplete script that was difficult to read, necessitating time spent in the studio that could have been more profitably spent elsewhere, was perhaps compounded by a high-handed attitude from its author when handing it over. Jim did have a marked facility at rubbing people up the wrong way – particularly during his early manhood, although it was not until late in his life that there was to be a noticeable diminution of that trait in his character. It meant that on this occasion both sides tried to stand by what they saw as their rightful position and only one succeeded. Although it is pure speculation, conceivably the sub-editor unconsciously felt the need to assert his authority because he had sensed it undervalued by Jim's demeanour.

And it was Jim's demeanour, which was thought to be 'to say the least of it, unfortunate', that the letter of reproval mentioned, together with a reminder that a condition of his contract was that his final manuscript was subject to the Corporation's acceptance. Addressed to his temporary residence at the Public Schools Club at 61 Curzon Street in London's Mayfair, it requested his side of the story. His reply was some time coming. Aware that he might have put further broadcasting in jeopardy, Jim requested a meeting with the Empire News Editor. The request was politely denied, being deemed it inappropriate until there had been a written response. Jim now succumbed to an unspecified illness and over the Christmas period and New Year several broadcast contracts requiring his signature were not returned. Quite possibly they were sent to one of the addresses where he was no longer in residence. At any rate, last minute substitutions had to be made which did not exactly help to improve the temper of his relationship with the BBC. Eventually, in the fourth week of January and while staying in the Palace Hotel, Torquay (for recuperation?), he penned his version of the events in the studio.

> As regards the matter about which we were corresponding before Christmas: the facts were, briefly these – I said, in essence, 'Now about the Rugby trial in Ipswich . . .', a remark or two, and then 'as for personal performances I have my programme in front of me, and I will just run through some of the names. I've marked everyone with . . . A, B, C, or D. I won't 'reveal' the Cs and Ds! But among those who played really well were . . .X . . .'. Then I discussed a player who did pretty well and added, 'I've put a B down for him.' I carried on for a minute or two, and then my guardian interrupted, and said, 'I'm afraid I can't allow that.' When I gathered the cause of complaint I am afraid I was somewhat heated. Technically, perhaps, I was quite wrong. But the situation would surely have tested Job himself. If I said anything to which he took offence please convey my apologies. The objection seems ludicrous in retrospect, but at the time I must say I found it too much to bear.

Conciliatory noises all round seemed the order of the day; however, a month later another letter was perhaps not unconnected:

> Dear Swanton,
>   It has been decided to change the scope of the weekly sports summary, and in the circumstances I am afraid that we shall not be sending you a further contract for the time being.
>   I take this opportunity to thank you for the excellent series of talks which you have been giving from time to time since I became Empire News Editor. I will certainly see to it that your name is borne in mind, as and when similar talks are required.

A prompt acknowledgement from Jim conveyed his sorrow at the tidings. He went on, 'I trust you may indeed remember that I will always be here, and willing to give talks on any sporting subject as and when you require.'

Jim seldom took time to look backwards and so, undeterred by outrageous fortune or any thought of whether he needed to take more care in dodging the slings and arrows that were coming his way with increasing frequency, once more took up the chase.

E.W.S.:

Dear Mr. Mackay,

   I am wondering whether you will be able to fit me in during the summer for any cricket eye-witness broadcasts. I shall be reporting fairly extensively for The Times and the Standard. I have done a good deal of Sports Talking for the Empire people, and I am having a Running Commentary test early in May. Perhaps if you are not wholly fixed up, I might come and have a word with you.

It was to Jim's advantage that the BBC had many mansions. This particular one was in the Regions. The reply was in the affirmative, the test was positive (nowadays not usually a desirable outcome in sporting circles) and eventually (and it was a long eventually) his persistence paid off. Throughout the summer of 1938 Jim inundated the BBC with letters offering his services.

   Would either Middlesex v. Essex (a vital championship match featuring numerous Test players) or Army v. Australians interest you during the next few days?

   On Saturday I am playing at Lord's for M.C.C. v. the Club Cricket Conference – whose team will be representative of all the cricket clubs in the South of England. The match will thus be of interest to any club cricketers, and I thought a report in the news might be a fresh note, and an antidote to the Test!

   The Test: a final summing up on Friday night?

Meanwhile, he was busy attacking on another front. Conscious that MCC were taking a side to South Africa the following winter, he was keen to broadcast on the tour. But in order to do so, he had to explore every avenue for work. Occasional pieces for the *Standard*, *The Times* and *The Field* would help; however, to make the trip a viable possibility he had to procure frequent broadcasting stints not only from the BBC, but also from the South African Broadcasting Corporation (SABC). Protracted correspondence ensued with practically every contact he had in the world of wireless: de Lotbinière, Snagge, McGregor, Standing, Boswell, Pooley, Dickson, et al. Names that, with but two exceptions, meant little to the public at large, but all potentially influential – or so he thought – in getting him the job he desired. Hardly a week went by without one or other of

these worthies receiving a missive from Swanton. In the modern era
the Mayor of London would have considered imposing a congestion
charge, such was the traffic. Never afraid to solicit senior stratas of
society, Jim even made overtures to the South African High
Commissioner! But at every turn he seemed to be thwarted. Nobody
was actually unhelpful, more politely unconvinced. The obstacles
were continuous both in commitment to the project and in how it
was to be managed. The questions went on a gyratory system. How
many commentaries and summaries will we need? Who is going to
pay for the lines? Do they (they being South Africa) look after the
technical side? Will they prefer to use one of their own people? Is
Swanton the right person? This last thought was barely voiced,
though it was noted that Michael Standing, a figure who exemplified
his surname in the world of broadcasting, thought Jim 'adequate but
uninspiring' and somebody else remembered that 'he had been
trouble in the past'. The real hindrance though, was the lack of
precedent. It had not been done before and nobody wished to
elongate their neck. Not that Jim would have been aware of all of
these bureaucratic rumblings; just that he seemed to be getting
nowhere fast.

Having asked Michael Standing if he could join him at the Oval
during the fifth Test between England and Australia, Jim at last made
the breakthrough he was seeking. The Test itself, of course, became
part of the game's historic tapestry because of Len Hutton's
monumental innings of 364 in an England total of 903 to 7 declared.
An enduring memory for Jim was of the ashen-faced young
Yorkshireman, his trousers grey with the Kennington dust, wearily
climbing the ladder to the broadcasting perch at the top of the Ladies'
Stand after he was out, to be interviewed by Howard Marshall. But of
far greater importance for his own career was being able to convince
Standing in conversation, and through him 'Lobby', that he was ready
for commentary. He was asked to commentate on the forthcoming
match between Surrey and Lancashire at the Oval, sharing half an
hour before lunch and half an hour in the evening with former Surrey
captain Percy Fender who was covering the Sussex and Yorkshire
game at Hove. In effect, this was a trial run for South Africa.

Never let it be said that the Corporation sent their young man to
the front unprepared. Standing, in an executive role and having
recommended Jim, was now anxious that he was apprised of the
pitfalls.

25th August, 1938

Dear Swanton,

There are one or two points which we have found useful in cricket commentaries, and some of which I don't think I raised with you the other day. Anyhow, here they are and I hope they will be a help in your broadcasts from the Oval next week.

1. The start: We give the score right away, and the individual scores of the two batsmen at the wicket. We then go straight into running commentary until the end of the 'over' which is in progress. In the first interval between 'overs' we try to give details of the score sheet to date, but it is important to avoid missing a description of even one ball bowled as we have been caught out before now by a wicket falling while we were summarising previous play.

2. Giving the score: The score of each individual batsman should be given every time a run is scored, and the total also should be given as it alters. If there is a 'maiden over' the total, together with the two batsmen's scores, should be reported at the end of it. Within reason, the score can hardly be given too often.

3. Ending: If you can, repeat again the details of the score sheet before cueing out, and always finish with the present score. Sometimes, naturally, you don't get time to repeat all the details, but it is something to be aimed at if possible.

All these points may seem rather pernickety, but I don't believe one can take too much trouble even over the more delicate 'nuances', and it always seems to be the minor details which involve us in criticism. At any rate, you can take these suggestions for what they are worth, and all that remains is to wish you luck with your efforts.

The commentator's position at the Oval is the same as that used for the Test Match, and within the next few days I will send you a Pass which will admit you to the broadcasting point during the three days of the match.

Unbelievably, with so much resting on his performance, Jim now took a foolhardy risk. He had been invited to be an usher at the wedding of his old flatmate Henry Longhurst at Dulwich and on the second afternoon of the match left the game for the nuptials. In those days apparently the journey from Kennington only took fifteen minutes each way. Eventually he returned 'full of bonhomie' in time to be 'filled-in' on the score and details (by Monty Garland Wells, the Surrey captain, no less) and settled as comfortably as possible into the tiny room beside the scorer's box that was used for commentary. The first fifteen minutes of the scheduled half-hour had been allotted to the match at Hove and Jim had just seated himself when he heard Fender say that due to rain there was no play at the moment and therefore he would hand over without delay to Swanton at the Oval.

'This was something the raw recruit hadn't bargained for,' recollected Jim years later;

> I wasn't worried at the prospect of talking for half-an-hour. Far from it. But nine Surrey wickets were down, and nothing was less likely than that Ted Brooks and Alf Gover would last that time. I had no idea whether between innings one should return listeners to the studio or keep going. In the event there was some mild fun to be had with the last-wicket stand – always good commentary material – before, inevitably, one of them got out and the field emptied. Ten minutes on the microphone can be a long time, especially with no Webber or Frindall to cough up 'records' and figure details. I'm not sure that we had scorers even in Test matches before the war, certainly I had none that day. What I talked about goodness knows, but out it came – 'associative material' as, I came to learn, it is known in the OB department. I ended by giving an over or two of the Lancashire second innings, and by the time I came off the air at six o'clock 'Lobby' had got through to the engineer with a message of appreciation.

Overnight any doubts about Jim's ability receded. A contract for South Africa was virtually assured although much remained to be settled. A recommendation from 'Lobby' to R.S. Caprara, SABC's Director of Programmes – 'we look on him as a knowledgeable and competent commentator' – allayed any doubts at the South African end. After that, ancillary requirements fell into place: cost allocation, the amount of coverage for the five Tests – either fifteen-minute or thirty-minute daily stints, the former consisting of a five-minute commentary on the closing overs of the day followed by a ten-minute eyewitness account of the day's play and the latter consisting of a twenty-minute commentary of the final overs with again a ten-minute summary (this was slightly revised later) – and contractual details. After a little haggling a fee of 120 guineas was agreed to cover the whole engagement. When Jim asked for an advance the BBC refused. When he threatened to withdraw, they made placatory noises and relented.

In the interim before going to South Africa there was a mild resurgence of the old tribulations.

Oct. 21st, 1938

Your Sports Summary last week contained the phrase 'it is a devil of a long time'. I am afraid that we rather bar phrases of this sort because, for all we know, they may be listened to on Sundays by devout listeners who may take offence at the language. So I should be grateful if you could avoid them in the future . . .

With a contract in his pocket Jim was emboldened.

E.W.S.:

Your strictures are duly noted. But I can hear Bernard Darwin now [*the eminent* Times *golfing correspondent and writer*], describing a golf match and using the awful word. However, perhaps he was reproved too. At any rate, I am sorry.

Once on board the *Balmoral Castle*, Jim found that William Pollock of the *Daily Express* was the only other journalist from Fleet Street – incredible as that may seem seventy-five years later. He was still much concerned about the cost of the trip for he had obtained hardly any commissions for written reports. Leaving aside his BBC fee here he had embarked with orders totalling £60.6s.0d. – no more. His return first-class fare by Union Castle to the Cape was £103.10s.0d. discounted by 20 per cent to £82.16s.0d. through the kind offices of his uncle Ernest, who was a 'name' in the shipping world having chartered a fleet of ships to lay cables between various Japanese islands after the First World War. Hotel and travel expenses in South Africa – for which he alone was responsible – were also predicted to be light, fortunately. But having joined the MCC party in Johannesburg Jim dispensed with dull care and was determined to enjoy himself. With six provincial matches out of the way the first Test was imminent. On Christmas Eve 1938 it began at the Old Wanderers ground and E.W. Swanton was able to make the first live cricket commentary back to England. The first day was inauspicious although Paul Gibb and Eddie Paynter made a painstaking stand of 184 during which there was much tedium when the former continued to block leg-breaks from Bruce Mitchell. For Jim, it was something of an anticlimax for he wanted drama to report. He was not to be disappointed:

The second day of the match was on Boxing Day and my luck really changed. At first it was much the same story with Mitchell himself doing the blocking this time, against Hedley Verity. Alone in my hot little box I imagined people falling asleep by the thousand after their second helping of turkey. But then, with about ten minutes to go before the close of play, Tom Goddard caught and bowled Dudley Nourse for 73. The nightwatchman, one Gordon, came in and was promptly stumped first ball. Tom was on a hat-trick and I was very excited. Young Billy Wade came in, a pretty good bat but a novice in Test cricket. He was obviously nervous. He took some time to take guard and look round the field and then, glory be, he was bowled first ball. It was only the fifth Test hat-trick by an Englishman and it was quite a story. At the end of the match Michael Standing sent me a wire. Congratulations on commentaries. Everybody pleased.

On the next day, Jim picked up commentary with two overs to be bowled.

Now here is Langton bowling to Gibb. Gibb played a forward stroke, it was well pitched up, and the ball is very well fielded by Melville up there at short leg. Gibb has once more come off and Edrich, I'm afraid, is out for ten. Now here comes Langton again, to Gibb, and Gibb this time plays back to short extra cover and no run is scored. And I dare say it's only human that Gibb and Paynter are thinking rather more now of being there tomorrow morning. Now here comes Langton once more to Gibb – his arm's over, Langton's slower one – and Gibb saw it in time and checked his stroke and played the ball again to the two short legs without any runs being scored. England haven't quite pushed the game on as we hoped they might, but they've got the chance to do that now tomorrow morning.

Now, here's Langton again, a good length ball, and Gibb has time to turn him round to square leg, the ball perhaps sitting on the middle of the leg stump, and again there were no runs scored. The ball went to Gordon, who has been a great standby for South African bowling and perhaps for the newcomers the one unqualified success so far.

Now, here comes Langton once more to Gibb. This time Gibb leaves the ball quietly alone, [it was] pitched well outside the off stump, and we have a few balls more of Langton's over. It's not quite certain that there will be another over, although I think there will be. There are three more balls to go now, anyway.

Now, here comes Langton again, and Gibb plays him forward – good stroke – but Langton fields the ball well, he's a very good fielder to his own bowling and everyone else's, and he threw the ball back to Wade, the wicket-keeper, in case Gibb, who's got rather a habit of walking out of his crease, had started to run. However Gibb didn't do so and now he's framing up to Langton again, and here comes Langton. Again Langton's . . . [raised vocal pitch] – Oh, that was very nearly a catch, very nearly a catch indeed. Gibb got there too soon, a little bit, and he played out round his leg somewhere. I didn't quite know where the ball was, and that Gordon had . . . well, I don't think it was quite a chance, but it went to his left hand and it very, very nearly was a catch. And actually they scored one run. So that's England now 96 for one, Gibb not out 49, Paynter, who now receives the bowling, not out 30.

Now here's Paynter again from Langton, and taking the ball round the corner for one run, and smart fielding by Dalton for one run – for two runs, and [excitedly] it's a very very sharp one, very, very sharp, with an appeal for run out. I don't know why Paynter went on that second run, but he did, and he just got home. There was very little in it. Dalton from third man. I think he was foxing him really, and he threw in very quickly, and he was very, very nearly run out . . .

And so Jim continued to the end of the day's play with England at the close on 103 for one wicket with Gibb not out 53 and Paynter not out 32. Both went on to score centuries on the final day of the match which petered out to an unsatisfactory draw after an unduly delayed declaration by Hammond. Although the commentary above is unremarkable in itself, with the spoken word having to be mentally listened to when read on the page as opposed to the written one which transmits automatically, it is noteworthy for another reason. The old 78rpm disc recordings of the first and fifth Tests of this series containing Jim's commentary have only recently resurfaced, having been lost to view for the last sixty-odd years. His words seen here are put down for the first time as part of what is now a new piece of archive.

After the first Test was over Jim took the long and dusty train journey down to the Cape. Over the New Year there was played another inconclusive Test Match highlighted by hundreds from Wally Hammond, Leslie Ames and Brian Valentine for England and Dudley Nourse for South Africa; and then on to Port Elizabeth where Jim felt very much at home on the golf links, which reminded him of other seaside courses such as the one at Deal. A civic lunch was memorable, if only for a speech where an ebullient Mayor either forgot, or pretended to forget, the England captain's name: 'I am very happy to welcome the MCC team and particularly their distinguished Captain, Mr . . . what's your name again? . . . Mr Hammond.' (Months later back in England, Jim gave a BBC talk which included this episode and made a reference to the Mayor 'getting on to his hind legs'. He was asked to delete the phrase and make 'a trifling change' as it was deemed a 'bit too frivolous and might offend some of them [and] just conceivably, it might distress some sensitive listeners!')

Jim continued his tour of Port Elizabeth's coastline with some excellent surf-bathing in the company of two of the South African side – captain Alan Melville and Pieter van der Bijl, who had both been to Oxford – before visiting the cricket ground where Len Hutton was being given net practice by an odd assembly of willing helpers including 'old men in braces, young boys in shorts, Indians and some Malays, including one rather elderly one with what I took to be a very doubtful action who (after they had been going well over an hour) claimed the shilling that Len had put on his stumps.'

In later years Jim recalled no impression of stark social injustice. During his twelve-week stay he spent much time in friends' houses where his minimal contact with non-Europeans was solely with their servants. Observing at the time only an atmosphere of benevolent strict paternalism, he later admitted he had been 'young and heedless'.

Having won the third Test in Durban by an innings and 13 runs with a double century from Paynter and another hundred from Hammond, England had to settle for another depressing draw in a rain-affected fourth game of the series at Johannesburg.

Once more the touring party all returned to Durban for the fifth Test and a match unparalleled in the history of cricket. After *ten* allocated days' play (one was rained off) the 'Timeless Test', as it came to be known, reached a farcical conclusion. On that last day, with the English side needing to catch the 8.05 p.m. train from Durban to Cape Town in order to make their departure on the *Athlone Castle* back to Blighty, the game was abandoned as a draw. During the match at least seventeen records were established. But for the full story let us go over to Jim for his final summary of the tour.

Hello Great Britain, and South Africa. The Test Match, the final Test Match here at Kingsmead, has ended, at last, in a draw. And so by a delicious stroke of irony nature determined that there should be a time limit after all. I feel myself, a personal view of course, that this is the proper result. England have won the rubber and South Africa have won much glory too.

The English score, second innings: Hutton bowled Mitchell 55; P.A. Gibb bowled Dalton 120; Edrich caught Gordon, bowled Langton 219;

W.R. Hammond stumped Grieveson, bowled Dalton 140; Paynter caught Grieveson, bowled Gordon 75; Ames not out, 17; B.H. Valentine not out 4; Extras 24; Total 654 for five wickets.

Well, we started off the tenth day of this amazing match this morning with 200 needed to win and England having seven wickets in hand. And we noticed at once that the wind – as on the third and on the seventh days, which were the two days that ended in rain – the wind was blowing from the south-west, from quite the opposite quarter from the other days. Well, it seemed from the start, to us who were watching, a question of runs against time. But, there were still, as I say, 200 needed, and for a long time Hammond and Paynter went along at a very modest pace, against the South African attack and South African fielding that was still, though very weary, very steady and keen.

The first hour of the match produced 37 runs. The second three-quarters of an hour – that's to say they played for an hour and three-quarters here before lunch – produced 45. Well, that makes 82. And so, at lunch we needed 118 more to win. And I can't think of any occasion during the morning when the batsmen seemed in any sort of positive difficulty. They had difficulty in getting the ball away, or rather they didn't attempt to get the ball away unless it was completely safe for them to do so.

Well, at lunch, as I say, there were 118 more, and soon after lunch I got a message through to the box from a listener in Umkumaas, which is thirty miles down the coast, and he rang up and said, 'It's raining like anything here, tell Mr Hammond, for goodness sake, to hurry up.' Well, just after that Hammond obliged by getting his hundred. But he didn't exactly hurry up, and at 611 he lost Paynter, who was caught at the wicket off the inside edge of the bat from Gordon's bowling. Gordon had just come on to use the new ball, and actually he was still bowling with the old ball when he got Paynter out.

Well, then in came Ames, and I must say I couldn't help wondering whether we should still be in this very tense position as regards the weather if Ames had come in last night and played his natural game instead of Paynter. The amount of time which was lost even by the fielders crossing over for the left hander, apart from all question of Paynter having scored slowly, was enormous. However, Hammond stayed there, and Ames came in, and the game went on with the scoring getting a little bit quicker and the clouds also getting much darker. Twice there was a little rain and the players had to come in. The South Africans stood the rain very well, but when it became too bad they did come in.

And then for the second time in the match, having scored 140, Hammond was stumped by Grieveson off Dalton's bowling. He was trying to push one on the leg side and he just missed the ball and Grieveson, as he has been in this match, was very, very quick about his chance.

Well, then Valentine came in – this was nearly tea-time now – and he nearly gave a stumping chance too off Dalton, his first ball. Well, then he hit a rather short run round to long leg for 4, and that's the very last thing that happened in the match, because then it began to rain very hard again.

The score then, as it was at the finish, was 654 for 5. There was just a spell during the tea interval when it wasn't raining, but as soon as the umpires were due to come out again the rain started and the light became atrocious, and within a quarter of an hour the rain was really whistling across that ground and there was no chance of any more play, not only today, but I should think really hardly tomorrow morning as well. The tarpaulin covers had even been blown off one end of the wicket where they cover the bowlers' crease. So that was all, and this ten days match has ended after all in a draw. They've been playing as far as I can work it out for roughly forty-five hours, and they've broken all sorts of records – I can't attempt to tell you half of them. One of them is that they've achieved a new Test aggregate of 1,981, they've taken the record amount of money for this Kingsmead ground – nearly £5000 – and Gibb and Edrich have made 280, which is the record partnership of England v. South Africa. Well, those are some of the things they've done.

And we're left just to reflect on what these timeless Tests, these modern Test matches do mean. It's my own view that modern wickets have made the modern Test what it is – a matter of stamina and concentration. It's not so much the fact of there being no time limit as that the wickets are so hopeless for the bowlers, and that the batsmen, they prefer to wait for the loose one and to grind the wretched bowler down. If the turf is faster, the ball comes more easily, more naturally under the bat, and the batsman is encouraged to make a stroke. Stamina and concentration, those are the things that count. They're the virtues that gave Len Hutton his 364 at the Oval in something over thirteen hours last August – and, incidentally, involved such a strain on him that I believe he slept for something like two hours in all in the making of it. And the sort of conditions, when a great maker of strokes like Hammond takes five hours and three-quarters over this 140 of his. And an aggressive, chirpy little man like Paynter, who we all know in

England so well, scores at a rate of rather less than 20 runs an hour.

This, please remember, is a personal opinion, but I do believe that more and more people are coming round to the same point of view. Prepare the sort of good fast wickets we used to have for Tests, I think, and we'll get back to the days when a man who scored 60 in an hour and a half was a hero, and when cricket was artistry – a fight between the bat and the ball. I should like to see a timeless Test on a fast wicket, and I believe we should get back to enterprising cricket again.

I hope that hasn't sounded too like a sermon, and I hope you don't run away with the impression that I'm unappreciative of the efforts of the players of either side. They've used the circumstances as they thought best, and shown great fortitude. Particularly, perhaps I feel it only fair to say, the English team, who bowled and fielded with the greatest determination and accuracy as long ago as last Thursday, if you can take your mind back to then, when it seemed to us that there was no hope left for them at all, and with South Africa piling up their lead into the 600s. But the England team tackled this gigantic task just from the first, as they really felt that they could make it.

From the South Africa point of view there is much to be glad of in that these last two Tests have shown that her team can fight England on level ground. The South Africans must come to England in 1940 full of confidence.

Goodnight Great Britain and South Africa.

There is something wonderfully comforting about hearing Jim say 'Goodnight', rather like an avuncular housemaster putting out the lights in the dorm. Again there is nothing exceptional in what he had to say, but even so his vocal DNA is unmistakable. The 'as it were's', 'as I say's' and 'so to speak's' were few, yet the measured pace, controlled exposition and rich timbre were present then as they were for the remainder of his life. Here he was, in his early thirties, a fully fledged summariser engaging every listener in a conversational one-to-one.

By this time, of course, his initial fear of having too little work had long receded. At the outset he had been engaged for twenty broadcasts. Very soon he had been doing two hours a day for the SABC domestic services and also writing for the *Argus* newspaper group. By the end of the tour he had done over 200 broadcasts. In fact, several of his friends made mock-complaints that they could not turn on their wirelesses without hearing his voice. Not surprisingly, in that last majestic summary traces of his extreme tiredness and a slight

hoarseness are just noticeable. One of his regular spots on SABC had
been a letters forum:

E.W.S.:

I'm trying to answer all who have sent names and addresses, but
some did not, and if any are listening tonight, just let me say thank you
very much. They were very encouraging to receive, and I hope if I refer
to one or two this evening, that the authors won't take it amiss.
There was the Cape lady, who after one of the early Tests said, I quite
like your broadcasts, but I think you're a bit hard on Bruce Mitchell,
and in case you don't know, in the Transvaal he's public heart-throb
number one. And then there was the chap from Port Elizabeth, who
hoped my voice would stand up to the strain of the timeless Test. As a
matter of fact, he had something of the detective in him, because he said
it wasn't so good on the Monday – that's one of the Mondays – and
that couldn't have been the strain, and perhaps I was suffering from a
weekend hangover. And then there was the Victorian lady who deplored
modern manners and morals, and wrote to me, as one who must have
known the world as it was before the war. Actually, the first thing I
remember was walking with my mother just before the war and asking
her what was going to happen. And she said that there might be a small
do between the Serbs and the Austrians. Well, this lady said what she
thought about the modern girl – their mouths, she said, looking as
though they were just a newly painted pillarbox, and all sorts of other
things like that. Very stern stuff it was. Well, she also sent her wishes to
Mr Hammond, and she said then, I recommend for the MCC no
evening parties, no cocktails and no cigarettes. Well, however much I
agree with her, and I certainly do, I think she was a little bit hard there,
because there's a strongish reaction, you know, after the strain of a day
in the field, and the party, of course a mild one, I think is the best way
to defeat it – I hope you'll agree there, Mr Hammond, would you?
[Wally Hammond, sitting alongside, replies, 'Absolutely.']

And then there was the man who contradicted me when I said that I
thought Newlands was the loveliest ground in the world. He said that
Brockton Point, Vancouver and [grounds in] New Zealand, were even
more scenic and that Don Bradman agreed with him. Well, I'm afraid
I've never been to New Zealand, but Newlands is good enough for me,
and as for the [unintelligible word] which he complains of at Newlands,
it doesn't really obtrude very much, and in any case for many people it
has very pleasant associations.

And then there was the lady who got rather irrelevant, as is a prerogative of her sex, and she told me about how she went to England with her mother, and they went to have a fiddle repaired, and the man who was repairing the fiddle said, 'I've just done a job for someone out your way,' and when she asked where 'out your way' was, he said Bombay . . .

As was usual with Jim, during his stay he had participated in a whirligig of activity. Interspersed with trips to the Victoria Falls and baboon-watching in the rainforest, and an excursion up the Zambesi in a launch to Kandahar Island to inspect the great crocodiles and tame monkeys, was the acceptance of a continuing round of generous hospitality. The cricket and broadcasting became almost incidental – but not quite.

Back home his broadcasts were adjudged to have been a great success. The tone of internal and external correspondence changed markedly. On his return, having delivered a talk about his experiences in South Africa, he received a congratulatory note:

Dear Swanton,
    This is just a line to tell you that the talk went admirably. I listened with interest and congratulate you.

Another communication also recognised his worth:

There is no doubt that his work was exceedingly popular with the South African listening public. I think you will find that he can deliver the kind of goods you want.

Mind you, not everybody was prepared to be pleased:

I was not impressed with his performance in 'Loose-Box'. He was fearfully lah-di-dah – effusively so – and did not seem to have any of the punch on which, I would have thought, S.A. would have insisted.

Support, however, was quickly to hand:

Be that as it may, he had something of a succès-fou with the South African listening public over a very long series of broadcasts throughout the MCC Tour.

And on his past rudeness:

I have always been puzzled about [that] because Swanton really is a very pleasant fellow indeed, and, I think, not unduly conceited.

Such a pleasant fellow was he that there were even murmurs that he might commentate at Wimbledon and even read the Epilogue. Unfortunately – some might have said fortuitously – Test cricket got in the way.

Jim had been rewarded for his efforts in South Africa by being given the chance to join Howard Marshall and Michael Standing in covering the Tests against the West Indies with ball by ball commentary. It promised to be a splendid summer, even though there had been an early setback. While in South Africa, Jim had written to the Editor-in-Chief of the *Daily Telegraph*, Seymour Berry, in the hope of landing the job of cricket correspondent which had become available. On his return, Berry offered Jim first refusal if Douglas Jardine declined. He didn't!

Never mind: George Headley's hundred for the West Indies in each innings of the Lord's Test; Learie Constantine's electrifying all-round performance at the Oval, including a whirlwind 79, the majority in boundaries, and which contained a stupendous six off the back foot down to the Vauxhall end; and the happy thought of a winter ahead giving broadcast eyewitness accounts, in conjunction with Teddy Wakelam, of the Wallabies' rugby tour helped to dispel any lingering disappointment. There was also the faint hope of travelling to India where MCC under the captaincy of A.J. Holmes were due to play three Tests at Bombay, Calcutta and Madras.

Neither the cricket nor the rugby tour were destined to take place, nor indeed was it possible to consummate an engagement offered by the editor of *The Field*. Brian Vesey-Fitzgerald had written on 18 August 1939:

Dear Mr Swanton,

I should be very glad if you would do our cricket for us next year commencing at the beginning of May at a fee of 5 guineas per week. We should require about 1,200 words each week and certainly not more than 1,500. This matter will have to be in our office by first post each Monday morning. We should also require from time to time during the winter, but at no specified times, further articles on cricket particularly during those winters when there are Test Matches abroad. In these circumstances we write to you for an article and we expect – and hitherto have always received – an article in return. I very much hope that you will accept this offer and let me know fairly soon.

This job had been Neville Cardus's and Jim was quicker than soon in accepting, but by 1940 matters were, of course, out of his hands. Commendably, the post was kept for him, awaiting his return from the war.

The 1939 cricket season, as many know, was truncated with the West Indian tourists returning home early, but of the games he had seen outside of the Tests, Jim had enjoyed particularly the University match at Lord's where the attendance over the three days was 9000 – a staggering total by today's standards. After the game, he was the recipient of another written salvo, only this time from an apoplectic naval commander:

Saturday, 1st July, Transmission 2, Inter-'Varsity Cricket Match: Mr. E.W. Swanton not only speaks indistinctly, but he omitted to give the names of the teams!! and although the commentary was limited to 15 minutes, this gentleman thought fit to waste (to us) precious time by bursting into poetry!!!

Oh, dear! He was obviously not aMused . . . However, for Jim, more lethal salvoes were imminent. The sabres were now rattling loudly around Europe. When war was declared everything was put on hold. On the top of Jim's personal pending file was a single sheet of paper. It was a contract from the BBC for a commentary on a rugby match later in the year that required his signature. In his adjacent in-tray lay another single sheet. The contract had been cancelled . . .

Chapter 5

Surviving in his own way

The sirens of war easily seduced Jim. Not literally, of course, for their haunting, eldritch wail was way off down the line. But rather in his eagerness to be involved once hostilities had been declared.

It had all started for him in the spring of 1939 on the boat back from South Africa. On board the *Athlone Castle* was a Colonel in the Bedfordshire Yeomanry, Stanley Harris, who had played rugby for Blackheath and England. At the bar one evening Harris had remarked: 'The harvest will be gathered in at the end of the summer and then it will all start. Mark my words. Why don't you come and join my regiment when it does?'

It was not really a question, more an offer and Jim *did* mark his words. After all, Stanley Harris was worldly wise and a man of many parts; besides his rugby distinctions, he had boxed in the Olympics and played Davis Cup tennis for South Africa. (Perhaps incongruously, he was too, a nifty mover in the world of ballroom dancing.) Harris, however, had added that 'you two [*Jim's flatmate Ian Peebles had also been present and included when the invitation was issued*] should first do a spell in the ranks as Territorials, in the HAC [*The Honourable Artillery Company*] or elsewhere.' Neither of the two had given much attention to the rider. But with Peebles having his hands full with the captaincy of Middlesex and Jim busy in the commentary box they had left their applications too late – the Honourable Artillery Company's lists were closed.

As the summer approached autumn and Ian Peebles's hands were less full and Jim was foreseeably less busy, they both suddenly became anxious. Surely the army was a sort of club which might at any moment declare itself no longer open with both of them excluded. For Jim such a thought was horrifying given his father's non-service in the First World War through a physical disability. He had never forgotten the comments he had overheard as a youngster regarding those who were thought to have evaded the call-up. The dreadful vision of being handed a white feather crept into the back of his mind.

The signing-on office in Victoria was dingy and the territorial recruiting officer supervising the formalities rather seedy. Never mind, for both Jim and Ian there was a sense of considerable relief. They were definitely *in*.

A week or so later Germany invaded Poland. On that day the two aspiring officers of the Crown enjoyed not so much a last supper as a last lunch. Both of them were experiencing a heightened sense of expectation, a mixture of apprehension and excitement as they exchanged repartee over the meal at the old International Sportsman's Club at Grosvenor House. Immediately afterwards they knew they had to set off for Uxbridge in Middlesex, where the unit to which they had been assigned was stationed.

As Jim recollected later, 'The car wheels were almost turning, when on a sudden instinct I slipped back into the club and sent a brief wire, which simply said that we two were on our way to Battery 999, RA, and that although it was probably now far too late the address was such-and-such if Lt. Colonel S.W. Harris of the Cavalry Club had any use for us.'

Once at Uxbridge they were soon immersed in the routines of regimental life. Both were intrigued by the vast metal 'ears' mounted on platforms ready to detect the sound of encroaching aircraft, but concerned at the dull prospect of a prolonged stay in 'Searchlights'. The wire had more or less been forgotten when just over a week later an archetypal bristling major sent for Jim and demanded to know why two gunners of his battery had applied for transfers and commissions in such an irregular fashion, Goddammit! Oh, and how did he come to know Colonel Harris of the Bedfordshire Yeomanry? Although removed geographically, Harris's rank ensured that ruffled feathers were not a sufficient reason to stop Peebles and Swanton soon making their way from Uxbridge to Dunstable. There they became young officers in the Bedfordshire Yeomanry, for the Yeomanry had been transformed as gunners in 148 Field Regiment, Royal Artillery, and which later became part of the 18th Division.

The '148' was a somewhat intriguing regiment. Colonel Harris was particularly anxious to acquire men with an athletic background. He liked distinguished sportsmen or the sons of distinguished sportsmen. His adjutant was the tennis player 'Dickie' Ritchie (son of a renowned player of the same sport, M.J.B. Ritchie) who eventually became Secretary of the Queen's Club. In other words, he too, looked upon his enclave in the Army set-up as a kind of club, with his sort of men.

The Regiment was, in fact, quite a close community – bankers, estate agents, auctioneers, and solicitors; in other words, professional classes on one hand, and on the other, an assortment of town and countrymen with their own skilled crafts. Territorials they were and territorially they were bonded, as many lived in the area of Dunstable, Luton and Leighton Buzzard and had known one another for much of their lives.

When Jim and Ian arrived at Dunstable in the autumn of 1939 they found a Regiment split into two Batteries, the '419' from the town itself and the '420' from Luton. Eventually, it was decided to expand the Regiment by another Battery, the '512', which comprised conscripted men augmented by key operators transferred from the '419' and '420' Batteries. Their places in the '419' and '420' were taken by militia men, who were brought in to fill the gaps.

Each of these Batteries consisted of two troops 'A' and 'B' and each of the Troops carried four guns. Overseeing the Batteries was the administration at Regimental HQ. Overall, there were around 400 or so personnel.

As a Second Lieutenant, Jim was put in charge of 'B' Troop, '419' Battery. 'A' Troop was in the hands of Lieutenant Price who eventually was promoted to Captain. Very soon Jim was to meet Eric Samuel who at the time was a Gunner. 'When Jim first came to the Regiment, he was billeted at Dunstable at Dr. Watkins. And Major Merry came up to me one day and said, "Gunner Samuel, will you do me a favour?" So I said, "Yes sir, what is it?" He said, "I want you to go up to Dr Watkins, just up the High Street where you will find two new officers. Will you be their batman until we can get something sorted out? Just look after them." And like a fool I said, yes. Well, it wasn't easy to be a batman to Jim. And I stuck it for I suppose about four weeks in Dunstable, then we moved down to Lowestoft, and I was still his batman down at Lowestoft, when we moved into the Victoria Hotel. And I thought to myself, you know, I didn't join the Army to be a batman and look after an officer, I joined the Army because I wanted to do something ... And I think it came to a head one morning. We were in a hotel – the officers were in bedrooms upstairs and we two or three batmen were downstairs in the servants' quarters.

Well, he rang down for me one day and said he wanted a bath. "I need you to run the bath," he said. So, I had to go upstairs to turn the tap on the baths, you know, and I thought, well, he could have done this himself. So, I put the plug in, turned the hot tap on and waited till it was about four inches from the top, turned the tap off and went downstairs. And he fumed. "It's too hot, I can't get in! What do you think you're doing?" And in the end, I said, "Well sir, to be quite honest, I don't want to be a batman, I want to be a soldier – that's what I joined the regiment for." Within about two weeks he got a new batman, who stayed with him right the way through . . .'

If not quite all the way through, certainly for a long time, Jim's batman was Gunner Douglas Cresswell, who died a few years ago. Second Lieutenant Swanton had obviously wasted no time in making his mark.

The 18th was an East Anglia Division and in a very short while Jim was supervising a convoy of impressed vehicles – lorries pulling the guns, trucks, civilian cars – on a journey around the windswept wastes of Norfolk and north Suffolk. Lowestoft, Hopton, Gorleston, Yarmouth, Caistor, Stalham, East Dereham and North Walsham were unexciting places for those geared for action. The Regiment was supposed to be guarding the coast and so was placed a mile or two inland in order to facilitate fire on any invasion force. The men were billeted in a strange array of accommodation – holiday camps, seaside hotels, under canvas and even at a rectory. Jim and other officers were, of course, either in hotels or private houses. 'Jim made sure we had first choice of billets,' said Eric Samuel. 'We always had a good billet – looking after my troops, that was typical Jim. In that sort of way he did look after us. Not many men liked him, but they respected him as an officer. You didn't have to like him to respect him.'

It was a time of manning promenades, taking part in training exercises and waiting for something to happen. Something, of course, never did, because the imminent invasion remained imminent. There was much building of gun-pits and firing of what was thought of as ancient weaponry: 16-pounders, 4.5 Howitzers and French 75mms. The 18-pounders the Regiment once possessed had been commandeered for the war in Europe and were lost at Dunkirk. Derek Gilbert, another Gunner, remembers that 'guns were dotted all along the coast, but the only gun we had never moved without a drag rope, because of its solid wheels. We were terribly poorly equipped.' Onlookers in a forty-year time warp could well have imagined they were watching an episode of *Dad's Army*.

Eric Samuel was by now acting as assistant to Jim at observation posts. 'We spent a long time practising. I think Jim and I climbed every church in East Anglia. It was the obvious place to have an observation point. He would be looking for any lies in the ground through his binoculars. When you get to an observation point, the first thing an Ack [*anti-aircraft telephone communications*] has to do is to make a sketch. He can then see a rough outline. You then mark out points on an Ordnance Survey map. For instance, at Lowestoft, a lighthouse would perhaps be a point, or a church steeple another point, and you would then work out where the guns were on the map. You knew where your guns were, you knew where the observation post was, and you knew these fixed things you could see. Then your job was to range the guns, establish their positions in relation to the set targets, that is, the distance aligned from the guns, because the observation point wouldn't be in line from where they were shooting. Having worked all that out from the observation point, you would relay the information down to the guns, and they would then lay the range on, as well as the angle, and begin to fire. With a bit of luck you would hit your target. Nine times out of ten you didn't, so you would then modify your range. OP [*observation post*] would say perhaps drop fifty yards or drop a hundred yards – 200 degrees right or left – and eventually they would get where they wanted to. Most people tried to get one shot in front and one behind and then you knew where you were. If you were good you would do it in half a dozen rounds; if you were rotten, you didn't.

'It relied so much on the terrain. I remember we did a firing camp in Wales, which is a bit rugged, and I was up the OP with Jim and our target was a patch of heather. We found out that the heather was right on the rising edge of a ridge. So, with the first round you fire – which is a little bit long – you don't see it, because it goes over the top. So what we did was to start well below and creep up to it. It's really interesting to be at the observation post – almost like playing a game of chess.'

On one occasion, it was even more interesting to be at the observation post. There was a firing camp at Larkhill. Jim was volunteered by all the other officers to take the first shoot. Normally, nobody would have minded being put in pole position, but there was a certain amount of trepidation as the exercise was taking place with live ammunition under the unforgiving eye of the divisional Commander, Royal Artillery, Brigadier Geoffrey Franklin, no less.

'With all the officers watching we were given a target,' says Samuel. 'We were fairly lucky, it worked out quite well. Half a dozen ranging shots, and then we were ready to put down troop fire, which means all the guns firing at once so you really saturated the area. The CRA then phoned through and said "Stop – we don't want to waste ammunition, that's OK." Well, the next officer came up and asked me to stay in the OP – he was a very nervous young Second Lieutenant . . .'

Jim himself picks up the story:

'Peebles, eh? Anything to do with the cricketer?' Ian pleaded guilty, and was duly given his target of copse or hedge somewhere well to our front. Calculations were duly made, and the orders given over the telephone to the troop of guns in rear – range, bearing, and so on, ending with the magic word – Fire!

So far on this day of days all had gone smoothly. We had seemed to know the drill reasonably well, and the shells from a range of somewhere between 4,000 and 6,000 yards had fallen in roughly the right area. But now! As the guns fired we raised our binoculars looking hopefully for the burst. Next second there was a fearful cr-r-r-ump and the OP was enveloped in dirt and smoke as the first shell exploded about a couple of cricket pitches to our rear.

'Stop!' bellowed the Battery Commander down the line. 'Stop!'

Yes, but would he be in time to prevent the next round, which might even now be whistling towards us in advance of the sound? In a word would near-miss be followed by direct hit? They were awful seconds before the cancellation was confirmed by the Gun-Position-Officer, and we breathed again.

The CRA's wrath at this escape was terrible to behold – as, for that matter, was the anguish of poor Stanley Harris, our CO. The verbal rockets spared no-one. Mr Peebles had made a gross error in the range, giving the distance from guns to OP instead of from guns to target. His Ack. was guilty of being a party to it. The GPO and his Ack. had failed to check and were equally guilty. So were all the officers at the OP, from the colonel downwards. Thus the day's sport terminated abruptly, and the CRA and his staff departed in a gleam of field-boots and fury.

Blame has been apportioned liberally by Jim. It is easy to judge as an observer. Anyway the ultimate result of the gun being literally jumped was that Ian Peebles was transferred out of the Regiment. He then proceeded rapidly to work in Intelligence with photographic security being his special province, until one night during a raid outside his M15 department in Queen's Gate, London, he came too close in proximity to a bomb and lost the sight of one eye.

Time passed slowly. The tedious repetition of the exercises with no end in view produced boredom. To relieve the frustration, for Jim at least, there was cricket once summer had returned. Throughout his time with the Regiment, he had still been engaged in correspondence with the BBC, suggesting this and that idea and announcing his availability to act as commentator or presenter. A missive from the Red Lion in Colchester in May 1940 informed them that he was free to play for the Corporation in a match against the Ministry of Information. Or as Swanton preferred to refer to it, 'the noisy service versus the silent one'.

There was a game, too, on the August bank holiday of that same year in which the Battery took on Ingham Cricket Club, or, in effect, a side full of Edriches. In the garden of The Grange at Ingham were a couple of howitzers, marked DP – for demonstration purposes and dated 1915! As Jim remarked, 'if the Führer's forces had chanced to descend on this portion of our sea-girt isle at that time he could have declared by lunch-time.'

The previous month Jim had been made up to Acting Captain, and then in October of that year, 1940, he was appointed Temporary Captain. According to his Record of Service the rank was never made substantive, although there is little doubt it would have been if events had followed a more normal course, and Jim had continued to be part of an accessible regimental unit. When eventually he left the Service he was accorded the rank of honorary Captain.

As the new year of 1941 began, the regiment was posted to Hawick in Scotland, which was where they received their G1098s, or in layman's language, the full equipment for battle. But even now, not yet unto the breach! The nearest thing to a confrontation was when the Regiment went into the rugby field to take on top quality side Hawick and predictably were slaughtered. Jim played at full-back.

After a snowy winter in Border country where the other ranks were housed in a tweed mill – steam-heated, so handy for pressing their gear – they all were sent down to Lancashire where Jim found himself comfortably ensconced in Lord Derby's residence, Knowsley Hall. While the men bedded down in the stables, Jim felt so much at home in the Hall that he promptly scored a hundred in an Army match.

Whilst at Knowsley, there was another game at the Gaye in Shrewsbury, which was situated below the Castle. The match was alongside the river, between two teams from the 148 Battalion, and Jim's opening partner was Bombardier Ronald Vearncombe. Having stunned a yorker from the opposition's fastest bowler and inadvertently almost trodden the ball into the damp ground with his foot, Vearncombe picked it up and helpfully threw it back to the wicket-keeper, who was still standing some ten yards behind the stumps. At the end of the over, Captain Swanton strolled up to him. 'Bombardier, if I see you do that again, I'll run you out.' As Vearncombe was to say later, 'My enthusiasm for the partnership suddenly died.'

At the end of the match, Vearncombe and a teammate made their way to the OR [*Other Ranks*] canteen to join a long queue for tea. After a few minutes they realised that to wait too long would mean being late for the truck taking them back to Knowsley. As they were on the point of abandoning the queue, suddenly a pregnant ATS girl keeled over and fainted. While his comrade helped the girl to a seat, Vearncombe carried on queueing and eventually collected a cup of tea before taking it across to the girl to help her recover. Having seen that she was all right, they both rushed off to the waiting truck. Swanton was counting off the numbers. 'You're late, Bombardier. I'll see you in the morning on a charge!'

The next day Vearncombe was marched by his Sergeant-Major to see the Captain. 'Cap off. Stand to attention!' 'Do you have any excuse for your behaviour?' The bombardier explained the dilemma of being torn between doing the decent thing and helping the girl, and keeping everyone waiting. He finished his explanation with, 'And I'm sure, sir, you'll regard that as a legitimate reason.'

Swanton looked up. 'If I thought you were . . .' His voice tailed off. 'Reprimanded!' Once outside, the Sergeant-Major could not stop laughing. 'I thought you were trying to pull a fast one and that you'd really be for it.'

But all these scores for and against Jim became nugatory when set alongside the tragic air raids on Liverpool to which he was witness. On the first Saturday of May, Swanton was named in the Liverpool side against Bootle in the Liverpool and District Competition for a match on the Aigburth ground. A major air raid on the city had taken place the night before. When he turned up for the game, he found the field full of shrapnel from the ack-ack shells. A small hole in front of the pavilion was a numbing reminder of a rogue shell that had killed an ARP warden in the unlikeliest of horrible accidents.

Even so the general feeling was that the match should take place. Jim went in first with Eric Greenhalgh of Lancashire and scored 60-odd before running himself out by over-ambitiously trying for a third run. That evening the raids on the docks continued, the second in a series of four on consecutive nights. Jim had an unwanted grandstand view from the Golf and Country Club at Childwall where he was staying.

Later that year, and from the same ground, Jim commentated for the BBC on a match between the Army and the RAF. BBC Archives reveal a letter that arrived soon afterwards, from the T.S. [Training Ship] *Mercury* anchored at Hamble, Southampton:

> Dear Swanton,
>   You may be amazed to hear that your broadcast on Saturday from Old Trafford or somewhere [*geographically not too far distant*] – with no particular objective material to put across – was the best I've ever heard on cricket.
>   All the best,
>   Yours truly,
>   C.B. Fry

In retrospect it seems incredible that, while he had been engaged with the Army in the fastnesses of East Anglia, the Border country and Merseyside during this long period of waiting for the big event, Jim somehow still managed to commentate or report on occasional cricket and rugby matches for the BBC.

Michael Standing, by now Director of Outside Broadcasts, often had difficulty keeping up with him.

> My dear Jim,
>   Thank you for sending your new address. On the other hand, I am not at all clear what you mean. Are you permanently at Monmouth now and temporarily at Trawsfynydd, or is Monmouth where you will be until Saturday, returning after that date to Liverpool? For a former journalist, you are singularly inexplicit.

Jim's peripatetic existence was obviously beginning to tell. Every communication from Standing's erstwhile and erring colleague during the past year had come from a different address: Shenley House, Lowestoft; Barton Wood Mill Farm, North Walsham; The Royal Norfolk and Suffolk Yacht Club; HMS *Excellent*, Portsmouth; and 100 Piccadilly!

Two of Jim's cricketing excursions were at Lord's; Army versus an England XI and Sir Pelham Warner's XI against the RAF. In covering these matches, someone called Elsie, in the Programme Contracts Department of the BBC, with perhaps only a vague knowledge of who Mr Swanton might be, had written to Jim explaining that he would be refunded for a third-class train ticket. An affronted Jim replied and pointed out stiffly that he was 'now an Officer'. Whereupon poor Elsie immediately capitulated: 'We didn't know – as a serving Officer you will, of course, be given a first-class fare.'

Back in the Regiment Captain Swanton was regarded as a stickler. 'Far too regimental, but he was respected as a good officer,' is the view of Jack Wragg, who then was a Gunner in Troop HQ. 'He made sure we were good soldiers and that's quite a thing, you know. He was very proud of his troops. We had to be the best. Basically, he was a decent man, but you had to be careful. I was on a parade one day and the last thing I'd done before going on the square was to sweep the room out. He had me up for having dusty boots. He really told me off.'

The Brigade were occupied with long divisional exercises in the Pennines as well as manoeuvres in Wales. On one drill order at Fennybridge they were trying out new armoured quads, which have the crew inside and the turret aloft. 'The front one overturned and the poor fellow driving it, a reservist called Selway, was decapitated,' remembers Derek Gilbert. 'He had stuck his head out of the top at the wrong moment. Well, Swanny rushes up shouting, "What the hell's happened here? Oh, look at my quad." He wasn't worried about the poor lad who was dead. He was not liked at all at that time.'

To be fair, Gilbert did concede that possibly Jim was not fully aware of the tragic circumstances. Unfortunately, as Eric Samuel relates, it was not the only accident on the firing ranges. 'On one firing camp, we had this young Irish sergeant-major – called McCormack – and he looked young, too,' Eric Samuels remarked. 'He was an immaculate soldier, couldn't fault him on anything, but he'd got no relationship with the men – he just didn't know how to handle them. He was a cocky little . . .! but Jim used to get on very well with him. You see, he had a father who was quite well up in the War Office [laughs] – wheels within wheels. Anyway, when we knew we were going abroad, we were at this firing camp up in Wales, and after the firing was over it's the job of the sergeant-major to collect up all the bags of cordite that are knocking about – cordite of course isn't very safe – and actually in the end get rid of them. Well, this sergeant-major got rid of them all right, in fact he blew them up in his face. He was very badly burnt, and so when we went abroad he was in hospital. But the funny thing is, Jim could see no fault in him at all. If Jim took to somebody, that was it.'

Back in their quarters in Liverpool another shock was in store. For some time Gilbert had been aware that letters from Jim were being sent to a rather effeminate-looking Lance-Bombardier. 'I know I shouldn't have done but I'd heard rumours and when this fellow was on guard one day, I went through his haversack and found these letters of Jim, you see. You'd think he was writing to his sweetheart.' The tone of one letter that was read left little doubt about the nature of the relationship: 'My darling . . . How I miss you . . .'

If confirmation were needed, it soon came. 'Jim was caught in bed with his boyfriend,' says Derek Gilbert. It was the talk of the Troop – though surprisingly, to modern ears, in a subdued, rather restrained fashion and not at all salaciously. After all, in those pre-Wolfenden days such an act, though rife – particularly in the Guards Regiments – bore the taint of illegality. Too much gossip could lead to an unwelcome and potentially career-ending appearance before a bewigged member of His Majesty's judiciary. Whatever was thought of Jim, nobody was malicious enough to wish that upon him. In fact, general opinion seemed to remain unaltered. 'We didn't think any the less of him because of what had taken place,' said Gilbert. 'It was just one of those things. We accepted he was that way inclined.'

What happened then? No one, it would seem, quite knows. Extraordinarily, given the Army's attitude to any kind of sexual relationship between officers and other ranks, nothing more was heard. Even in today's army, one would surely expect some kind of punitive action under some classified sub-clause of a heading such as 'serious misconduct'. However, the Army's real concern about the liaison would have been with the difference in rank. In other words, not so much the act of commission as the gulf in commission between lance and lieutenant: in reverse order, the haves and the nons.

In Jim's book *Follow On* he mentions that he turned up late for a match in which he was playing against Southport in the Liverpool and District League.

> Some business connected with a court-martial prevented my arriving until around 3.30, and I hustled in, struggling with a cricket-bag of pre-war size, urged on by sympathetic spectators near the gate.
>
> 'Eh oop, laad, that's late, tha knows.'
> 'Liverpool will have missed thee.'
> 'Let me carry tha' bag.'
> The score on the board was 10 for no wicket, with Liverpool in the

field, and I concluded I'd missed surprisingly little. Not so – we had already been bowled out (one short!) for 15! I never missed my innings either before or since, apart from declarations – but at least, unlike Ian Peebles in his youth at the Cape, I was not reported in the press as 'Absent Bathing'.

The thought occurs that Jim was lucky it was not his own court martial that had detained him. It was not long since when for serious misdemeanours the culprit was literally 'drummed out' of the Regimental gates in shame as the figurehead of a full parade with side-drummers beating a tattoo, or at the very least simply discharged from the Service because his moral turpitude might endanger the welfare of his brothers-in-arms. Surely even someone with as seemingly impregnable an edifice of self-esteem as Jim must have had qualms. It is, of course, just possible that it may have been an isolated occurrence and thereafter he was scared into celibacy. Who knows? Though one cannot help but speculate that the necessity of maintaining secrecy in such an environment, with the ever-present risk of discovery, would have intensified both excitement and apprehension in the relationship and been part of the attraction. For Jim, knowing that in public at least he had to impose constraints on such yearnings – not just in this one instance, but possibly with other associations in his life – would have led to inner strain and tension and could account for much of his prickly behaviour.

The only visible aftermath was that a couple of months after this episode the Lance-Bombardier was promoted to Sergeant. There were a few wry smiles within the Regiment. It did not take long to make a connection.

Army Personnel Records which might divulge details of such aberrations are closed for a period of 75 years, but it is much more likely that Jim's close friendship with Colonel Harris helped the matter to be conveniently forgotten. After all, what was the alternative? A full judicial enquiry? That was in nobody's interests, especially for Harris, for whom paramount would be the good name of the Regiment. After all, there were far more pressing and important concerns – for instance, the little matter of a war to be won . . . Oh, lucky Jim!

For a time Jim was lost to sight – moved elsewhere apparently. He was not seen by the Regiment until they had decamped to Monmouth, their final billet on British soil. On the forecourt of the Castle, they all paraded before King George VI, who was accompanied by Major-General Beckwith-Smith. Nothing was said, but everyone realised the significance of the event. As so it proved. At long last they were off.

The departure from Monmouth produced some tears. A few of the men had married local girls. It did not take long to decide in wartime.

For most of the other ranks, weighed down with full kit, sleep was impossible on the trains journeying throughout the night to Liverpool. A chill autumnal wind added to the shivers of suppressed apprehension and excitement as they boarded HMS *Andes* the next day. As the ship picked up steam and the twin towers of the Royal Liver building began to fade into the distance, many wondered aloud whether they would ever be coming back.

Meanwhile, on the upper decks Jim and his fellow officers started to enjoy some of the perks of what he referred to, as 'the lavishly appointed cruise ship'. Apparently, a vast amount of alcohol embarked, but did not survive the voyage.

On the lower decks the men did not fare so well. Food arrived in huge dixies and was distributed by the NCOs. The 'heads' or toilets soon began to flood. Cabins with bunks were preferable to haphazard hammocks, but both were too close to the throb of the engines to allow other than fitful sleep.

However, the heavy swell of the Atlantic Ocean was no respecter of position and many stomachs soon began to somersault. The *Andes* was in the centre of a convoy escorted by two destroyers from the British Navy, who circled continuously on the lookout for German submarines.

After two or three days, when the convoy was just off the southernmost tip of Greenland, new escorts appeared. The American Navy had taken over. Never known to stint in numbers, the Americans had provided an aircraft carrier, two battle cruisers and eight destroyers to protect seven English ships and one Polish, the *Sobiesky*. As the two English destroyers turned back to England they sent a signal, 'Goodbye and Good Luck'. Many wished they were returning with them.

During the voyage and in between bouts of physical training on deck, Jim and other officers gave lectures on their possible role in desert warfare. The rumour was that they would end up at Basra in the Middle East.

After ten days the shelter of shore began to ease the bitter cold. The first impression on reaching the harbour at Halifax, Nova Scotia, was the stink of fish – never had the smell been more welcome. A young lady in a well-filled bright orange jumper leaned out precariously from an office window and gave a wave. She was rewarded with a lusty cheer from thousands of throats.

At this stage, early November 1941, the USA was supposedly uninvolved or rather non-belligerent; Pearl Harbor was a few weeks away. Therefore the transfer to an American cabin-class cruiser was a surprise to say the least. Jim found the *Wakefield* cramped, uncomfortable and dry – in comparison with the *Andes*. His men thought the opposite. 'We couldn't believe it,' said Derek Gilbert. 'After the *Andes* we were treated like lords in the American boats; they really fed us up [laugh]. We had a tremendous send-off from Halifax – planes, ships and sirens going.' 'It was like coming from the slums of the East End to the luxury of the West End,' wrote Henry Dixon in his account, 'It was Goodbye and Could have been Forever' as he embarked on the *Mount Vernon*. 'I could not believe my eyes. It was all equipped with bunk beds and I was allocated to the coffee room at the stem of the boat on Deck level. It was all a dream with iced water on tap all the time.'

The *SS West Point* was the third of the American ships which had been stripped and refitted for the sole purpose of carrying troops. For this operation there were approximately 6000 men on each ship, which together with ancillary vessels had the same escort as that which had accompanied the convoy on the second half of the voyage across the Atlantic.

The ships now proceeded south, hugging the east coastline of America, with a short stopover at Port of Spain, Trinidad, for fresh water and refuelling. Although there were instructions to stay on board, Jim's enterprising spirit could not be contained and he ventured ashore, no doubt seeking cricketing habitats. Onward once, more, with a zigzag course past the West Indian islands to avoid German U-boats, before leaving the security of the South American shore with a crossing of the South Atlantic towards the Cape.

Suddenly there was dramatic news. Two days from Cape Town an announcement over the ship's Tannoy told how Pearl Harbor had been attacked by the Japanese Air Force and that, as a consequence, the United States was now officially at war. Jim thought that the pervading frosty attitude of the Americans on board changed little. Below stairs, as it were, they disagreed. 'Limeys' became 'Buddies' and if you happened to win one of the endless games of Tombola or Housey Housey, the prize would be Camels, Lucky Strikes or Philip Morris cigarettes.

On reaching Cape Town the harbour was ablaze with lights. The welcome was rapturous with an embarrassment of entertainment being thrust on all and sundry. As always with Jim, even in the most alien of circumstances, cricket was never far from his thoughts. On the same day as the Pearl Harbor attack had been broadcast, he had sent a cable from the boat to 'Sport Pienaar', a famous figure in the cricket and rugby world of South Africa, and one of those amiable entrepreneurs who knew everybody and could arrange everything. The cable ran: '5th Brigade challenge Western Province to a Match'. A positive reply had soon been forthcoming and the game was played at Newlands where the home side were duly defeated. The Province borrowed a couple of sailors from the aircraft carrier *Hermes* to make up their team – distressingly, it sank shortly afterwards with total loss of life. As if to show that he had not forgotten his officerial duties, Jim marched his battalion round Newlands to give them exercise.

The one sour note to surface from the short stay came when one of his original '419' Battery, Jim Porter, had seen a black woman with a baby in her arms begging in the street. He had given her a threepenny bit. A white South African lady, in name only, who chanced to be passing by had given him such a verbal lambasting that he wished he had given the poor beggar woman considerably more. Apartheid did not wait for official sanction.

To the boats again and up the east coast of Africa while their ultimate destination was being decided in exchanges between Churchill and the Australian Prime Minister, Curtin. Was it to be the Middle East or Malaya? In the event, one Brigade went to Malaya and the other two were sent to Singapore, but not before an interlude in India.

Having disembarked at Bombay just after Christmas there were a few days spent under canvas at Pashan Camp, Kirkee, before taking the train to Poona. Poona was dubbed 'the Aldershot of India', but the stiff route marches to dispel boatbound lethargy soon gave way to exercise in the Services Club swimming pool or on the hockey field. As for Jim, he once again donned his flannels – would you believe he had brought his full cricket bag with him – and 'in marvellous dry heat' bowled all afternoon from lunch to tea against gritty opposition provided by league cricketers from the York and Lancaster Regiment and King's Own Yorkshire Light Infantry.

All too soon it was back to reality, in this case Bombay, and incarceration in the dreaded, for him at least, *Wakefield*. Heading south and then east on a circuitous route round Ceylon, as it was then called, through the Sunda Strait which divided the islands of Sumatra and Java, towards their destination. It was hoped that by taking this route, rather than proceeding more directly through the long and narrow Strait of Malacca, there would be a chance of arriving undetected. It was to prove a vain hope. In the Sunda Strait they were spotted and the Japanese air force unleashed a bevy of bombs, all of which, fortunately, fell into the sea. It was a grim warning of what was to come and a cue to make haste. 'We didn't even know the Japs had invaded Malaya until then,' recalls Jack Wragg. 'Swanny went down to get some instructions. When he came back he'd got his baton and a map with him. "Right, I'll give you the situation," he said, "the Japs have got there . . ." He did not really need to say more. The *Wakefield* and another ship were fastest in the convoy, so we went full throttle and got to Singapore before the rest of them.'

As the *Wakefield* berthed, a twenty-seven strong Nippon bomber force came straight at them in arrowhead formation. Surely, as a static target, there was no chance of survival. But just as they were almost directly overhead the planes veered away and dropped their lethal load on a target nearby, which was thought to be the gasworks. Jim, and presumably most of the rest, felt it was their first insight into the Japanese mentality: obedience at all costs. But was it? At the time, Keppel Harbour was experiencing a tropical deluge; possibly the ships had been, at least, partially obscured.

'We were sitting ducks,' said Derek Gilbert. 'We got no air support whatsoever. We were pretty shattered by it.'

As fast as they could the troops hustled ashore. It was with some dismay they noticed, coming up the other gangplank onto the ship, a number of civilians carrying children and all their personal belongings: also some nurses and RAF personnel. If they are leaving, why are we arriving, was the unspoken thought.

The Australian truck drivers who took 54 Brigade of the 18th Division at breakneck speed to a staging camp told them they had arrived too late. As they were shaken about in the bone-crunching TCVs [*Troop-Carrying Vehicles*] there were bewildering glimpses of a teeming city that, in appearance, was part European, part Oriental: the clatter of Chinese clogs on the pavements, the street vendors crying their wares and the musical clack of bits of wood being knocked together by the sellers of ice cream. But any feeling of normality was quickly dispelled by the bomb craters on some of the roads.

As the troops moved in under canvas in a small Chinese village called Tek Hok, Jim tried to get in touch with Army HQ at Fort Canning. The official communication suggested nothing untoward. In a letter from the Deputy Provost Marshal there was a request for duplicated photographs of the entire Brigade in order that identity cards could be issued. Jim did not believe it. Bureaucracy still rife when by the weekend the Japanese were likely to be at the Johore Bahru Strait which divided Singapore island from the Malayan mainland. It did not help when he recognised the signatory of the letter – Lt. Col. Brian K. Castor, who before the war was secretary of Essex County Cricket Club.

The following days were to be disillusioning for the entire Division. After two years preparing to get to grips with the enemy, it was the enemy who were about to get to grips with them. The whole force were now to be sacrificed on the high altar of expediency, left totally exposed, defenceless and in hostile hands. How on earth had it been allowed to happen?

Field Marshal the Lord Bramall not only had a hugely distinguished career in the Services including several years as Chief of the General Staff, he also after the Second World War occupied Japan and therefore had a direct interest in the unfolding of events.

'The point was that, of course, we spent no money on defence whatsoever in those years between the wars, and something had to give. And the result was that the Far East was neglected even more than anything else. And the Chiefs of Staff and particularly the Navy, of course, were getting quite concerned about Japan, because Japan had powerful naval forces. I don't know why, but they didn't expect any land invasion of Singapore; but they did expect that Japan might sweep down with its naval forces. And so most of the guns defending Singapore were sited to fire out to sea to the south and there was not much to the north.

'Then eventually they did send, which they could ill afford, two battleships or battle cruisers out to the Far East – the *Prince of Wales* and the *Repulse* – and provided a deterrent to the Japanese fleet. And, of course, in the early stage of the conflict they were both sunk, which left no naval support. And also they had very few aeroplanes out there and so the whole thing rested on the ground forces. And the ground forces, when the Japanese attack came through Thailand from the north, really didn't do terribly well. They didn't realise that they ought to know the jungle to be able to fight in the jungle. They were very road-bound. The planters up there said to them can we teach your people about the jungle – we live in it. And they said oh no, we know all about it, and the result was they were road-bound. The Japanese were not road-bound, the Japanese used to outflank their position, and then instead of perhaps standing firm and sort of sticking it out, and possibly getting re-supplied by the odd air drop, or even just holding out and producing a thorn in the side, as soon as the Japanese came at them they pulled back, before they were cut off. And the Japanese did it again. And before they knew where they were, they were right back at the causeway on Singapore island, having been pushed back there by a far smaller Japanese force.

'Then, of course, it was deemed to be too late, because the only people who then would have suffered were the enormous civilian population, and so the superior force surrendered. But just before this happened, and only just before, Winston Churchill – who suddenly woke up to the fact that the whole of this great presence of our Allied forces was collapsing – relocated the 18th Division, which had come round the Cape into the Indian Ocean and was going to the Middle East, and suddenly said we'll send that into Singapore. Well, by the time they arrived it was shortly before the surrender, and they really didn't do anything at all except to be taken prisoner.

'Wavell was technically Commander-in-Chief [*based in Java, of ABDA – Australian, British, Dutch and American forces*] and exactly what part he played in it, I don't know. But he was under pressure from Churchill. Of course, Alanbrooke stopped Winston doing exactly the same thing in France. They were going to send the whole British Corps into France, and Alanbrooke said to Churchill, "It's no good resuscitating a corpse." And at the last minute the decision should have been taken that Singapore was going to fall and it's no good sending in forces at this late stage. But they didn't. It's difficult to tell sometimes why these decisions are taken. And so this fine division just went in to become prisoners of war. Which was terrible. If the battle was going to be won at all, if the Japanese were to be delayed, it would have had to have been done much further north up the Malayan Peninsula.'

After the war Jim became a friend of 'Dwin' Bramall. No doubt he would have taken issue with Bramall's point about the Allied forces having superior numbers. On paper that may have been so, Jim would have opined, but in practical availability to be deployed . . .? The Japanese also had tanks and the mobility of some of their troops on bikes carrying food in rucksacks. Fundamentally, though, amidst the stumblings of a top-heavy administration, the decision had been made to write off both Hong Kong and Singapore, even if pride and expediency prevented such an admission. Inexcusably, the deployment of a division had been a face-saving exercise.

Fifty years later in a programme for BBC Radio, Jim told me, 'The whole of the battle of Singapore was a ghastly muddle and a tragedy of the first order. We got to Singapore just at the end of January 1942.

We were in action with the Japs coming through the other side of the island on the Australian front line in the early days of February. We had to go back and join in with the line, although on the north-east side of Singapore we weren't actually attacked. But we had to go back to defend the city and so we were in a losing battle really, because apart from anything else they had taken the reservoirs and therefore there was no water.'

In an article for the *Spectator* in 1992, Jim gave a precise and vivid account which enlarges the picture.

The shape of Singapore Island is much like a full-blown rose, twice as wide as it is deep, with the city on the southern coast. The naval base and the causeway connecting with the mainland lie centrally, with the military area of Chicago to the north-east.

This was the area assigned to our 18th Division, which was composed of Territorials from the eastern counties. With what remained of the Indian 11th Division, we took up positions on the 31st, the battle-weary Australians and the other Indian and British troops who had been fighting a gallant, hopeless retreat on the mainland being deployed on the left flank. Churchill, in Book IV of The Second World War, notes that there were no permanent fortifications on the landward side and, what was 'even more astounding', no field defences had been attempted after the war in the East had begun. This is the exact truth. Not a coil of wire did we find, and when we sent to the RAOC depot on the afternoon of Saturday the 31st to get some, we found they had closed down for the weekend.

We made what defensive provisions we could in that first week of February, and provided some custom to an Officers' Club bar with well laundered staff down by the shore. I signed my last chits there (thinking a bottle or two of whisky would come in handy) on 8th February, the very night that the Japs (after a strong bombardment, in small craft and with blood curdling cries) penetrated the north-west coast.

'The 18th Division,' wrote the Prime Minister to General Wavell, the Supreme Commander, on 10 February, 'has a chance to make its name in history.' Vain hope! After two years of hard home training, commanded by General 'Becky' Beckwith-Smith, in whom we had confidence and who held the affection of all, we were denied any such glory. Leaving us unscathed, apart from spasmodic bombardment from the air and artillery on the mainland, the Japs made such inroads in the north-west that by 11 February (my 35th birthday) all troops east of the causeway were withdrawn to a circular perimeter in defence of the city. Units were thrown in piecemeal to plug the gaps. Beckwith-Smith saw his beloved division dismembered bit by bit.

Those early days of February were harrowing. The stark snapshots were retained in the minds of the British troops for the remainder of their days. Order, in the sense of a cohesive and integrated overall plan of action, was glaringly absent. Chaos reigned. And the disjointed accounts of those who were there reflect the sorry state. Always re-active, never pro-active responses to events outside of their control. Individuals together, yet separated. On their own. A disconnected sequence of images in retreat. Desperately trying to plug holes in a gaping defence. Cries for help. Now! Now! . . . before it is too late. It is too late.

Eric Samuel: 'The poor old Australian 8th Division who had done their stint – they got them, as well . . .'

Derek Gilbert: 'We lost four of our guns in the harbour at Singapore. But we did have one gun that was on the front lawn of a Malay policeman's house – I remember he had a Chinese wife – and I was actually the layer of the gun. I used to fire it every day for about two weeks. My ears used to bleed and we had no protection whatsoever. I've got terrible tinnitus now.'

Eric Samuel: 'We had a gun post in a Chinese cemetery. Jim being Troop commander was observation officer. Everywhere we set up our gun positions, Jim was up the front, directing our fire in front of the guns but behind the Infantry, that is, if we had any . . .'

Derek Gilbert: 'We were firing a 25-pounder at the Jap troops and tanks over the Infantry – a range of a few thousand yards.'

Jim Porter (from *3½ Years of Hell*):
The tombstones provided excellent cover for us as we were constantly bombed, shelled from the sea by their navy and they had a balloon up for observation on a cable in use as an observation post for their artillery which was extremely accurate.

During the course of our retreat back to the outskirts of the city, we had to pass through the clubhouse of the Singapore Golf Club. In an outhouse at the back were crates and crates of spirits.

My CO Jim Swanton took one look at them and said to me: 'Bombardier, smash that lot, we don't want to leave them for the Japs, do we?' With a feeling of almost sacrilege I found myself an axe and commenced to smash the lot. With a heavy heart I watched the precious liquid trickle down the nearest drain.

I did not even loot one bottle. Bottles of Johnny Walker, Gordon's Gin and Four Star Brandy all received my attention. I was standing in the doorway surveying my handiwork when a shell landed close by and a red hot piece of its casing buried itself in the frame of the doorway where I was standing. It was about six inches from my right hip, so I thought: 'I'll never have a closer shave than that,' and off I went to rejoin my Battery.

E.W.S.: 'In seventeen days, I never recognised a single Allied aircraft, only Japs either bombing from high altitude or, in the final days, spotting disdainfully for their guns almost at tree-top height. They even had balloons doing the same job. Denied any vestige of air support, even the finest fighting troops would have been pressed to maintain morale.

'On 12 and 13 February, the 25-pounder guns of 148 Field Regiment supported the centre-right of the perimeter defence of the city facing the MacRitchie, the southernmost of the three island reservoirs, with the Bukit Timah golf course just west of it. From a convenient observation post, I had the satisfaction of directing heavy concentrations of fire from the twelve guns of 419 Battery at and in the area of the clubhouse and down the Sime Road.

'The left of the line came under the heaviest enemy pressure, and on 14 February we received orders to conform to a further withdrawal.'

Jack Wragg: 'Swanny was a good officer when we were fighting. He would be up at the observation post and keep communications going between the guns. I remember I had to roll the wires out with Harold Williams, and we were taking it up on a big roll, unwinding it, going up to the Chinese cemetery. Actually we'd been there once before. And then all of a sudden we got shot at by a trail of mortars. We rolled down into a ditch and took cover. Jim could see us being shot at by the Japs and all of a sudden there he was standing up above us wearing a big white sweater. As we were crawling along he said, 'Wragg, what are you doing down there?' I replied, 'Keeping my head down, sir – they can see you up there.' I must admit he came down pretty smartish – he didn't realise they were as close as that. Soon afterwards he got shot himself, in the arm . . .'

E.W.S.: 'It happened on 13 February [laugh], Friday 13th. I was trying to establish a new OP, when I came to grief. The wireless communication between OPs and guns was extremely unreliable, making archaic telephone lines absolutely essential. While my OP Ack was away directing the signallers laying the wire, up an adjacent tree I saw a pair of spectacles glinting in the sun. Using my Ack's rifle, I aimed a few shots into the foliage, but nothing happened. I must have forgotten about him. I was very tired, and had gone down to see my signaller who was bringing the wire up. Anyway, this chap winged me in my right elbow. I suppose it was about an inch below the funny bone. It went through, but did no real harm, but I had to go back to the dressing station, obviously. I was numb in this right arm, and bleeding and so on, and was succeeded at the OP by my battery commander, Major Bill Merry. Well, during the night of the 14th/15th the situation on our front rapidly deteriorated, and in the early morning of the day of surrender poor Merry, in the act of rallying some straggling infantry, was killed.'

Derek Gilbert: 'Our Major, Major Merry, was a very brave man . . .'

Jack Wragg: 'What happened was Swanton had come along to the troops, and said to me and Tom Jones, because we were the two signallers, "Major Merry wants you." Well, having got that message, we went to another observation post nearby, and found Major Merry. "Get out, the Japs have broken through," he said. We all tumbled into a truck with Major Merry in front, and got down the road a bit. Suddenly there was a lot of firing, shouting and screaming, so we went down an embankment into some woods before Merry stopped us and said, "I'm going to find out what's happening." He got his revolver out and was creeping down, and went out of sight. I never saw him again. I reckon he was captured. They never did find his body. The screaming stopped, it suddenly went all quiet. We were all in this ditch with our rifles, and eventually we came up. After a long time another officer from our Regiment arrived. I'll always remember what he said: "The Artillery never retreats" [laughs]. Oh really? Just give us a chance, mate, we thought. We stayed there for a long time. I reckon there had been a Jap raiding party. Somebody said they found Major Merry's watch, but I don't know if that's true. I know the other officers questioned me afterwards. I just told them he left and that we didn't see him any more. He was either captured or he was blown up – I don't know. We were on the outskirts of town in Singapore and so we came back to our gun position in the town. And then, Swanny took over as acting Major when Merry went. Perhaps he appointed himself, I don't know . . .'

Eric Samuel: 'Captain Uttley should have been the Major, but at the time he was at RHQ. Jim would have been with his troops and they probably never saw one another. Jim would have known very quickly what had happened to Merry, because he would have been up at the OP.'

In fact, Jim was not at the observation post when Merry was killed, he was still at the hospital having his wound dresssed.

EWS: 'I was keen to get back to my own unit. I'd have been still more keen if I'd known that the Battery commander was dead, because I was then in charge, but I didn't know that. [*Presumably the upgrading in the event of such a happening had been cleared with Colonel Harris at some point.*] But anyway, I wanted to get back, naturally. And I got some police who hadn't been rounded up to take me in a car to where I knew my own unit was and I rejoined them there.'

Derek Gilbert: 'And then we had the order to smash all our guns, blow them up . . .'

Jack Wragg: 'I didn't really know what was happening. Just before capture I buried my rifle and shoulder straps and sling with my name and number on it. I left a shell in the muzzle. It was all a muddle. Some big General – Wavell or somebody – said that on the Sunday the sky will be black with American planes. Of course, there weren't any. We never saw them, of course, and we had no planes. One or two Bristol Buffaloes, I think they were called, but you never saw them up. We were constantly waiting and watching for Jap planes coming over low. You could see the pilots. You just hoped that they hadn't seen you . . .'

Jim Porter: 'When I got back I was given some bad news, the pride of the British Navy, the *Prince of Wales* and the *Repulse*, had both been sunk by the Japanese. They had sent over torpedo bombers and they had sent these gallant ships to the bottom with a frightening loss of life.

'Whoever sent these giant vessels out to Malaya without RAF protection wanted their brains examined. Here we were with no aircraft to shoot down a Japanese observation balloon, and they were so stupid as to put those two great ships into such a suicidal position.

'It was just another example of the tremendous number of tactical errors of judgement made by persons in high office who should have known better but didn't.'

EWS: 'Once the Jap had gained a foothold on the island, surrender was inevitable. I found there a medley of emotions: frustration ("We were thrown away," says a staunch bombardier, recalling the moment), indignation in some, indifference in a few, and in many – for those at the guns' end had had no direct contact with the enemy – sheer surprise. For our losses were negligible: four killed out of 202, one of them our battery commander.

'So the white flag was hoisted and shortly after dusk in the Ford factory at Bukit Tamah, General Percival acceded to the demand of unconditional surrender made by his opposite number, Lieutenant General Yamashita. The Jap army had shown all the military virtues, as well as a capacity to inflict acts of unbridled savagery that boded ill for their captives. After the action at Muar, non-walking wounded were massacred in cold blood. At the Alexandra Military Hospital at Singapore two days before the surrender, many patients and medical staff were executed.'

Derek Gilbert: 'We had a twenty-four hour wait before the Japanese marched in. We had to line up all along the road while the Japanese marched through. I couldn't believe it, because the first battalion of Japs were midgets. We couldn't believe that we had capitulated. But they were wonderful jungle warfare soldiers. And then we all had to march to Roberts Barracks in Changi – the airport's there now.'

EWS: 'The feeling that we were implicated, however helplessly, in the humiliation of Singapore, coupled with the sudden change from normal food to a diet exclusively of rice and jungle vegetables, did nothing for morale in the early days of captivity. I recall a dark moment in March or April when a string of heavy Jap cruisers – we counted eleven in line ahead – steamed past Changi to the naval base. Our release, at that moment, seemed a very long way off.'

And a very long way off it was to prove. The cup of defeat was a bitter one to swallow. There was a general feeling of utter helplessness. They troops were all marched to Changi – and herded in there for several weeks. Gradually the new captives began to learn of the temper of their captors. Or, in some cases, very suddenly. The Japanese were unprepared for the speed of their victory and confronted with hordes of prisoners often reacted violently. They had their own code which was remotely connected to the ancient Way of the Warrior, but Bushido was light years away from the humane principles of the Geneva Convention.

> EWS: 'The Japs found some Sikhs who had gone over to the enemy from the Indian Forces who simply guarded a wire which they flung round the top segment of Changi. They had naturally removed all the boats and small craft which hadn't already taken off with various civilians and other escapees in them. And so there we were, and they threw a few bags of rice now and then over the wire and I think they probably came into the camp with lorries, but the food was very scarce and very, very bad. And the first impression one had was, for the first time in one's life really, being absolutely paralysingly hungry. The change from a European diet to fourth class rice and damned little else, meant that we soon began to grow a few vegetables . . . Unfortunately, there was any amount of food in Singapore, but it was all tinned stuff and the tins had all been pierced by bayonets by us before capitulating, so that the Japs couldn't use it: many lives would have been saved if that food had not been destroyed.'

After a time there was some kind of reorganisation. With such a vast amount of clearance work to be done around the docks of Singapore, the Japs started to make use of their prisoners of war. Working parties were formed to clear up the mess. There was no shortage of volunteers – not that volunteering was an option – for any sight of the outside world, however restricted, was welcome. It was also an opportunity to regain a little self-esteem by trying to outwit the Japanese guards who were supervising the work. And in this the British were quick to take lessons from their resilient Australian comrades in captivity on such fine arts as under-the-counter trading and exchange. And, in some cases, straightforward scrounging. Any initial qualms of conscience or worries about discovery were usually quelled by the pangs of hunger. Sometimes, when it came to bartering for goods, sleight of hand was essential.

'I was in a working party down by the docks, and we were marching back in this column,' remembers Eric Samuel. 'And my friend, Leslie Webster, who was also a Sergeant, was marching with me. And these Malay traders would be running alongside trying to keep up and offering their wares. We would mutter through clenched teeth, *"Kitna budgie hai?"* – well, that's what it sounded like, anyway – How much? – How much? We had a little money – the Japanese gave us a few Jap/Malay dollars – and we each managed to buy two tins of Marmite – which lasted for months – and Zambuk – which is based on herbal remedies and which will cure anything. I'm sure that's what kept me alive to the end of the war. We quickly slipped the tins down the inside of our shirts – we still had them then – because we'd have been beaten up if the guards had seen us.'

In one instance, two of the British working party were fortunate not to lose their heads, though here the Japanese were not involved.

'I was working in a copper mine,' said Jack Wragg, 'and it collapsed on me, dust falling, and I did a running dive and was out into water. My legs were scratched and cut, but I managed to get out. You would think I'd have been a trembling wreck, but then it was just one more lucky escape. The fellow with me had been digging, and had taken the basket outside – big fellow. Suddenly about a hundredweight fell from the roof. When he came back – he'd gone to the tip – I said, "It was lucky you moved."'

Many could recount similar experiences – of standing to attention with the contraband (as some of them called it) stuck precariously down the inside legs of their shorts; of demanding petrol from a Jap guard to make a steamroller work, and then selling the allocation to Chinese traders for a handsome return in dollars; and of numerous ruses to make their captors look thoroughly imbecilic. What they constantly had to be aware of, though, was the consequence of discovery or, quite simply, of the savagery that could be unleashed without any apparent provocation.

Derek Gilbert: 'I was ordered to go with a working party into Singapore. About forty of us, to clear up after the battle. You can imagine the terrible stench down there with dead bodies: arms and legs sticking out of shallow graves. It was while I was down there, I was up on the back of an army truck that had been hit by a shell. On it there were about thirty soldiers, all killed, and we had to put them in plastic bags. The Japanese cleared out of the way, even though they had got masks on, but we hadn't. And it was while we were on top of the truck that I saw all these other trucks driving onto the beach, and off the back of these other trucks came a lot of Chinese men. As they got towards the sea, they were all machine-gunned down. I found out after the war was over, that there were many thousands of those lads massacred there. Not only the men, but the wives, mothers, sweethearts, who were running after them – they were all machine-gunned with them. But that didn't satisfy the Japanese.

They cut the heads off a lot of those Chinese, and wherever you went in Singapore you would see them stuck on spikes with all the blood dripping down. I will never forget the sight of those heads . . .'

Astonishingly, amidst all this carnage, there was an attempt to introduce culture. Away from the working parties Lieutenant-General Percival and Major-General Beckwith-Smith had helped promote a kind of university in the 18th Divisional area.

EWS: 'We had a theatre and every unit fixed up talks, technical courses and so on. For myself, I very quickly discovered a surprising thirst for knowledge among men whom one had seen before only in the practical capacity of gun layers, ammunition numbers, signallers and so on. You could go round and see a flock of gunners listening to a lecture on the modern history of Europe, or a Shakespeare play reading. There was some cricket and even football for those who had the stamina for it. We grew lean and necessity made ascetics of us all. Unfortunately, for most of us, this phase didn't last very long.'

But while it did, the cricket matches had been organised affairs and had taken place on a matting wicket on the *padang* of Changi camp. One of the games was between the 18th Division and the Royal Artillery for whom Jim turned out quite regularly. He was amazed to see bowling for the opposition someone he thought he recognised. 'When he saw me bowling, he thought it was Bill,' Geoffrey Edrich told me shortly before his recent death. 'He was a Major, and I was a Sergeant in the Royal Norfolk Regiment.' Geoffrey Edrich, of course, eventually was to become a top-order batsman for Lancashire and his brother Bill – W.A. Edrich of Middlesex and England fame – was, at the time, earning his DFC in the RAF.

'I can't remember quite how long the illusion persisted,' observed Jim many years later in *Geoff Edrich's Benefit Book*, 'but, of course, it was Geoffrey. Their figures were extraordinarily similar, and Geoffrey that day, in spite of a baking sun and the more or less exclusive diet of rice which our cooks then had no notion how to cook, was propelling himself to the wicket with his brother's bustling energy, and that peculiar slinging action which suggested that he might at any moment throw himself down the wicket as well as the ball.' With so many Australian servicemen in captivity with their British counterparts, a so-called 'full Test' series of five matches was soon promoted by Lt. Col. A.A. Johnson of the Suffolk Regiment. Heading the AIF [*Australian Imperial Force*] team was none other than the former Australian wicket-keeper, Ben Barnett. Jim, with his injured arm, was unable to take part but, as was his wont, he kept an eye on the 'England' batting order. He also busied himself by keeping the score on a blackboard. Beside Geoffrey Edrich, Len Muncer of Glamorgan played in some of the matches. 'The Tests' created a tremendous amount of interest with between 4000 and 5000 spectators urging their sides on, to the bemusement of the Japanese. They were played on Sundays and there were a set number of overs for each side. Apart from anything else, the 'Tests' acted as a morale-booster for the troops and were a lively topic for conversation throughout the week. 'England' won the series, 2–1, with the other two games drawn.

Eventually there was a move from Changi – no more organised cricket – to the River Valley Road Camp which was some eighteen miles away across a small river from the centre of Chinatown. It was here that Jim expanded a role as so-called camp Welfare Officer. The historian of the Thailand–Burma Railway, Sibylla Jane Flower (daughter of Lt. Col. H.S. Flower, Royal Northumberland Fusiliers) explains what happened: 'It was Jim's idea to give everybody something to occupy their minds. While most were engaged in clearing up the debris in the roads of Singapore, the storm drains and the bodies and so on, he asked any of these parties going out of the camps to look for books, with the incentive that to join the library and reading club, any person would first have to produce two books. And so began the first attempts at building a library. Most of the books were scavenged from private homes. The 1939 *Wisden* which he had brought with him from England was borrowed, at one time, every six hours. It had the Japanese stamp on it in purple "Not subversive". When Jim got to the last camp but one, the hospital camp at Nakhon Pathom in Thailand, it was re-bound by two bookbinders who were in the camp, called Forster and Gould. The book was re-bound in gascape and rice paste, and it lasted throughout the time he was a prisoner.'

Which is more than can be said for Jim's precious notes on his progress through the war, which he had scribbled on rice paper. Those who did not recognise the archival value of such weighty prose used them to make and light their cigarettes. He was not pleased.

When, in the autumn of 1942, came the tortuous journey to Thailand, these commandeered books (two to a haversack) were in the possession of men the majority of whom had never once set foot in a library. Their thoughts on J.B. Priestley, Evelyn Waugh, John Galsworthy, Arthur Bryant, H.V. Morton and John Gunther can only be imagined.

Derek Gilbert: 'We got the orders to go down to the railway station at
Singapore – Jim was with me then – and we got on to these steel railway
trucks – thirty-six men to a truck. The doors were shut with a clang,
and we had a four-day train journey with only one stop every twenty-
four hours for rice and a bowl of water. And we had two men in our
truck with dysentery, so you can imagine the stench. At the end of that
journey, we lost one of our men. He died. After that, we had a day's
rest. Jim was in a truck with twenty-two officers.'

Whereas the other ranks could only huddle and lie down in turns, the
Officers' truck with under two-thirds the number were able to enjoy
the luxury of just being able to stretch out full length head to tail,
albeit like sardines in a tin.

'Talking of sardines, a few of us brought a tin of them which we soon
ate,' wrote Jim, 'and the smell of fish and tomato sauce lingered in our
airless corner for the four days of our journey. We must have been
travelling backs to the engine! From time to time the train stopped at
a station, and we were served rice and water from pails on the platform.
We tottered out at last at the railhead of Banpong, and forthwith set
out, with such belongings as we could carry on our backs and slung
on bamboo poles, to march westward towards the distant hills.'

Derek Gilbert: 'Jim was marching with the troops all the way on the
120 or so kilometres to Tarsao. We had to go through the jungle during
the monsoon. All of us were carrying very little because everything was
taken from us. If any of the men fell sick, we'd try to carry them along,
but some of them couldn't make it and they would just collapse and die.
We all tried to help our mates as much as we could, though, because
the Japs would whip the stragglers ... We were wearing shirts and
shorts and old army boots, which were in a bit of a state because of the
humidity. Eventually, of course, everyone walked around barefoot for
two and a half years. Once our clothing had worn out, that was it, no
more whatsoever.'

'Here, on the march, the Japs – or, as they were universally known, the
Nips, were thick on the ground,' continued Jim, 'halting us for
interminable roll-calls, and generally getting excited. On the third,
fourth and fifth days our route led over slippery raised ridges of paddy
fields and then through jungle tracks in which often the guards lost
their way, and we were no sooner enclosed in these than it came on to
rain cats and dogs. Drenched to the skin we slipped and slithered on.

Our cup of woe, in every sense, it might have been thought, was full and brimming over, but as if spontaneously a strange thing happened. The men had borne the heat with terrible curses. Now suddenly they began as one to sing. Everyone grew cheerful. Maybe they were reminded of home. Anyhow I will never forget the look of utter, fearful mystification on the face of our own particular Nip. We were altogether beyond his comprehension – and so, in general, were all Europeans outside the understanding of all Japs. And vice versa. Apart from the language difference we were as much a mystery to them as they to us.'

Having spent a few weeks at Tarsao, they all retraced their steps to camps at Wampo some sixteen kilometres further back, to begin work on what has become known as the notorious Thailand–Burma 'Death' Railway. After their arrival at Wampo, Gunner Gilbert managed to corner what, in relative terms, was a cushy number.

> **Derek Gilbert:** 'While I was at Wampo, the Japanese allowed one batman to every six officers. So, I was batman to Jim Swanton and Captain Price – he was one of the others from '148' – and also about four other officers. It only lasted for a few weeks, because the Japanese officers got very jealous.
>
> 'I used to boil this sweetcorn for Jim – he used to love this sweetcorn. At that time, if you had money, you could buy stuff from the Thai people. He had some money and he used to buy eggs and bananas, and of course this sweetcorn, and he'd give some to me, but it didn't last long. The money ran out.'

The Wampo camps were where the troops helped in the building of a viaduct for the railway. The solid limestone rock embedded in a precipice adjoining a bend in the river made the work extremely dangerous.

> **Derek Gilbert:** 'We were working hammer and tap, before they got pneumatic drills, and we were told we would have to drill two metres before we could get back to the camp, and sometimes the days would last as long as eighteen hours. We had to put our own dynamite charges in – the Japs would give us a lighted cigarette and then they would blow the whistle, and we had to light these fuses and run like hell into the jungle. But a lot of lads got killed by flying rock, and some of the rock used to fly a very long way, right down into our camp, which was in a hollow by the river. You had about a couple of minutes to get away before an explosion. You had to get behind a tree somewhere to avoid being struck by those flying rocks.'

The ill-fated 18th Division were the largest military formation on the railway which was to stretch all the way from Nong Pladuk in Thailand across the Burmese border at the Three Pagodas Pass to its terminus at Thanbyuzayat, close to Moulmein, which in all was approximately 415 kilometres. Construction began in June 1942 in both Burma and Thailand and was to last approximately sixteen months until October 1943.

> **Jane Flower:** 'When Singapore collapsed, the Japanese were aghast at the sheer number of prisoners, because they had no administration available to take responsibility for the camps. So initially they used the Allied officers to run the camps, and the officers would work to the Japanese. Eventually, after July 1942, the Japanese managed to form an administration, a POW administration in various areas. There was a Thailand administration, a Burmese administration, and a Malayan administration, and they were all autonomous under senior officers. But they retained the allied officers' battalion rank, so that they would remain in their military formations. They then removed all officers of the rank of Colonel and above, and they were taken to first Taiwan and then elsewhere. Therefore the Japanese worked through battalion commanders – lieutenant colonels and majors – and it placed an enormous amount of responsibility on these officers.'

There is, of course, little point in retelling the well-documented story of that time unless there is a direct or indirect correlation with Jim and those who were part of his circle. At the beginning of his captivity he was in a mixed gunner battalion, known as 'F' battalion, which was a section of Group 4. The battalions and regiments of which the troops were a part in the United Kingdom bore little relation to the groupings within each POW camp in Thailand.

They all had been split up. (They were fragmented initially at Changi when the Japanese had simply demanded the use of 800 men.) Comrades who had served together for years now lacked mutual support and the comfort of familiar faces. One should add that this did not apply to the Australian units, most of whom had been brought up together, trained together, and fought together.

During his three and a half years as a guest of the Son of Heaven (otherwise Emperor Hirohito) Jim either existed in, or visited briefly, no fewer than sixteen camps. Some of the men he had known since joining the Bedfordshire Yeomanry were with him in some of the camps, some he saw hardly at all. A good few had seen him last in Singapore and met up again on the boat home. It was pure chance.

In one way, Jim was fortunate in that his first lengthy incarceration as a POW took place at Wampo. Wampo was not a typical camp, inasmuch as initially there was a cooperative relationship between the two senior British and Japanese officers. In civilian life Lt. Col. Harold Lilly (5th Sherwood Foresters) was director of a large paper-manufacturing company. But more to the point, he was one of the most remarkable and admired commanders in Thailand. His opposite number, Lt. Hattori, a lawyer who had studied at Tokyo University, had been conscripted to the Japanese Army because of his knowledge of English. Hattori, however, was basically indolent and content to leave the decision-making to Lilly. He was fond of quoting passages from J.M. Barrie, on whom he had written a thesis, and declaiming the speeches of Lloyd George. In the evenings, the bantering relationship between the two was good enough for them to play bridge together. The three battalions in the camp included a large number of volunteers – Malayan lawyers, chartered accountants and businessmen. Jim would remark that the sheer range of talent in that camp triggered remarkable conversations. Therefore the acclimatisation process for him was gentler than for others elsewhere. There was even a football match of sorts at Wampo:

> **EWS:** 'I remember they said that on Christmas Day there must be a football match between the guards and the prisoners. And Colonel Lilly said to Hattori, "I'll play if you play." Which, I suppose was a challenge to Hattori. He would have lost face if he had refused. To say that he played was going a bit far, but he was on the field and I can see him there now smoking a cigarette out of a holder and taking a few sort of desultory kicks at the ball whenever it got anywhere near him. But this Hattori seemed to us to be a perfectly reasonable fellow.'

Further upriver at Kinsayok, where Jim spent time, Hattori had changed: 'It was much nearer the Burma end, and we found him then to be difficult, unapproachable, and as really unpleasant as he had been relatively pleasant before. I don't know, perhaps he'd had the tip-off from someone that he was being a little bit too pro us.'

Hattori's relationship with Lilly also altered. Increasingly, the young Japanese commander's position had been undermined by an unpredictable and vicious regular soldier with years of Army service in China, Sergeant-Major Hiramatsu, 'The Tiger'. Lilly thought this disastrous and made his feelings clear. Hattori's weakness, of course, had also undermined Lilly and all the advantages that he had been able to obtain for his men.

It was 'The Tiger' who could have cut off Jim's head. At Kinsayok Jim had helped organise a sort of open-air church, inasmuch as there was a table which served as an altar and where a Padre could take a Communion Service. Basically, it was a place where everyone foregathered.

Derek Gilbert: 'Jim Swanton was taking a service for a harvest festival, and some of the Korean guards brought bananas and eggs and gave it to Jim for the service. This terrible Jap officer called "The Tiger" found out and called him up before him, and he got a terrible beating up, really severely beaten up, and eventually was moved down to Tarsao. He got beaten with his fists, and the flat of the sword, almost unconscious – if you read Jim's account in the *Spectator* it was just a few slaps, but it was far more than that. At one point he had his sword raised above his head and I thought he was going to cut Jim's head off. He was really angry. Anyway after he'd gone, we poured some water over Jim and helped him up. He soon recovered, and made light of it.'

As Gilbert says, when speaking of the event subsequently Jim would dismiss it as 'a sort of mildish beating-up. They thought I was testing the loyalty of these Koreans who had told me they were Christians. After that they dismissed me from the camp which they thought was the worst disgrace and sent me down river with a couple of guards in a little boat we called a pom-pom, because of the noise it made.' Jim laughed deprecatingly: 'And that would all have been very pleasant if it hadn't been that I was being reported to the Jap Commander at Tarsao, which was the headquarters, and I thought that I might be in line for something unpleasant.'

If the dreaded Kempei-tai (the Japanese Military Police) had got hold of him, no doubt he would have been. 'But oddly when I was brought before the Tarsao fellow he thought nothing of it and so that was that. Thereupon I was added to the strength of the camp at Tarsao.'

Jim's adherence to ecclesiastical ritual had brought trouble before – this time with British officers. Once when conducting a service he had noticed Captain Henry McCreath (Royal Northumberland Fusiliers) and two other commissioned officers failing to bow to the altar. He had put them on a charge which, not surprisingly, was laughingly dismissed out of court by Colonel Lilly.

Mostly the moves to other camps were dictated by the progression of the railway. Sometimes this involved a leapfrogging pattern whereby one group of workers would pass beyond another group to make sure that the momentum in making a path for the railway was maintained. But at Tonchan Main, a few miles up the track from Wampo, for a time there was hardly any work done at all. Jim had been at Tonchan Main before a move to Kanyu and then Kinsayok, which, as we now know, is where he came into conflict with 'The Tiger'.

Incidentally, many of the prisoners' taskmasters had been given labels according to their unattractive behavioural habits and physiognomy: Jim would have known Lt. Usuki 'The Kanyu Kid' and Korean Iwaya, 'The Mad Mongrel', both of whom were hanged at the end of the war for their inhuman treatment of POWs.

When Jim arrived at Tonchan Main he had found the camp in a shocking state. Torrential rains had made the ground 'a glutinous mess' and the poorly made huts, with no linings, leaked persistently. The best tents had already been given to the Tamils in the adjoining camp. Very soon there was disease. The Tamil camp was upstream and poor hygiene and sanitation infected the water supply. In spite of the unceasing efforts of the British and Australian doctors, cholera spread rapidly.

> **Eric Samuel:** 'You could go out to work in the morning, and when you came back both your mates who had been sleeping on either side of you would be dead and buried. It was as quick as that with cholera. As far as I understand it, the body dehydrates, and the blood can't get round the body, and you die with cramps in the stomach. Absolute agony.'

Inevitably, the railway construction fell behind schedule and the frantic Japanese, themselves under the whip from on high, sent down to the lines enfeebled men with barely enough strength to be able to lift a pickaxe. 'By this time officers were working on the line,' remembered Jim. 'I have a vivid memory of one "Speedo" job on a bridge when British and Dutch officers, the British and Dutch ORs [other ranks], Tamils, Chinese and Malays, Jap engineers and a collection of elephants were all at it together. The casualty lists were enormous and men evacuated downriver were still dying from the effects of this period nine months later.'

While at Tonchan Main, Jim was involved in a disciplinary procedure. A member of his original Troop, Jim Porter, had a good friend from one of the sister batteries, '512', a gunner called Roy Whitehead. Whitehead was close to death from a combination of dysentery and beriberi.

'Whilst Roy lay dying an event took place which made me very angry indeed,' observed Porter. 'Someone had stolen his boots. Things like blankets and boots to us were very precious, because when your boots wore out the Japs did not give you a replacement, so you went barefoot. I kept my eyes open and spotted a chap from another battery wearing them. I reported the matter to our Sergeant-Major, and he in turn brought the man up on a charge. My battery commander, Jim Swanton, sat on a log in the jungle and listened to the evidence. The man admitted stealing the boots and Major Swanton offered him a choice – he could lose ten days' pay or receive six cuts across his backside with a thin bamboo. He chose the latter punishment and the Sergeant-Major administered the strokes. To his credit the man never bore me a grudge, so I let him keep the boots.' Jim must have imagined he was back at school. The continual daily beatings of the prisoners by their guards had become contagious.

When at Tarsao Jim met up again with his former batman. 'I had lost contact with Jim for a little while and then one day he appeared and said: "I've just had some bad news – your brother died at Kinsayok." Because I wanted to get up there Jim managed to get me onto a barge which was taking rice, and so I got onto the boat and became one of their handlers. When I got to Kinsayok I made a bamboo cross for my brother's grave – he was buried in a rice sack beside the railway. He died of beriberi, and only lasted nine months – he wasn't as strong as me. I was very fit, having played water polo, while he was very studious. Also he couldn't stomach stuff like I could, such as snakes, rats, dogs, monkeys, and so on – he tried to live on rice alone, you see. I could eat anything, I could, even eat the guts of the rats. I used to wrap it round a bamboo and grill it, and eat it like a kebab [laugh]. I could stomach anything, I could. We were working on the railway one day and the Japanese saw these two baboons go into a cave. And they called me and another soldier over and they gave us their rifles. [*The thought must have crossed their minds momentarily of shooting the guards, but escape was virtually impossible in the jungle.*] And they told us to go and shoot these baboons. You know, baboons can be a bit fierce when they're cornered. Anyway, we shot them, and dragged them out of the cave, and each of us got part of a leg. The Japs had the rest, because they were also very poorly fed you know, mostly on rice and fish, so that was very acceptable, that was [laugh].'

One of the daily responsibilities for the POW sergeants was to ensure that the thirty gallons of water contained in the huge woks called Kwalis was sterilised. 'You had to get up well before 6 a.m.,' recalled Eric Samuel, 'in order to make sure the water had been thoroughly boiled, before being poured into every man's dixie which was his supply for the day. I was Orderly Sergeant on this particular morning and when I woke up, it was still dark and I couldn't see what the time was on the Camp pocket watch which had been given to me. We were sleeping in five-foot high bamboo atap huts and so bent almost double I crept towards the embers of the bonfire which was just outside the entrance at the far end. Half-asleep and groping in the dark I stepped over the fire, missed my step and fell into the latrine pit. Well, I was only wearing a G-string and I just managed to hold on to the watch, but I was in a terrible mess. So I went to find the Camp Sergeant and got his permission to go down to the river to have a wash. By the time I got back I was very tired and fell straight asleep.

'I woke up and there was still just enough time to light the fire, but when I got there I found that the man whose job it was to leave the wood to light the fire had cut only green bamboo – I couldn't get it to light. So, the water wasn't ready. Well, RSM Mannion, who was an officious little . . ., said, "Sergeant Samuel, I'm going to put you on a charge." And there I was, cap off, up before the Camp Officer, who was Swanton. He said to me, "Sergeant, I understand you didn't get the drinking water ready for the men this morning. Why?" And I explained. After my explanation he paused and he said, "I don't know quite what I shall do with you. You realise how serious this is? If men going out to work, do not have water to drink?" "I fully realise that, sir," I replied, "but if I could have got it ready, I would have done. The bloke before me is as much to blame as me – he didn't leave me dry wood to get the fire going." And then I added, "There's one thing, sir – you won't confine me to barracks, will you?" Swanton smiled. "No," he said, "I don't think we can quite do that while you're here. We'll put it down to experience, but you must realise how grave a situation this is."

At Tarsao, it would seem Jim's direct or indirect interaction with the men never ceased.

Derek Gilbert: 'On the first day I was working in the railway in Tarsao, a Jap officer called me over and in an American accent said, "Hey, you there guy, I've been looking at you, and you remind me of my young brother who was killed in the Battle of Singapore. How would you like to come and cook for me?" Well, I thought if it gets me out of this job,

I'll do anything. So for several months, I was cooking for these Japanese officers. I was shown exactly what to do. But before I did so I had a word with Jim Swanton, because I was very worried about appearing too Jap-happy, you know, and Jim said "It's up to you, but if you feel you want to do it, carry on."

'Anyway, I decided to do it after speaking to Jim, because this Japanese officer was giving me food to take up to the hospital at Tarsao, which was very acceptable. There was a big hospital up there with bamboo slats, and I remember being in it myself after having been severely beaten up. One day I'd roasted a little pig for these officers, and on that evening they had been drinking a lot of saki, and I used to sing to them, all the old Paul Robeson songs, like "Ol' Man River" and "Swing Low, Sweet Chariot". Anyway they used to have these young Korean girls up there, comfort girls they called them. They were very young, these Korean girls, sixteen, seventeen, eighteen years old. After they'd finished this pig I was called over, and the Japanese officer said, "Take your pick." Well, you see, they had left all the trotters of the pig, and so I said, "Thanks very much, but could I have those four trotters instead?" And he couldn't stop laughing. He said, "They're yours," and so I took them up to the hospital. He was the one good Jap I would have liked to have met again. I don't even know his name – I used to call him Yankee. And I've been to Japan recently, but there was no chance of finding him without knowing his name.

'Now only Jim and the two sergeants knew that this was happening, and now, of course, they are all dead. It was not the sort of thing you'd want everybody to know was happening. In the end the Japanese officer apologised to me and said, "We've all got to go up on to the front line in Burma, so now you'll have to go back on to the railway," which I did. People didn't know where I'd been.

After enjoying the delights of Japanese desserts, Gilbert went down with dysentery and malaria: 'Every morning that terrible officer called "The Tiger" would call in. He had a ferocious temper.' (*Hiramatsu did not discriminate in his brutality.*)

Derek Gilbert: 'While I was at Tarsao I went down with dysentery and malaria, and I was in this hospital hut, and every morning we had a visit from "The Tiger". He'd come round the hospital hut and pick out people – and I was half dead really – and he made me on this occasion go out on to the railway. As I said, I'd got dysentery, and so I kept nipping backwards and forwards into the jungle with this dysentery you see. And every time you did that you were supposed to get permission from the Japanese sergeant who was in charge. Well, once I didn't ask, and he called me over. He was sitting on a chair. And then he got two other Jap soldiers to lift up a sleeper and I had to stand and hold the sleeper above my head. I was too weak, I could only hold it for a few seconds, and it fell down onto my neck – I've got a prolapsed disc there now – and then it fell down and caught him on the foot. He went berserk, and dug his bayonet into my leg about four times, and I've now got some terrible scars there. Then he got his rifle butt and smashed my knee. I had to be carried back to the hospital hut then. For weeks I was out of action. But as soon as I could limp, I was back on the railway again.'

Gilbert's was a common experience. Illness rarely left the prisoners. Eric Samuel even went so far as to list the ailments he suffered throughout his tenure in the camps: between March 1942 and August 1945, scrotal dermatitis; dengue fever four times; bacillary dysentery twice; diphtheria; beriberi; five attacks of VT malaria; septic scabies; tropical ulcers; avitaminosis twice; ordinary dysentery and debility. How on earth did he survive? 'I just made up my mind I was going home. You'd scrounge what food you possibly could and that was another day gone. Some hospital wards were terrible. The ulcers were worst to look at. They'd put maggots in them to eat them out to keep them clean. Maggots will eat all the putrid flesh and not so much of the decent flesh. I've seen small ulcers scooped out with a sharpened teaspoon. Some ulcers were almost as big as the cheeks on your backside – you could see the shin bone. When that happened they usually died, because the body simply couldn't take it. If only we could have had some iodine or something like that, most of these people could have been saved.'

When Jim had come down to the Number 4 Group Headquarters Camp at Tarsao in November of 1943, he found a hospital of 2000, the doctors striving to do their best with only a handful of drugs and a general atmosphere of squalor. 'Here it was possible to get the talks and such-like diversions going again in the wards,' he remembered. 'There was a natural sort of amphitheatre too and the convalescents would come out and listen to talks on every topic under the sun. Personally I found that anything about cricket was certain to find an audience and some of my pleasantest memories are of evenings with a mixed crowd of British and Australians shooting questions from all angles and barracking sometimes in a friendly way from The Hill – that's a reference to The Hill at Sydney Cricket Ground.'

Although still suffering from the effects of malaria, Australian POW Desmond H. Jackson had been invited by his fellow Tasmanian, Reg McWilliams, to the weekly 'Radio Newsreel'. Invariably produced by Jim, who was on the Camp Entertainment Committee, it was an occasion not to be missed. The simulated broadcast incorporated realistic sound effects produced by a small team of willing helpers. Many years after the war, Jackson would write about this evening in detail. He would have been the first to agree that therapy can arrive in unexpected ways. We can but give a flavour of the experience:

With the authority of the Japanese, the committee had created an open air theatre, utilising a small concave hill which rose steeply from a flat area at its foot. A stage of bamboo and covered with matting was built on the flat land and the POW audience simply sat on the slopes of the hill.

On Tuesdays, a structure shaped like a huge radio set was placed in the centre of the stage. Also made of bamboo and matting, it was about nine feet tall by seven feet wide. Some two feet from its top, a rectangular section had been cut away and crude lamps burning peanut oil were placed on a ledge behind and below the aperture to give the impression of a lighted dial. Under that, there was a 'speaker' – a large round hole covered with hessian – while wings of high bamboo matting extended from each side of the radio set to the edges of the stage, effectively screening actors and assistants from the audience on the hill.

The weekly 'Radio Newsreel' programmes were entertaining documentaries, read by performers who stood behind the 'speaker' of the radio, and 'The Life of Bradman' promised to be of particular interest, especially to the Australians and the British.

When Reg and I sat down on the hill, it was already crowded and there was a loud hum of excited conversation. Not so different to a theatre at home, I thought. It was a cool night but the sky was cloudless with no wind and most had brought something to sit on as a defence against the early dew. At 7 o'clock, all fell silent and the well modulated voice of an invisible announcer opened the show.

'Good evening. This is the Allied Broadcasting Corporation transmitting from Tarsao and tonight Radio Newsreel brings you a cricketing feature about the world's greatest batsman. Our programme is "The Life of Bradman" and will be presented by the well-known sporting personality, E.W. (Jim) Swanton.'

After some warm applause, Major Swanton's pleasing English voice came clearly through the speaker.

'Donald George Bradman was born at Cootamundra in New South Wales on the 27th August, 1908. He was the youngest of five children and in 1911, the family moved to Bowral, about 85 miles south-west of Sydney . . .'

Already, the audience was warming to the subject. 'In his early childhood, he enjoyed music and showed promise at a number of games – tennis, rugby, athletics and, of course, cricket.'

Swanton then described how Bradman gradually developed his batting talents by throwing a golf ball against a curved, brick tank-stand and hitting the rebounding ball with a cricket stump and by employing a similar method to sharpen his fielding. By this time, each man present was so engrossed in the performance that he had quite forgotten his problems and his unhappy lot.

Jim had captured his audience. The men on the hill were now completely enthralled. Outlining Bradman's early life and Test debut, he eventually covered the momentous 1930 tour to Britain and the third Test at Headingley.

'Only one run but that's enough and Foster's record is broken. Bradman is smiling broadly and the England players are all round him, shaking his hand. Now he waves his bat to the crowd.'

The noise of applause increased and as it slowly died away the prisoners began to clap in spontaneous appreciation of the exciting commentary and sound effects which Swanton and his small band of helpers had so cleverly and unexpectedly produced.

The Major went on to describe the remainder of the 1930 tour and pointed out that Australia regained the Ashes by winning the series 2–1 mainly because of the predominance of Bradman, who made 2960 first-class runs during that summer at an average of 98. In Tests, he totalled 974 runs at 139, figures which clearly demonstrated his formidable influence.

After summarising The Don's great success against West Indies in 1930–31 and South Africa in 1931–32, Swanton added a romantic touch by mentioning Bradman's courtship of a lovely Sydney girl, Jessie Menzies, whom he married in April 1932.

Then, with great tact, because the audience was about half-English and half-Australian, he dealt with the notorious England tour of Australia in 1932–33.

'That series caused a great deal of controversy and bitterness and I don't propose to say much about it. England won back the Ashes by 4 matches to 1 largely because Bradman's average was reduced to that of a very good batsman. Some said he failed: yet in 8 innings, he scored 396 runs for an average of 56. It would have been an excellent result for anyone other than The Don. He was unable to play in the first Test through illness but listen to this recording of his performances in the second at Melbourne, which Australia won by 111 runs . . .'

Suddenly, there was silence . . .

Immediately, I saw two guards standing beside the stage. We were back to reality and all knew that if the show was to continue, normal formalities would have to be observed and quickly at that.

The Allied Camp Commander, Colonel Harvey, was sitting close to the stage and rising to his feet, he gave the order 'kiotske'. The audience stood and came to attention.

'Keray,' called the Colonel. All bowed and the guards acknowledged the salute by inclining their heads slightly.

'Nowray,' called Harvey. It was the order to come back to attention. The guards went behind the screen and we hoped that they would not find something to cause them annoyance. They didn't and shortly afterwards, they reappeared, called 'OK' to the Colonel and stomped away. Protocol had been satisfied and amidst a buzz of conversation, consisting mainly of rude comments about the Japanese, we sat down.

Major Swanton resumed his absorbing story as though nothing had occurred to interrupt it . . .

All too soon for the prisoners, the Newsreel was reaching its conclusion:

'He has already made 92 centuries – about one in every three innings – and about 23,000 runs at an average of 95. Incredible figures. Let us hope that before long, when the war is over, we will all have the profound pleasure of again seeing or hearing Donald George Bradman at the crease in Test matches, displaying once more his extraordinary skills.'

After a short pause, the announcer's voice came through the speaker. 'The Allied Broadcasting Corporation at Tarsao thanks you all for tuning in tonight and I hope you have enjoyed the programme. This station is now closing down, but first a reminder that the next Radio Newsreel will be presented at the same time next Tuesday night. Make sure that you are listening.'

Well before the end of the announcement, the whole audience was on its feet, applauding with great warmth. Everyone appreciated the excellence of the performance which, by stirring so many exciting and nostalgic memories, had enabled each man to forget for a brief period the awful conditions under which he was being forced to exist.

While Reg and I were walking back to our huts I said, 'Great show, wasn't it?' 'Wonderful,' replied Reg.

We said no more for our minds were strangely at peace and we knew that we had just experienced something that we would always remember.

In April 1944, Jim moved south after eighteen months in the jungle and enjoyed not only the sight of a flat plain but actually being able to watch the sun set. He was bound for the base hospital camp at Nakhon Pathom and it was there, some eight months later on New Year's Day 1945, that rather than trying to simulate cricket for an audience, he could settle down as one of the spectators for another unofficial tussle between England and Australia.

The scene is not easy to put before you, but I must try. The playing area is small, perhaps sixty yards by thirty, and the batsman's crease is right up against the spectators, with the pitch longways on. There are not runs behind the wicket, where many men squat in the shade of tall trees. The sides are flanked by long huts, with parallel ditches – one into the ditch, two over the hut, in fact all runs by boundaries, 1, 2, 4 or 6. An additional hazard is washing hung on bamboo 'lines'. Over the bowler's head are more trees, squaring the thing off, and in the distance a thick, high, mud wall – the camp bund – on which stands a bored and sulky Korean sentry. (Over the bund no runs and out, for balls are precious.) In effect, the spectators are the boundaries, many hundreds of them taking every inch of room. The dress is fairly uniform, wooden clogs, and a scanty triangular piece of loin-cloth known (why?) as a 'Jap-Happy'. Only the swells wear patched and tattered shorts. The mount at long-on is an Australian preserve, their 'Hill'. The sun beats down, as tropical suns do, on the flat beaten earth which is the wicket. At the bowler's end is a single bamboo stump, at the other five – yes, five – high ones. There is the hum of anticipation that you get on the first morning at Old Trafford or Trent Bridge, though there are no score cards, and no 'Three penn'orth of comfort' to be bought from our old friend 'Cushions'.

The story of the match is very much the story of that fantastic occasion at the Oval in August 1938. Flt-Lieut. John Cocks, well known to the cricketers of Ashtead, is our Hutton; Lieut. Norman Smith, from Halifax, an even squarer, even squatter Leyland. With the regulation bat – it is two and a half inches wide and a foot shorter than normal – they play beautifully down the line of the ball, forcing the length ball past cover, squeezing the leg one square off their toes. There seems little room on the field with the eight Australian fielders poised there, but a tennis ball goes quickly off wood, the gaps are found, and there are delays while it is rescued from the swill basket, or fished out from under the hut. As the runs mount up the barracking gains in volume, and in wit at the expense of the fielders. When at last the English captain declares, the score is acknowledged to be a Thailand record.

With the Australian innings comes sensation. Captain 'Fizzer' Pearson, of Sedbergh and Lincolnshire, the English fast bowler, is wearing BOOTS! No other cricketer has anything on his feet at all, the hot earth, the occasional flint being accepted as part of the game. The moral effect of these boots is tremendous. Captain Pearson bowls with shattering speed and ferocity, and as each fresh lamb arrives for the slaughter the stumps seem more vast, the bat even punier. One last defiant cheer from 'the Hill' when their captain, Lieut.-Colonel E.E. Dunlop, comes in, another and bigger one from the English when his stumps go flying.

While these exciting things proceed one of the fielders anxiously asks himself whether they will brew trouble. 'Should fast bowlers wear boots? Pearson's ruse condemned – where did he get those boots? . . . boots bought from camp funds. Official denial . . . Board of Control's strong note . . .' headlines seem to grow in size. Then he remembers gratefully that here is no Press box full of slick columnists and Test captains, no microphones for the players to run to – in fact, no papers and no broadcasting. The field clears at last. As he hurries off to roll-call he thinks of a New Year's Day six years before when the bund was Table Mountain, the field was the green of Newlands, and he decided that even the South Africans who jostled their way cheerfully back into Cape Town that evening had not enjoyed their outing more than the spectators of this grotesque 'Cricket Match'.

All too soon, it was back to reality. For all of them. The endless roll-calls; 'Tenko' – ichi, ni, san, si, go, toco, sutchi, hatchi, coo, jon, jack, Queen, King, Ace . . . Humour was a godsend. There was a sense of revenge in being able to make a mockery of their captors. Did the Japs realise? For the prisoners, their mind-set was like a cipher that could not be decoded. As Reginald Burton points out in his book *Railway of Hell*, 'the language barrier was always a source of mixed laughter and frustration'. 'Orru Maine Musk Rearn Japanese Ranguage'. And if they happened not to know the words to say, some of the Japanese marching songs, a severe slapping could quickly follow. The secret wireless sets, illicit traffic in money and medicine, and the hourly tests of will made captivity dangerous and exhausting. That, together with the interminable clearing of the jungle, eternal digging of the red clay sand and the carrying of it in baskets to build up embankments and the blasting and drilling of the rock only added to the burden. But while the men toiled, Jim led a comparatively easy existence working behind the lines, even when there was a deadline for the completion of the railway:

EWS: 'Then everybody on two legs had to go out and do his stuff. The officers were never idle because they did all the camp administration, when I say administration that's probably rather a grand word, building latrines for instance, open latrines have got to be dug and maintained and finally, of course, filled in and started again. There was always hut building going on which we had to do. There were all sorts of chores to keep a camp going. The camps varied so much in size, some of them might be only just a hundred or two, others of them were nearer a thousand. But they were all built of bamboo, that was the only substance ever used in building a camp, and a good deal of hard work went on in maintaining them. But of course it wasn't the hard physical daily slog that the troops had from the start on the railway. Eventually after a protest – because according to the Geneva Convention I believe officers are not supposed to work when they are prisoners of war – the officers consented to work on the railway. They did it really for the sake of the men more than anything else, and also because, I think, there was no doubt that some of them would have been killed just to make the others a bit keener. [*In fact, most officers were forced to work during the building of the railway.*] That was very, very tough going indeed. I did a little of it, but I didn't do very much.'

Billy and Lill, Jim's father and mother. With feline company in the garden at Catford Hill.

Great-grandfather Friend 'Wendy' Westover. A grocer by trade, he looks as if he wouldn't tolerate any pipsqueaks! He lived in the same house opposite St Mary's Church in the village of Lewisham for about 60 years until his death aged 72 in 1935.

Grandmother Elizabeth Ann Swanton (née Westover) who died in 1938. 'A fine old lady, impressively built, big-boned and not dissimilar in size to her grandson.'

Vancouver Road, Catford. Jim's birthplace. Two young friends, Haydon Fergasson and Kenneth Pickett, at the gate.

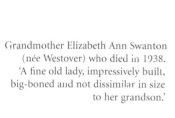

Forest Hill Cricket Ground – the Pavilion. Mama helped with the teas while Papa was treasurer and sang in the concerts. Jim lay in his pram unaccountably mute – at least, when W.G. Grace was batting...

Proud mother with her baby son already setting his sights on the way ahead, 1907.

Well-groomed schoolboy.

School report, Form IVa, Lent Term, 1922. His Form Master thought Jim was 'a trifle lacking in originality', whereas his House Master – who adds three months to his age – was 'expecting much of him in the future'.

A protective pose with his younger sisters, Tina and Ruth.

Walking off at Forest Hill Cricket Club after a strenuous time in the field.

An officer in uniform with his hands in his pockets – put him on a charge! Some time spent with sister Ruth at South Wootton in Norfolk while manning the coastal defences in 1940.

Jim's report of the match at Ipswich caused a squall in the studio.

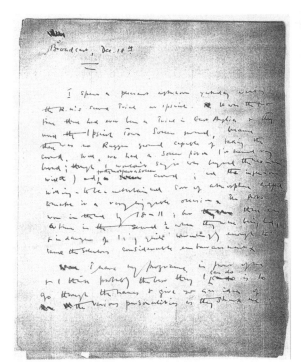

RUGBY FOOTBALL UNION

SECOND
INTERNATIONAL TRIAL

PROBABLES
v.
POSSIBLES

Ipswich Town Football Club Ground,
Portman Road,
IPSWICH
SATURDAY, 18th DECEMBER, 1937
Kick-Off, 2.15

Official Programme · · TWOPENCE

SMITHS, SUITALL PRESS, IPSWICH.

His illegible handwritten script.

PROBABLES (White)

15	+R. A. GERRARD (Bath)		Full Back
14	J. A. MACDONALD (Cambridge University & Blackheath)		*Threequarters* Left Wing
13	F. M. McRAE (St. Mary's Hospital)		Left Centre
12	+P. CRANMER (Moseley)		Right Centre
11	+E. J. UNWIN (The Army and Rosslyn Park)		Right Wing
10	W. S. KEMBLE		*Half-backs* Stand-off
9	+J. L. GILES (Coventry)		Scrum
8	+R. BOLTON (Harlequins)		Forward
7	C. THOMPSON (Harlequins)		Forward
6	+W. H. WESTON (Northampton)		Forward
5	+T. F. HUSKISSON (Old Merchant Taylors)		Forward
4	+A. WHEATLEY (Coventry)		Forward
3	+H. F. WHEATLEY (Coventry)		Forward
2	+H. B. TOFT (Waterloo)		Forward
1	+R. J. LONGLAND (Northampton)		Forward

+ International

POSSIBLES (Blue)

15	H. D. FREAKES (Oxford University & Harlequins)		Full Back
11	+A. OBOLENSKY (Oxford University & Rosslyn Park)		*Threequarters* Right Wing
12	+R. LEYLAND (The Army & Aldershot Services)		Right Centre
13	B. E. NICHOLSON (Harlequins)		Left Centre
14	G. E. HANCOCK (Birkenhead Park)		Left Wing
10	+J. R. AUTY (Headingley)		*Half-backs* Stand-off
9	P. COOKE (Oxford University)		Scrum
8	P. K. MAYHEW (Oxford University & Old Haileyburians)		Forward
7	J. R. SPEAR (Durham University)		Forward
6	J. T. W. BERRY (Leicester)		Forward
5	D. W. STANDEVEN (Halifax)		Forward
4	R. W. MARSHALL (Oxford University)		Forward
3	+R. E. PRESCOTT (Harlequins)		Forward
2	W. O. CHADWICK (Cambridge University & Blackheath)		Forward
1	G. T. DANCER (Bedford)		Forward

+ International

Referee: R. B. HUNT (Eastern Counties)

The marked programme for the match with his 'A' and 'B' categorisation of players' performance.

Descending from the tree-box, Newlands, Cape Town. Jim made the first cricket commentaries to and from South Africa during the 1938/39 MCC tour.

Looking just spruce and dandy.

A match at Lakenham in 1951 to celebrate the Festival of Britain. Jim is batting for F.G. Mann's XI against Peter Softley of Norfolk. He scored 53 and 12 in a drawn game. *Norfolk Newspapers*

'B' Troop, Knowsley, Liverpool, 1941, shortly before departure to the Far East. Jim showing his stiff upper lip *(sixth from the left on the front row)*. *Jack Wragg*

Lt. Kishio Usuki, 'The Kanyu Kid'. An alcoholic, he was one of the worst of the Japanese war criminals and later hanged for his brutal ill-treatment of POWs in numerous camps. *Irene Janes*

Korean guard Iwaya, 'The Mad Mongrel'. Vicious and unpredictable, he was similarly dispatched for multiple maltreatment of POWs. *Irene Janes*

The huge trench dug for the grave of POWs at Kanchanaburi, Thailand, 1945. The atomic bombing of Hiroshima and Nagasaki came just in time. *James Noble*

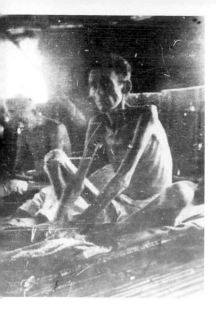

One of the many sufferers of severe malnutrition and no doubt much else in the hospital at Tarsao.
Irene Janes

Tarsao Camp Hospital, June 1943. Derek Gilbert (*the first left of those sitting up*) with a swollen and battered knee two weeks after it had been badly damaged by a Japanese guard (*see p. 112*). The remainder of those pictured died of cholera or other diseases. *Derek Gilbert*

Surrounded by old comrades from the 148 Field Regiment at Sir John Paul Getty's ground at Wormsley, 1993. (*l. to r.*) Jim Porter; Jack Wragg; Eric Samuel; Don Janes; Leslie Webster; Ken Holland. (*front*) Geoffrey Munton (Royal Engineers), the father of Sally Munton, PA to Sir John Paul Getty; E.W.S.

Bowled for a duck by G.N. Peters when playing for Cross Arrows against Hampstead at Lord's, September 1953. *MCC*

Confidently waiting for his cue.

'Three happy commentators at the Oval are we!' E.W.S., Brian Johnston and Peter West after England had won back the Ashes. Equally elated is Bill Wright, senior cameraman, BBC Television.

That fact did not go unnoticed. For a long time Jim carried his left arm in a splint.

Jane Flower: 'I'm afraid Jim was the subject of animosity and ridicule when he was on the railway. A lot of the officers were not convinced that he had a genuine wound. Initially he had been in hospital in Singapore with his wound from the sniper and was declared unfit up there, and then at the end he did go to the hospital at Nakhon Pathom. But on the other hand, there were too many people who noticed the moment the war ended the splint disappeared. A few years ago when I first went to see Jim, he looked at me and leant over his desk and said, "Tell me, what are people saying about me?" I knew exactly what he meant, but I couldn't touch on it, so I thought quickly and replied, "Everybody is asking, 'Have you seen Jim Swanton?'" He cackled. Well, you see, the men would not have seen this. He asked me to go and speak to the remaining gunners of "148", who still lived in the Bedford/Luton area, and I did that, and they were devoted to Jim and his memory, but very few of them would have been with him all the way on the railway. They would have been in different camps because of this system of splitting up units.'

When asked about sickness and incapacity during an interview for the Imperial War Museum in 1980, Jim replied:

'I had mild dysentery all the time, but it was not really awful. And I had something called dengue fever once which is rather a tiresome thing to have. You get great soreness, splitting headaches, a great soreness of the arms and back and neck so that you really can't even brush your hair. The use of your limbs is very restricted for a while. And then I had what I thought was dengue a second time, but it turned out not to be dengue but polio, but where I was so frightfully lucky was that it simply attacked my left shoulder deltoid supraspinatus muscles and they don't function now, so that I can only move my left arm a few degrees from the perpendicular. One's got to live with it, but I was frightfully lucky that it just stopped there. But in order to try and get the movement back, or to offset the wastage there, they put me in a sort of an improvised wooden frame so that my arm was horizontal . . . And I went about the camp in this rather clumsy frame for quite a long time, but it didn't do any good because the nerve had gone and therefore nothing could be built up again.'

Jane Flower: 'I hadn't realised until recently how long Jim had spent in the jungle camps where the conditions were appalling. From going to Wampo in November 1942 and then Tonchan in April 1943 to Kinsayok in the August of that year and then Tarsao from November 1943 to April 1944, Jim was in the jungle much longer than most POWs. It shows a resilience which is remarkable. No wonder he succumbed to illness.'

Not that that attracted any sympathy. Some officers regarded what they thought of as his 'phantom incapacity' as merely an excuse to avoid going down to the lines. Major Ronnie Archdale of 'B' Battalion, who knew of Jim's indiscretion at Knowsley, once voiced an opinion of Swanton in most undiplomatic terms, 'a shit and a sponger', and in an interview many years after the war was over, even spoke of cowardice. It was an opinion shared by Brigadier Sir Philip Toosey who, of course, was unforgettably portrayed by Alec Guinness in *Bridge Over the River Kwai*. (Although Jim and many fellow prisoners felt the film to be a calumny.) As part of the oral history of the British POW in the Far East, Toosey's recollections, amounting to around 470 pages of manuscript, now reside at the Imperial War Museum, originally having been recorded by his biographer, Dr Peter Davies. When asked about post-war reunion meetings Toosey replied:

> Another who doesn't come out well, as a matter of interest, is that great broadcaster from the *Daily Telegraph,* the cricket correspondent who was prisoner with me the whole time, Jim Swanton. He was a miserable so-and-so, I've met him once since and once only and he deliberately tried to avoid me.

Davies: *That's funny, as he comes over as a very cool, calm sort of countryman.*

Toosey: Don't you believe it, he was a coward.

Davies: *And what rank was he?*

Toosey: He was a Lieutenant Colonel.

Davies: *Was he? That's very interesting, I didn't realise that.*

Toosey: He was a useless so-and-so and nobody in our organisation has anything but the greatest contempt for him and this also goes for that great rugby footballer down in Wales – I'll think of his name later on. But it was a very odd thing, these great sportsmen who were very highly skilled and had been used to the worship of crowds of people – Wooller was the name – a cricketer, not a rugby footballer [*he was, of course, a rugby footballer – one of the greatest centre three-quarters of all time*] – somehow they can't take hardship, they get used to adulation and this I think faults their character. This is one thing that we can't do, of course, we can say how good people were and name them, but we can't name people who didn't live up to expectations. It wouldn't do; besides, we might be had up for libel. Well, that's one point and the other thing is, of course, it's a bit unfair. I'm not talking about Swanton now, I don't know him except I see him on television and hear him on the radio, but there may be other people who didn't come up to achieve the heights and without talking to them personally and asking them their side – I mean there may have been circumstances which we don't know – who are we to judge? – everything I've said to you is the personal opinion of P. Toosey. It isn't necessarily other people's opinions.

Such a serious charge cannot be allowed to pass unchallenged. To be accused of cowardice strikes a numbing blow at the very heart of any person's self-regard and in military terms has been terminal. There are both instantly dismissable resonances of school playgrounds and ineradicable echoes of First World War battlefield firing squads in such a slur on character. So what did Toosey mean? Before one seeks an answer, it should be noted that his remarks are muddled, incorrect and therefore unreliable. Jim was never a Lieutenant Colonel and after the war he frequently attended reunions. And at one such, he even play-acted a Tenko and allowed a pint of beer to be poured down the inside of his trousers in the best traditions of slapstick.

Besides appearing to backtrack towards the end of his testimony, Toosey also undermines his case by trying to bracket Wilf Wooller with Swanton. Although both Jim and Wilf on occasion were reportedly distinctly uncomplimentary about each other's behaviour and views, and neither suffered fools gladly, they were very different people. Incidentally their paths crossed rarely in the camps. Wooller's intrepidity was renowned, he was a forceful personality and an uncomfortable antagonist. And although much the same could be said about Jim, they had totally dissimilar independent minds and were cast in unmatched moulds.

Even given Toosey's inconsistencies, though, there is no gainsaying his lasting impression. And within it, we can perhaps find a clue to his outburst. Neither Swanton nor, it would seem, Wooller conformed to his stereotyped expectancy of what an officer should be, or behaved in the way he felt an officer should behave. The patterns that embroidered their lives were not ones he was able to recognise. Jane Flower once more:

> It makes me very angry to hear what Toosey had to say. It is most unfair and he had no right. In the camps, he was only with Jim at Kanchanaburi in 1945 so he wouldn't have known at first hand what Jim did. In the main, his remarks must have been hearsay. And one should not forget that this lengthy debriefing by his biographer, which took many sessions, was not until many years after the war and not all that long before Toosey died in 1975. His memory so long afterwards was likely to be defective.

Jim had other detractors too, for instance lawyer Gerald Kidner with unsubstantiated comment to bookseller Timothy D'Arch Smith decades after the war had finished: 'Swanton didn't do a stroke of work and he bribed the guards.' But what evidence is there of that? And if so, was it done for a reason such as to enable the likes of Lawrence Moody, attached to the Cambridgeshire 196 Field Ambulance, to steal out of camp at night to go down to the barges and barter for cheaper eggs and other goods? 'Jim gave me twenty dollars once and I bought gula sugar, Malacca peanut toffee, bantams' eggs and four ounces of tobacco at 2.50 each,' Moody told me. 'I would have been shot if I had been caught.' Without being too defensive of one who is unable to defend himself, all it is possible to say is that the verdict is most definitely non-proven.

There was an occasion where camp boot repairer Bill Nicholson of the Royal Northumberland Fusiliers had heeled the knee boots of Hattori, who was the Japanese officer in charge of Wampo, with a solid piece of bamboo as a last. 'I was invited to dinner at his house as a reward. There to my surprise were two British officers. One of them was Major Swanton. We had a good yarn over the best meal I had as a POW.'

Now, at surface level, such an encounter could be interpreted many ways – particularly by those of mischievous intent. But an explanation is straightforward. Col. Lilly and other officers did on odd occasions dine with Hattori, who was an educated and humane man. They were not in a position to refuse, and it was in everyone's interest to promote as harmonious relations as were possible amidst the degradation. No one should suspect that there was ever a hint of collusion. It is true to say that in some respects the Japanese were as much prisoners of the situation as were their captives.

However, there is no doubt that Jim was adept in avoiding many of the worst aspects of life as a POW. And one of these concerned the lines, where there was the greatest potential for conflict with the Japanese engineers or Korean guards. In 1992, Jim had sent an article that he had written about the war to Archdale seeking his view. Archdale's curt rejoinder merely said, 'Dear Swanton, I've no comment – Archdale.' And yet Archdale, who was not alone in his assessment of Jim, contradicts the opinion of the troops who saw him in action, which admittedly was brief. Ken Holland, who was one of Jim's Dunstable battalion, thought 'he was an extremely brave officer and always looked after the men', and many others spoke of him similarly. Conversely, Captain Henry McCreath of the Northumberland Fusiliers felt that Jim 'always made sure he was all right and was a law unto himself'. An authentic comment, but it is probable that most of the officers never saw Jim at his best, whereas his men did. 'We respected Jim,' said Eric Samuel. 'The officers used to think he had usurped their chance of promotion. He was a pusher, was Jim. They knew he had got into the Regiment because of Colonel Harris and that didn't go down well.'

A small minority of officers possibly envied Jim's reputation as a cricket commentator; certainly several felt he was beneath them; of a 'different social class' and with no pedigree.

There is no doubt that, at times, Jim could be his own worst enemy. He once confided that during his lowest moments in the camps, he used to promise himself that if he ever managed to survive and return home, he would do all he could to live as comfortably as possible for the remainder of his life. Now, of course, there is nothing too much wrong with that. The trouble, in the eyes of so many of his fellow officers, was that he began practising for that enviable state while still a prisoner.

Jim could not be ignored; he was too big a man for that. Nor did he idle docilely on the sidelines. He was articulate, if not voluble, certain of his opinions and he liked to hold court. How irksome it must have been for those in close contact to put up with his elevated manner, while they were stretched almost beyond bearance to the limits of their physical and mental capacity. There also was the question of rank. The fact that Jim was an acting Major, by default as it were, who had assumed that rank on his own initiative, caused considerable resentment. Other regular officers of far longer service and greater experience were incensed by something they thought of as entirely unethical; and therefore it coloured their judgement of whatever he did. Being a Major made Jim, in effect, a field officer and anybody of that level or above generally attracted a greater degree of respect from the rank-conscious Japanese. They were given light administration duties, as opposed to Captains and below who, when the pressure to finish building the railway was at its height, were forced to do strenuous labour with the other ranks. Hence the antagonism.

The legendary 'Weary' Dunlop, the Australian with Scots ancestry, whose unswerving courage and unsparing skills as a surgeon saved so many lives on the Railway, mentions Jim a number of times in his famous *War Diaries*. He notes his enthusiasm to embrace all kinds of recreational activities: concerts, entertainments, quizzes, competitions, talks etc., and also arts and crafts. But one also senses a certain displeasure when he writes, 'Major Swanton by Lt. Colonel Harvey's instruction also went to the lines, but is apparently the hospitals amenities officer'. Which meant that somehow Jim had managed to extricate himself from a job which could have meant that he got his hands dirty.

On the other hand, Dunlop's batman Milton 'Blue' Butterworth, now in his eighty-fourth year, says that 'Weary' thought the world of Jim. 'I remember the dear old bastard walking up and down the camp at Nakhon Pathom carrying a book and reading aloud to himself. We all thought he was saying ta-ta's and had gone doolally.' In all likelihood, Jim was preparing for his next cricket talk or camp funeral.

Religion was another bone of contention. On 3 December 1943, Dunlop's diary entry reads:

> An amusing half hour listening to Marsh, Father Bourke, McNeilly and others after going to bed. Marsh explosively and violently took exception to the fact that Maj. Swanton, Turner and one other were taking advantage of their position on the hospital welfare committee to proselytise their views as 'Christian fascists' (i.e. Anglo Catholics) and to that end depicted Franco as a knightly soldier of God! Padre Bourke took up the cudgels on behalf of Franco and swept in a mighty blow by saying, 'Seeing that you for months have taken advantage of similar welfare committees to proselytise your own views to troops, I hardly see how you can take exception to others doing it!' How extraordinary that so many of our enthusiasts in politics and social economy etc. should

devote so much time in evangelistic fervour, addressing these poor shipwrecked devils.

Jane Flower: 'Jim's faith was forged, he told me, in the tragic camps like Tonshan and Kinsayok, especially during the period called "Speedo", when the guards would be screaming at the men and would drive them to work with wire whips. It was then with the men that Jim tried to bring religion and faith. He didn't have a very high opinion of the padres, particularly the Anglican ones. He said, "The problem with many of the conventional military padres of these battalions meant that they were middle of the road Anglicans, and they really turned into officers' padres, they were not really interested in the men." He added to me that he didn't think the ability of the ordinary Anglican padre could relate to the conditions that they were meeting, and that they were not inspiring. He also said that he thought the Dutch Roman Catholics were the persuasive power, and he particularly admired Padre Marsden from Sydney, a Roman Catholic, and also Father Bourke from New Zealand, and also the work of the Church Army, people who were not ordained but who had prayer meetings in the camps. Something Jim never did was to overlook the plight of all the Asians – the Tamils, the Javanese, the Malayans – some of whom had been working in the rubber plantations with their families and children, and who were enticed up to the camps with the prospects of good work and pay. Two or three hundred thousands of these died. Jim never forgot that.

'Jack Marsh, who was a very individual officer, and who became a senior figure in the Institute of British Management, was an agnostic. He told me he would never ever forgive Swanton for the way in which he exploited his views on Anglo-Catholicism.'

In this fevered atmosphere every strong controversial view became almost dynamite. There was a lot of quarrelling and in-fighting among the combatants. Because there was so little to talk about, these arguments became overheated and angry.

Jane Flower: 'Marsh felt Swanton went way beyond the boundaries of good sense, and that he caused great dissension and unhappiness. Whereas Father Bourke would always talk to the men and have great revivalist meetings in some of these camps – he was very much an old-fashioned "Hell and Damnation" priest, of enormous power – Jim would preach without really having the authority to do so.'

Several tried to dampen the hostility, feeling that in their parlous situation, polemical views should be toned down. Dissension, they felt, could provoke outrage. In another camp, to give an extreme example, there was a member of the British Union of Fascists who gave talks on Anti-Semitism. He was stopped.

Jim, of course, practised his faith by taking religious services and officiating at the frequent funerals. 'In fact, they were such regular occasions as to attract little notice,' he wrote. 'At times all that could be done was a mass burial, with no accompanying words from the Prayer Book.' At a later date he said to me: 'But just to be there was something.'

> **Jane Flower:** 'Jim was able to draw huge strength from his experiences, but he had nightmares, he was haunted by it all. Yet he was able to come to terms with it through his faith.'

Jim's attachment to his Church attracted not just enmity but also levity. His ostensible foe, Archdale, once commented: 'James, by the grace of God, Major.' Another gave him the nickname 'Pig' because he said that was what Jim reminded him of, both in looks and in the way he behaved. A friendly voice from amongst the commissioned ranks is that of John Cook, of the Cambridgeshire Regiment: 'Jim did not endear himself with all the officers because he was a bit of a walking encyclopedia, with his lectures on "The Life of Churchill", "Test Cricket" and so on, and the fact that he would always be going round the huts and talking to the men. He certainly didn't like to get his hands dirty. I composed some satirical lyrics to the hymn "The Church's One Foundation". You remember the words – they were by Samuel John Stone, "The Church's one foundation is Jesus Christ our Lord, She is His new creation by water and the word. From Heaven He came and sought her to be His holy bride, With His own blood he bought her, and for her life He died." It doesn't need much imagination to see how we altered the words to caricature Jim. All very sacrilegious, I'm sure, but at the time it felt appropriate.'

In November 1999, there was a letter published in the *Daily Telegraph* from a member of MCC's Committee, Oliver Stocken:

> Sir, last November I attended the memorial service of a friend, who had been a prisoner-of-war with E.W. Swanton on the Burma/Siam railway. [*The service was for Peter Fane, who had just died.*] Just before the service began, up the church aisle walked Jim. On a cold autumn morning, at the age of ninety-two, he had travelled across the country

from Kent to attend the service of a younger officer from the Bedfordshire Yeomanry. After the service he stayed on, well after many had left, talking to family and friends. This single act of loyalty to a former friend and colleague demonstrated to me just what a great man E.W. Swanton was.

Jane Flower: 'And yet Peter himself would ponder and consider the behaviour of Jim in captivity, and find it impossible to reconcile with the man he was friendly with after the war. Peter Fane felt Swanton had not come through the war as a brother officer should have come through. But at the same time, he would have accepted that Jim's contribution to POW life was very great – in the commentaries he gave and so on. He was always friendly with Jim. The loyalty of one officer to another was such that he would never have pointed that out to Jim and Jim knew in attending that service what Peter felt about him. Archdale wouldn't have contemplated shaking his hand. Jim would have known why.'

Before the necessary ventilation of opinion on Jim's war conduct, we had left him at the base hospital camp at Nakhon Pathom, residing in relative comfort. In many ways Nakhon Pathom was a showcase camp: its wooden huts had been built to allay international fears about the treatment of POWs. But Jim was not to see out the war there, for eventually he was to be part of another mobilisation. In January 1945, all allied officers in Thailand were sent to a camp at Kanburi (Kanchanaburi). The stay was to last eight months.

In August we were again being moved, in batches, to somewhere deep in the interior where we could be quietly liquidated in the event of invasion. Of this we had little inkling, for some time after the defeat of Germany our wireless gave out, and in the last vital months we were without news. My party were due next to move when one evening, on Wednesday, August 15 to be precise, the hut commanders were called to camp headquarters. This was next to the one confined to field officers (majors and above) which was politely known as the Imperial War Museum.

Looking through the ventilation gap between the atap walls and roof we saw the officers march in, bow from the neck in salute in the prescribed manner, then listen to a statement from a visiting Jap. Our men then turned and left without making the obligatory bow, and it was at that moment we knew they had been hearing the news that the war was over. We had been prisoners three and a half years to a day.

As is well known, the Japs were ordered to maintain their guards and be responsible for our safety until allied forces could fly in, and so there followed a varying period before we could taste the full sweets of freedom. Small parties took it by turn to visit the cafe in Kanchanaburi which belonged to the trader Boon Pong. When my turn came, a friendly Thai went to a large radiogram standing on the earthen floor, and twiddled the knobs to get the BBC programme in our honour. Next moment we were at Old Trafford, listening to a commentary on the fifth of the Victory Tests between England and Australia and, dammit, a fellow unknown to me called Cristofani was about to get a hundred. Now we really believed that life at home was returning to normal. But what about the commentator? It was a certain Rex Alston, a master at Bedford when I left England, for whose MCC side I had sneaked off to play a war-time game against the boys.

Excitements now followed apace, beginning with a mercifully short spell as commander of a camp at Petburi on the Kra Isthmus, several thousand strong, containing all ranks, British, Australians, Dutch, East Indians, and a particularly difficult bunch of Americans, this with no sanctions whatever for the enforcement of discipline.

I had endured some days of this when, as I was reading a news bulletin to the assembled camp of two or three thousand, an American Air Force officer burst in, followed by a Chinaman with a tommy-gun whom he introduced as his bodyguard. He asked leave to make an announcement, then clasping his hands above his head and shaking them like a successful boxer acknowledging a cheering crowd he told us that the American Air Force was flying in to the nearby airstrip right away to fetch us out of this goddamned place, yes, sir.

Eric Samuel: 'When we were liberated in Thailand we were taken by lorry down to Bangkok, and after we were stationed there for a bit we went to the airport, and were waiting for planes to fly us up to Rangoon, where we were going to have our medicals. Well, the planes come in, and they line us all up, and they were all old Dakotas – no seats, just benches each side and everything – and there was a little old RAF bloke, no stripes or anything, who was seeing us POWs being loaded onto the planes. And all the planes were queuing up to take us out, and he was counting us off. And he turned round, and there was Jim standing there, and he said, testily, "Come on, come on, get onto the plane," and Jim said, "I'm an officer." And the little RAF bloke said, "You're a bloody POW – get on the plane!"'

The atomic bombs at Hiroshima and Nagasaki had saved all their lives. In the camps, trenches had been dug by the men, who were convinced they were destined to be their own graves.

Homeward bound – Rangoon, the SS *Corfu*, Southampton and Waterloo Station. On the platform, Jim's father walked straight past him. His mother could not restrain her tears. They could hardly recognise him. At 10½ stone he had lost a third of his body weight. But, as he said, he had lost a lot physically; but gained much in other ways, which could not be easily defined.

And there we prepare to move away from a harrowing few years. One reads and listens to their accounts with bleeding eyes. The divergent views, particularly of Jim, are not easy to equate. When life is stripped of its civilising varnish, responses are usually in black or white and are rarely shaded. And for those who look back sixty years on, the wounds are still raw. When Emperor Akihito came to Britain in 1998 to be dubbed by the Queen as an Extra Knight of the Garter, many found it impossible to exonerate his countrymen of their crimes, and turned their backs as the procession made its way down The Mall. At the time and in an article for the *Daily Telegraph*, Jim supported the language of reconciliation. 'We were as much a mystery to them as they to us. We cannot forget, but can we forgive?' A flood of letters arrived within days which either agreed with the moderation of his words or were vehemently opposed to any such pacification.

It is not for us to be judgemental – we who were not there. They all had to get through the only way they knew how or could manage. The barbarism of their captors made it one of the lowest points of twentieth-century inhumanity. The horror of the ordeals suffered by the unprepared prisoners, together with the inadequate rations and virtually non-existent medical provisions are beyond normal comprehension. Conversely the courage and fortitude of those who endured such hardship defeats any conventional expression of admiration. We can only stand back . . . and try to draw breath . . .

Eric Samuel: 'People survived in their own way. I've seen men who've said, "Well, that's it. I've had enough." And they won't eat and they won't drink and they just die. They just decided it wasn't worth it. It was survival of the fittest.'

Derek Gilbert: 'I always knew I was going to come back – I knew I was going to survive. I was determined to . . .'

Jack Wragg: 'You just lived for the day. There was a great camaraderie. We suffered, but it taught us a lot. It taught toleration and to help other people.'

Jim: 'It might seem a strange thing to say, but I would not have missed the experience for anything.'

'Weary' Dunlop: 'Surely some increased understanding should emerge from a tragic conflict in which when all is said and done, Japanese losses vastly exceeded our own. If not, I reflect with Macbeth as to what is life:

> *It is a tale*
> *Told by an idiot, full of sound and fury*
> *Signifying nothing.*

There was much to admire in Japanese courage and deadly earnestness of purpose. Their contempt for those who surrendered to an enemy steeled me to a resolve to at least never show them fear in facing death and, still more testing, not to flinch as it came.

We can find much to admire in modern Japan in the way of industry, integrity, ability and patriotic fervour, which has rebuilt a shattered country and transformed a wrecked economy. This has lessons for the 'Lucky Country', where old and proven virtues appear to be declining whilst we treat the perilous path down which other civilisations have gone whose fault was 'giving too little and asking too much'.

In Japan there is much of sensitivity and creativity, but I have sensed that the single-minded loyalty gives the system some of the defects of an insect society, with a pattern of blind, unswerving acceptance of leadership whether towards good or evil.

This, too, marches with the Germanic brooding madness of the *Götterdämmerung*, 'The Twilight of the Gods', with desperate overtones of self-immolation. It is difficult for those with such intensity of purpose to temper their actions or to direct humour to them.'

Art historian David Piper was also a prisoner. His coming to terms with the experience led him to write a piece twenty years after his release that somehow contains everything that needs to be said:

For a decade after the war I was haunted by the need to formulate, precipitate the essential character and significance of our prison existence, and frustrated by the apparent impossibility of translating it into a form comprehensible to anyone who had not shared it. Only in 1955 was I released from this need, when I saw Beckett's *Waiting for Godot*. That play for me was a near-perfect statement of the prisoner's condition of suspension in stagnant time, and I recognised it with profound gratitude. It deals of course in rather general terms, and does not touch upon some specific facets of my own experience, especially hunger. Acute hunger, stretched over the years, is beyond the normal scope of Europeans and Americans. In practice, it becomes quite quickly paramount; it strips the body to a bleak anatomy, and dissolves mind and spirit within one ravenous physical appetite. Below a certain subsistence level, other considerations vanish – for three and a half years, for example, the needs of sex were nil. On the other hand, the urgency of hunger was the essential governor of survival, its insistent concentration surely the reason why so few prisoners went mad. Only when it faded could despair overwhelm fatally; known in all Far Eastern prison camps was that stage in a prisoner's illness when hunger failed; then the man would turn his face to the wall, and simply surrender life and die – not necessarily for pathological reasons, but because he had no longer any incentive to live. But twenty years later, I can no longer feel, even remember, this state of being hungry, of living as hunger.

I still have my rice bowl, three and a half inches across, two and a half inches high; at bad times this, filled with boiled rice three times a day, was our total food ration. I use it as an ashtray.

We had then for years waited for Godot. Now many of us were dazed, distracted by inexpressible elations, but also by new fears. We had entered into our waiting through catastrophe and defeat, we had become attuned to perpetual catastrophe and yet now we would be free. No one knew how Godot would reveal himself, what the face of freedom would prove – whether it would even be bearable. For we had become conditioned by captivity, and sickly secure in it. One might die, one might be beaten up by one's captors or bombed by one's allies, but there was nothing whatsoever one could do about it, there were no decisions to take. Now decisions would be thrust upon us . . .

Chapter 6

The Church's one foundation

It has been a surprise to many that religion played such a large part in Jim's life. Those who were surprised were conscious, perhaps, of the views of the ascetic nineteenth-century cleric, Cardinal Manning, who had only converted to Catholicism when in his forties. Manning disliked the ideal of muscular Christianity and of a heaven where cherubs played curates at cricket indefinitely. Once when questioned about his opinion of athletic priests, Manning replied with a question of his own: 'How would you like to appear in the next world with a cricket bat in one hand and a chalice in the other?' Well, Jim, for one, would have done.

Whether or not Jim would or could have become a priest or held some other position in the ecclesiastical hierarchy is a moot point. Certainly a few have likened his august presence and the resonant sounding-board of that beautifully produced voice which carried the consonants and vowels to the furthest corner of any room in irreverent terms. 'There but for the Grace of God goes God,' was not a rare observation.

As we know, Jim had always gone to church. And, according to his sister Tina, he had always preferred Anglican High Church to any other denomination or sect. In *Sort of a Cricket Person* he professes to having been 'an instinctive, but ignorant Christian – duly baptised and confirmed but in the 'thirties an indifferent church-goer'. He goes on to say that he was able partially to educate himself thanks to some appropriate books and in discussions round the jungle fires. 'My acceptance of Catholicism during the years of captivity embraced also the position of the church of England as an essential part of the one holy Catholic and Apostolic Church, as the creed proclaims.' The Nicene Creed formulated by the Council of Nicaea under the watchful eye of the Emperor Constantine was produced in AD 325. Why look back to the fourth century for an understanding of the position of the church today?, was the thrust of more than one heated argument as the embers sparked then died.

Having returned from the extreme rigours of captivity in the Far East, Jim tried to settle down to something approaching normality in London. But it was not easy. The old routines could not be re-established in quite the same way. The gay 1930s were no more. The world had changed, and so had the people in it. Gradually, though, Jim recovered from his physical debility while living with his parents in their home in Beckenham. He also renewed work contacts and tried to regenerate his broadcasting and writing careers. But the mental bruises were not so readily healed. Recuperation was in order.

An introduction from fellow POW Lawrence Turner (later to be MP for Oxford) to the Principal of Pusey House, Canon Frederic Hood, was a kind of salvation. Hood offered Swanton two rooms in which to stay: 'There, with the staff of few priests and a changing resident population of undergraduates, some about to be ordained, others not, I was due to be based for six happy years, abroad often, elsewhere in England, often doing my job, but with Pusey as my only home, in the university but not of it, enjoying much of the life of Oxford at an amusing and stimulating period.'

Pusey House was named after one of the leading figures of the Oxford Movement, Edward Bouverie Pusey, who, before his death in 1882, had been for fifty years Regius Professor of Hebrew at the University and a Canon of Christ Church. Although a shy, sombre, unprepossessing, scholarly figure who was reputed rarely, if ever, to have smiled, Pusey spoke out courageously against the persecution of Catholic priests under the penal anti-ritualist legislation in the 1860s and 1870s.

'The Oxford Movement was an attempt to recover what committed Anglo-Catholics believed to be the fundamental nature of the Church of England – that is a Catholic Church as part of the universal Church. In other words, they were seeking to restore the Catholic belief and doctrine of the Church before the Reformation.' The words of Father William Davage, Priest Librarian and Custodian of the Library at Pusey House since 1994.

'The House was founded to be the centre of Catholic worship, teaching and practice, and as a place of scholarship and learning in the University of Oxford,' Davage went on. 'The theological Library alone contains around 80,000 volumes and specialises in Church History, Patristics and Liturgy and as a repository for theses for Lambeth degrees and diplomas. And although never a monastic order it was certainly a religious house in which the community lived very much a collegial life.

'Now when "Freddy" Hood was here, he had a tremendous range of friends; in a way his ministry was realised through his hospitality. During Swanton's time, there'd be a butler, a house boy, cleaners, staff in the kitchen and all the meals would be prepared and taken communally in the dining room. You could also have guests and there would be a guest night once a week during term.

'Hood had a tremendous irenic approach to things with lots of intellectual activity, so, in a sense, Swanton would be getting an education simply by being here.'

Given Jim's lifelong fascination with Oxbridge and in particular his allegiance to Oxford, he would have felt he was getting the next best thing actually to being an undergraduate.

'It's certainly true that here he mixed among academics,' continued Father Davage. 'For much of the time when Swanton was living-in, Tom Parker was Priest Librarian and he was a great historian of the Reformation. Eric Mascall, not a member of the Chapter but very much in evidence in the House, was a leading philosopher and theologian and a renowned expert on Thomas Aquinas. Eric Kemp, who went on to become Bishop of Chichester, was an eminent Canon lawyer and was actually writing his doctorate while he was here. So certainly he would be very much part of an intellectual elite as well as a social elite and an Anglo-Catholic elite. Visiting scholars would come in either as guests at dinner or to give talks and papers.'

Canon Frederic Hood's diaries contain numerous entries mentioning Jim at dinner and/or coming to his (Freddy's) room after the meal. The entries are bald and unforthcoming, and were obviously intended purely as an aide-memoire for a later time. A few extracts give the flavour:

18 January 1946 (Friday)
Major Swanton arr. [ived] today as a lodger.

19 January 1946
Coffee party in my room after dinner. Eric Kemp, Kenneth Jones, Swanton, Michael Lane. John Hester came later.

23 January 1946
Swanton came to my room after dinner.

31 January 1946
Swanton had David Macindoe (Captain Varsity Cricket) to dinner.

20 February 1946
C.B. Fry came to lunch with Swanton. Coffee party in my room. Sebastian Comper and Frank Knight called and later John Betjeman.

11 May 1951
Jim Swanton returned after being away for some time: he came to my room for an hour after dinner.

24 May 1951
Guest Night: Jim Swanton's guest Nick Stacey.

15 August 1951
Arranged [for someone] to occupy Jim Swanton's rooms for a month.

27 October 1951
[Speaker unable to come] so Jim Swanton arranged for the film of the MCC's Australian tour – Elusive Victory – to be shown in the Darwell Stone Room. Jim made some remarks at the beginning and answered questions at the end. 63 there. Devotions [at] 10 [p.m.]

9 January 1952
Bath Club (where we met Jim Swanton).

The Bath Club, sadly no more, was to be found next to Claridge's in Brook Street in London's Mayfair. It had a certain cachet alongside the more famous White's, Boodle's and Brooks's, and as a social club attracted what might be termed a fairly exclusive upper crust membership. As a member himself, Jim no doubt would have felt he was mixing in the right circles.

The diary entry mentioning John Betjeman is a reminder that both the poet and MP Tom Driberg were to be churchwardens during Hood's time as Priest-in-Charge of the Guild Church of St Mary Aldermary in the City of London. Betjeman's reminiscence of Pusey House in 'Summoned by Bells' underlines the quandary posed by its theological stance between Canterbury and Rome.

Silk dressing-gowned, to Sunday-morning bells,
Long after breakfast had been cleared in Hall,
I wandered to my lavender-scented bath;
Then, with a loosely knotted shantung tie
And hair well soaked in Delhez' Genêt d'Or,
Strolled to the Eastgate. Oxford marmalade
And a thin volume by Lowes Dickinson
But half-engaged my thoughts till Sunday calm
Led me by crumbling walls and echoing lanes,
Past college chapels with their organ-groan
And churches stacked with bicycles outside,
To worship at High Mass in Pusey House.
Those were the days when that divine baroque
Transformed our English altars and our ways.
Fiddle-back chasuble in mid-Lent pink
Scandalized Rome and Protestants alike:
'Why do you try to ape the Holy See?'
'Why do you sojourn in a halfway house?'
And if these doubts had ever troubled me
(Praise God, they don't) I would have made the move.
What seemed to me a greater question then
Tugged and still tugs: Is Christ the Son of God?
Despite my frequent lapses into lust,
Despite hypocrisy, revenge and hate,
I learned at Pusey House the Catholic faith.
Friends of those days, now patient parish priests,
By worldly standards you have not 'got on'
Who knelt with me as Oxford sunlight streamed
On some colonial bishop's 'broidered cope.
Some know for all their lives that Christ is God,
Some start upon that arduous love affair
In clouds of doubt and argument; and some
(My closest friends) seem not to want His love –
And why this is I wish to God I knew.
As at the Dragon School, so still for me
The steps to truth were made by sculptured stone.
Stained glass and vestments, holy-water stoups,
Incense and crossings of myself – the things
That hearty middle-stumpers most despise
As 'all the inessentials of the Faith'.

When at Pusey it is thought that Jim occupied the Sacristan's room together with the adjoining guest room on the second floor. Although with differing configurations each room is compact and rudimentary, and with far less space than would be found in the Colleges of the University itself. Every morning, to reach the bathroom, he would have had to walk the length of one wing and half the length of the next which is situated at a right angle, in what were originally three eighteenth-century houses that had been incorporated into the entire building at the end of the First World War. Those who were there at the time of Jim's sojourn record an abundance of cold water with which to wash!

Almost certainly Jim regarded Pusey House as a sanctuary. Nobody came through the hellish existence of a POW in the Far East unscathed. The unremitting brutality and suffering affected everyone – even those who had tried to keep an arm's length distance – in some way. Minds were fractured as well as bodies. Jim's public front hid a private self; one which he would have had difficulty in revealing to even his nearest and dearest family and friends. The cloak of self-containment buttoned by the cultured gruffness of a man's world was nurtured early no doubt, as was the case with so many, by the necessity of some form of adopted protection in the rough and tumble of a boarder at a public school. The softer emotions were not for open display; such behaviour he would have thought indulgent and unnecessary. Therefore, an innate warmth and kindness would often remain trapped underneath the more dominant forces of his own personality; unseen by most who judged from only a cursory glance. But the inhabitants of Pusey were the good Samaritans who gave him more than a cursory glance, and so the House and, in particular, 'Freddy' Hood, provided a process of therapeutic healing – not a concept that would have been expressed in that way then. In those late night chats after dinner we can but speculate what demons were quietened or even exorcised.

Pusey House also provided protection within the walls of his tiny rooms. Secluded and safe, the nightly hauntings that recreated the worst moments of the recent past could be dispatched in the knowledge that he did not have to be seen to be making a point or striking a pose. Here he could be more anonymous than at any time in his life – if he sought to be so. During the early days of his stay and with his future in the outside world uncertain, Jim probably came closest to pursuing a vocation within the Church.

For a time Canon John Hester lived in the next room to Jim at

Pusey and always thought that he would be ordained. 'We had some very pleasant conversations and I assumed that his future lay in the Church. I liked Jim very much, he was a delightful person under the grand manner. I remember he drove a rather splendid Bentley and several times we would go to the theatre together – plays, musicals – usually at the New Theatre in Oxford. Later on, he would invite me to the commentary box at Lord's.'

The Right Reverend Dr Eric Kemp was Priest Librarian at Pusey House from 1941 to 1946 and a Governor from 1955 until 2002. 'Although I did not have much to do with Jim Swanton when he was there, I found him to be a very pleasant, friendly person and enjoyable to be with. He was not at all arrogant in any way and he entered very much into the life of the House. There would be three Communion Services in the morning – all optional – at 7.15; 8.00 and 9.00. Breakfast afterwards, which was a silent meal, and then lunch and dinner where the community met and talked.'

'High Mass would be on Sundays or greater Holy Days,' carried on Father Davage. 'Jim would have seen a three-person High Mass. The priests of the time explored a range of possibilities: Tom Parker would have said his Mass in Latin from the Roman Missal; "Freddy" Hood in English from the English Missal and Eric Kemp would have used the Book of Common Prayer. Then, of course, there would be the ceremonial and ritual which is a beautiful thing aesthetically to behold.'

Father Davage then ventured into a description of the building. 'Pusey House is interesting architecturally. Outside it looks a rather dull and forbidding seminary. Having pushed that heavy and rather daunting outer door open, you come into an extremely unfriendly gaunt foyer, which tells you very little of what's going. But once you've come through the archway into the quadrangle you see the House for what it is – a most wonderful building. And inside, both the Chapel and Library have been blessed with the most beautiful architecture. Designed by Temple Moore, a Northern architect, and built very much in the English Gothic tradition with a spareness of detail on the Benedictine model, the beauty comes from the spatial relationships. It is rather a small chapel with a sunken expanse before you come to a series of steps up to the altar. Beyond that is the Blessed Sacrament Chapel with a wonderful stone screen and then further on the space narrows to give a sense of distance and there is an exuberant golden altar in bold *baldacchino* beneath the east window. It's simply magnificent and was designed in the 1930s by Ninian Comper, an

English baroque architect. You go in there and think, here is the very gate of Heaven, it is so beautiful. So you see there is a combination of an austere Benedictine feel to things, the colour and drama comes from the music, vestments and ceremonial, and then the other chapel and altar in the *baldacchino* canopy which takes you out of yourself. The Library is built in the Oxford mould on the first floor to protect the books because of the flood plain. In all, the House is a hidden treasure disguised by the rather prosaic external aspect.'

With such a vivid description it is hardly any wonder that Jim was enamoured of the place: 'Personally I find worship made easier in a setting of beauty and dignity. If one believes that God is present on the altar in the Blessed Sacrament, surely only the best is acceptable in reverence of ritual, in music, and in the externals of service? Yet these things are matters of individual taste and preference. Many are happy only with the simplest expression of worship. What has always seemed particularly odious to me is a denial to other people of the liberty to worship in the way that suits them best.'

Few would take issue with that. Jim left Pusey House in 1952, more or less at the same time as 'Freddy' Hood moved to London to begin exercising pastoral care over those priests who were under discipline. Hood shared Swanton's penchant for the company of celebrities and high achievers both lay and ecclesiastical, or perhaps it would be more correct to say that the Principal had been his guest's mentor in that respect. He had come from a wealthy family in South Wales who had made a fortune in steel, and was generous in digging into his own pocket to support the finances of Pusey House. Hood enjoyed sporting a Daimler car which was perhaps his only indulgence not shared with others. As David Williams, author and businessman, wrote of him: 'he was a good friend and priest in every sense, approachable, human, an "aristo" by birth and upbringing, but a snob only where it came to manners and tested values.' The latter aspect again could be said to have been shared by Jim, who many times would have heard that mannered, melodious, deeply rolled, guttural pronunciation of the letter 'r' as Hood bade farewell: 'Say your purr-er-airs, won't you?'

The principal reason for Jim leaving Oxford and buying a house near to Lord's at 17 Loudoun Road, St John's Wood, was the declining health of his mother. In the past few years she had suffered more than one stroke and was reduced to moving around in a wheelchair, so Jim decided to take both parents under his wing and into his new home. The house, incidentally, was next door to that of the renowned concert pianist Solomon, who was most concerned that his practice did not disturb his new neighbours. A married couple was employed to keep the Swanton household ticking over – Jim was, of course, frequently away on the cricket circuit – and the plan was eventually to install Mrs Swanton in the St John's and St Elizabeth Hospital nearby. Sadly, before that could take place, at the beginning of January 1953, she had a final stroke and died.

Jim always had been extremely fond of his mother, but as usual hid his deeper emotions from the outside world. 'Jim's mother was a pretty woman,' remembers John Kitchen, who for a short time was a kind of amanuensis for her son on the cricket circuit. 'She would call Jim "Jumbo" and she would make a great fuss of her cat whom she had named "Sally Whiskers". When she used these names in front of visitors he would get highly embarrassed and chomp and tut-tut in that manner of his – "Really Mummy, really". She liked to tease him.'

By now Jim was attending, as often as his commitments allowed, another great tabernacle of the Catholic tradition within the *Ecclesia Anglicana*. Variously described as 'an exotic and mysterious cavern' and 'a kind of parish church for the world', All Saints, Margaret Street, is tucked away in one of the less frequented thoroughfares close to Oxford Circus in London. Sir Roy Strong, author and historian, and former Director of the Victoria and Albert Museum, describes the overwhelming impression that seized his mind from the moment that he swung open the door and was engulfed by the gloom:

> I was treading on holy ground. Not an easy feat within a few yards of Oxford Street. The retina of the eye adjusted to unfold a world vibrant with glorious imagery: friezes of saints in ceramic, an abundance of mosaic in alabaster and marble, patterns in brick and tile covering every surface, painted images and guttering candles and, above all, the haunting cavernous chancel and sanctuary, with its flights of steps, huge altar, banks of baroque candlesticks and the silver Sacrament House hovering aloft and lit from within, shining like a solitary star in the night sky before the vast gilded reredos. The odd stray beams of light that somehow struggled in through the stained glass almost seemed an intrusion.

All Saints likes to think of itself as 'authentically eccentric'. Unlike many other pulpits of Anglo-Catholicism, the William Butterfield masterpiece has never been drawn Romewards for its inspiration. A visiting priest who once requested the use of a Roman Missal was rebuked by Cyril Tomkinson, the vicar at the time: 'The rule here is music by Mozart, choreography by Fortescue, decor by Comper . . . but libretto by Cranmer.'

Jim had periodically been to services at All Saints since his youth, often in the company of his sister Tina, and was to continue to do so throughout his life, latterly being joined by his nephew, the respected singer, Martin Nelson. He was to marry Ann de Montmorency at All Saints and he always thought of the church with great affection.

Chronological leaps are, of course, unavoidable in sketching Jim's Christian life. When, after their marriage, the Swantons were spending time in Barbados for their annual holiday, St James's or St Mary's would be their places of worship. The island has a strong Anglican tradition and for a long time the priest training college, Codrington, was run by the Mirfield Fathers from Yorkshire. Both churches are packed to the rafters for every Eucharist and the hymns and psalms are always sung with great gusto. When attending St Mary's, which is in the capital Bridgetown, the Swantons would be driven the seven miles each way by a retired policeman who lived quite close to where they stayed and who was a churchwarden. Ann Swanton was to write: 'We would probably be the only white people [there] and the "peace" is given to us with such enthusiasm, not only from our neighbours in the pew, but from many outstretched hands from the pews two or three rows behind ours. It is their way of welcoming us.' Jim would occasionally be asked to read the lesson.

He would, of course, do the same at St Clement's, the Parish Church of Sandwich, where he and Ann had their home in England. Leading the Intercessions at the Eucharist or reading the Epistle, the Swanton voice could not be quelled. The local Rector, the Reverend Mark Roberts, recalls how only forty-eight hours after their arrival, he and his wife were invited to dine with the Swantons. 'The after-dinner conversation in his study was far more gruelling than the original interview for my new job! Somehow, I must have passed muster!

'He was a long-serving and distinguished churchwarden and after his retirement from that office he still nearly always managed to find a reason to invade the clergy vestry on every occasion right until the end . . . I don't think he always had his own way, although I came to regard selection to read or pray at the morning Eucharist on a Sunday – the rotas for which he organised – as akin to selection for the England Test side! Jim loved his parish church and cared deeply for it. He worked tirelessly and supported so generously its Restoration Appeal. And he was also instrumental in what we call our "Churchwatch Scheme", which provides a large team of people to meet and greet visitors, and enables the church to be open for the majority of the year.'

During 1987 and 1988 and for the Sandwich Parish Magazine, Jim felt led to produce a series of seven articles which he called a layman's sketch of 'The Anglican Church, from its origins to the present'. The articles were published as a booklet to coincide with the 1988 Lambeth Conference at Canterbury where the vast company of 500 bishops from the twenty-seven Provinces of the Anglican Communion met together. The then Archbishop of Canterbury, Dr Robert Runcie, wrote the foreword. He finished by saying, 'In these pithy, readable, informative and balanced chapters, Jim Swanton has put us all in his debt. I am encouraged that a distinguished layman from my own diocese and a very loyal friend should have written this during the Lambeth Conference year and hope that this book will have a deservedly wide circulation.'

In writing the foreword, Runcie was, in a sense, repaying a debt, although neither he nor Jim would have thought of it in that way. Three years earlier in the letters column of the *Daily Telegraph* under the by-line 'The frailties of an archbishop' a Miss Joan Whatmough had stated her view:

Sir – According to your report of the General Synod, Dr Runcie stated in his presidential address that the Press mistakenly regard his position as being similar, within the Church of England, to that of the Pope.

I suggest that the Press is not as misguided as Dr Runcie would wish. Although the Queen is Head of the Anglican Church, the Archbishop is the spiritual leader whose job it is to lead.

Dr Runcie states that he is the chief bishop and then slips out of his responsibilities by saying that he regards himself as one of the bishops and that he has a fraternal approach to the others.

Thus he is able to dispense with his very obvious duties. One very major duty of an archbishop at the present time would surely be to take a firm stand against the blasphemous attitude towards the basic Christian Gospel being stridently proclaimed from positions of authority within the Church.

Since Dr Runcie is only one of the bishops the way would seem to be open for some of the other bishops to rise up and make a stand for the truth of the Gospel. Such action could not make matters worse since the Church is rapidly disintegrating. It would bring hope to those who look to the Church for leadership and action in this and many other grave problems of our present society.

E.W.S. wasted no time before wielding the cudgel on behalf of his friend:

Sir – Miss Joan Whatmough must have been flattered to see her letter with its offensive belittling of the Archbishop of Canterbury and her allegations of a 'rapidly disintegrating Church' leading your correspondence columns.

It is inevitable, no doubt, that the Establishment as represented by the government of the day, the Church of England or, for that matter, the MCC should be used by the disaffected as a cheap Aunt Sally. And loyal Anglicans in particular have been long inured to insult.

Most of it comes, though I do not suggest so, in this case, either from professed agnostics or others with little or no knowledge of the Church, its formularies of its worship.

In the five years since his enthronement, the Archbishop as *primus inter pares* within the wide-world Anglican communion has travelled widely and assiduously to listen, to learn, to inform and to preach.

As to external relationships, those with the Roman Catholics – as witness the Papal visit and the conclusions of the Anglican-Roman Catholic International Commission – and with the orthodox, thanks to the archiepiscopal triumvirate of Ramsey, Coggan and Runcie, have never been more cordial or promising.

At home, faced with problems, some inevitable, some surprising, he has stood surely as four-square defender of the Church of England, Catholic and Reformed. Within our own diocese, I sense that all who have met him have found a man of our times, compassionate, approachable, and spiritual above all.

Of course, the Church of England has difficulties and divisions to face, as, according to the Acts, did the Apostles themselves. But we may hope that they are debated in the spirit of that 'unity in fellowship' of which the Queen spoke at the opening of the General Synod.

It was the Archbishop's turn now to write a letter, though this time a public platform was not required:

My dear Jim,
Thank you so much for standing up for me in the *Daily Telegraph*. Characteristic of you and I don't deserve it.

Now we are all being labelled Marxists, so that a report which is uncongenial to some will now be read by many of those who would approve of its reasoned tone and well argued case . . .

Another friend of Jim's whom he met while he was wearing cricketing whites rather than clerical cloth was the Right Reverend Lord Sheppard of Liverpool. In 1950, David Sheppard had not yet been ordained. 'I remember him bowling at me in the nets at Fenners – he kept a length. He'd spotted some of us who were some good and he wanted to get to know us. People spoke of him as being a bit lordly and as the Baron or the Emperor, in those words. I know he started to cross-examine me about my faith, because shortly before I'd had an evangelical conversion while at the Christian Union in Cambridge. He wasn't at all sure of whether he approved of this, because he was, as you know, an Anglo-Catholic. And he had doubts about my experience and my faith, and I suppose he was wanting to test whether it was genuine. I don't think he put me down, but anyway he became more tolerant about a lot of things as he got older and also about that. I remember that when I got to Australia Jack Fingleton, who was a Roman Catholic, asked me about my faith and said, "Does Cardinal Swanton approve of this?"' [laughs].

David Sheppard went on to talk about there being a Party Anglo-Catholic as there is a Party Evangelical and to say that Jim would have been firmly in the former camp. 'There is part of that which would have made him very critical of the Church of England, but Robert Runcie won his heart. Jim admired Runcie and gave him his full support [laughs]. After all, there is nothing like being in his diocese and knowing the Archbishop of Canterbury.

'I think there was a very ambitious bit of Jim that wanted to be a big figure – and that wanted to be the best authority on the game. There was an arrogant streak, but it mellowed a lot.'

Dom Felix Stephens, OSB, once of Ampleforth, now of St Mary's Priory, Warrington, first met Swanton when scoring '80 something' for the Authentics in a game against Jim's own side, the Arabs at Oxford in 1965. 'I recollect Jim fielding at mid-off and John Woodcock at mid-on and my partner and I managed to get a lot of singles when pushing the ball in their direction. Actually, I think Jim quite approved.

'When he came up to Headingley I got him to come to Ampleforth two or three times because I'd spotted straight away that this chap was interested in the spiritual thing. Most of our conversations were about either cricket or spirituality.

'I remember once when he came to the Abbey – in 1973, I think it was – he left the First XI cricket match early to have a bath and change before Vespers [Evensong] and Benediction, which was followed by the simple formula of a silent monastery supper.

Afterwards Jim was taken to what we euphemistically call a "horse-box", which cannot have been much bigger or less basic than the space he had as a POW of the Japanese. Several of us still recall his simple devotion at Benediction of the Blessed Sacrament. While we rather routinely carried out the well-oiled ceremony with a bland acceptance of its truth and our adoration, Jim was fervent in his praying with his well-thumbed little prayer book. You see, he said his prayers, but more than that, he was a man of prayer – and the two are not the same. He ever remembered the Abbey: "It was for me, as I suppose it is for many people, a haven . . . the serenity of it all."'

Father Felix went on to expound on Anglicanism's being very deep in the psyche of the English: 'It goes back to the twelfth and thirteenth centuries in terms of people's piety and in that culture the Swanton religiosity is medieval. But I don't think Jim ever quite analysed his Christian belief. It was something he felt. That was reflected in his Anglican booklet – it was devout, sincere and much appreciated, but lacked analytical depth. But he radiated conviction about the centralities of the Christian Faith. If he ever wavered, it was private. It was no secret that he fretted about woman priests because he could never really hide something about which he felt deeply. He started from the position, it's not of the faith, therefore I can't accept it and I do not approve.'

'They have their own ministry of service, heaven knows,' wrote an exasperated Jim, 'both inside and outside the religious orders. To give countenance to the idea of admitting women to the priesthood for the first time after all but two thousand years, in the knowledge that the idea is anathema both to Roman Catholics and the Orthodox Churches at the very moment when at least a degree of reunion has become substantially nearer than at any time since the Reformation, would seem to be lunacy . . .'

'And yet Jim supported women's membership of MCC,' I remarked to Father Felix, introducing a touch of bathos to our conversation. 'Ah, that was different,' he replied. 'Well, how do you explain the huge contradictions in Jim's character,' I went on, changing tack, 'some of which were most unchristian-like?'

'Let me tell you a story which illustrates that paradox,' Father Felix continued. 'We had a monk at St Benet's Hall in Oxford who was very like Jim. He was absolutely wedded to the Establishment and vain beyond belief.'

'Ah, but Jim could revolt against the Establishment at times,' I interrupted.

'Fair enough, but he never revolted against the culture into which he was born, did he?' was the rejoinder, 'which I think is to his credit.

'Anyway, I remember this monk coming into the Common Room – this is a Jim sort of story, remember – as a young master with his MA gown billowing out having to go to a meeting with the Heads of College at Oxford. He breezed in. "How do I look? How do I look?" Now, that was Swanton all over. Although I'm not talking about him in this instance, I'm transferring the characteristics. And yet we knew that this monk was one of the humblest men in our community with a penchant for vanity and a weakness for the Establishment. Now, how could I say that? He was deeply prayerful and he would drop everything to help other people. It didn't matter from what class they came. He would look after them and he never talked about it – he just did it. And if you think about it, Jim was very similar.

'I remember meeting him at Sandwich one Saturday afternoon after a Rugby International. I was going to preach at St Clement's the next day. Now, all of Sandwich will recall Jim's Jaguar. But not many, however, will have known that in the boot were a dustpan and brush and a duster. We went up to the church. "You take the brush and I'll use the duster," he said. A lot of people would not imagine that Jim Swanton would so demean himself as to take his turn to clean the church. But he did.

'You see, people didn't see this other side. He did lots of things for people that was never publicised. Now, that is humility, Christian humility.

'The other thing, and this is the paradoxical bit: if you think deeply about Christian spirituality, the ability to show your weakness in public and not to be afraid of it, is actually the mark of a humble man – if it is deliberate. Which in the case of this monk and also with Jim, it was. In other words, his weaknesses, which often caused mirth and irritation in equal magnitude, I think, we were privileged to see. And some chose to be disdainful of it and others chose to love him for it.

'He didn't cover up. One, because he couldn't – it was the nature of the beast. And two, because he wasn't afraid of being the person he was. Runcie was right when he said that Jim had no self-doubt. But he also had no self-doubt about his limitations. Those who hide weaknesses are usually far less attractive characters. Jim really stood out because he was humble enough to do so.

'I know the pomposity of the man annoyed a lot of people and you were right earlier when you said Jim could take an opposite view to that held by the establishment. The Establishment is all-powerful.

David Sheppard was hurt by it dreadfully in his stance over South Africa. Sheppard is known for his integrity and self-discipline, and that was the position he took over Apartheid. He suffered for it, possibly because he was a figure in authority, whereas Jim was respected for his stance, possibly because he was only a commentator.'

'I was grateful for Jim's support over South Africa,' Sheppard had remarked. 'The *Daily Telegraph* had a very clear line and Jim was not of the same opinion and stood his ground. I was in the firing line and friendships were lost. Peter May and I had been the closest of friends. Some called for a special meeting and I proposed a vote of censure. Afterwards Mike Brearley and I said we ought to try and mend some fences. But Jim's backing meant a lot. He was a man of conviction and I think the issue of justice had a lot to do with his faith.'

Father Felix finished our conversation by telling of a letter that he had received from Jim towards the end of his life. 'I have it in mind to join the Roman Catholic Church,' wrote Jim.

'We had a serious discussion about that,' said Felix. 'You see, the high Anglican is very much Church of England by law established, where the Roman Catholic is stuck with Rome and Pontiffs and all that. Now, when Jim talked to me I have no doubt that in terms of the doctrine of the faith Jim was a true Roman Catholic in every respect – faith, benediction, the Virgin Mary, the nature of the Church – absolutely. But in culture and tradition and upbringing the Church of England is, as I've said, by law established. "Jim," I pleaded, "I've thought about this and I don't think you should change. I think it would crucify you to leave St Clement's and go down to the barn [the Roman Catholic Church and the Mass] with a different clientele with whom you would not feel comfortable and in a setting which you'd find distasteful and with the sort of liturgy which, in fact, is a disaster compared with what you've been brought up with." Bold words indeed. "So, if it is a question of the faith of the Church which overrides your conscience in every respect, then, of course, you have to move over, but if you are part of this Church of England by law and statute you are part of this culture and its traditions. For goodness sake – don't change! You are a Catholic, so ease your conscience on that, but why having given your life to the Church for fifty, sixty, seventy years should you have a miserable decade incarcerated in the wrong lot?" There was a long pause . . . Eventually, a short laugh. "I think I agree with you," he said.'

It was an example of how doubts can assail the most determined of minds.

When he was a prisoner of the Japanese in Thailand, Jim had made the acquaintance of a young Lieutenant in the Argyll and Sutherland Highlanders called James Noble. About thirty years later Noble got in contact once again. 'I'd remembered that in the camps Jim sometimes got the unkind name of "God" due to his not being a clergyman but conducting services,' said Noble. 'With his voice and big size there was a fraction of the bully about him, but at the same time he had humour. He did have this ability to upset people, perhaps because he always got everything right. But he did have some good ideas and as I had set up "The Company of Speakers" I wanted his advice.'

Noble's idea, which proved highly successful, was to take the very best public speakers in Britain to talk to schoolchildren all over the country; thus relieving harassed headmasters and school teachers who had long since emptied their stock of general knowledge subjects upon which to address their charges. 'Jim helped enormously with contacts for names I could use and also by getting financial support from such as the Getty Foundation,' continued Noble. 'We had 246 speakers in the end and went to about 300 schools and we charged nothing for doing so, not even expenses. There was a great range of speakers from elderly politicians to young nuns, but the proviso was that they all had to be exceptionally good. Jim never spoke himself, but he was always there in the background. "Leadership in POW camps as it affected junior officers" I recall was one of the lectures, and also "Religion and Politics: do they mix?" It was nearly all state schools, but also private and public establishments such as Canford and Radley College.'

And it was to Radley, just outside his beloved Oxford, that Jim ventured forth on a winter night in 1980. The visit had nothing to do with 'The Company of Speakers'. This was an independent mission outlining his beliefs and hopes for a new generation:

May the words of my lips and the meditations of my heart be always acceptable unto Thee, O God, our strength and our Redeemer

I've always seen eye to eye regarding lay sermons with the great Dr Johnson when (amending just one word) he said: 'Sir, a layman's preaching is like a dog walking on its hinder legs. It is not done well, but you are surprised to find it done at all.'

He said in fact a woman's preaching – but that is an emotional side-issue much best left alone.

For your sins, then, you've got a layman this evening – someone who has spent his life writing and broadcasting about cricket. Perhaps, by the way, it should give me a little (badly needed) confidence that so many of you are familiar with the television cameras, and in starring roles too. If the BBC ever wanted a new chairman of *Mastermind* they haven't far to look. ('I have started, so you may answer.')

But to my subject – and in due course to my text.

I wonder if you will cast your minds back about two years and consider what happenings in the world have made, over that time, the biggest impact on your hearts and minds: the agonies of the Boat people; the continuing killing of innocents in Northern Ireland; the brutal aggression of the Russians in Afghanistan; the brave struggle for human rights in Poland. The world as usual is full of conflict and suffering. And, with peace between east and west so precariously in the balance, we have just had, surely, the gruesome charade of the American General Election.

Bad news always makes the headlines, and it is hard not to be depressed by it. Yet in these last two years a figure has arrived on the world stage, a spiritual figure who has grown in stature as his pilgrimages have taken in country after country, drawing to his presence some of the largest, the most devout, the most enthusiastic audiences ever seen.

Pope John Paul went first, after his election, to his native Poland, and the atheistic masters of that much-afflicted country were utterly powerless to prevent the simple message that he put across: a message of love and smiling tenderness, of duty to the Church and to one's neighbour. The Poles' fervent response to their Pope echoed round the world. Suddenly its statesmen seemed pygmies beside him.

He goes to the Americas, to the United States and to Brazil; to Africa, to Kenya, and the Ivory Coast and Zaire; to Turkey and West Germany; close at home, to Ireland. Everywhere the response is the same, so that one marvels at the divine force which is driving this saintly man tirelessly on. One can scarcely comprehend the humility and grace which he communicates to all who see and hear him. And, when the television watchers are included, one realises that these are infinitely the largest audiences ever drawn together by one man.

The new Pope then is the Good News of our time. Said a *Daily Telegraph* leader: 'If we are Roman Catholics we may indeed feel pride and joy that such a shepherd has been put over us: and, if not, we may feel a twinge of envy, or even yearning.'

Even yearning! I suppose that almost all who call themselves Christians – be they Presbyterians or Baptists or of any other Protestant persuasion – will have been greatly moved by this personal mission to a strife-riven world, on which the Pope has embarked and which, by God's grace, he clearly intends to continue.

But in the hearts of very many Anglicans – even most of those who heed its Church's teaching and cling to the Sacraments – is 'yearning' too strong a word? I think not.

Thus I come, belatedly, to my text. The words are those which are recited constantly in this chapel; which are being said and sung today and every day, wherever English is spoken and in many other languages, in many thousands of churches all over the world: I BELIEVE IN ONE HOLY, CATHOLIC AND APOSTOLIC CHURCH.

Oh, yes, runs the argument of the Protestant-minded: but Catholic here means only just one universal body of Christians. For most of the time since the Reformation, it could be broadly said, the Protestant element in Anglicanism has taken precedence over the Catholic. Yet for a century and a half since the start of the Catholic Revival within the Church of England which had its roots almost here – at Oxford – in 1833, we Anglicans have been emphasising more and more strongly our conviction that, when the break with Rome came at the Reformation, the essentials of our Faith were preserved: we inherited our Apostolic Succession; the doctrines enshrined in the Nicene Creed. We believe that, despite differences of emphasis, our Church is essentially One, essentially Holy, and essentially Catholic and Apostolic.

You here at Radley must be specially conscious of our Catholic heritage for it was to the Oxford Movement that you owe your foundation: you were founded only fourteen years after it burst upon a sleepy Church of England to preserve and strengthen its traditions.

I hope that amid all the clamour of school life today, in the intensity of it, you may come to realise, as I believe old and young are coming more to do – especially perhaps the young – that the spiritual and the material must be kept in balance. You Radleians are fortunate in the strength of the Christian tradition here – in contrast, I just possibly might whisper, to some other schools of your standing. If you wish to pursue it, you have the opportunity to turn to apologetics – which means just the rational argument for Christianity – as well as algebra and anthropology.

But before I close – and I am grateful to a young friend of mine who told me, 'It doesn't matter what you say after ten minutes because they won't be listening' – we should be thankful for all the recent evidence of the fact that that which unites Christians is infinitely greater than the things which keep us apart.

No doubt many of you will have seen the recent magnificent

enthronement of the Archbishop of Canterbury, and I hope you may have been inspired, as I was, by it: not least by the presence of leaders from all the churches, Catholic, Orthodox and Protestant, and by the warmth of the Archbishop's greeting to them and the sincerity of their response. It was said that not even before the Reformation had eight Cardinals of the Roman Church been seen together in Canterbury Cathedral.

Such a scene would have been highly unlikely twenty or even ten years ago. Equally improbably would it have been that a cardinal Archbishop of Westminster should come, as Basil Hume did, and preach to us at the famous Anglican church of All Saints, Margaret Street, and tell of his yearning for unity – with such warmth and humility that at the end of his sermon a packed church stood and applauded.

There are many difficulties still in the path towards reunion. The way will be neither quick nor easy, but with Dr Runcie at Canterbury and Archbishop Hume at Westminster the climate must be auspicious surely for the visit of Pope John Paul to England the year after next.

A little story in parenthesis. Archbishop Hume was until recently Abbot of Ampleforth and a great lover of cricket. When I saw him after his sermon at All Saints he said: 'You know, David Sheppard' – he was an England cricketer and is now Anglican Bishop of Liverpool – 'comes and stays with me when he is in London. He stayed last night, and I said: "Now, David, I want to talk to you about two things, the ordination of women and Geoffrey Boycott." But I'm afraid we never got further than Geoffrey Boycott.'

I couldn't resist this true tale because it illustrates how priests and laity need humour and humanity as well as holiness. But let our last picture be of Pope John Paul standing before the world beckoning in that simple, compelling way of his for more recruits – and more fervent ones – to that One, Holy, Catholic and Apostolic Church to which we all belong, and to which I pray you may cling all your lives, despite the indifference, or maybe the danger, surrounding you.

May it guide you into all truth, and in the knowledge and grace of Our Lord Jesus Christ. AMEN.

Chapter 7

Self-appointed Oracle

While still residing at Pusey House, Jim must have felt he was leading a Jekyll and Hyde existence. On the one hand, the cloistered calm and tranquillity of an ecclesiastical community and on the other, the endless endeavour and fray of a competitive world with the pressing need to earn a living.

The juxtaposition was confusing. Which way was he to go? He could not stay at Pusey for ever. A career choice had to be made. Was it to be the pulpit or the press? He had put off making a final decision for as long as possible. His father confessor Freddy Hood had gone to pastures new. He should too. Or, at least, to a pasture he knew.

Jim's mental turmoil, if so it could be described, was not visible in his work environment. That he would not have allowed. Nor was there any time for letting the dilemma impinge upon his mind when dealing with his copy and outside commitments. But when back at Pusey, and that was increasingly less often, he realised that it was becoming obvious that he was using the House as convenient free 'digs'. After all, five or six years was a long time to remain a guest.

Middlesex and England cricketer J.J. Warr, who saw a lot of Jim during this period of his life, has an interesting observation: 'He was very close to going into the Church, you know. Very close. But it wasn't a question of seeing the light, it was rather the light going out. A sort of reverse conversion. I think he suddenly decided his life was much better spent reporting cricket than sermonising to a few people in an obscure church somewhere. He just didn't see it as a vocation. But he was still very religiously inclined.'

Was there also a sense in which Jim felt he had served his penance for actually surviving the war? Had there been a moment during those awful years in the Japanese camps when he had made a prayerful commitment on the lines of, 'God, help me survive this fearful incarceration and I will serve thee faithfully for the rest of my days'? And with the gradual receding of the horror had there also come a lessening of the resolve? If so, it would have been a very human condition. The Church and cricket provided two predominantly male brotherhoods which had great appeal to Jim. But cricket had larger arenas. And Jim's ego needed a big arena.

Before experiencing that contrasting existence at Pusey and in the work places outside, he had, with his usual impulsiveness, tried to get up and running too soon. The knowledge that Rex Alston and others had been occupying the commentary box during the 'Victory Tests' of 1945 had made him very anxious to re-establish his presence within and without the portals of Broadcasting House. He therefore had decided to register the fact that he was now back in circulation with the BBC's Head of Outside Broadcasts, 'Lobby', which, as observant readers of previous chapters will know, was a necessary and convenient abbreviation of Seymour J. de Lotbinière. 'Lobby', at six foot seven inches every bit as lanky as his name was long, was normally nothing if not decisive. But at the meeting, which took place a few weeks after Jim's return from captivity in the Far East, he was noticeably non-committal. He did, however, promise an early chance behind the microphone the following season.

During Jim's time as a POW, his father William had written to Jim's old colleague Michael Standing, who was then the BBC's Director of Outside Broadcasting:

Prisoners of War Post
Service des Prisoniers de Guerre

Capt. E.W. Swanton, R.A.
Bedfordshire Yeomanry
(attached to Royal Artillery)
BRITISH PRISONER OF WAR
MALAY CAMPS   YOUR OWN ADDRESS HERE
c/o Japanese Red CrossGreen Heys
TOKYO   70 Birchwood Avenue
                                     Sidcup
                                     Kent
                                          March 25th, 1942

Dear Mr Standing,

I thought you might like to cheer Jim up with a letter, knowing how much he would appreciate hearing from some of his friends. Perhaps you would be kind enough to pass this on to any mutual friends you are in touch with.

Above is the correct way to head a letter to him. Address the envelope as in the left hand corner; no stamp is necessary. THE WHOLE LETTER must be typed or written in block letters, and on one side of sheet only.

A reply was soon forthcoming:

Dear Mr Swanton,

Thank you for letting me know where I should address a letter to Jim. I will certainly write him and follow your instructions about the method of address and posting.

I hope that you have reasonably good news of him.

After the fall of Singapore, there was a report that Captain E.W. Swanton was missing and it had been some time before his whereabouts was established. It is doubtful that letters had got through to any of the camps in which he was a POW. Ken Holland, one of Jim's original troop, says that 'When letters arrived they came in batches and that happened only twice during all the time we were out there. The *real* problem was in sending letters the other way. We were allowed only twenty-five-word cards, which were heavily censored. Fortunately, before going out there, I had calibrated a map of the world into figures rather like ordnance survey maps and similar to my regimental army number. So by putting digits in a certain order, I was able to let my parents know more or less where I was.' Indeed, an ingenious device.

To return to Jim's present. 'Lobby' was as good as his word and the following May (1946) Gloucestershire versus Lancashire at Gloucester and a Wally Hammond century provided plenty of action for a good appraisal and very soon Jim was contracted for the Test Matches. Later on, 'Lobby' confided in Jim that he had been taken aback by the latter's debilitated appearance and that his hesitancy was the result of wondering whether Swanton's faculties would be sharp enough for broadcasting.

Whatever 'Lobby's' doubts, when Jim was once again behind the microphone, he had been totally supportive:

Thank you very much for your message of encouragement yesterday: the later commentaries went more confidently as a result of it. I felt there were some incoherent moments due perhaps to rush which I hope to eliminate tomorrow.

Further support came from C.B. Fry on the TMS *Mercury*. Addressed to Mrs Davy, BBC Pacific Talks, it read:

> Dear Davy,
>   Please, if you know 'em, tell your Sports blokes that E.W. Swanton is, beyond dispute, a very good broadcaster on cricket indeed. I can see everything when he describes a match. His technical knowledge is excellent and he has, to my mind, a curiously attractive microphone manner.

Encouraged by such positive feedback, Jim was soon clamouring for more broadcasts. Soon there came a missive from BBC cricket correspondent Rex Alston:

> 'Lobby' has asked me to tell you that your persistence has worn us down and he has allocated the Varsity match to you. It will be heard on the HOME service, not the Light, and will involve probably two commentary periods per day, except for the Saturday afternoon where there may be two or three break-ins. I was going to do this match myself, so mind you do it well.

The inevitable response from Jim was sent from the Majestic Hotel in Folkestone:

> Mystified by directors' reported comment about 'persistence'! I did indeed mention in passing that I had broadcast the match in 1939, that I had not missed a ball in the match since 1926, and will this year have played either with or against all the players. I hope that isn't undue pressure . . .

In the same merry month of May, Jim also had been engaged to man the public address at the Oval for a celebratory one-day match between Old England and Surrey. This was a delayed Centenary match for the County Club and of the Oval itself, which in normal times would have taken place in the previous year. For a few hours, time stood still, as in front of a riveted crowd of 15,000, including

King George VI, the legendary knights of yore once more took to the field a decade or so after nearly all of them had retired: Woolley (Jim's very own hero), Hendren, Sutcliffe, Sandham, Fender, Jardine, Freeman, Tate, Knight, Allom, and with Ted Brooks, the only non-England player, filling-in as wicket-keeper. Their average age was just over fifty and yet they still managed to make 232 for 5 in reply to Surrey's 248 for 6. Jim took some pride in the fact that he had convinced his friend the Surrey captain, Errol Holmes, to make sure the pitch was covered; thus ensuring a benign wicket for the 'golden oldies' to be able to show off their strokes with a degree of confidence.

The day following that special occasion at the Oval, Jim's life changed for ever. Not that he was to realise it at the time. He had been invited to meet the Hon. Seymour Berry at the offices of the *Daily Telegraph*. The *Telegraph* were urgently looking for a replacement for Sir Guy Campbell who had found he was unequal to the demands of covering the cricket circuit. Unknown to Jim at that stage, the papers had also approached his long-term friend the golf correspondent Leonard Crawley, who rather than trying to embrace another sport on which he was eminently qualified to write, had generously suggested E.W.S. as the person for the role. The meeting went well and soon Jim was a 'Special Correspondent' for the Test Trial at Lord's. Obviously he passed his very own trial and was shortly to be hired on a monthly basis for the rest of the season by the Sports Editor, Frank Coles.

Two months later in mid-August 1946 Jim wrote to Coles on Devonshire Club, St James's, SW1, headed notepaper:

Dear Coles,

May I put on paper my feelings on the matter of the contract, which we discussed on Friday evening?

You mentioned a new arrangement, to cover the Australian tour and to be operative until the end of August, 1947. I am very happy to put my full energies at the disposal of the paper in return for the figure we spoke of. The only difficulty concerns the question of my connection with the BBC.

As you know I have worked for them since 1935 [*sic*], and have been one of their Test commentators since the MCC tour in South Africa in 1938/9. I realize that it will be necessary, in order to do the job as I would wish for you, to curtail my BBC activities very drastically. I am however reluctant to agree to cut them out altogether in exchange for a short term contract.

I feel that for me to do a few matches for them next summer would be good publicity, and would give me some safeguard against the possibility of my contract with you not being renewed. I suggest it should be understood that my work for the *Daily Telegraph* came first, that I agreed a programme with you at the beginning of the season, and that the BBC chose from that list of about thirty matches a maximum of, say, six for me to cover in the home programme. If it was preferred, these need not be the Tests, or indeed any of the bigger matches. At the end of next season we might then review the position.

I would not suggest this if I thought it would interfere with my writing at all. On the contrary, by giving a new angle on the game, as well as from the point of view of publicity, I feel it is likely to be beneficial. It has been proved this summer what an enormous listening public there is for cricket. Having heard one's voice and opinions occasionally over the air, would not an enthusiast be more likely to read one in the paper?

As regards Australia, perhaps you will let me know when we can have a conference on the subject of treatment, policy, and the technical side also.

Ten days passed in which further discussion took place before the financial director of the *Telegraph* wrote to Jim c/o the Savoy Hotel, Strand, WC.

Dear Swanton,

This puts in black and white the arrangements we have reached – outlined by you to me in your note of August 27 – i.e. that for the forthcoming MCC tour your engagement provides for:

(1) Salary £100 per month.

(2) Expenses at a rate of £200 per month for the first two months – revision to be made, if necessary, on your report to me after the first Test Match, December 5.

(3) Preliminary equipment and expenses on chipboard to be rendered separately.

(4) Our decision on any future contract to be made known to you by Christmas.

(5) The *Daily Telegraph* to have exclusive rights of all your work in England.

(6) You undertaking not to broadcast home to England, but you are free for broadcasts within Australia.

Within a few months Jim's horizons had widened beyond his most optimistic expectations. He had intended spending the summer writing a weekly piece for *The Field*, compiling a diary for publication, pursuing openings for possible broadcasts and playing club cricket. And now here he was about to embark on the steamer *Stirling Castle* to Australia. On Friday, 30 August 1946, he was allocated three long columns on the sports pages by his new employers:

What Fortune Awaits Our Test Team in Australia?

by
E. W. SWANTON
DAILY TELEGRAPH
Cricket Correspondent
who, as announced on the front
page, sails with the MCC team
tomorrow to report all
its matches in Australia.

The question which exercises the followers of cricket at present is the measure of skill of the team which Hammond leads from home tomorrow. There are some factors which are better set down now than when the battle is joined.

The most important is that this tour, undertaken relatively so soon after the close of six years of war, takes place specifically because the interest of millions of Australians and Englishmen seemed to the authorities to demand it.

There is no need to disguise the fact that many would have liked to see our cricketers tuned up for the business by the full dress series of the Test matches due to be played over here against the South Africans next summer. The gap of six seasons has prevented a whole generation from showing its mettle, and the older players from keeping their skill from going to rust.

The English golfers, one may note, have declared a two-year truce before continuing engagements with their enemies from America. But cricket's spotlight has a brighter and more powerful beam. It must be added that Australia, too, have had their losses and their interruptions. Further (what we often overlook) their source of supply is a small fraction of ours. The population of Australia can still be contained within that of Greater London.

Where the selectors of the present side have been particularly handicapped is in the generally low standard of our cricket this summer.

It is an inevitable thing, but none the less tiresome, that long scores made against many of the counties in 1946 have been valueless from the point of view of appraising the likelihood of a batsman's success against Australian bowling on Australia's wickets. Equally, it is little criterion that a bowler may have taken eight for 45 against Blankshire, or even captured 100 wickets and be sixth in the averages.

On the face of it, as many have written to point out, it must seem strange that few of the bowlers chosen are anywhere near the top of the averages. What the selectors have insisted on is good fielding, and wherever possible batting ability as well. I doubt if any side to visit Australia has had fewer real passengers in the batting line.

As for the fielding, there are several fine natural athletes in the party and few real weaknesses. But they will have a tremendous standard to live up to. A.P.F. Chapman's team did not miss a catch in Australia until the rubber was won. I believe that D.R. Jardine's missed only one. In two series Ames missed only one chance behind the wicket. Here, in his Kentish successor, Evans, I think we are still well provided.

It is generally agreed, I think, that the selectors were a little hasty in announcing 12 names in the first batch. My personal opinion is that there are two specially lucky choices, perhaps three. But no side has ever left these shores approved by one and all. It is enough to say that the team as a whole will carry the confidence of English followers, from the captain down to the youngest member.

Two weeks after an ecstatic welcome for the whole party (including fourteen press) at Fremantle, Jim put his Sports Editor back home in the picture:

October 6th.

Dear Frank,

Herewith a line to give you something of the atmosphere of the tour, since we have been ashore all but a fortnight. From your point of view I fear things have been very tame. It has been just a marking-time (due to the early sailing time), with no cricket and little happening to justify D.T. space. The show begins really on Friday next.

At the moment there is one major snag: accommodation. Jeanes, of the Board of Control, has been able to do little with regard to hotels for the later journalists to join the party, and as I write I am not booked for Adelaide, and have only an offer of a place 30 miles from Melbourne. The Cup is on, and wool sales, and heaven knows what else, and the whole hotel problem here is very difficult indeed. It might be a help, incidentally, to have the names of our correspondents where they exist. Would you be good enough to cable the names of our men at Adelaide and Melbourne? As regards addresses however the hotels I have given you should stand, and I would like letters sent on to them, marked c/o MCC, and I will call for them.

The team has gone down well so far – as a unit it is very friendly, and there is among most a real effort towards sociability. Offsetting this a little, Hammond has not quite caught on with the press. The first ship interview was rather sticky, and ever since he has been rather suspicious and defensive, except in the case of those he knows well. I think he tries to create a good impression, but is very self-conscious and anything but an easy mixer. So far as I am concerned he has been wholly cordial (as a matter of fact I have just come in from a game of golf with Denis Compton, Jack Fingleton, and himself): the only thing I fear is he may be going to ask me to do some sort of press liaison work.

I will not, by the way, be doing much, if any ABC broadcasting. I did a talk from the ship on arrival, with the captain and manager, and an introductory talk on the team, both of which apparently went down favourably here and in the Eastern states. But they are over-loaded with six commentators already signed up for the Tests.

One item may interest you. We have formed an Empire Cricket Writers' Club, to be open to all who write or broadcast about cricket. The idea is to play matches, in the countries where Tests are being played, to entertain prominent people, and help the development of cricket generally. Menzies is being invited to be the first President, and the secretaries are Arthur Mailey and Bruce Harris. I think it may develop into quite a powerful body. I, for my sins, am Chairman. The project really is Mailey's – a great Anglophile. We have already played several matches, mostly against public schools, and applications are coming in fast from the east.

By the way, I sent today a cable about cuttings. I hope it won't be too much bother for anyone, but it really is essential to know what is going on. I have not seen an English paper in Australia yet. I suggest a weekly packet, sent each Thursday or Friday to the appropriate hotel on the list, allowing a full 7 days transit.

Please remember how valuable any suggestions would be regarding the coverage of the tour. I have several ideas for articles with a news interest when the cricket is under way. But of course I will not know what is appearing elsewhere – that is one way in which a tour differs from work at home.

Very best wishes to you all.

Dear Jim,

Many thanks for your long and informative letter. I would have replied sooner than this but have been taking a spot of overdue leave and am only just back at the office.

So far as this end is concerned everything is going according to plan. We have no difficulty with your cables and the matter is easily the best appearing in the London dailies. That is an outside-the-office view as well as my own.

The Powers That Be are as quiet as mice, which you can take as an excellent sign. No comments and no criticism. Keep going as you have started and all will be well. Very soon now you'll be running into the big stuff.

You'll be interested to know, by the way, that the office is thinking so hard about the Tests that we are to publish the Close of Play scores each morning on a whacking great board outside the Fleet-street office. The old D.T. is waking up, what?

So far none of your contemporaries on the tour has got away with a scoop or attempted to put over a sensational story. Who's been doping Mr. Dale?

I hope your Empire Cricket Writers' Club is going strong. We managed to get a Peterborough para in today's issue as you will see from this cutting.

By now I suppose you will have seen some copies of the D.T. The larger size (8 pages twice a week) has led to a little more recognition of sport, but actually we have run into the dull autumn and winter season and there's not a lot doing. Praise Allah for the Tests – and Jim Swanton . . .

Now don't fuss yourself about your work. I do assure you it is tip-top, and obviously pleasing everybody. So carry on as you've begun. I will write to you again after the first Test and let you know the reactions here.

In the meanwhile, the best of luck to you. Lainsor and the lads join me in that thought.

Yours sincerely,
Frank

The 'Empire' was very soon dropped from the Cricket Writers' Club and so Jim became the first chairman of an organisation that is still flourishing today. The correspondence continued:

My dear Jim,

First I want to thank you very much indeed for the splendid parcel of 'eats' which arrived safely yesterday, and the kind thought that prompted the most welcome gift.

Now about the Tests, I have cabled you today asking for a rehearsal. We want to publish in our late (4 a.m.) edition as much of the pre-lunch play each day as possible, and have been assured that messages will reach us within 15 minutes of dispatch if you will let us have a series of short flashes filed Urgent Press.

Get through as many short messages as you can of the play before lunch, and flash the lunch-time score, e.g. 'England 150 for two Hutton not 50 Compton not 40'. The early wickets we shall get from the P.A. Service.

These instructions will apply to all the Tests, and are of course independent of your usual summing up of the day's play. The experiment with W.S.7 match should be instructive.

Your work is much liked. A day or two ago I sent you a cutting of an appreciative letter we published from Charles Fry. Very soon now Stowell will be getting busy on the question of your future with the D.T. I will let you know at once a decision is made.

In the meanwhile keep going on the present lines.

The best of luck to you,

Sincerely,

Frank Coles

Dear Frank,

Thank you for your letter with its encouragement. How very kind of Charles Fry to write! I showed the cutting to Arthur Mailey, who was sharing a room with me at Melbourne. How nice, he said, but a pity he spoilt it with the Latin at the end . . .

The side goes fairly well but badly needs a kind, stern sergeant-major. There is very little positive direction or advice. I'm afraid the manager is rather weak, and the captain remote from all. He is still a very fine player but the personal limitations would never make him what is needed for this job. However, he isn't likely to make any active antipathies, which is something. (Incidentally, you've only misinterpreted me once – due to cable-ese: I wrote "Hammond like good captain" did something. That is on a specific occasion. This was amplified into "the good captain that he is". However I marvel and am grateful for the general accuracy of the stuff.)

Coles was not the only recipient of a splendid parcel of 'eats' sent by Jim. Colleagues at the BBC, friends, fellow POWs from his Battalion including the wives of those unfortunate men who had not survived the Railway, were all delighted to received unobtainable small luxuries (such as bags of sugar) in a severely rationed Britain and while a 'feathering the nest' motive could have been perceived in some cases, his generosity was never forgotten. In years to come Jim's propensity for enjoying creature comforts became part of the legend – the best hotel, first-class travel. Always he was aware of standards of service.

The food was good on the train, the drink likewise, though the average Australian, like most of Anglo-Saxon stock, does not exactly aim to head the field as regards grace of service. We leave the refinements to the Asiatics and the Latins. In these egalitarian days it's rather that you, the customer, have to win your way into his regard, than vice versa.

I had an example on the train of varying standards in this respect that makes me laugh as I recall it. Before my first lunch aboard I ordered a pink gin and was politely and correctly served, the barman first rolling the angostura bitters round the glass in the prescribed manner. A day later I approached the bar with the same request which was quite differently received.

'Pink gin?' said the man indignantly, 'we don't have any pink gin.' It was as though I'd stepped into a small hotel and nonchalantly asked for pink champagne. I said, 'I think you'll find you have – I had some yesterday.'

'Yesterday?' he cried, 'that's got nothing to do with it. The New South Wales blokes were on yesterday. We've got no pink gin.'

I remembered that the train is staffed by different state railways as each border is passed – first NSW Railways, then South Australian (to which this chap belonged), then Commonwealth, and finally Western Australia. However, he was too aggressive for my taste, and so I said quietly, 'Look, you only had to say you were sorry that South Australian railways didn't carry pink gin, and I'd have understood.'

'Sorry?' he asked. 'I'm not sorry, I'm bloody glad.' E.W.S., fascinated by now, and puzzled at this: 'Tell me, why are you bloody glad?'

'Because it'd be more for me to bring on the train, that's why.'

I thought of telling him the size of a bottle of angostura, but, as I settled for a plain gin, delivered instead a few well-chosen (and no doubt horribly pompous) remarks about courtesy to the customer. This seemed to silence him, but when I asked my dining neighbour whether he'd heard this lively exchange he said as he was a bit deaf he hadn't caught it. 'But when I went up to order mine the bloke said, "Cor, that Pom was a bit cranky, wasn't he? Reckon it was because England lost the Test!"' He'd had the last word after all.

Two days before Christmas Jim wrote to Coles again:

Dear Frank,

I'm getting this off tonight so that with luck it will arrive just before the Third Test begins.

(1) D.T. Cricket

As I expect you know Stowell has written to say he hopes I will carry on with the cricket on my return. But he has made no proposition regarding an annual salary. I have asked for this mentioning the hearsay figure paid to Guy Campbell.

(2) Third Test

I see that for the final editions of the Second Test play a good deal of matter other than mine appears under my name, presumably agency work: notably something about 'a sporting gesture' by Hammond (Dec. 16), followed by an 'interview'. Again (Dec. 13) there is something about the wicket being apparently full of runs, which is a foolish comment before a ball is bowled, was not justified by what happened as readers will have known by the wireless before reading their papers, and further had not been predicted by me the day before.

What seems to have happened is that more is needed than I supply. Your last instructions dated Nov. 25 say that for pre-lunch cables '300 words definitely maximum'. Do you now want more? The point is if we are building up a reputation for reliability and good writing it is a pity to spoil the picture with agency stuff – which, so far as this tour goes, is far from reliable. Believe me I am not unappreciative of the general handling in which I know I have been well and generously looked after. Incidentally it is worth remembering that to revise your requirements you can get in touch with me at urgent rates in a few minutes.

(3) Australian Cricket

I thought that while MCC were in Tasmania you might have room for thorough review of Australian cricket situation. If so, please write to me at Hotel Windsor, Melbourne.

The tour continues to go tolerably – but so much less well than it might have done under more inspiring management and leadership. But since both concerned are probably giving their best one can hardly be frank in print.

I am looking forward to my rest after Jan. 7 more than I can say, feeling for some reason very done up. Best New Year wishes to everyone.

Dear Jim,

Things have been moving at a pretty fast pace since your letter to me of December 23. I will deal with your points right away.

(1) D.T. Cricket.

The question of your annual salary will be settled satisfactorily, I feel sure, on your return. If I were you I would not worry about it now. The point is that you are established as our cricket correspondent for 1947.

(2) Front Page Test Stories

If you were in this office at 3 o/c in the morning, and not a line had arrived over the cable about the current day's play, you would realise the difficulties of the man in charge in building up a page one Swanton story.

I admit that the odd sentence you would not agree with has appeared under your name, but please give the sub-editor, racing against the clock, a chance!

(3) Review after Third Test

Yes, a thorough review of the situation after the third Test match will be grand. I am writing this before we have lost the 'Ashes'.

There has been a tremendous lot of nonsense published on this side about bad umpiring. While you as a good cricket correspondent ignored the squeals, it was necessary that we should come down one side or the other on the controversy. Hence the cable you received from Stowell on January 3.

Your answer to the criticism on umpires is well balanced and appreciated, but we must not ignore this anti-Australian angle, which I am sure starts among the smart boys in the Press Box.

I do not expect to hear from you again, apart from your 'inquest' story on why we failed to win the 'Ashes', until the end of the month. Have a good rest in the sun. If you were here tonight you would be quite happy to die. It is snowing and sleeting, and we all have our collars up.

One gets a sense that Jim, feeling more secure of his position, already is testing the boundaries of control. The perfectionism in his make-up – more apparent after being indoctrinated with regimental disciplines during the war – was both a strength and a weakness. For those who had to deal with it on a daily basis, more often it was just a bloody nuisance!

Nevertheless the *Daily Telegraph* seemed generally content with what they were getting. Phrases in letters such as: 'We have been very pleased with the work you have done for us and the way in which you have got away with your stories in slick time' left little room for doubt.

When it came to the subject of his salary, Jim made a proposition: 'I believe my predecessor worked on the basis of an annual salary, which one gathered from hearsay to be £1500.' The reply was a model of tact and discretion. 'I have the best possible precedents for the figure I do not name, which is £1000. You can be assured that I am not wishing in the least to undervalue your work, and if, as I hope, you do well with us in the ensuing twelve months, I shall be the first to recommend an upward revision.' Throughout his working life both with the BBC and the *Telegraph*, Jim always negotiated strongly for the highest achievable financial rewards. Files over an inch thick in both organisations testify to his perseverance. At the *Telegraph* he had a comrade in arms, namely the golf correspondent, Leonard Crawley, who dubbed Jim 'Lord Sockem'. With regard to their employers, they had both agreed to sock 'em for expenses; though, of course, Jim would never have admitted to doing so:

> My dear Lord Sockem,
>   On the basis of my beginning on the pay roll twenty years ago and two and a half times the cost of living today, my pay has gone backwards. And my base allowance and car allowances are really disgraceful. We must stand together on these questions and I am relying on you to keep me informed . . .

When touring Jim would charge travel (Air, Steamer, Car, Local Transport and baggage charges); Hotel and Living Expenses; Hospitality (to MCC Team, Officials etc.); Facilities (Messengers, Assistance, Postage, Wires and Sundries; Excess Baggage, Heavy Baggage (sent by sea) and on several occasions a payment of £25 to Mr W. Ferguson, MCC Baggage-Master for services rendered during the tour. There could also be a receipt enclosed for the purchase of tropical clothes during a stop at Colombo.

When at home, there would be the cost of a telephonist, secretarial assistance, and garage allowance for his car. In 1953, and feeling, one surmises, that he had more chance of acceptance by going to the top, he explained his modus operandi to none other than the Rt. Hon. Lord Burnham, CB, DSO:

Dear Lord Burnham,

I thought it best just to set on paper, if I may, the points I put to you about allowances for hotel and subsistence and for my car.

It is necessary generally to stay with the players and officials, and at these hotels the average run of prices (often raised beyond the quoted tariffs for matches and Tests) is roughly thus: Bed and Breakfast 25/- to £2; luncheon 6/6 to 10/-; tea 2/6; dinner 7/6 to 12/6. Add 5/- to 7/6 a day for gratuities, and the total for subsistence comes to at least £3 before considering the question of drinks.

I usually like a drink or two after a day's work, and in any case the bar or the hotel lounge is the common meeting-place. It is not a question of dispensing lavish hospitality at the paper's expense, but rather paying one's own way. When one is in the company of younger games-players, especially of course professionals, one has to be careful to do one's full share. It is of course these occasions of contact which help one to get the 'feel' of the situation, and to know the people one writes about.

All in all one tends to spend an average amount of £1 to 25/- a day on hospitality, including of course one's own drinks. The total thus is about £4 to £4.5.0, which is what I charge – although, as you pointed out, my method of accounting was not all it might have been. I hope it will be in order for me to charge an all-in amount of £4 to £4.5.0 a day. When hotel prices were even steeper than usual the account would be supported, as you ordered, by a hotel bill.

On the question of the car the difficulty is to deal on the basis of a hypothetical car which in fact would by now be worn out: the 16 h.p. Austin which I bought with the assistance of the office five years ago. In 1948 the rate of depreciation was very small, and the £75 a year allowance that I received at first covered the loss in value. If I had kept it and sold now I should probably have received a sum well below the difference between the original cost and the £375 I have had for depreciation. In addition I should now have had to come to you for help to buy a new car.

What in fact I have done is to buy, three years ago, a larger car which still gives good service, but on which repair and maintenance bills are inevitably higher for my having done 37,000 miles. Incidentally the secondhand value of this car has decreased very sharply, but that I realise is my own risk.

I gave you the figures for my car expenses for the six months August '52 to January '53 inclusive. For the year January '52–January '53 inclusive I find I travelled 8,080 miles for the office, out of a total mileage of 11,000. The office proportion is almost exactly four-fifths.

The total expenses of the car including fuel, garage, insurance, tax, tyres, washing, service, and repairs, was £410. Four-fifths of this is £328. I received from the office, on the 5d. a mile basis, £185.6.6, so that I was out of pocket upwards of £140.

To this £140 I must add the difference between the £75 received for depreciation and, say, £225 which seems a fair present-day depreciation figure for the sort of car which is recognised as suitable by the office. On this basis my total loss last year works out at about £300. Obviously I cannot afford to run the car on this basis.

I am sorry to have burdened you with so much detail.

I think that you appreciated the gist of all this when I came to see you; but as there are, for me, quite important sums involved it seemed best to be as specific as possible.

A few weeks later he received a reply – but it was not from Lord Burnham:

Dear Swanton,

The matter of your expenses has now received the attention of the Management and it is proposed to institute the following schedule:–

*1. Test Matches and Internationals. £4 a day to include hotel, hospitality, meals and taxis.

*2. County Matches & Rugby Club Matches. £3 a day to include hotel, hospitality, meals and taxis.

*These allowances will be reduced by £2 a day for matches within a 40 miles radius of London.

3. Invitations as Guest Speaker. Travelling expenses plus £1 per meeting for entertainment.

4. Entertainment of Celebrities and Receptions. Name to be given and a separate claim for expenses made. This also applies to contributions to Benefits.

5. Secretarial Assistance. £52 a year.

It is also considered that a telephonist is not necessary except at Test Matches.

I should be glad if you would base all expenses from the 1st April next on this schedule.

I would also mention that the Management do not consider we should be called on to make any contribution for entertainment at the University Match.

Whilst writing may I also deal with the question of the car. Had you retained the Austin 16 car you purchased in January, 1948, I assume that it would be worth between £350 and £400 today. The original cost was just under £800 and in five years you have received from us an allowance for depreciation amounting to £375. Taking into account that you used the car privately to the extent of one-fifth it is only fair to add a further £75 depreciation, which would leave the value of the car today at just under £350. In the circumstances I do not think you have any complaint.

The minutiae of monetary detail in all of the above veers towards tedium, but its inclusion is necessary in order to show the extent to which Jim would go in trying to benefit the exchequer. Some would see only venality in his method, but really he was only protecting to the utmost what he considered his right. Though at times, Swanton's assessment of his place in society's firmament seemed to exceed the wherewithal of his own pocket and the expectations of his masters' purse. Gracious living came at a price.

Jim's other bone of contention was the sanctity of his copy. During the Test match at Trent Bridge in 1947, he was dismayed to find that his article had undergone major surgery. Writing to the Managing Editor, he complained that 'there was much besides the South Africans' performance that therefore received inadequate recognition.'

Dear Mr. Swanton,

I sympathise very fully with your jealous desire to make the best possible showing in the paper. We all feel the same way and are, equally with you, meeting with a good deal of disappointment. We have only a ridiculous amount of newsprint for the amount of news to be covered and all we can do is use it to what seems to be the best adventure. Whether we succeed in that will always be a matter of debate, since there are so many interests to cover and opinions on their importance are bound to differ.

I have looked up your copy of Sunday night and have noted what was cut out. There are two main excisions. I have never found a writer to agree with a sub-editor about the treatment of his copy, but to an impartial observer it seems to me that the first cut did not matter, having regard to the necessity of saving some space. Part of the second cut would have been better left in, but on the other hand, the sub-editors added something about a new record which was not in your copy and which they thought to be of interest.

Your own solution of the difficulty that a guaranteed space should be given for cricket is an ideal one. Unfortunately, newspapers have to be made as the day goes on. If they were like a house, where you can call in a quantity surveyor to assess the exact amount of material required, life would be much easier. We do, of course, attempt to do this in the morning, and it is on the first estimate of the paper that Coles gives you a wordage to write to. We never know what will turn up, however, and estimates have to be revised in the light of important news which we do not anticipate.

The *Daily Telegraph* has always had a reputation for cricket reports and you may be assured that we are as anxious for your credit as you are yourself. If only we could get some more paper we should both be able to do the job thoroughly.

Yours sincerely,
Arthur Watson
Managing Editor

Dear Mr Watson

I must thank you for your letter about the cutting of my cricket reports. I appreciate indeed that most correspondents labour under difficulties similar to mine. I would only wish to leave the impression that just a little extra for the main report would make such a considerable difference, and that it is the cutting of these two hundred words which is apt to take out so much of the character.

Eventually, our man's persistence (on one occasion, he even threatened to resign) managed to establish a platform. After an article on a Rugby Trial had been scissored drastically in November 1955, Jim's complaint found a sympathetic ear: his old colleague Frank Coles:

The last thing I wish to happen is the slightest loss of confidence among our very fine team of writers in the sub-editorial staff.

Treatment is wholly my responsibility and you may rest assured that I will take steps from now on to ensure that your copy is not cut except in exceptional emergency. If and when the situation arises I will handle it personally.

Mention of the Test Match at Nottingham in 1947 is a reminder that it was not only 'the South Africans' performance that received inadequate recognition'.

John Arlott was in his second season as a commentator and in his first, as such, on BBC national radio. The endemic snobbery and class distinction of those days, which was particularly noticeable in some of the upper reaches of cricket, grated with his liberal, egalitarian instincts. As he wrote of himself in the third person: 'Some of his colleagues did not disguise their opinion of this down-market interloper.' During this Test at Trent Bridge, Jim and John had a difference of opinion over who had booked the commentary box.

John told me: 'I was in there doing a recording and not understanding or caring who I was he came in and told me to get out. So I stood up, shut the microphone off, and said, "If you don't go away I'll throw you off the top of this pavilion." There were no adjectives interspersed – I was too much of a copper for that.'

'It was a silly thing, really,' recalled Jim some forty years later. 'I much regret that it ever happened. I was wanting to make a recording and it was over who had the rights of the box. It was the only altercation we ever had. I wouldn't say we were blood brothers, but I think we respected one another.'

Both were innately too sensible and too professional to let a feud develop. They had, after all, to work together. But the locking of horns led John to pen a somewhat snide squib which rapidly went the round of the press box and produced many a smirk.

> *Stately is my manner and Swanton is my name,*
> *and in the* Daily Telegraph, *I write about the game.*
> *I was never at Oxford or Cambridge,*
> *But I think that my accent will pass;*
> *and I've got a check suit and deer Michael,*
> *and that's in the Bullingdon class.*
> *I've dined out with all the best people,*
> *and I thought I made quite a hit;*
> *So why should mere cricket reporters*
> *declare I'm just a big journalist?*

Each of the two, in his own uncopyable way, was to help make the broadcasting of cricket a national institution; Arlott with his commentaries and Swanton with his summaries, though, as we know, Swanton also gave extensive commentaries in his time. Was there anything finer that Jim's masterly coverage of the day's events, when it seemed that everything possible had already been said many times over? With very little time at his disposal (often less than four minutes) he would, off the cuff, assess the game in its overall context, putting it in a totally fresh perspective. It is easy to see now how, in delivery and sound, one voice so perfectly complemented the other, and how two such disparate personalities from such dissimilar backgrounds could only extend the range for the other. But at the moment of confrontation they could have been seen as potential rivals, though Jim, having been writing and broadcasting since before the war, had a head start on John.

'My first impression of John was that he was different,' Jim Swanton told me. 'There was no Arlott prototype, so to speak. You can imagine Alston, the schoolmaster, the steady orthodox performer. John was not orthodox – as it seemed at that time. The thing about him, of course, was that he produced a personal idiosyncrasy of style – if not idiosyncratic way of talking. He was a very good reporter with a gift for colour . . . was "quick on the ball" to spot anything off or on the field, any quirk of a fielder, that sort of thing. He was unconventional in his way, I think . . . You must realise, of course, that there hadn't been that much running commentary in broadcasting until 1946. In 1946 it took a different form altogether . . . I suppose he thought I was very much an Establishment figure, but I think he may have revised that opinion after my attitude to the South African question which, of course, happened years later.'

That may well have been true as seen in print, because near the end of his life Arlott wrote a reasoned, balanced judgement of Swanton for the obituary files. But when I put to him that Jim was sorry for the episode, there was a long silence. When pressed for a comment, he grunted and said finally: 'Can you imagine what it must be like to write as much as Swanton did over so many years without leaving one memorable sentence?' Which, of course, might be recognised as prejudiced comment, for Jim's fluent command of the English language was widely admired. As Gideon Haigh has written so perceptively, 'As a prose stylist, Swanton makes a fascinating study. There have been many more felicitous phrasemakers and more memorable aphorists. Yet a passage of Swanton is unmistakeable.' There was a sense though in which Arlott was giving his view as a poet, and of the relaying of prose being subsumed by something far deeper which was the result of imaginative vision and interior monologue. But then, Jim came from a different stable. In this case, however, John's usual magnanimity took second place to that of his erstwhile mettlesome colleague.

As did several broadcasting journalists, Jim had to be careful when juggling with his commitments. When he first had started working for the *Daily Telegraph*, the paper had been wary about his broadcasting duties. They had tried to insist on a name check for each of his appearances, but this the BBC had refused to countenance, concerned that to do so would make a precedent in terms of their charter. However, given that the written imprimatur could not be countermanded, individual producers on Outside Broadcasts had allowed the name of the paper to be mentioned once only in a discreet fashion on several occasions. Eventually – and it was an eventually that lasted all of a decade and during which Jim experienced what it was like to be 'piggy in the middle' between unaccommodating organisations – the issue was settled with a reference to the paper at the beginning and close of the day's play. Near the end of the saga, Jim displayed an adept negotiating skill as a servant of two masters by telling his superiors on the *Telegraph*: 'since everyone now knows who is interested enough to listen to cricket that I am the correspondent of this paper there is surely no more value in regular mentions than in the indirect publicity we get from the persistent mention of my name. I hope you find yourself able to subscribe to that view.'

From the BBC's point of view Jim was esteemed. But that esteem was not unqualified. Antony Craxton, who in a distinguished Television production career covered many high profile occasions, had reservations, as can be seen in a memorandum of 1955 that is discussing commentary allocation:

I would be very reluctant to drop Peter West whom I consider in many ways to be the best of our cricket commentators. This is not only my personal opinion but the opinion of many people with whom I have come in contact during the past two years. He is considered a better summariser than Swanton who annoys people by his pomposity. He has a very considerable knowledge of the game, certainly much more than Johnston and not much less than Swanton and above all he is far more produceable than Swanton and no less so than Johnston. It may interest you to know that this year we have had many more complaints about Johnston's continued irrelevancies, primarily from those interested in cricket though I have no doubt that the fringe viewer rather enjoys his quips.

We have certainly not got an ideal cricket commentator, one who knows the game from A to Z and who is a first rate television commentator, but I would put West as being the nearest of the three to this perfectionist. It would therefore seem logical to reduce Swanton to two Tests and to give West three. However, I know that if we suggested this we would lose Jim altogether and I think this would be a bad thing in the long run. As you know he considers he is

indispensable and I am afraid no amount of talking will dissuade him
from this view . . .

Peter Dimmock, Head of Television Outside Broadcasts, replied:

I agree with all you say about Swanton, but the fact remains that he is
popular, and I think that it would be very unwise to reduce his number
of contributions in 1956. On the other hand I note what you say about
West and we should I think try to retain him if we can.

In effect, this was a rehash of an ever-present allocation issue that
had stirred Jim's ire three years earlier. As always, Jim began at the
top, this time with a letter to 'Lobby'.

Dear Lobby,
    When you kindly referred to me as 'the doyen of cricket
commentators' at the Outside Broadcasts conference, I did not suspect
that at the age of 45 I was being nudged gently towards the shelf.
    I have had from Antony Craxton the TV offer of cricket
commentaries for the season, as well as an outline of what Rex Alston
requires for sound. The outcome of these two offers is that my fees for
1952 look like being down more than one-third on my post-war
average – a diminution considerably greater, I imagine, than can be
accounted for by economy cuts.
    I am most seriously concerned with my status as a TV commentator,
so I will deal with this first. As you may know, I have acted as one of
the commentators for every Test ever done on TV, except one arranged
late for which I was previously booked by Sound. Thus I feel I have had
the opportunity to do rather more than anyone else to build up TV
cricket technique. As I mentioned to you in the autumn, I do not think
the present system gives quite as good an answer as we should be able
to achieve, and I have been hoping that you will find time before the
new season for a few of us to talk the thing over. But judging by
comments and many letters received, the public seem pretty well
satisfied.
    I have been offered only two of the four Tests, and one other match:
three bookings out of the fourteen available for the seven matches
being covered. I gathered that Brian was to be offered all four Tests,
and Peter West two. This puts me in a subsidiary position which, with
all respect to those concerned, I am afraid I cannot accept. I am not
going to try and sell my wares to you, but I must naturally look after

my professional reputation, which has been built up over a longish time.

I quite see that other people must be given experience, but by the suggested arrangement I should have only three days practice before the first Test and then nothing more for two months. Equally it seems right to look out for new people; but you have at least five already, and there should be better opportunity for that when the Australians command more attention next year.

Both my TV and Sound offers have no doubt been affected to some extent by the need for economy. As regards this, might it not be as well to discover whether broadcasters outside the staff would be willing to accept lower fees (like Cabinet Ministers) before giving listeners and viewers such a large dose of BBC men who are, and need to be, 'all-rounders'?

I suppose I hardly need to add that my telephone conversations with Rex and Antony were on a thoroughly friendly note. Rex has always been scrupulously fair and extremely co-operative in all his dealings with me, and Antony went out of his way to write appreciatively of my work last year.

As I naturally don't want to go over anyone's head, I hope you will approve of my sending copies of this to them both . . .

On receiving his copy, Antony Craxton's comment had been: 'My own personal view is that it would not be a great loss to television if we found that he did not wish to partake in any commentaries this year. However, knowing Jim, I am pretty certain that he will accept the position although not without protest.'

Unfortunately, like many broadcasters, Jim assessed his own worth from different criteria – the response he was getting from the public, the letters that landed in his in-tray, the things people said to him on a personal level. An intermittent and valued supporters was the redoubtable C.B. Fry who on one occasion had benefited from a gift in kind:

Dear Swanton,

Thank you very much for sending me your book which came this morning.

Evidently, as I judge from perusal of salient points of it, you maintain your high standard of knowledge of the game and of ability to write the English language.

Your publishers have done you well in the matter of production. In this, the book easily excels anything I've seen lately, at any rate on the subject of cricket.

> Your inscription is more than kind. But I cannot remember any possible 'service' except that once in a moment of exaltation, following on debasement, I did approach a High Level at BBC House with my opinion that you were the only commentator that enabled me to see anything that went on in the field!
>
> No doubt this was true – Alston and pre Arlott and at a time when I knew what I was talking about.

There is an element of give and take in that acknowledgement, the praise being rather evasive as in the book's title: *Elusive Victory: with F.R. Brown's Team in Australia*.

As we have noted, Jim's roller-coaster ride with the accountants was not confined to the *Telegraph*. By the mid-1950s, the BBC Head of Outside Broadcasts (Sound) Charles Max-Muller had taken over the case:

> In view of the trouble which we have had this year over Swanton's *expenses*, namely, that he gets us to pay expenses for him as well as the *Daily Telegraph*, I do not want any verbal commitment made with him for next year's Sound broadcasts of cricket matches until the whole matter of expenses has been thrashed out. I think that it is entirely wrong that anyone gets expenses from two sources unless there is some very good reason, i.e. because of broadcasting he has to take his secretary with him. This perhaps could be admitted for Test Matches when he has to be available to us for long periods, but I do not think it should apply for County Matches when he is only wanted for one or two short pieces.

Back came Jim:

> I had supposed that the explanation I gave you would be sufficient in itself. After all, so far as I can see, what you needed was a bone-fide reason which, so to speak, satisfied the Corporation's conscience: an assurance that I was not 'making' an extra set of expenses. As I said, I cannot possibly broadcast and write on the same match unless I have an assistant present for telephoning the copy etc. etc. The position is not greatly different whether it is a Test match or some lesser event. The *Daily Telegraph* want a considerable proportion of my work before close of play. I cannot telephone it if I am tied to the microphone.

The BBC reluctantly acquiesced. Once more, Jim had the last word:

> I have always found the BBC so thoroughly fair in matters financial and
> otherwise; and I am naturally very pleased that you have seen the
> matter of my expenses in the same light as myself.

It was not only the groats and guineas which captured his attention.
Here he sallied forth on a matter of peripatetics.

> We are holding the issue until it is known whether the commentating
> facilities there would enable me to do my writing without a constant
> procession from one end of the ground to the other. I don't at all want
> to seem contumacious about this issue, but the difference in terms of
> time and energy involved is considerable.

And later:

> Dear Charles,
>   Having experienced the luxury of the Oval sound broadcasting point
> (not Television!) I have been having a look round here at Lord's to see
> what can be made of the situation here. Jim Dunbar is quite prepared to
> 'play' on a carpentering job, and I certainly think there should be an
> improvement. To broadcast a full day from Lord's is the refinement of
> torture, and the bigger you are the worse. As I have fifteen more days here
> this year I am, I suppose, more personally concerned than anyone else.
>   I thought if I got this off today someone from the department might
> possibly be able to get up to Lord's tomorrow and talk the thing over.
>   One other point while on the question of commentators' positions. You
> have persuaded me to do the extra sting at Trent Bridge. Brian Johnston
> says that there is a small room in the palatial new premises intended for the
> no. 2. He thought I might be able to write there from a table without
> inconveniencing anyone else. I thought I would ask for this via you. You
> may remember the difficulty at Trent Bridge is that the press box is at the
> very furthest end of the ground so this would be a great convenience.

Yet another letter to Charles:

> Thank you so much for facilitating my work at Trent Bridge, with the
> collaboration of Michael Hastings.
>   As you may have heard, we had a meeting with Jim Dunbar on
> Saturday morning at Lord's, as a result of which he is expecting to get

in writing exactly what we would like done in preparation for the Test Match. As far as I can see it will involve raising the floor, so that one's feet are on the ground (v. important) and a sloping desk, replacing the narrow parapet. That would make a very considerable difference to the commentator's comfort – and therefore his efficiency. I believe the good Richard is arriving with a tape measure and specimen chair this morning.

Yours in haste,

P.S. One further thing about Lord's: I hope you may agree to ask for say one visit per session by the upstairs catering staff for an order. At present, as you know, we have to queue with the members for a cup of tea, or a gin and tonic – during which time Tyson may be doing the hat-trick!

There is little wonder that Jim needed sustenance when looking at his itinerary for the summer of 1956:

E. W. Swanton – Itinerary – Summer 1956

Date	Engagement	Address at first post
Sat Apr 28	DUKE OF NORFOLK'S XI v. AUSTRALIANS (Arundel)	c/o Duke of Richmond and Gordon, Goodwood Park, Goodwood, Sussex
Sun Apr 29	Commentary	
Mon Apr 30	BBC Lunch to Australians: Savoy	17, Loudoun Road, N.W.8 (MAI 3098)
Tu May 1	Foreword for Wednesday	-do-
Wed May 2	WORCS v. AUSTRALIANS (Worcester)	Raven Hotel, Droitwich (Droitwich 2224)
Thu May 3	-do-	-do-
Fri May 4	-do-	-do-
Sat May 5	OXFORD U. v. YORKS (Oxford)	Pusey House, Oxford. (Oxford 573321)
Sun May 6	Commentary: R. P. Kirk's XI v. Boar's Hill	-do-
Mon May 7	CAMBRIDGE U. v. LANCS (Cambridge)	-do-
Tu May 8	-do-	University Arms, Cambridge (2223)
Wed May 9	YORKS v. AUSTRALIANS (Bradford)	-do-
Thu May 10	-do-	Midland Hotel, Bradford (Bradford 25663)

Date	Engagement	Address at first post
Fri May 11	-do-	-do-
Sat May 12	37 Loudoun Road, N.W.8 (MAI 3098)	
Sun May 13	Melford Commentary	-do-
Mon May 14	MIDDLESEX v GLOUCESTER (Lord's)	-do-
Tu May 15	-do-	-do-
Wed May 16	SURREY v AUSTRALIANS (Oval)	-do-
Thu May 17	-do-	-do-
Fri May 18	-do-	-do-
Sat May 19	MIDDLESEX v SUSSEX (Lord's)	-do-
Sun May 20	Commentary	-do-
Mon May 21	MIDDLESEX v SUSSEX (Lord's)	-do-
Tu May 22	-do-	-do-
Wed May 23	R.C. Robertson-Glasgow's XI v Corpus Christi (Oxford)	-do-
Thu May 24	-do-	
Fri May 25	-do-	
Sat May 26	MCC v AUSTRALIANS (Lord's)	-do-
Sun May 27	Commentary: Hampstead sv Butterflies	-do-
Mon May 28	MCC v AUSTRALIANS (Lord's)	-do-
Tu May 29	-do-	-do-
Wed May 30	OXFORD U. v AUSTRALIANS (Oxford)	17, Loudoun Road, N.W.8 (MAIda Vale 3098)
Thu May 31	-do-	Pusey House, Oxford (Oxford 573321)
Fri Jun 1	-do-	-do-
Sat Jun 2	Arabs v Oxford University Authentics	-do-
Sun Jun 3	-do-	-do-
Mon Jun 4	37, Loudoun Road, N.W.8	
Tue Jun 5	-do-	
Wed Jun 6	Foreword for First Test	-do-
Thu Jun 7	1st Test: ENGLAND v AUSTRALIA (Trent Bridge)	Black Boy Hotel, Nottingham (41531)

Date	Engagement	Address at first post
Fri Jun 8	-do-	-do-
Sat Jun 9	-do-	-do-
Sun Jun 10	-do-	-do-
Mon Jun 11	-do-	-do-
Tue Jun 12	-do-	-do-
Wed Jun 13	English Speaking Union: Debate	17, Loudoun Road, N.W.8
Thu Jun 14	-do-	-do-
Fri Jun 15	Lucifer Golfing Society dinner (Savoy Hotel)	-do-
Sat Jun 16	? Horsham Cricket Club: Dinner	-do-
Sun Jun 17	Commentary: Arabs v Sandhurst Wanderers	17, Loudoun Road, N.W.8
Mon Jun 18	SURREY v YORKSHIRE (Oval)	-do-
Tue Jun 19	-do-	-do-
Wed Jun 20	Foreword for Second Test	-do-
Thu Jun 21	2nd Test: ENGLAND v AUSTRALIA (Lord's)	-do-
Fri Jun 22	-do-	-do-
Sat Jun 23	-do-	-do-
Sun Jun 24	E.W. Swanton's XI v Cranleigh Village	-do-
Mon Jun 25	2nd Test: ENGLAND v AUSTRALIA (Lord's)	-do-
Tue Jun 26	-do-	-do-
Wed Jun 27	Household Brigade v MCC	-do-
Thu Jun 28	Diocese of Canterbury v Diocese of Southwark (Oval)	-do-
Fri Jun 29	ETON v WINCHESTER (Eton)	-do-
Sat Jun 30	MIDDLESEX v LANCASHIRE (Lord's)	-do-
Sun Jul 1	Melford Commentary	-do-
Mon Jul 2	ESSEX v HAMPSHIRE (Westcliff)	
Tue Jul 3	-do-	
Wed Jul 4	-do-	
Thu Jul 5	-do-	
Fri Jul 6	Foreword for University Match	

Date	Engagement	Address at first post
Sat Jul 7	OXFORD v CAMBRIDGE (Lord's)	17, Loudoun Rd., N.W.8 (MAI 3098)
Sun Jul 8	COMMENTARY: Arabs v R.M. Stow's XI	-do-
Mon Jul 9	OXFORD v CAMBRIDGE (Lord's)	-do-
Tue Jul 10	-do-	-do-
Wed Jul 11	Foreword for Thursday	-do-
Thu Jul 12	3rd Test: ENGLAND v AUSTRALIA (Leeds)	Old Swan Hotel, Harrogate (4051/2)
Fri Jul 13	-do-	-do-
Sat Jul 14	-do-	-do-
Sun Jul 15	-do-	
Mon Jul 16	-do-	-do-
Tue Jul 17	-do-	-do-
Wed Jul 18	GENTLEMEN v PLAYERS (Lord's)	17, Loudoun Rd., N.W.8
Thu Jul 19	-do-	-do-
Fri Jul 20	-do-	-do-
Sat Jul 21	Arabs' 21st Birthday Match	-do-
Sun Jul 22	COMMENTARY	-do-
Mon Jul 23	-do-	
Tue Jul 24	-do-	
Wed Jul 25	Foreword for Thursday	-do-
Thu Jul 26	4th Test: ENGLAND v AUSTRALIA (Manchester)	Midland Hotel, Manchester (Central 3333)
Fri Jul 27	-do-	-do-
Sat Jul 28	-do-	-do-
Sun Jul 29	Benefit match for K. Grieves at Didsbury	-do-
Mon Jul 30	4th Test: ENGLAND v AUSTRALIA (Manchester)	-do-
Tue Jul 31	-do-	-do-
Wed Aug 1	LANCS v NORTHANTS (Blackpool) or LEICS v SUSSEX (Leicester)	c/o County Secretary (Address later)
Thu Aug 2	-do-	-do-
Fri Aug 3		
Sat Aug 4	LANCASHIRE v YORKSHIRE (Manchester)	Lymm Hotel, Lymm, Cheshire (Lymm 83)
Sun Aug 5	Melford Commentary	-do-

Date	Engagement	Address at first post
Mon Aug 6	LANCASHIRE v YORKSHIRE (Manchester)	-do-
Tue Aug 7	-do-	-do-
Wed Aug 8		
Thur Aug 9	Arab tour v Lincolnshire Gents.	Pettwood House, Woodhall Spa (3182)
Fri Aug 10	-do-	
Sat Aug 11	Arab tour v Yorkshire Gents.	Monk Fryston Hotel, nr Selby, Yorks. (South Milford 369)
Sun Aug 12	COMMENTARY: Arab tour v Yorkshire Gents.	-do-
Mon Aug 13	Arab tour v Catterick Services	-do-
Tue Aug 14	Arab tour v Eton Ramblers	
Wed Aug 15	MIDDLESEX v KENT (Lord's)	17, Loudoun Rd., N.W.8 (MAI 3098)
Thu Aug 16	-do-	-do-
Fri Aug 17	-do-	-do-

As far as his writing was concerned, by the early 1950s Jim had built on his reputation for sober and reasoned judgement. For cricket lovers his column in the *Daily Telegraph* had become the one to read. Even by this stage of his career it was evident that he was a kind of self-appointed Delphic Oracle, a position that had been attained imperceptibly, but not by stealth. His seat at the organ of the right wing enabled him to play all the right tunes to capture a place deep in the English psyche. In other words the chords he produced had an agreeable resonance for his readers – most of the time.

In the winter months Jim also covered rugby, having been persuaded by the paper to take on the joint role soon after he was established as their cricket correspondent, but there was never any doubt as to which sport was his priority. By judicious planning always he contrived to be one of the press party on important MCC tours abroad, and it was only to the Indian sub-continent that he found sufficient reasons not to go.

In December 1952 E.W.S, as was his wont, addressed a matter of moment which, even some fifty years later, still divides opinion:

AUSTRALIA'S EXPERIMENT WITH TEST WICKETS
Change will Take Variety Out of Game

It has been decided, with the concurrence of MCC, to cover the wickets in Test matches the next time an English side go to Australia, which is in 1954–55.

On the surface, as it is not difficult to see, there is a fair prima facie case for covering. On recent tours there have been a lot of ruinous wet Saturdays. And in some instances there probably could have been cricket if the whole wicket area had been effectively covered.

When in response to a direct request from Australia to agree to the covering of the wickets over there, MCC sought the opinions of many famous English players and discovered that they were pretty well equally divided for and against, there seemed little alternative but to concur, at least for the next tour.

MCC have held on as far as they could, out of respect to the views of many of their most experienced and distinguished members, by agreeing to the coverings as an experiment.

One must admit the plausibility of the case for covering, though personally I abominate the idea on principle, and on practical grounds distrust it. As to the latter objection, experience has shown that when it really rains in Australia all forms of cricket covering so far devised are futile. At Brisbane six years ago when the heavens opened the tarpaulins might well have been found wrapped round the boundary pickets.

Covering when it is effective must tend to destroy that prospect of variety and hint of chance to which all the cricketing philosophers ascribe the game's unique appeal. And in my view it is the very sameness of the scene which is tending to limit interest in Australia. In other words in the long run I believe covering to be against Australia's best interests.

The argument of those in favour of covering, that no batsman has a fair chance on a real Australian 'sticky', I would neutralise by taking away the crease covers which under present regulations in Australia v. England Tests give the quicker bowlers, as it were, a firm firing platform.

They bowl straight half-volleys, or should do, and the wicket more or less does the rest for them. That at least is the theory, though certain eminent batsmen led by Hobbs and Sutcliffe, in their day, have upset it.

If neither the creases nor the rest of the wicket were covered, the bowling, when play became possible after rain, would have to be done at first by the slow bowlers, who could get a firm footing. Under present arrangements they do not get put on. That solution conjures prospects of an infinitely fascinating battle – and surely a fair one.

However, there it is, the deed is done, temporarily at least, artifice has triumphed over nature, and we must accept what is certainly the most fundamental difference there has ever been in the laws and match regulations as between Test matches in England and in Australia.

Don Bradman, Australia's favourite son, to whom Jim had sent a copy of his thesis, picked up the theme:

I think it is important that those who have the responsibility of legislating for cricket, should know what people like yourself think, and I was very interested in your attitude towards the question and the various angles put forward.

Without any doubt at all there is a difference in the conditions applicable to England as compared with Australia. A wet or sticky wicket in England in most cases is definitely one upon which a batsman can exhibit a considerable degree of skill and he may even, within reason, be able to master these conditions.

In Australia it is still true that some batsmen will handle the conditions better than others, but I do not think it is true that any batsman can master such conditions where the crease covers are allowed and the bowler has a firm foothold. It was this part of your article which really prompted me to write this letter. So far as I know the primary reasons for wishing to cover wickets in Australia were:

(1) The fact that if one side batted on a firm wicket and the other got caught on a sticky wicket, the variation in conditions became so great that the weather and not skill decided the issue.

(2) The necessity to gain the maximum financial return from the matches.

It was this later consideration which I think was responsible for legislations agreeing to cover the bowlers' footholds whilst leaving the wicket uncovered.

It is difficult to say whether cricket has been possible because of covered footholds where otherwise there would have been no play. I think generally speaking that if the wicket is fit to play on, then slow bowlers could certainly operate even if the fast ones could not. It is this aspect of fast bowlers sending down their thunderbolts from firm footholds into a sticky wicket which has made the batsman's task hopeless. If we could have a return to the old idea of a slow left-hand spinner pitting his skill on a wet wicket against the batsman, we would have a really interesting duel, but the existing set up helps nobody.

I very much doubt whether the Aust. authorities would agree to take the crease covers away, because the majority view here seems to be undoubtedly that we should have completely covered wickets, but there is no denying your argument that this does bring a sameness to matches which tends to blunt the edge of public interest. It will be interesting to follow developments, but I do not known how things will go.

Over the years the Don and Jim continued to have a regular correspondence on all sorts of public and private matters. Where their concerns embraced cricket, one is left with an impression of two of the most influential voices on either side of the globe together trying to sort out the future of the game. There is no question that both cared deeply about cricket. But when Jim's views were paraded on the pages of the *Telegraph*, the pontifical tone sometimes tended to obscure his own solicitude. On the 1953–54 tour to Australia, the MCC manager Geoffrey Howard a number of times was exasperated by what he read:

'Jim seemed to disapprove of so much that took place on that tour. He didn't really think that Hutton should have been captain – it was the professional/amateur thing. When Len put Australia in at Brisbane and we had no spinners he called it "a sort of midsummer madness". Then he criticised us for playing Denis Compton a few days after his plane had crash-landed at Karachi – saying it was stupid to play him and so on [Compton scored a hundred] and also he had a go about the lack of urgency in the Sydney Test.'

In *At The Heart of English Cricket – the life and memories of Geoffrey Howard* as told to Stephen Chalke a diary entry reads:

Sydney, 2 March. Jim Swanton is after Len again. He never misses a chance to take a dig at him! It's all so silly: the Lord Protector of English Cricket. He has not made a great deal of progress out here, and people are beginning to tire a bit of his stuff, I think.

'I do remember saying to Jim one day – look, you may be critical, but you are fortunate in the sense that you don't really have to make any decision. What you're doing is commenting on people who have to make decisions, right or wrong. Your decisions are basically a choice of words as to how you express yourself.'

Shortly before his death Geoffrey Howard retreated a little from that position.

> That's a little unkind. I never thought his criticisms were unfair, and his bias was always to uphold the best traditions of English cricket.

The previous year Hutton had had a difficult time when captaining the MCC in the Caribbean. The reactions of his side to what they viewed as incompetent umpiring had severely strained relations on and off the field, which the press were quick to exploit. As a result Jim was asked to manage a side to the West Indies during 1955–56 in order to heal the rift – more of which in another chapter.

> It would be dishonest to conclude that Len Hutton's influence on English cricket was unreservedly admirable [*wrote Jim in* Sort of a Cricket Person]. 'Apart from his attitude to the opposition – which derived partly at least, I believe, from a patriotic reaction against the failures of the early post-war years in Australia and the West Indies – he must have either originated or connived at the slowing-down of the over-rate as a tactical ploy. I blush now to recall the prolonged booing of the New Year's Day crowd of 65,000 at Melbourne as England spent the whole five hours getting through 54 overs. Neil Harvey was the chief threat to England in that 1954–5 series, and he was palpably irked if the natural tempo of the game was reduced.
>
> Yet what man who has achieved anything can look back on his life without regrets? I do not doubt that Hutton, like the rest of us, if he had his time again, would have ordered some things differently.
>
> But what has he not got to show on the credit side? He brought England back to the forefront of world cricket, and showed to his fellow-players a perfection of technique and a dedicated example that were faithfully followed by his young disciples, Peter May and Colin Cowdrey. Both of them likewise saw in their first touring captain, and followed in their turn, the dignity and reticence he brought to the job. These attributes did not desert him when after retirement came the blandishments of newspapers and publishers to 'reveal all'. Len felt the lure of t'brass keenly enough, but unlike most of his professional contemporaries he never yielded to the temptation to depict his career and times in the sort of language that the 10% agents could have made a small fortune from.
>
> May for Hutton was the obvious succession in the England captaincy, and it is extraordinary how similar was their approach in so

many respects. Both were serious, reserved, difficult to penetrate – and both in turn had the added burden of carrying the England batting on their shoulders.

'I don't think Len ever worried in the slightest what Jim wrote about him', said John Woodcock, the distinguished former cricket correspondent of *The Times*. 'But the same cannot be said for Peter May, although it was what Jim had written about Doug Insole that upset him so much. Peter was captain in South Africa in 1956–57 and Doug was his vice-captain and he didn't think Jim's reporting of Doug's batting had been fair. He'd said something like no one could make batting look more painful, and that unless he changed his approach he had little hope of success on South African wickets. Doug had a method all his own and it had precious little to do with the textbook, he was very bottom-handed, very much leg-side player, but it was very effective. In fact, he went on to have a very successful tour. Anyway there was a serious rift between Jim and Peter and not only Peter, but most of the team. It was childish, really.'

Wisden's report of Insole's performance on the tour is illuminating:

> The highest Test average for either side, 39.00, was achieved by Insole, the vice-captain, who also finished second to May in the full tour record. Somewhat ungainly in style and often suspect outside the off stump, Insole improved tremendously as the tour progressed and proved his splendid temperament and fighting qualities on several vital occasions. A powerful on-side player, he made the most of his fine eye both as a batsman and fieldsman, usually at slip where he held many brilliant catches. His success proved most popular for he was an excellent tourist, being full of humour off the field and extremely keen on it.

During the tour there were many hard-fought games (the five Test series was shared 2–2), not least at Pretoria, where in early December a South African XI ended MCC's one hundred per cent record up to that time and also consigned them to their first loss on a turf pitch in South Africa. Insole was MCC captain for the game and at the end of the third day's play an unusual incident occurred. McGlew, the South African XI captain, ran off the field to see Insole about extra time. *Wisden* again: 'Bailey and Lock, the not out batsmen, walked in with the umpires with the rest of the fieldsmen standing their ground. The batsman had to return, having been under a misapprehension about the rules existing for extra time.'

True to form, Jim could not resist building mountains. The repercussions rebounded to Lord's and soon Jim was the recipient of a letter from the universally liked Assistant Secretary, Billy Griffith:

My dear Jim,

Thank you for your letter of the 12th December and for the enclosed press cuttings from South Africa in regard to recent unhappy events. As you say, my letter of the 3rd December now reads somewhat sadly – unlike you I am occasionally, of course, wrong.

Before touching upon the cuttings which you sent, I would like just to say a word or two about your comment 'I have had so much evidence that the MCC simply don't want to hear what I say about happenings on tour . . .' This is, of course, utter nonsense and I am sure after some thought you will agree. In my experience any criticism or comment upon a touring side coming from you, or indeed anybody else who has some experience of these matters, is regarded with the greatest interest. It is well appreciated here at Lord's that you are in a unique position in so far as the number of tours that any member of the Club has been on. We may be stupid, but I do not think quite so stupid as to utterly ignore your views on both behaviour and play during an MCC tour. I do, therefore, hope that we do not have any more remarks such as these which are totally unworthy of you and I know give a wrong impression of MCC's true feelings in the matter.

To return to the incident . . . We understand from all reports and letters from all concerned that this unfortunate matter has been settled, or at least attended to, by the Captain and Manager. No attempt has been made at excuses and from this end the matter has been attended to with great firmness, leaving no doubt in the minds of any members of the team what the outcome will be of a repetition. It is, of course, desperately unfortunate that the thing has happened at all but it would appear that the trouble, as it were, was nipped in the bud before any really fatal harm had been done.

I have, of course, been enjoying your writings immensely and they continue to be a joy on these damp, gloomy December mornings. I was, however, – and I am sure you would wish me to mention this – a little bit shaken by your virulent attacks upon the Vice-Captain as a result of his handling of the side during the match at Pretoria. I know he was the root of the trouble which subsequently finished the day off, but I didn't think it quite fair to attack him so virulently on things which had gone before. However . . . I am sure you have your reasons for doing this but it seemed as one who is a pretty close student of the great man that this was not your normal form . . .

My dear Billy,

A short note – and no adequate answer to your most interesting letter, but I am in the middle of a Test Match.

About Doug. I have what I wrote rather on my conscience. Unfortunately, it had to be got off at much speed, directly after the Bailey walk-off, when I was highly indignant with MCC's performance. I said that 'MCC missed their Captain in every possible direction'. In fact, of course, they did (a) as a batsman – no question; (b) as a tactician – Lock 5 for 112 on a dry crumbler, mostly off the edge past short third man and leg slips; (c) as a disciplinarian. On this last point consider this. There was bad language from our people on the first day. On the second day it came from the acting Captain, involving an apology. On the third comes the walk-off, the ignorance about Playing Condition, and the quibble about playing on. Bailey, though requested by the Umpires to remain, not only went off the field with Lock, but took his pads off!

Shades of West Indies and Pakistan! Do you begin to understand my feelings?

There was one thing I didn't know until later, and it alters the situation in some degree. That is that Tayfield had spoken out of turn at the moment of the Richardson incident – 'Now you know the sort of umpiring that we had to put up with in England' – which was what provoked Doug. That being so, it seems that we ought to have handled the situation so that any apologies were mutual. There was no need for us to have been put in the wrong, so far as the press account was concerned. 'MCC say "Sorry"' is a damaging headline, you'll agree.

I have had a long talk with Doug, and have told him I am very sorry to have caused him distress, that I will cover the matter rather differently in my book, and that having supported his claims for the vice-Captaincy, I will do all I can in this respect out here. I am not sure, to be frank, that he has always shown quite the right idea of the form on tour – but I am possibly being hyper-critical.

I note your fury when I say that Lord's is not always very keen to have my criticism about touring affairs. I am unrepentant. I do not mean you – but I cannot forget that no-one wanted to hear anything I had to say about West Indies. It was apparently more palatable to swallow Palmer's version – with the result that very few people (i.e. only one or two who believed what I told them!) knew the truth about our performance.

Just off to the play, in some apprehension (27th, a.m.) Will you please, and very kindly, make sure that Gubby sees this letter, as I wrote

to him briefly from Pretoria before I knew about Mr. Tayfield's
performance.

Yours, as ever . . .

G.O. 'Gubby' Allen was Jim's soulmate. Nobody was more attuned to
the thinking at cricket's HQ where he was a sort of *eminence grise*.

My dear Gubby,

You will not, I hope, have thought it too unfriendly that I haven't
written thus far. But I've known you were pretty well briefed and from
all points of view I was determined not to write back anything of a
critical kind about the management – which rather precludes gossip
about the team and the tour. I'm not departing from that now – but in
view of this evening's box-up, following the field row on Saturday, I
thought a comment or two amplifying what will have appeared in
tomorrow's D.T. might be timely.

Frankly there's nothing to tell you to lighten the general picture
except that Peter seems in remarkable order considering what's gone on.
I've just talked to him on the 'Phone, and he said 'to think I thought I'd
have a rest.' What has come over Doug I can't say, but he is certainly
very lucky that (as far as I know) it hasn't appeared in print that it was
his Anglo-Saxon invective that provoked McGlew's complaint. Fancy a
manager having to apologise for his vice-captain – and what price the
authority now of the latter with someone like Lock who was talking out
of turn and in the vernacular when bowling in the first innings.

Frankly without going into personalities further I think Peter
deserves a great deal better advice than is available to him . . .

I hear word from my father that you agreed with all I wrote on this:
he may have got this wrong, of course, as he sometimes does, but that
was the message in his last letter. I hope even now you may send an
extra body, even though he can hardly be available for Newlands.
There's no margin whatever now – and neither Insole nor Oakman look
like Test batsmen. Nor has Taylor shown any form – in the Test sense,
in either direction.

You will probably have deduced by now that I feel your presence
could do a lot in several directions, but particularly as a source of
strength to Peter. I have found him 100% delightful, and when just a
few times (for instance on the matter of the additional batter) I've given
my view unasked he has been as nice and apparently appreciative as
could be. But I can't help him much, except by giving him a pat on the
back whenever possible – especially as Freddie would very quickly

notice and resent any such thing. If Billy's common-sense and instinct were on the spot all would be different.

Peter told me this evening he is going to dine à deux with Jackie McG during the Natal match, and I hope they may straighten out a few things. I like and trust McG, and as he said yesterday when talking about the on-field happenings of Saturday he has a great admiration for Peter.

'The lads had taken umbrage,' Doug Insole told me recently. 'Peter May and Colin Cowdrey and many of the rest had decided that they didn't want anything to do with Jim. You see, he had written to the effect that anyone of any intelligence would have altered his batting method long before then. The result of it was that Jim, who always liked to get the views of the captain or vice-captain before the game – like how was the wicket going to play, or what sort of side were they going to pick – was unable to do so. That effort on his part was laudable really, but he was always lurking around shortly after the toss. Of course now he was cut off – a bit draconian really. Strangely enough, during the tour he had actually had an operation for a cartilage in Johannesburg and I was the only one of the team who went to see him. It all wore off in the end and a few years later I wrote a book and in it I gave him a bit of stick. He was rather hurt and said "You've got your revenge," but I said, "No, I don't need to have revenge." Eventually, of course, we got on very well. I became a selector and got to know him a lot better. And after he got married he was a much more rounded person. It's water under the bridge really.'

In May 1956, some six months or so before the South African tour had taken place, Jim, flushed with the success of his own international side's recent tour of the West Indies, had sent an essay to his friend Viscount Cobham, who in 1954 had been President of MCC.

17 Loudoun Road
London N.W.8
12th May 1956

The Viscount Cobham,
Hagley Hall,
near Stourbridge.

My dear Charles
I feel moved to unburden myself of some thoughts on the future of MCC tours with special reference to their management, and I hope you

will forgive my selecting you as the recipient. If you think the following has any value by all means let anyone see it whom you think fit. I have written frankly about people, but not, I hope, unfairly. At all events I feel the good name of MCC is more important than individual considerations.

If the history of recent MCC tours is examined with the object of avoiding past calamities and mistakes I have at least some claim to be listened to, for I have accompanied the last seven major tours beginning in 1938, three to Australia, two to South Africa and West Indies; all in fact except those to India and Pakistan. No-one else has done that.

Looking back, one sees everyone setting off each time with high hopes, and being received with fair words; but promise has generally fallen woefully short of reality, and most of the tours can only be described as disappointing, either from the playing angle or the angle of social contact or both. I would say the chief reason was that there was not nearly sufficient strength at the top, taking the captaincy and management together, nor, in several instances, a proper realisation of the issues involved.

Going back to 1938 in South Africa we had a combination of Hammond and Jack Holmes. I needn't go into Wally's obvious limitations, and perhaps in theory it was fair to hope that his manager would give a gloss to the party which it might otherwise lack. As it turned out Jack counted for pretty little beside a much stronger personality, and the personal popularity of people like Bryan Valentine, Norman Yardley, etc. had to make up for the fact that Wally did not go down at all with the South Africans, and only with certain of his own side.

Knowing of his form on this tour I fervently hoped MCC would appoint a strong character to go with Hammond to Australia in 1946/7. Yet they sent Rupert Howard, who had been perfectly satisfactory as a sort of secretary to Gubby ten years earlier.

As you may know, captain and manager toured round Australia in Wally's Jaguar, and the rest tagged along under the guidance of 'Fergie'. It was heart-breaking to see morale, which had started so high when we sailed, sink into a general state of disillusionment. You can still detect the cynical influence of Hammond reflected in a few of the players today.

Next we had MCC in West Indies (1947/8), when Gubby faced a tougher proposition than anyone could quite envisage in advance, and injuries finally almost broke the tour. Billy Griffith did a notable service as player-manager, and helped hold the players together in a way the captain could probably not have done on his own because he really belonged to a different generation. Between them, one might say, they made the very best of a bad job.

South Africa in 1948/9 was a happy and successful tour, run in a different spirit from anything since. The combination, you will remember, was George Mann and Mike Green, but it was George and Billy (as vice-captain) who really ran the show.

In 1950/1 in Australia Freddie Brown had two managers, Messrs. Green and Nash, the former more or less covering public relations, the latter admin. John Nash performed efficiently enough, but Mike cut little ice in Australia, certainly not with our players, and least of all with the Press. The point here is that the captain, even after the experience in Australia in 1946/7, was merely presented with the appointments. He had no say at all – though he was obviously in for a pretty rough ride one way and another. The Australians had much respect for Freddie, whom I should rank as distinctly the most popular English figure in the three post-war tours there. The relations between the sides on this tour were more friendly than before or since (post-war).

Next West Indies in 1953/4. Len Hutton was presumably an automatic choice as captain. I happen to know whom he wanted as manager because I was asked by the Treasurer to sound him confidentially – since I was going North just before the thing was coming up. Len said 'Griffith' unequivocally.

My belief is that Hutton was quite aware of his own limitations, and wanted a proved success as a diplomat and disciplinarian, whom he had seen on the job on two previous tours. MCC sent Charles Palmer who made scarcely the slightest impact either on Len, or on the side, or on the West Indians. The result was a diplomatic and sporting disaster of the first magnitude which, I am quite sure, could have been averted by the right man.

Even after the West Indies tour MCC, for Australia in 1954/5, persevered with the policy of appointing as Hutton's manager a county secretary whose function was more or less subsidiary. Geoffrey Howard did perfectly adequately – within the old limitations of a manager's job.

My conviction is that in these seven tours between 1938 and 1955 only in South Africa in 1948/9 did the MCC team reach their full potential on the field and acquit themselves creditably off it. Even they lost a few marks by comparison with the Australians in South Africa the following winter. Hassett and Dwyer were much the best captain-manager combination I have ever struck.

The problem of social contact is a ticklish one for various reasons. The 'old sweats' are inclined to expect everything to be laid on for them, and to take all hospitality for granted, as though it was they who were conferring the favour by appearing: not all of them, but most. The players are inclined to grumble if too many parties are laid on, and to complain when they have nothing to do. Many of the Northerners are naturally reticent and not 'easy' – compared, say, with the Australians and South Africans. Only a manager with authority, for whom the players have respect (and perhaps some awe), can handle this side of things.

He must first, nowadays, combat the Hutton–Bailey philosophy whereby the other people are disparaged and belittled from some muddled notion of tactics or gamesmanship. In West Indies Len from the start of the tour was saying: 'these black —— don't like us.' Leaving out the word 'black' he said the same in Australia.

I soon had first-hand evidence in West Indies that the younger players had been 'indoctrinated' against fraternising with the West Indians. It may seem too childish to credit, but it is perfectly true.

In short the manners in West Indies were shocking. As you know the West Indian umpires, in three out of the four Test centres, complained about behaviour on the field. It was consistently embarrassing off the field. Here is one example among many. At a dance after the first day's play in Granada a coloured woman, a doctor who had taken her degrees in England, said to Crawford White: 'Please don't bring any more English sides out here unless you can bring nicer men.'

It transpired she was in charge of the meal arrangements for the teams, including getting volunteers to serve. She said she could have got any number before the match, but she was having to beg her helpers to continue on the second day as the MCC were so rude and unappreciative. Not all: she named as exceptions just the ones you would expect.

It was at a private dinner party at the plantation house of Jeffrey Stollmeyer's father that I heard an English Stollmeyer daughter-in-law, provoked by some deplorable remarks by —— [*a member of the touring party*], say: 'I can only think you do not realise the harm you are doing to our cause over here.' When —— answered 'I can only say I never want to come and play in West Indies again', —— [*another member of the party*] in my presence agreed with him. This while receiving hospitality from the father of the West Indies captain.

Ian Johnson heard this story when he was in West Indies last year, and he tells me —— was concerned in a similar sort of scene in Australia.

The Australians are not so sensitive as the West Indians, nor was the 1954/5 tour marked by the ructions of West Indies a year earlier. But the team, with exceptions such as Alec Bedser and Colin Cowdrey, remained generally aloof. You probably heard of Peter May's remark to

Gubby, at least semi-serious: 'Is there such a thing as a nice Australian?'

At the end of the tour I said to Colin Cowdrey I had scarcely heard any of the side say anything complimentary about Australia or Australians. He said something to the effect that he liked them well enough, and had made a lot of friends – but that he would think twice before saying so in the dressing-room.

This remark fits well with the equally true story told me by an Australian player who took one of the MCC side to lunch and for a game of squash, and was asked afterwards not to say anything about it because Len was all against their fraternising.

After the last day's play of the Fifth Test Johnson, Miller, and Hutton were taken to a broadcasting studio where each made an appeal for the N.S.W. Flood Relief Fund. Len said the conventionally polite things about Australian hospitality; but when the broadcast was over he told the captains of Australia and New South Wales what he really thought of it, and was, I believe, extremely uncomplimentary. They made light of the situation, which could obviously have had embarrassing repercussions. But they have not forgotten it.

Hutton nursed this peculiar complex, and encouraged others to think the same way, including our prospective captain in South Africa.

I must take the risk of your thinking it somewhat petty to 'gossip' in this way. But illustrations such as this may help to give you the picture. At any rate it is all thoroughly authentic, and I am perfectly happy to be cross-questioned on anything I have written.

So much for a view of things which if it is a fair picture, as I believe, surely demands that MCC look into the question of control of touring sides before making the appointments for South Africa. If the Pakistan business, which I know about only at second-hand, has this result some good may come out of evil.

There are a lot of people concerned, at Lord's, who have never been on a tour abroad, and who therefore cannot really visualise the situation. Some of them perhaps are happy to accept the reports of captain and manager as gospel, and leave it at that. There may be more evidence at hand after tours than I know about. I assume the Colonial Office might have supplied some data about West Indies.

At all events I had the feeling that as soon as it was known I was critical of the team no-one seemed very interested in my opinions. Although I was the only member of the Club on the tour outside the team my evidence was not asked for. (Yet George Duckworth's apparently was, on the Pakistan business.)

There are several reasons why, as it seems to me, MCC cannot continue to pick the sort of manager who has recently functioned more or less as a secretary: an administrative fellow from the counties.

Firstly the players themselves have got to be made to see their full responsibilities on these tours, and that can only be done by having someone as manager who himself both realises what is at stake and has the authority to keep everyone up to the mark, including, if necessary, the captain.

In the 'old days' the problem was much simpler. The professional had a sense of discipline, and, normally, of respect for the amateur: at any rate he was in some awe of the captain. Now all is different. Everyone considers himself as good as everyone else, and amateur and pro. are often more or less indistinguishable. With so many easy-going amateurs and elderly pros. (wanting chiefly a comfortable time) as county captains the sense of leadership and direction has been largely lost from our cricket. A man like Surridge is considered something of a freak.

I believe the average young pro. today is an admirable fellow – so long as he is led sensibly and firmly. Whoever captains England today needs at his side a manager who can help him run the show.

Secondly, wherever MCC tour nowadays it is preferable to have someone of sufficient prestige to be able to speak for the Club, and, if needful, to make sure the team get a fair deal, in all respects.

Thirdly, the manager should be someone at ease with the Press who is sympathetic to their problems, and able to take this particular load off the captain's back.

I can imagine you saying: 'is such a paragon to be found?' or even: 'are these tours so difficult as not to be worth while?' Well, MCC are committed to them, anyway. Personally I am sure they have as great a potentiality for good as for ill, and that they can be run without risk of friction or disorder by the right person. Preferably he should be a cricketer, and of a generation not too far removed from the players. Anyone with a tinge of the 'Blimp' would not do.

Before the Australian tour I told you I could see three 'ace' possibilities: Griffith, Mann, and yourself. I believe neither you or George could consider it. There was still Billy, who has a unique popularity with overseas cricketers and officials, and who has the admiration of our own players.

Personally I believe the best answer lies in a rearrangement of duties at Lord's which would release him for these tours. It is a matter surely of priorities. Nothing is so important to the prestige of MCC. After West Indies, and Pakistan (where, from all I have heard, the manager cannot be entirely absolved), we simply cannot afford another flop. It might be possible among the MCC membership to find someone suitable who was able, in return for the right fee, to leave his job for six months. But there could be no question of taking a chance with anyone short of the highest credentials.

One last word – and I'm afraid all this has run to a great length. Do not think I suspect Peter May's ability to make a success in South Africa. That is not so. I like and admire him, and I think fundamentally he is sound enough, and strong enough. But the environment of two tours under the influences I have mentioned has had its effect. He is not at present as gracious-minded as one would like to see an England captain abroad. Anyone chosen as a touring captain nowadays needs a strong right-hand man: he especially in view of all that has recently occurred.

Yours ever,
    Jim

My dear Jim,

I quite agree, and indeed I think that the more people on the MCC Committee who see your letter, the better, and anyway I am sure that the Chairman of the Selectors ought to have it.

I think that it will do nothing but good, if only because it will shake up those who pooh-pooh all such reports from overseas, and insist upon maintaining that everything in the garden is lovely, and if it is not it is the fault of the other side.

I went to Worcester a couple of days ago, and had a long talk with Peter Richardson – an exceptionally nice boy by the way, and one who is determined to 'fraternise' to the best of his ability, which is considerable. But, my dear Jim, what a state of affairs when a word like this should have to be mentioned about our guests from Australia!

I remember Stanley Jackson telling me how in the old days he always started a match by walking into the Australian dressing room and pulling Hughie Trumble's leg, and asking him what 'that damned old scoundrel Trumble has got in store for us today'.

Peter Richardson entertained the Australian side in their dressing room during the match, and I think that the Australians enjoyed it, but he was a little saddened by a remark of Ray Lindwall's as he left the dressing room – 'Oh, well, we shall remember with gratitude another side who will talk to us. After 7th June, there is not much fraternisation', or words to that effect. This has simply got to be stopped. It really is too childish to think that you can only play cricket successfully by hating the opposition.

Yours ever,
    Charles

In August of the same year Jim played a variation on his theme in a personal letter to the England captain, Peter May:

Old Trafford. Wet!
My dear Peter,
   I'm taking the chance of the usual Old Trafford scene to expand a bit on what we were talking about in t'Board Room here at the Test, and, as you were good enough to say you could bear a general comment or two, to stick down what comes into my mind about South Africa. A bit about some of the characters as well – for your ear and eye, and knowing we both have at heart only one thing, the success of the tour in all its aspects.
   My feeling, as I tried to elaborate the other day, is that all the post-war MCC tours have suffered, more or less, from the same weakness – a lack of sufficient weight and strength at the top, taking captain, vice, and manager together. I'm sure that nowadays the captain wants not only a tough manager to keep the press and other people at arm's length on occasions, and to help him enforce discipline in the side. He also wants, it seems to me, a friend as vice-captain whom he can turn to for help, and whom he can turn the side over to with confidence if he wants to take a few days right off. I don't think it essential that such a chap should necessarily be a certain starter for the Tests at all. Both Doug and J.J. [*J.J. Warr*] appeal to me as strong personalities who would back you up 100%, keep anyone in his place who needed it (? Messrs Evans and Bailey), and incidentally inject some much-needed humour into the proceedings – when you pull up at dawn at some dorp and have to cope with an Afrikaner mayor, or – well, you can think of any number of situations when the right word means everything.
   My first pick would be J.J. because I think, rightly or wrongly, that he's just about the sanest and shrewdest and nicest chap in cricket – present company of course excepted. Incidentally I am writing in the dark as to whether he's available. I believe the marriage is imminent: but I'm plumb sure he'd jump at it if he could. Perhaps it might accelerate things!
   Assuming Doug can't go the alternatives, I suppose, are Washbrook, Cowdrey, and Bailey. As to Cyril I've always thought him an excellent chap, but my goodness he's not a very clever captain, is he? Also of course it doesn't advance English cricket any from the batting view-point if he goes. At least six years ago he got into all the tangles in the world coping with Ram and Val. Presumably you don't want Cyril and Denis, and if Bill Tucker still holds the opinion he expressed early in the

spring Denis needs warmth and bathing for 'the knee', and if he gets it he ought to be much stronger and more mobile next year than this. I would have thought that after a South African summer, giving him a reasonable amount of rest, he would have been the best spec for keeping the W.I. spinners at arm's length next year. Presumably you might want to make the party 17 if Denis goes, but if it were put to the South Africans I'm sure they would agree he'd pay for the extra keep several times over in the 'gate'.

There's no better person than Colin, and from many points of view he'd be a very good understudy, but my impression is he doesn't rush for responsibility, at any rate for the moment: also he can be extremely diffident at asserting himself with people his senior – as many would be. I would rather him than Trevor. Indeed I suppose Bailey's general outlook (though it may have mellowed a bit) and his record puts him out of the hunt. If I may say so it looks to me as though you've kept him in the picture very well this summer, and if I were you I'd certainly want his brains on a selection committee.

Thus one comes back to old Warr. Of course he's not an ace performer, but he'd flog himself to death in the lesser matches, and is quite good enough to get wickets outside the Tests. You may or may not think it helps his case that although the choice of Warr as vice-captain would not stop part of the press deploring Trueman's omission (assuming that) it would at least give a fair reason for it. Otherwise he's plainly been found wanting for reasons other than cricket – especially if Moss is out of the hunt. As to Alan I rate him a top-class tourer – but you can judge yourself from West Indies.

Looking at the general picture if this tour is like all previous ones to South Africa getting runs will be easier than getting them out. No-one, of course, knows how the Johannesburg wicket will play because it's only just been laid – and there are two Tests there. But generally speaking the wickets are terribly easy. However, though things are probably a bit better now, they aren't great stroke-makers, apart from the odd fellow: e.g. McLean. In other words they have to be winkled out. That means someone using the air. Also of course you want wrist spin if you can get it. I've seen Greenhough up here only bowl a few overs on dead wickets. He certainly spins it. He seems an extremely pleasant young man, like most if not all the Lancashire side. For the air who is there but Wardle? I wish I could suggest an alternative.

I imagine you may be a bit dubious about Tony Lock's success. He wants to knock the stumps down six times an over, and in West Indies seemed still under the impression at the end that he could pitch on the leg-and-middle and hit the off. But if you don't take him to Africa how can you know whether he'd be any use in Australia next time? I think, by the way, that Alan Oakman could be coached to do a useful job outside the off stump, making them fetch it, as a fifth bowler, if he quickened up a shade, and really got down to practice.

Well, I've imposed rather a lot. But it was difficult to talk freely at Old Trafford, and I did want to make a case for John because it occurred to me that most of the selectors might not be looking far beyond the people who have played for England this summer, and this tour seems a different operation altogether.

I dare say we may not meet before the Oval Test: if not all good luck therein. We must make it three, preferably on a good wicket all through. Personally I rather hope you do without Denis, partly because he's a liability at the moment in the field, and also because on what I've seen he's now hard to run with in a different way: I mean everyone stands ten yards deeper, knowing neither he nor his partner can take the average single – which makes it very hard to keep the score moving, especially with someone like Peter Richardson at the other end.

However I see the temptation. It would be a great coup if it came off – and the selectors apparently can't go wrong! I prefer to see him ending up against Australia not out when the rubber was won, at the Oval and Adelaide.

Yours ever,
Jim

In retrospect, the undeniable influence of Swanton in matters which were not directly his concern is nothing short of amazing. He had, in effect, become a self-assigned custodian of cricket's virtues. Behind it all, though, one can see an ambition that was secretly rampant, though perhaps one should omit the adjective.

Around this time, when all these machinations from the Master were taking place, a letter was sent to the Editor of the *Daily Telegraph*; not a few would have agreed with the sentiments expressed therein:

Dear Sir,
    Don't you think that the time has arrived for your cricket correspondent to be quietly disposed of, stuffed, and placed in the Long Room with the curved bats, the sparrow, and the other freaks of the noble game?

Chapter 8

Marriage maketh the man

While surveying Swanton's public utterance and professional life, it would be easy to neglect his filiation and friendships.

Since Jim's father was widowed in 1953 he had not enjoyed the best of health. William Swanton suffered from a respiratory condition which led to emphysema, and a physiotherapist had been engaged to help him cope. In the fullness of time the engagement to help became an engagement to be married and so Jim's father moved in to join his bride at her flat, at 26 Iverna Gardens, Kensington, which is situated just behind what was the Army and Navy Stores in the High Street. The new Mrs William Swanton, née Helen Baker, had been born in 1908 and therefore was about a year younger than Jim who, of course, was now her stepson. Helen was the second of four sisters in a family that had moved to the West Country from Tynemouth. Her mother was illegitimate, the result of a liaison between a Danish sailmaker and a serving maid, and in the best traditions of Victorian novelettes 'had been adopted by a lady in the big house'. Given the circumstances of her upbringing it was not surprising that her mother, who was called Margaret, tended, in old-fashioned phraseology, to 'flirt a fan', and her behaviour impacted on her daughters, particularly Helen, though in a contrary way. Whereas Margaret, invariably dressed in navy and white with spotted scarf and pearl hatpin, would drop the *manière* by lounging in an armchair smoking Craven A and reading the *Daily Sketch*, Helen never did.

'Helen used to dress a little tweedily, but with Kensington flair,' remarked sometime acupuncturist, yoga teacher and writer, Mary Horsley, who was her niece. 'She had been an archetypal spinster, and was always very formal and rather snooty. Everything had to be perfect and my brothers and I, who were young children, were a bit of an inconvenience when we visited. I don't think our manners came up to scratch. You had to psyche yourself up to go and see her, because she was so prim and proper. She had a dog's bottom mouth with a pouting lower lip and she was full of affectation. You know, the sort of English women who practise "prune" and "prism" to get the right sound. God knows how she managed to afford that flat in Kensington, because she didn't have a great deal of money.

'Uncle William was a sweet old man, soft and gentle and also generous. I really liked him. He was always pretty poorly with this chestiness and Aunt Helen – it was always Aunt, never Auntie – would have to thump him on the back, because he was awash with phlegm. He was a bit of an invalid, really. The family feeling is that the marriage was a disappointment to her. She had expectations after having been wined and dined by what she thought was a fairly rich man and was deeply shocked shortly after they had married to find that there wasn't much money after all. Any money William had he spent on wining and dining Helen. She had always kept herself rather separate and now she was landed with this old man in his late seventies who wasn't in the best of health.'

Mary Horsley's elder brother Michael was a town planner. His remembrance of Helen and William is a little different. 'I thought they were good together, although basically she was not the marrying kind. As I understand it, he wanted to share a bed, but she wasn't having it.'

With the physio side of the therapy obviously having certain limitations, Jim's father and stepmother were eventually to leave Kensington and move to a cottage at Upper Welland, in the shadow of the Malvern Hills in Worcestershire. There Helen busied herself with local art, music and history societies while William still made the occasional visit to his old offices in London which were at 2 Copthall Buildings, Throgmorton Street, in the City. Soon after returning to Britain from his imprisonment by the Japanese, Jim had used this office as a postal address while recuperating.

Jim often referred to 'Papa', as he called him, as 'The Father of the Stock Exchange' and in one sense that was probably true. There were elected members with greater longevity, but as far as sheer service went, from the age of fourteen as not much more than a tea-boy to well into his eighties as a partner, few could have out-distanced William. Throughout that time he worked for the one firm, William Norton & Co., whose telegram address was 'Teacup Stock, London', which does not leave much need for erudition when deciding where lay the concentration of their shares.

On the eve of the First World War there were around 1000 firms and 4000 to 5000 members on the Stock Exchange. William Swanton was elected in 1919 and would have acted as a broker, being an intermediary between the client and the quick-witted jobbers on the Floor. His sedate journey from office dogsbody to clerk to senior clerk to broker to partner was as predictable as it was long. David Kynaston, who has recently written a deservedly lauded multi-volume history of the City, outlined several alternative methods by which a partnership in a stock and share brokers could be obtained:

> First of all there is the blood route, father to son or close family relative; then by bringing in money to bolster the firm's collateral; another way is with connections to individuals or institutions which provide the chance of regular business; much rarer is to have the brain power which is an asset in itself; and then every so often somebody who has been hard-working, reliable, hasn't speculated wildly, made sure the clients have paid their dues on time and who is decent company and a good chap, is invited to become a partner. If he doesn't bring in much money, obviously he will not get a big percentage of any profits, but in a way, it's a reward for long service and loyalty.

It is not hard to see into which category William Swanton would fit. Never overloaded with funds and always renting rather than buying properties in which his family would live, the nervous breakdown he suffered in the 1930s was almost certainly brought on by financial pressures. Not even his recognised skill and speed with figures (he was inordinately proud of having won the Maths competition in Catford in the 1930s) could offset that.

His end was not unexpected. Emphysema and heavy smoking have an unwelcome relationship. The death certificate produced on 21 January 1966 at Malvern General Hospital gave compounding causes: coronary thrombosis, atherosclerosis, hypertension, cerebral thrombosis. In naming so much contributing causality no doubt the doctor reasoned there was a chance of getting at least one right. William Swanton had passed his eighty-seventh birthday by three days. His wife Helen survived until 1995 when she died at virtually the same age.

In his will William left just over £3000, including small pecuniary legacies to ten relatives. He also bequeathed '(free of duty) to my son

Ernest William Swanton my gold watch, my platinum chain and my gold matchbox.' To his wife Helen he left solely, 'my gold cigarette case'. One wonders, was that an irrisive rejoinder to her nagging him about his nicotine habit? To Jim, his father had been 'a marvellous chap in his way, but he wasn't distinguished. I owe to him my love of cricket – he had very bad eyesight and therefore he was no good himself, but he taught me to play.' The importance Jim seems to attach to the fact that his father was not distinguished is telling.

When it came to Jim's own personal life, his predilection for the male form (there is nothing sinister or inferential about that comment), as evidenced in his continued interest and championing of the gilded youth of Oxbridge, had not hindered a great deal of discreet heterosexual relationship. Jim's correspondence files are laced with missives from the Lornas, Julies, Marys, Marions, Marjories, Paulines, Valeries, Elizabeths and Bettys of his acquaintance. As they are invariably addressed to 'My dear Jim', he obviously inspired affection. One letter though, went straight to the point:

> You may remember you asked me to the theatre. Well, Mr Swanton, cricket means far more to me than the stage, and since I started playing cricket seven years ago – that makes me sound very old – I have had two great ambitions; one is to go inside Lord's Pavilion and I have tried several times to get a ticket for a Test, but so far have been unsuccessful. I expect you can guess what's coming!

The lady never did disclose what her other ambition was, but as for Jim it seemed he never could get away from the game.

Among all these burgeoning bonds, however, there was one relationship that seemed especially close.

Born in Stanmore, Jacqueline Gordon was one of the leading lady amateur golfers of her day. She had played in the Curtis Cup against the USA in 1948 and also against France, Ireland and Wales. She had also either won or been runner-up in a great many tournaments. The German Ladies Championship in 1956 led to a letter from Frankfurt:

> My dear Jim,
>   A line to tell you how I'm getting along over here . . . The golf course is very long, stock par is 76 . . . I was very pleased to reach the final, winning 8/6 in the first round, 5/4 over the German No. 2 lady, 5/4 over the Belgian Champion, and 2/1 over Angela Ward.
>   The final yesterday was played in very hot sun, strong wind, and on a

rain-soaked course. Bridget Jackson went round in 74 in the morning, I was 80 (with a 6 at a par 4) – in the afternoon I was 1 over par for the eleven holes and 2 more down!! A rough day, 5 over par for 29 holes and beaten 8/7! She had 5 birdies running in the morning, so I lost them all, to my own bogeys – she had four 2's! Obviously not my lucky day. However, I feel I've justified my existence, by beating three internationals running. I know I'm destined to be a runner-up always, this is my 6th silver medal! The Girls, the British, the English, and two French!

I haven't seen an English paper since I left, how is the cricket going?

We fly to Copenhagen on Monday, do drop me a line there – at the 'Belle Vue Hotel, Ringsted, Denmark'. No hospitality given up there, a pity.

I'll be home on the 27th, so will give you a ring about Lord's. Hope you are well.

Love from Jacqueline

That Jacqueline Gordon had stirred deep feelings in Jim's bachelor breast is confirmed in an epistle from his idiosyncratic, quixotic golfing friend Leonard Crawley – the man who had dubbed him 'Lord Sockem'. On this occasion, Crawley uses his other moniker for E.W.S.:

Mr dear Lord Cowson,

I was very much touched, that you took me entirely into your confidence the other evening to discuss with you, most private affairs.

But, we are great friends and – like me – you know the value of friendship.

Elspeth and I talked for a long time about you and Jacqueline and we want you to know that if you decide to marry her, we shall do everything in our power to make your marriage the greatest possible success.

We both hope and pray that you will do nothing in a hurry for many good reasons.

You have become a prominent figure with your journalism and broadcasting and at your age and with your considerable charm of manner you must be a more than eligible bachelor.

J, poor girl, as I explained the other evening, has had a lot of bad luck from time to time and it is no use mincing matters, she has made herself very unpopular, and she also, do not forget, is a public figure.

Think very, very hard about it old fellow, for no-one can afford to marry the wrong person, particularly when they have the type of life that you do.

> But do remember – once more I must stress it – that if you marry her,
> we shall pray for your happiness and remain your staunch supporters
> and friends.
>   All good wishes,
>   From,
>   Leonard

Make what you will of that, dear reader – there appear to be many
swirling undercurrents. According to one of the foremost players of
her day, Maureen Garrett, who played with and against Jacqueline
Gordon many times, Crawley's comment regarding her lack of
popularity can be explained by her tactlessness: 'She was her own
worst enemy. She would make stupid remarks. She once said to me, "I
can't play with anybody that wears a beret". She thought she was
superior.' Oh, dear, that sounds familiar. Now, where have we met her
male equivalent . . .?

For whatever reason matching like with like did not lead to love
and Jim's indecision seemed to be final. Sadly, Jacqueline Gordon was
destined to die of cancer relatively young in the early 1970s.

In an interview with Naim Attalloh for *The Oldie* in 1997, Jim was
asked why he had not got married before 1958, when he was over
fifty. Had it been a case of just not getting round to it before then, or
what?

> Before the war I suppose I was having a very good time as a bachelor
> in London. I had a great liking for women, but I never really got near
> marriage before the war. After the war I had to struggle to make my
> place in the world again. I didn't have any money, and so I was really
> too busy on my career. The greatest bit of luck in my life was meeting
> Ann who became my wife.

It had all started at a Golf Foundation Ball at Grosvenor House in
Park Lane. Ann Carbutt, a highly attractive widow in her mid-forties,
was attending the Ball in a party of ten as a guest of Brigadier-General
A.C. Critchley. Critchley was not only a very good golfer, but also the
initiator of greyhound racing at White City in London. Ann, too, was
a very good golfer, playing at championship level with a four handicap
and having inherited her skill from her father, a celebrated golfer and
cricketer of pre-war days, Reymond Harvey de Montmorency.

De Montmorency (the family line went back to the Norman
Conquest) was born in Gondar, India, in 1871. A member of the Royal

and Ancient at St Andrews and Sunningdale among a host of clubs, he had played against the legendary Bobby Jones in the inaugural golf match between Great Britain and Ireland and USA at Hoylake in 1921. An Oxford blue for golf, cricket and rackets, he eventually became a housemaster at Eton. Among his feats was to capture the 6th hole at the Western Course, Gailes; the 4th and 13th at Sunningdale, the 4th at Rye; and the 3rd, 7th and 11th holes at Stoke Poges, each in one stroke. He played last in the Open Championships in 1930 in his fifty-ninth year.

Ann was the younger of de Montmorency's two daughters. Her brother, also called Reymond, and heir presumptive to the Montmorency baronetcy, became a regular RAF officer and was killed piloting a Blenheim in an early raid over Germany in 1940. Her first husband, George Henry Carbutt (they married in 1934), who as a midshipman had lost a leg in a wartime accident at Scapa Flow, was to become a chartered accountant. With Carbutt, Ann had two sons: Francis, known as Billy, and Edward Reymond, known as Eddie, who also were to become chartered accountants. She also brought up the daughters of Carbutt's first marriage: Diana, who became the wife of the distinguished violinist Manoug Parikian, and Sue, Mrs Peter Guinness. Carbutt died in 1956.

Ann went to school at North Foreland in Thanet where she showed considerable musical ability as a sensitive exponent of the keyboard, before proceeding in due course to the Royal College of Music. There she rather dismayed the purists with her liking for jazz and what was dismissively called 'light music'. She became a devotee of Carroll Gibbons and of the music of George Gershwin, and during the war with the singer Helga Mott played in London at regular concerts for servicemen, especially Americans wounded and on leave. As if that were not enough, Ann had a list of compositions to her credit including a 'Rhapsody for Piano and Orchestra'; specially commissioned music to the Diana Wynyard/Godfrey Tearle 1948 production of *Othello* at Stratford for the Royal Shakespeare Company; and published popular songs such as 'Sometimes I Think of Spring' which was featured in broadcasts by Geraldo and his Orchestra.

Of all this, of course, Jim was totally unaware – his own musical tastes were largely underdeveloped and confined to Gilbert and Sullivan and the *English Hymnal*. He had first seen Ann when together with J.S.F. Morrison she had won the Central England Mixed Foursomes at Woodhall Spa in the 1930s. From a distance he had admired her stylish weatherproof golf trousers and during a later round her unconventional mackintosh skirt. He had noticed her again in the mid-1950s, when she was runner-up to Wanda Morgan in the Kent Ladies' Championships.

Anyway, as the Ball drew to a close Ann helped her host Critchley, who was blind, into the foyer of the hotel and towards the door in search of a cab. She too was intending to leave as she had not totally recovered from a recent bout of flu. Suddenly Jim materialised, seemingly from nowhere – he had, in fact, been in the bar area with golfing correspondent Henry Longhurst with whom he had spent the entire evening – and led the way to Critch's taxi. At the same time he ordered Ann not to go and get her coat. When, naturally, she demurred, he told her to 'go straight back to the table'. Obviously Jim's required bedside reading had not included Dale Carnegie's famous treatise. Ann herself laughingly said to me that: 'He'd ignored me for the whole evening and I said to myself, "Shall I? Shan't I? Shall I? Shan't I?" And obviously if I'd stood my ground, gone and got my coat, I should never have seen him again, but I didn't and that's how it all began.'

The Golf Ball took place on 11 December 1957. One month later, on 11 January, Ann and Jim became engaged and then a month after that, on 11 February, Jim's fifty-first birthday, they married.

To say that the marriage had been a shock to Jim's friends and colleagues far and wide would verge on understatement. It had all happened so quickly – they had had no warning. Universally, Jim had been thought of as *ein gefleischter Junselle* (a not inappropriate phrase considering his part-German ancestry) – he who was intended to be single. The response to the news was immediate and widespread, both before and after the nuptials.

A typical letter came from Australian writer and journalist Ron Roberts, who was in Durban covering the Australian touring side's visits to South Africa:

Mr dear Jim,

I was delighted yesterday to receive your letter with the news of your marriage on February 11th; and is it not a case of your birthday, too? May I take this opportunity of wishing that you are both as happy as Maureen and I have been. As a recent runner in the matrimonial stakes, I thoroughly recommend the action. Life seems to have so much more purpose, even if at times it seems more hectic!

I wrote to Woodcock and suggested that Swanton, Bannister and

Roberts in one year was a notable treble, and wondered whether he and
the Bedsers would be capable of bringing off a similar coup in the
ensuing year . . .

In fact, Jim had had some fun with Alec and Eric Bedser not
long before, when trying to tempt them into a wager on who
would be married first. Now understanding why he had been
so eager to make the bet, they wrote to Jim offering their sincere
congratulations and best wishes for good health and happiness: 'We
shall look to you for advice on this "marriage business" and tell us
how it is done.'
Even 'old flames' were delighted for him:

My dear Jim,
   Do not answer this – it is merely to say that it is the most wonderful
thing you are marrying and I do hope you will be blissfully happy . . . It
is truly the only way to live and one will never be able to live long
enough. Somehow problems almost cease to exist, when one knows
beforehand that they will be halved when they arrive, and somehow it
does work like that. Any 'joy' is certainly doubled. Ann is a lucky
person . . .

Jim's old benefactor, the Revd Canon Frederic Hood, also got into the
act with a note from his new abode at Wesley Street, London W1:

Mr dear Jim,
   I am delighted to read my *Times*.
   Is it your Australian widow?
   Anyhow, my best congratulations. Could I creep in to the wedding?
   Love, Freddy

Finally, Jim's bank manager made his presence felt:

Dear Mr Swanton,
   Thank you for your letter of 16th May. First of all, let me
congratulate you on your marriage, – far more important to you, I am
sure, than red figures at the Bank or even perhaps cricket! May I wish
you every happiness.
   Having been in Fleet Street now for over six years, I am quite used to
seeing this continual struggle between red and black, and my
forbearance has been due to the knowledge that the BBC provides a

'long-stop' around this time each year. May I express the pious hope
that the ball won't ever reach the red boundary. Having been married
thirty years myself I can appreciate that this colour struggle is now
going to be even more heavily weighted against the more sombre hue.

With kind regards . . .

Shortly before Jim took his marriage vows, he had become concerned
about the financial implications of his new responsibilities. A letter to
his boss at the *Telegraph* reveals the state of his mind:

My dear Frank,

What I wanted to talk about, if you had been able to come last
Friday, was this idea which has been turning over in my mind before the
immediate affair of my engagement, though the latter makes it more
urgent.

Do you think you could bear me as Deputy Sports Editor, working
with you much as we do now where matters of policy and coverage are
concerned, but giving me a bigger share of the responsibility, especially
at such times as you did not feel in good enough form to control things
on first hand.

As you will see from the attached letter to Lord Burnham I should
like to justify a salary increase, and feel this is a way that might appeal
to the management if it was agreeable to you.

After more than 30 years of reporting (apart from the war period)
I've rather lost my zeal for all but the big stuff, and you've been very
understanding in allowing me to shape the cricket and rugger
programmes, and give plenty of the good games to Melford, Marlar,
Roberts etc.

Now that I'm to be married I certainly won't want to do more
reporting, perhaps even a little less if I can make up for it by writing
more Commentary pieces and, if you like this notion, of helping you
with the expanding admin. of the sports pages. (I realise, of course, that
I shall be wanted for the major tours and am naturally happy to do
them, at any rate if I can manage to take Ann too.).

You don't get any younger and neither do I – 51 next month – but
there's no-one with anything like our experience, yours, of course, much
longer than mine. I feel we might carry on a happy and profitable
partnership for a long time.

Apart from days when you were off and I was on, I visualise a
weekly morning meeting to plan ahead and exchange ideas for stories
and articles. To my mind we now have the best games pages in

London – but that's not to say that a lot of effort is not required to keep up the standard – and indeed perhaps to improve it.

Incidentally, it's not perhaps a great point in making the decision but if you decide on shifting to Kensington Close (which has a lot of merits as a place, by the way) we should be pretty close, as I think it's highly probable that I shall move to Ann's flat in South Kensington.

I don't know when his Lordship will want to see us, but could we have a talk some time before the end of the week, either here or at the Russell, whichever suited you.

I'm sure the days are long past when you might have supposed I was trying to 'muscle in' to your detriment. I hope I don't need to add that is very far from the truth: in fact the complete opposite, because although I naturally like the prospect from my own point of view I do also feel I can relieve you of a certain amount of strain and worry.

At any rate, my dear Frank, that is what I would hope to do.

Believe me

    Yours very sincerely . . .

Surely this was one of those offers that could not have been refused, and yet Coles obviously found it comparatively easy to do so.

Many have speculated that Jim's marriage to Ann was one of convenience. Here he was in his fifties without a recognised partner. In the circles in which he moved such singularity could have been thought to be a serious obstacle for someone such as he who had social aspirations. And so, went the reasoning, he needed a homemaker and a place to give and reciprocate hospitality: after all, marriage was a necessary asset.

There is no surviving evidence that Jim thought any of these things. With his father's second marriage having taken place shortly before, it is likely that he started concentrating on his own position perhaps in a way that he had not done previously, but certainly the marriage with Ann was founded on love and affection.

How can one be so sure? Certainly those who knew them over many years and saw the way they behaved together, need no convincing. But unassailable attestation of their love is seen in a letter from Ann to Jim not long after they became husband and wife.

Normally, even the natural foraging instinct of a biographer would shy away from displaying a missive so intimate. Yet this communication is of such sweet and tender sentiment, that it would be the greatest disservice to their memory not to do so:

My darling Jim,

You wrote me your first love-letter for my birthday, so I decided to write mine. It's not easy without being sentimental, which, I know, covers you with confusion, but for once, you must be confused.

It's extraordinary to think that although we've been married nearly 5 months, engaged for 2, we have never had to write to each other. When I think of the risk you took in marrying (for the first time) someone you had known for such a short time, someone you really knew so little – I blanch.

Was it that you had supreme confidence in yourself (as you have in most things) that you could make me happy or did you receive the telepathic message I put out from the start that I wanted to marry you.

I, for one, have not been disappointed in the way it has turned out – in fact, I would go as far as to say that I am astonished at my own peace of mind, my supreme happiness, my complete contentment and my desolation when we are parted.

Now what have I done for you? Goodness knows. Re-organised (maybe wrecked) your household, introduced a small proportion of femininity into your otherwise masculine existence, created a new hairstyle for you (which I may say, has been noticed on the telly from the Sandwich quarter), usurped your telephone, wasted your time in bed till 10 am, but on the whole, I think it would be admitted, I have made you a little less prim, less embarrassed at talking of matters which have hitherto been considered shocking, resulting in a more human, lighthearted, and to me, perfect man.

I hope when we've been married quite a time and our married life inevitably becomes humdrum, you will remember that I once did feel like this – I love you darling, so terribly and I always will . . .

There is general agreement that Ann made Jim a better man; mellowed is the word used universally. The spikiness in his nature, fuelled by his perfectionism, to a degree was smoothed out over many years. It certainly did not happen overnight. But he became a more rounded individual who enjoyed being nurtured by his wife. He also enjoyed and took pride in her accomplishments (such as the fact that she was the only person to have played piano duets with both Don Bradman and Noel Coward) and in her success with painting, which she took up after having ceased to play golf when she finally became disenchanted with Jim's swing.

After their marriage they had short spells in St John's Wood, at Melton Court in South Kensington and Ann's cottage, 'Two Trees', Bowling Street, in Sandwich, before becoming established at the nearly adjacent Delf House, where Ann used her skill in interior design in helping to renovate what had been a rather run-down lodging for homeless men. The property dates back to at least 1700 and is an integral part of the historic Cinque Port. Along the front of the house runs a moat, in fact a section of the Delf Stream, which functioned as the town's main water supply and sewerage for nearly 700 years up until the end of the nineteenth century.

Delf House and its ambience inextricably became part of Jim and Ann. The House was right for them and they were right for the House. Almost, it was as if it had always been theirs. As for the town, Sandwich is a surviving bastion of olde-worlde England, seemingly remote from inner-city callousness, and flush with evocatively named byways such as Knightrider Street and Holy Ghost Alley. It is from Sandwich that the Crusades left many centuries ago. Somehow, one feels that they should have waited for Swanton.

Chapter 9

The Reigning Chief Scribe

If Jim was supposed to have mellowed after marrying Ann, nobody had thought to tell the man himself. Letter after letter still spilled out of his questing mind, every one suggesting either this, or complaining about that, or more often than not trying to manipulate something else.

The words flowed from him with a kind of controlled messianic fervour. 'Jim absolutely loved dictating and sending letters,' laughed his old friend and fellow correspondent John Woodcock. 'A day would not be complete for him unless he had done so. He much enjoyed writing to all and sundry and stirring the pot. In a way, it was a hobby. For myself, although I did think of writing letters about many things over the years, in the end I mostly couldn't be bothered.' Bothered Jim nearly always was, about anything and everything to do with cricket and its component parts. And a lot of people to whom he wrote were bothered by what he had said – they felt he was meddlesome and, at times, intemperate. On many occasions it would have been better if he had adopted Woodcock's sensible approach and not been so keen to interfere. The impression left is of someone who could not bear to let events take their course without the benefit of his considered input, whether in public print, personal typescript or handwritten note. Often, though, an exchange of letters had been initiated by his correspondent. That redoubtable all-rounder Gerry Gomez, who was to become an influential figure in the administration of West Indian cricket, rivalled Swanton when it came to long-windedness in bulletins through the post. In November 1957, the recent tour of England by the West Indies during which May and Cowdrey had successfully employed pad-play to combat the wiles of Ramadhin and Valentine, obviously was very much in his mind:

My dear Jim,

There is one other feature regarding the Test Matches which I would like to offer as a basis of discussion and that is the tendency which has crept in amongst Test match batsmen (particularly Colin [*Cowdrey*]) to allow the ball to strike the front foot with unfailing regularity. This attitude springs mainly from the preconceived idea amongst 90% of umpires that in such circumstances the batsman is free from dismissal by the lbw rule. If these circumstances are applied to the normal county game which is played on wickets which invariably do a lot more, there is every justification for this outlook in umpires. I do feel, however, that on the better prepared surfaces which are made for Test Matches (and particularly in hard wicket countries like Australia, West Indies, South Africa and India) there is every justification for the bowler to have leg before decisions in his favour with the ball striking the front pad (that is of course if it satisfies all the normal requirements of the rule). I have done some personal experiment on concrete and I have found to my own satisfaction that a large number of balls pitched on or outside the off stump when intercepted by a pad thrust well forward actually hit the stumps. I think you will agree with me that quite a number of the wickets prepared in the majority of countries mentioned are very akin to concrete and I am taking steps to have the Umpires body in England go into this matter fully in order to reduce to some extent the virtually hard and fast rule which operates at the moment. Another feature of this matter is that it spoils the game of cricket and makes it rather unpleasant to watch. I do appreciate that on quickly turning wickets it is certainly one avenue of escape from conditions which are very much in favour of the bowler. The closing stages of the first Test Match was definitely a case in point in that the majority of balls bowled during the last half hour were allowed to hit the pad and some of the appeals seemed to be fairly well justified according to my reckoning. It appeared that the stage had already been set by the fact that the umpires made it very clear that as long as the ball hit the front pad playing forward, the decision was always in favour of the batsman. I felt and still feel that the Birmingham wicket offered little assistance to bowlers of all types and in fact the ball hardly deviated at all for the majority of the match. This preconceived idea on the part of the umpires certainly allowed the players to turn the game into a football match and I feel fairly certain that unless a new interpretation and outlook is applied to this particular feature of umpiring, many a match in the future is going to be spoilt. Again, English players find it very difficult to accept as honest, leg before decisions received at the hands of umpires who officiate in games where the wickets allow little or no deviation.

I would appreciate your considering these remarks as there has been and there will continue to be much weeping and gnashing of teeth over the matter of leg before decisions with the batsman playing forward. It is my opinion that the determining factor is to a large extent dependent on the texture and behaviour of the wicket being used.

This ought to give you something to think about during one or two winter evenings and I look forward eagerly to your most knowledgeable comment on this matter.

Over two years were to pass before Gerry Gomez received Jim's 'most knowledgeable comment' and then only after another letter of amplitudinous proportions:

My dear Gerry,

When you write you certainly say a mouthful!

About the playing forward. I am sorry if I kept silence on this – I can't remember you wanting my views, but I am duly flattered! I find your comments most important and revealing and unexpected. I hope you have sent a copy to Lord's, and I should also make quite sure that Walter Robins, Peter May and Colin Cowdrey (who is still sometimes an offender in sticking out the leg and not playing a stroke) see what you have written. To be frank I think you have suggested a rather complicated procedure on the drag question, and hope the white disc will be used as in Australia and as agreed for England in 1960. But generally I do congratulate you warmly on the notes and think they will be a great help . . .

Nine years later, in 1968, and with a change to the existing lbw law in the offing, a letter arrived from Don Bradman:

Dear Jim,

On May 3, 1968, when Jeff Stollmeyer advocated a re-think on the LBW law, you sat up and took notice. But when ASB did it in 1932, in a letter to MCC, trying to find an answer to bodyline, it was ignored. I have been advocating it ever since and am delighted that after 36 years someone is seeing the light.

Who has once gone to cricket to watch a batsman pad up to save his wicket? What right has a batsman ever had, since the laws were promulgated, to this protection? Why has MCC since its solemn resolution about the turn of the century, to stop this menace 'by every means in its power', failed to face up to the problems?

Please get a copy of my book *The Art of Cricket* and read carefully what Larwood says, page 155, and then what I say – pages 197 to 205.

Surely Jim you must at last be convinced that in this day and age there is no longer any room for the man who only survives by manipulating his legs.

The off-side is the place to start . . . because we must bring the bowling back to the off-side and to do this we must rework the bowler for switching his line.

Not only that but technically it is right.

The curse of modern cricket is the incessant attack of medium fast bowlers at the leg stump with 5 or 6 on-side fielders.

Jim there is no shot on to this stuff, but they bowl it because they can't get an LBW outside the off stump.

After this dreary summer perhaps is a wonderful chance to try the off side LBW. Go your hardest – cricket will be in your debt if you can make the powers that be see the light.

Cheers,

Don

Bradman, Gomez and Jim were automatic confidants when serious issues affected cricket. 'Throwing' was one such, when during the late 1950s and 1960s the South African Griffin, the Australian Meckiff, the Englishman Rhodes and the West Indian Griffith were all thought to have suspect actions. The Don typically went straight to the point in November 1959:

Dear Jim,

Thank you for your letter of Oct. 20th. Since then the MCC have pronounced a further judgement on throwing and dragging. The throwing definition means the same as ours, but frankly I like yours better because I think it simpler and clearer.

Nevertheless, I don't think a definition matters much because the umpire will no-ball a chap or otherwise according to his judgement. And if he passes the bowler that is the end of it.

I notice Pakistan are passing Meckiff. That means every country but England and will make it difficult for anyone else to query his action.

Your use of the white disc for dragging is pure machinery and doesn't affect the principle.

In July 1965, Gomez also was exercised. Although never 'called' during the West Indies 1963 tour of England, their destructive opening bowler with the awesome physique of a heavyweight boxer, Charlie Griffith, was widely believed to have 'thrown'. Gomez wrote to Jim in the latter's capacity as Editorial Director of *The Cricketer* magazine:

Dear Jim,

The copy of *The Cricketer* dated the 18th June contained an article entitled "MCC and the 'throwing' controversy'" – which was positively disgusting.

The *Cricketer* magazine discharges a particular responsibility to the game and cannot at any time allow itself to slip to the level of the cheaper elements of Fleet Street. I found it particularly distasteful to read 'that in England, umpires are itching to right the wrong done in 1963'. This is a horrible blow to all that cricket stands for, and indicates quite clearly that English umpires wittingly condoned contraventions of the laws. To state also that: 'Griffith can hardly play Test Cricket or indeed any first class cricket outside his country again' is a vicious, unwarranted and scurrilous attempt at discrediting West Indies cricket. This, to my mind is the end, and I am absolutely flabbergasted that such debasing utterance could get past the scrutiny of your editor into the columns of your reputable magazine whose main purpose in life is to safeguard and protect the interests of cricket.

I trust that in the future we will be spared such harmful comment and no doubt you will see to it that greater vigilance is exercised or you might even have [*Frank*] Rostron contributing to your editorials.

Now, on more or less the same subject in slightly different vein, I would like to take this opportunity of telling you confidentially, what action has been taken regarding Charlie Griffith.

Copies of the film taken during the 4th Test Match in Barbados were passed around the Board members and I have not yet had all the comments in order to assess the situation fully from a general Board viewpoint.

It was my personal impression that there were a number of occasions on which Charlie contravened the law and in casting my mind back to the pictures taken prior to selection of the team for the 1963 Tour, I have noticed some deterioration in his bowling action, particularly when he is tired. It was obvious from the presence of O'Neill and Lawry at the wicket that these pictures were filmed late on the second day of play by which time Charlie had done quite a lot of work. At this point in the 4th Test Match, after a fairly tiring colony game, it was obvious that Charlie's co-ordination suffered considerably and that on many occasions when exerting the extra effort to bowl a bouncer or a yorker, his action definitely contravened the law.

This being the case, I rang Tom Pierce and strongly recommended that John Dare should take this film to England, and allow it to be used along with films of other first class bowlers as a basis of discussion in first trying to improve the wording of the law, and secondly, to allow the examiners to satisfy themselves as to whether his method of delivery is illegal with each delivery or whether there is an occasional contravention of the law. [*Both Pierce and Dare had turns as President of the West Indian Cricket Board.*]

Another point that I stressed is that some effort should be made to induce in umpires the thinking that if a man throws he should be called whenever the umpires' assessment of the delivery suggests such action. At the same time, umpires need to be persuaded from the deterring thought that a bowler called for such offence is immediately outlawed.

If of course it is the considered opinion of a large majority of umpires that there is chronic failure to meet the demands of the particular law, then the player must withdraw from the game.

Tom Pierce agreed with this proposal and I am hoping that John was able to carry out on our behalf the type of positive action which this present situation clearly demands from our Board.

I do look forward to having your comments on some of the contents of this letter and also about any information regarding the current English season . . .

Dear Gerry,

Thank you so much for your charming letter of congratulation on my award. It is our 210th letter or wire and one of the most appreciated! [*Jim had been awarded an OBE*]

Now, with regard to your letter of the following day about the *Cricketer* article. I have much sympathy with you, and think that the phrase about the umpires was highly unfortunate. I cannot see everything but an Editorial Director must accept responsibility. I have had a similar complaint from Jeff [*Stollmeyer*], but without saying exactly what he disliked.

Please accept this as an acknowledgement of your letter rather than a complete answer, as at this moment I have so much on my hands I do not know where to turn. I would only say then that I am grateful for your confidential information on the action you have taken regarding Charlie Griffith, and I hope that John Dare has brought the film to England – though I have not heard of it.

I believe that you are in an extremely awkward position, and as you

know I have bent over backwards to avoid inflaming opinion. At the
same time you say 'his action definitely contravened the law'. There is
not a single West Indian opponent I have heard of who considers
Charlie a fair bowler, and I believe the image of West Indian cricket will
be tarnished so long as you continue to play him. We come back to the
old cliché – the game is greater than the player. Incidentally, it does not
help your cause that several of the West Indian players – and also
Frank – are freely quoted in conversation by the cricketers of other
countries as admitting privately that he is a chucker.

If, as I expect, you will be seeing Jeff in the near future, perhaps you
will show him this letter. I am so sorry it isn't fuller.

Incidentally, I don't think I can agree that bowlers who are
occasional throwers should be allowed to continue in the game. It is the
occasional one that does the damage and if such a ball takes an
important wicket in a Test Match confusion would reign again.

The most natural thing in the world for Jim would be to show all the
correspondence to his great friend 'Gubby' Allen, who regarded MCC
and Lord's as his fiefdom. A few months later a reply from Allen's
stockbroking office at South Sea House, 37 Threadneedle Street,
London EC2 wended its way to Jim's mat:

Dear Jim,

I have read the enclosed with great interest. Gerry may be right about
a bowler's action deteriorating when he is tired, but in my opinion
Griffith's action is at fault, admittedly in varying degrees, in every
delivery in the films taken last winter, which we have.

The part of the letter which intrigued me was about what John Dare
was supposed to be going to do in England this summer. So far as I am
aware John brought no films to Lord's, nor made any effort to discuss
the situation. He made a statement at the I.C.C., which everyone
thought was rather stupid as in the main he simply accused others of
'persecution'. Billy and I intended to tackle him, but he slipped out of
England without our knowledge.

I am sure they are heading for trouble, and as you said 'The game is
greater than the player.' In my opinion they have been warned. BUT
only unofficially.

Hope you have a wonderful trip.

Yours ever,
Gubby

By 5 December 1965, Jim was in Melbourne covering the England tour of Australia. Further bowling controversy – although not for 'throwing' – reminded him that it was time to appraise Gerry Gomez of the latest episode in the saga:

> Dear Gerry,
>
> This comes to you immediately before Ann and I go up to Brisbane for the Test: Aussie weather positively awful – much hotter in Sandwich before I left! – but the Poms' performances better than we dared hope . . . By the way you'll be interested in the extreme action taken against Jones. Having been warned twice for running into the 'box' now laid down as a guide in the playing conditions a certain umpire Burgess banned him for the innings. Bad luck in that it was quite accidental, the boy trying to deliver (left arm fastish from nearer the stumps) – whereas it's often been a ploy as you know. However the ump. was quite justified, and I'm all for umpires being given tangible help in the way of boxes or whatever rather than expect them to act on vague phrases. However, that's by the way . . .
>
> Thought you'd like to know I heard recently from Gubby when I asked whether John Dare has made an approach at Lord's on the Griffith matter, or had brought over any film for anyone to see. You'll remember you told me you had made this suggestion to Tom Pierce. Well, Gubby's sure John brought no film, nor made any effort to discuss the situation. At my instigation Gubby asked Everton to go and see a game and I believe they had a talk but I didn't ask any questions.
>
> As you know I've declared in public with great emphasis the comments of O'Neill and Dexter. The fact is however that they have said what all opponents and many of your own side privately thought, and although I still think his throw is very difficult to pick from square-leg it must be difficult at times not to have doubts – and according to the law doubts are still all that are necessary.
>
> This doesn't mean I don't realise what a difficult situation you face as selectors, and the Barbadians also. I only hope he fails to show form in the Shell matches, or that if he does go full out (which, by the way, he didn't do in England in September) Jordan earns himself a medal by calling him once more . . .

That remark in Jim's letter a little while back enumerating no fewer than 210 letters or wires between Gerry and himself underlines the friendship between the two – and also the Swanton penchant for meticulousness and order.

One letter to Gerry in July 1964 held particular interest:

My dear Gerry,

I must say that when you do put pen to paper you do it properly!
Your views I found extremely interesting and in most cases acceptable –
though not all! Let us have a full-scale meeting to resolve the problems
of cricket when I come out in the winter. I am glad to say our house in
Barbados will be finished at the end of the year, and we shall be out
there in late January or early February, preparatory to my watching the
first three Tests against Australia.

I have one serious suggestion to make to you regarding West Indies
cricket and the appointment of Garry Sobers. As you know, he was with
me in the Far East and I like him very much. I think also that he is quite
shrewd, both in the cricket sense and outside it. At the same time,
considering what he will have to do on the field, the Board have asked a
tremendous lot of him, and he will want (and is entitled to expect)
much help and good counsel.

I have always thought the West Indies' system of appointing a home
team manager for each island a source of weakness to you.

Surely now is the time to try and get Frank Worrell to undertake the
whole job? It should be done by a member of the Board who knows his
cricket and cricketers: why not the man with the most prestige, who
would have (I would have thought) the strongest influence on the
players? I dare say this is no new thought but sometimes people from a
distance can see things more clearly than those on the spot. There it is,
at any rate, for your consideration.

I agree entirely with you [*replied Gerry*], and at the same time I hasten
to express my appreciation and thanks for the considerable interest
which you have always taken and continue to take in our cricket. There
is every indication that given the right kind of support this young man
can in time, become the greatest cricketer that has ever set foot on a
cricket field. However, there are one or two rough edges in his makeup,
and in view of your deep interest in his welfare, I would appreciate your
providing him with some fatherly advice. The fact is that he is a
shocking correspondent and that letters, cables etc., are either entirely
ignored or given very belated attention. I sensed during his short visit
here after the last tour that there was a slight hint of unhappiness when
dealing with our Board and its members. There might be some area of
discontent which I have not been able to discover and I would
appreciate your sounding him out with a view to improving his
personal relations with the Board and its members during the
forthcoming season, and it would help if the little chip was removed.

I am pleased to hear that your house will be finished at the end of the year and above all that we will have the opportunity of seeing you again in these parts after your protracted absence.

On this occasion, Jim wisely stood aside:

I am glad you agree with me about the desirability of Garry Sobers being given the best kind of right hand support. Frank has a remarkable way with all these chaps, and I have no doubt that his influence would make all the difference to your prospects. The Australians are very limited in bowling but you know far better than I the difficulties of keeping the best West Indian team in a hundred per cent trim in a home series. In fact you have generally done far better away.

Jim's interest in the Caribbean and especially Barbados surprised many who recognised only his undoubted snobbery and grandee conduct. That immensely original writer Robin Marlar, who knew Jim better than most, realised in the 1950s that he had fallen in love with the island. 'In a way it extended Jim's power base because it was much easier to get some influence with the establishment in Barbados and by extension the Caribbean than, for instance, over here in England. He knew that this would help in the cricket world, but he really loved Barbados and he and Ann bought a house in the grounds of Sandy Lane and went there every year.'

With Jim and Ann spending so much time in Barbados, it had seemed a sensible investment for their future to have a house *in situ* and avoid the financial outlay involved in staying in hotels. 'Coralita' suited them admirably, it was somewhere they could entertain and also it was on the doorstep of the world-famous hotel with its rich social mix of international high-flyers.

I asked Mike Brearley for his view on Jim's Barbadian connection. 'Maybe one of the things about the West Indies, or indeed Africa, is that there is a kind of spontaneity and liveliness that can help to bring someone out of their English stiffness. You're not at your own home and you don't have to meet the expectations there and maybe he did feel a little loosened. I think he was much better when people didn't take him at his own estimation of himself. There was much more of the human being coming through and maybe the West Indies were partly deferential and partly affectionate and partly because they had their own spontaneity and life he could laugh with them.'

If Jim felt that he was not so much on parade in the Caribbean, there was no such feeling in England. Never for a moment did he seem to relax his vigilance over his self-chosen task of guarding the moral welfare and efficient management of cricket. Often he was fighting battles on behalf of his press colleagues with regard to passes and adequate facilities, notably, in different eras, with Brian Castor and Commander Babb at the Oval. At another moment he would be crossing swords with Billy Griffith at Lord's after an unguarded comment in his *Daily Telegraph* column berating 'cricket authorities who seem to be bent on killing first-class cricket'. In his commentary in the paper also he might pick up a letter from a reader:

My God, what a shambles in Lord's Pavilion now they have opened the flood-gates. A pair of field-glasses pinched – not mine, but a friend's. Another chap told me he'd had a valuable pipe pinched – who'd want to smoke someone else's pipe, however valuable. My companion put two cushions down to bespeak a couple of seats; they were immediately appropriated and sat on. A character, straight from the Oval Members, sitting behind me complained that my pipe-smoke was blowing in his face. Well, that's fair enough; so I got up and said, 'Well, I tell you what; you take my seat and I'll sit behind where you are.' He exclaimed loudly, 'You take yer 'ands off me; nobody don't do that to me.' Shades of Lord Harris.

That was the sort of epistle that might have elicited a half-smiling harumph from Jim if feeling abnormally *lese-majesté*.

One signally acrimonious exchange occurred in May 1958 after Surrey had trounced the touring New Zealanders by an innings and 163 runs. The home side were indebted to a magnificent century from Peter May, but the pitch, described as 'fiery and fast' in *Wisden*, contributed significantly to the match being all over by twenty to three on the second afternoon after only eight and a half hours' play. Former Surrey captain H.M. 'Monty' Garland-Wells, who was now a committee member, was not best pleased to see that in Swanton's report in the *Telegraph* the wicket had been described as 'a cart track'. He complained bitterly to the Editor of the paper and to Jim himself:

I have always considered that you were one of the very few upon whose reports I can rely for a fair and honest approach to a particular contest and the 'game' in general. Your last two efforts, however, have caused me to think that my faith may have been misplaced.

Our man was not short of a riposte or nine:

Dear Monty,

Herewith now some thoughts on your letters to the Editor and myself on the matter of wickets at the Oval. First a few questions.

1. Do you suppose the wicket for the New Zealand match was a good one?

2. If not why were the touring side, in fine weather, not given a good batting wicket?

3. Apart from Melford's opinion on the wicket have you had any other good disinterested opinion? I don't know how much you would value Charles Bray's view, but you would no doubt accept George Duckworth's. Both thought it a quite unworthy wicket on which but for Peter May's brilliance neither side would have reached 100 in either innings.

4. How do you account for the fact that the Gloucester wicket directly afterwards, in similar weather conditions, was a beauty, bearing no relation to the other, either in appearance or in the way it played?

5. Have you ever seen such a Test wicket as the West Indies were asked to play on last August?

6. If the groundsman was going to do such a risky (an almost unprecedented) thing as to put a thick marl dressing on a Test wicket ten days before the match why was not the elementary precaution taken of preparing an alternative?

7. Did you know that [Bert] Lock had expressed the view that this would be a first rate wicket which would get better as the match progressed? [Alf] Gover quoted this prediction on the air before the game, which finished early on Saturday afternoon.

8. Did you know that when Sussex came to the Oval two years ago in fine weather, David Sheppard thought the wicket was disgraceful, and said it was 'the worst but one' he had ever played on?

9. Why do you think Surrey (whose batting has generally been second to none ever since the nineties [1890s]) have gone for 12 years without producing a Test batsman? (May learned to play on the wickets at Charterhouse and Fenner's.)

My personal view (shared, I believe, by some of the players) is that Lock often seems extremely hazy as to what sort of wicket he has prepared. I do not know, of course, under what instructions from the Ground Committee Lock operates. But if he were simply carrying out orders in the case, for instance, of the New Zealand and West Indies wickets I think a statement should have been made regretting the wickets and exculpating him. If not I feel on the face of it he is lucky to have kept his job. And if the ground committee were re-elected this year I think they were lucky too.

The phrase you disliked so much referred to 'a wicket', not the whole square, as you suggest. I wanted to make the point as strongly as I could, and I am very pleased it has created attention at the Oval, not because I like making a stir but because I think that, whether wittingly or not, touring sides especially have been given an unfair deal.

I know Laker and Lock have taken more wickets away from home than at the Oval, and I don't at all think all Oval wickets are bad ones. But there are too many mistakes, and when they affect the touring side the thing has Commonwealth implications which one appreciates the more one travels abroad.

I see you say you would like the Surrey Committee to give me a chance of 'exchanging views'. You are in a good position to arrange this if you wish. Perhaps my questions here might form a basis for discussion. I am coming to see the Lancashire match.

As usual with so many of these verbal eruptions it all quietened down with honours reckoned to be more or less even. On a much calmer note and in the following winter with May's side in Australia, E.W.S. once again became the voice of his colleagues in the press by writing to his old friend the Prime Minister, no less. Robert Menzies, Companion of Honour, later favoured by HM the Queen as a Knight of the Thistle, cannot often have had to address such an important matter of state during his time in office:

My dear Prime Minister,

You will have received, I think, by about this post the copy of a letter to Ian Johnson, the Secretary of Melbourne Cricket Club, about the new Press Box in which they are proposing to inhabit us all for the Test Matches. I am one of the six Australian and English press signatories, those six forming the executive committee which has been dealing with press arrangements on the tour. I am not at all sure that you will forgive us for even acquainting you with the matter, when you have so many infinitely weightier things to worry about. However, you are a member of the MCC Trust, and since the Cricket Club seem to us to have shown such little awareness of their responsibility to us – and through us to the cricket public, who whether they like it or not have to seen the cricket through our eyes, as it were – it was thought proper to bring things to your attention, and also to that of the Chairman, Mr Caldwell.

As for me, I thought if you were going to see my name at the bottom of the document it would be civil to send a private note first apologising for the presumption and also giving a brief idea of the background to the trouble. The proposed site of the box, which is at the very back of the second storey of the new Olympic stand, over long-off, was first heard of by the main body of cricket writers at Perth. Fingleton thereupon wrote saying that first reports from the Victorian press were unfavourable, and that we should like to talk over the position with the MCC on arrival at Melbourne for the State match. We found Johnson prepared to defend not only the site but also the furnishings which could only have been designed by someone with a diabolical hatred of all newspaper men and their works. The knees of the man behind in your back, your knee in that of the man in front, a fiendish wooden bar in the wrong place, a beastly little sloping bit of wood to write on – and so on. He asked to see the committee, and Ian produced Messrs Chadwick and Rigg, whom we put through the torture, and with whom we discussed possible alternative places. The best was probably about thirty yards further forward on the same floor, but was in the open and would have necessitated awnings. The architect now finds that such awnings would interfere with 'sight-lines': in other words a certain number of seats in rear would have an incomplete view. So although we are now to have chairs to sit on and apparently even a decent sort of desk to write and type on, the position is to remain – unless other pressure can be brought. Now as to the position: I would say it was 160 yards as the crow flies from the far stumps. It is right up in the sky – so that one seems to be watching very small men playing a remote game with the ball almost out of vision. (Keith Miller has great difficulty in following the flight of the ball – so you will imagine how much the older gentry see of it!) It is impossible to get 'the feel' of the game from such a distance.

I am surprised that Chadwick and Rigg have not found a better solution because they seemed sympathetic and understanding of our difficulties; but it seems as though the Committee and Secretary are prepared to stick the Press away in such a remote corner as will not inconvenience the members, forgetful that the cricket writers contain at least a pretty fair percentage who need to be able to watch and work in a decent position. You may possibly remember that the old Press box was at very deep mid-wicket, in the back recesses of the old Grey-Smith stand.

As you probably know I have worked in all the Press boxes of the world's Test grounds, India and Pakistan excepted. Wherever a new box has been built in recent years – for instance at Lord's, at Leeds, at Brisbane, and at Johannesburg – the siting has been good and the amenities in accord with the larger numbers who now are sent to cover the big games. But at Melbourne, which in one sense at least is the greatest of all Test grounds, they are proposing to install what would be the worst Test Press Box I at least have ever sat in anywhere.

I suppose you will have heard enough, and to spare! Forgive this, and I need scarcely say it would be well understood if you took no action of any kind in the matter. Some of us rather presumed to feel that in its restricted sphere it was an Australian affair, rather than a local one, and that if it were an Australian cricket affair you would at least care to know what was afoot. I hope we may meet before, but in any case look forward to the really big game at Canberra in February!

With warmest if belated congratulations on your latest Test win.

Jim's policy of going to the top 'to get things sorted ite!' was put to the test in further upsets in the world of broadcasting. A spate of memorandums and letters goes to the root of the problem:

27 May, 1959

The time has come, and none too soon, for serious action to be taken with regard to Swanton. His attitude and manner during the MCC v. India match has been such that I feel it is going to be difficult to work amicably with him in the future. His whole approach to his work has become so self-opinionated that life for the producer, commentators, scorers and others is being made impossible. His attitude towards Denis Compton is expressed in Swanton's own words to Brian Johnston – 'Compton has only been in the game for five minutes' and his views are not worth hearing. The feeling between Compton and Swanton is so red hot that an explosion is inevitable before the season is out.

Yesterday, in a heated exchange with Brian Johnston, Swanton insulted him by saying that he was only there to provide entertainment, implying that Johnston has no standing as an expert. When Peter Webber took over production from me on Monday, Swanton made it clear, by implication, on the air that he wasn't getting the pictures he wanted from the producer. Webber told him in no uncertain terms who was boss.

Swanton has a three year contract. There are clauses, however, which would enable us to terminate at three months' notice. I believe a very strong letter should be sent to him, and if there is no improvement we ought to consider termination. I know of no member of the Corporation, Sound included, who would regret his departure. There are limits, it seems, to how far one can go in employing a man who may be an expert but who is impossible to work with. It is clear that his work with the *Daily Telegraph* comes before broadcasting, and as this implies, he is most unwilling to use up material in his summaries which he clearly has earmarked for next morning's edition.

I would suggest that a meeting between all interested parties in Sound and Television, before the season gets under way, would be very advisable.

Peter Dimmock, the Head of Outside Broadcasts in Television to whom Antony Craxton had sent that memorandum, wrote a courteous letter to Jim saying how unhappy he was to hear of the disagreement, that Compton was employed specifically to give his views and that the producer on site had the final say in deployment of personnel and pictures:

My dear Peter,

I had your letter last evening on returning from the country, and as my assistant is away today I'm putting my thoughts on paper before going off to Nottingham, as I don't think it a good thing to allow misunderstandings and conflicts to develop if it can be avoided. I have put a carbon in for Antony and Brian, so that they can discuss this letter with me if they wish up there. If after that it seems, either to them or to me, that we should all have a round-table talk with you there ought to be time to fix it before the Second Test. I'm doing this one for Sound.

I've been clearing away a lot of BBC correspondence since moving into this flat following Australia, and the letters I've been sorting from Cecil McGivern, Antony, and Ray Lakeland following the various Test series, all writing very generously about my TV work on the cricket, seem to suggest that any lack of harmony so far as I'm concerned is a recent thing. It boils down, I think, to MCC v India the other day. I also was unhappy about one or two things that happened there, and thought of writing to you but decided against it because I supposed that on reflection those concerned would see my point of view – or we could talk it over at Nottingham.

Now that Antony (I assume) has ventilated the matter it seems necessary to go into a certain amount of detail. On Monday he was away in the afternoon and evening with Brian on a Serpentine programme, and I therefore performed for three short sessions with Peter Webber. When I came in to the box on Tuesday Antony said in the presence of Brian, Roy Webber, and a young Scots SM whom I hadn't seem before this match that P. Webber was very sore with me because I'd been 'trying to tell him how to produce'.

These are the facts. On the Monday I made two suggestions over the second mike (Commentator to Producer) – one was to ask him to try and get a shot either on the oblique camera or one of the main ones showing the slips as well as the batsman as the latter was obviously going to give them a catch any moment – as shortly happened.

The other thing I suggested was an alternative shot to the most boring one of all, namely the back view of the fast bowler as he trudges back to his mark. I said to Antony that this sort of thing was exactly the reason why we started the second mike several years ago, and that if I had been in Webber's shoes, not apparently having done very much if any cricket work before I'd have welcomed suggestions from someone who was supposed at least to know something about it. Antony agreed.

I'd have preferred Antony to have discussed Webber's remarks with me privately, but there it was. In the afternoon it was pretty clear that we should have to improvise something for the 6.20–6.35 session as the game would be over, and the obvious thing was the choice of the new England XI in relation to the play we had seen at Lord's. Antony said: 'We think you must choose your Test side. Denis will do the same, and you can then discuss each other's.' My first instinct was to demur at this, thinking the time (15 minutes) might be better used. Thereupon Brian said I was never prepared to stick my neck out, that I ought to do it, and that if I wasn't prepared to state my side I had no right to criticise the selectors in the paper. This seemed somewhat beside the point, but what was not beside the point was that for the second time in a few hours I was being criticised in a very pointed way with three others present. If Antony had said: 'We've got this very good listening time at our disposal, now what are we going to do about it?' that would have been a different approach altogether.

As a matter of fact since I'd had the best part of a couple of hours with the Chairman of Selectors only the night before I could not have had a better idea in my mind of the players under consideration and of the general policy. So far as the vacant Test places went I know that the off-spin job, for instance, was 6/1 the field, and that there were any number of good candidates in the other categories with more or less equal claims. The thing to do, in my opinion, was to give a picture of the situation as I saw it in the light of Australia (where I had been present) and of the West Indies tour this winter, to discuss the selectors' difficulties and problems, and to go through the many names in their minds and say something about as many as I had time for.

If I had thought of it in time I would have got a message through to
you, asking you to listen if you could, to get your reactions. I felt myself
that the viewers got far better value than if I had followed Denis's piece
about his team with another on the same lines. I think I mentioned
about forty names in all – including seven I rated as certainties – so
quite a few viewers must have heard something about their local
favourites!

Now, with that lengthy and perhaps rather tedious narrative off my
chest, about Denis Compton. I like working with him and think he
certainly has something to contribute in the way of first-hand
knowledge of the players and great experience of Test cricket. It is the
job of the commentator to bring that out, and I think this is normally
best done by giving him a moment's warning, either in a whisper or
over the air, to collect his thoughts. My experience is you generally get a
worth-while comment that way, whereas the sudden question probably
produces a platitude or something that doesn't quite add up. Above all,
I think he's more effective if used say every three or four minutes rather
than brought in continually. I have been moving a lot these last few
days among keen cricket-followers and the one thing that seems to
irritate them more than anything is a perpetual two-way waffle. Brian
naturally tends to use Denis rather more than me, because he is not
often prepared to advance a technical opinion. My own view is that
sometimes his commentaries develop into something like a conversation
piece with Denis. The Sound way of getting the pithy comment from the
'expert' seems to me the best one – but I am, of course, perfectly
prepared to fall in with any formula we jointly decide on.

Following on from this I think the ideal positioning in the box is for
the commentator to sit in the middle with the scorer on one side and
Denis on the other, so that one does not have to communicate with the
latter behind Roy Webber's very ample back. I assure you my DT duties
practically never keep me away during transmission times, and I think it
would be a very good rule if, normally, both commentators were
present and that there were two rules: silence and no visitors.

The difficulty too often is that there's no comfortable place for the
man who's off duty. I use the glasses a great deal, and therefore need a
table for the elbows and for one's note-book. At Lord's there is only a
high stool with one's feet off the ground. In preference to that I usually
move to the Press Box. If before the Second Test a low platform (in view
of the front row, which will only take three) plus table and chair could
be produced that would be the answer.

I accept your letter, of course, as a friendly one, designed to produce the best team effort, and in this I will naturally co-operate all I can. The remarks about 'taking it out' of anyone, and of criticising while on the air I simply cannot accept, and I think you must have misunderstood Antony or Brian or whoever has been discussing the subject. If that is a serious charge you ought to have me on the mat in a very big way. In fact it was I who came away from Lord's feeling somewhat aggrieved, and I have known the two of them so long that I was rather surprised and hurt. However under stress things better left unsaid are apt to slip out, and I don't claim to be any less guilty than the next man.

May you have (?be having) a very good holiday, and I hope we may see you at the TV point, if not in conference before.

On the very day that Jim had sent that reply, Craxton had put his colleagues, Ray Lakeland in Manchester and Philip Lewis in Birmingham, in the picture:

Since you will both be working with Swanton on the Tests this year, I thought you ought to know that as a direct result of his behaviour at Lord's during the MCC match, Dimmock has sent him a letter. In this he intimates that Swanton is becoming increasingly intolerant and apt to dictate towards all and sundry. As we all know, this is nothing new – Swanton has been throwing his weight about from the start. This warning, if it can be called that, has been long overdue, and he must now do as he is told and not dictate to you or the other members of the team.

Denis Compton is one of Swanton's big bones of contention. Swanton is, I believe, excessively jealous of Compton's position, and feels he has usurped his position as the expert. I believe the public are more interested in Compton's views than Swanton's, and I have told Compton that he is at liberty to comment when and as often as he pleases, though notifying the commentator that he is going to do so. There is no need for Compton to feel he has to be brought in every time. I personally keep his microphone up all the time during transmissions so that he needs only to signal to Brian or Jim before he speaks.

Again, if you feel like using Compton for visual summaries which are, as you know, less than five minutes, you are free to do so. To get a two-man summary in this time is, I believe, out of the question, and Swanton has no prior right to be used. I am proposing to use Compton for a short summary at the lunch interval and Swanton at the end of play in the evening.

To sum up, be as firm as you can with Swanton, and if you have any trouble with him do not hesitate to let us know.

The next season Jim was the one who complained to Dimmock, probably on the basis that those who have been thought to have been wrong also can be wronged:

Dear Peter,

I had intended writing you directly after the Lord's Test but for my secretary getting involved in a car accident, which put me in greater chaos than usual. However, answering today an indignant viewer who pleads for 'a fairer crack of the whip for the cricketers', and with another *Grandstand* imminent on Saturday I am typing these thoughts quickly before getting off for Trent Bridge.

I think it correct to say that everyone working at Lord's felt that *Grandstand* centred at Wimbledon could have been (a) more enthusiastic in its hand-overs to Lord's as well as (b) more generous in the time allotted. The impression one gets is that they are not specially interested, nor very knowledgeable. Let me give two examples of what I think you may agree is very poor team-work.

(1) On the first day we were told there was no play at Wimbledon, and we would have to fill in the tea interval. At Antony's command I therefore wound up at 4.15 saying that after getting a situation report from Wimbledon we would be back for an interview between Brian Johnston and the Australian captain, Richie Benaud – giving Richie a brief build-up. The commentator taking over at Wimbledon began: well, after all there may be play here so WE WON'T HAVE TO HAVE THAT – i.e. the interview. Those were the words. Could gaucherie go further? Not specially polite to me, but very slighting to Benaud, awaiting his cue. I can't remember what the tennis was, probably a Rumanian lady fighting it out with a Latin American . . . Seriously, is this good TV?

(2) Saturday afternoon, South Africa follow-on, and we ask for the first few overs by Statham and Trueman – which of course were likely to be particularly vital. The message back was that they would come over 'at the fall of the first wicket' – as if anyone could tell when that would be. In fact they arrived after half an hour with the score 14 for none. I began by saying that we had been watching a 'gripping' half-hour duel between the England fast bowlers and McGlew and Goddard, as indeed it had been. Whereat the director's comment came back for all to hear over the cans: 'What a ridiculous comment. How can 14 runs in

half an hour be gripping?' As you can imagine there were various adverse comments on this – including that of the S.M. (I think) who said that by that line of reasoning there wouldn't be any excitement in a goalless draw!

One year later the positions again were reversed:

There is no doubt whatsoever that Swanton is one of the most knowledgeable men on cricket not only in this country, but throughout the cricket-playing world. There are many instances that I could quote where his advice has been taken not only by the selectors, but by the captains of the Test teams – there was an example of this in the last match. However, Swanton has never been and never will be the easiest man to work with in television. This is simply because he is just not prepared to adapt himself to the technicalities of the medium. For instance, for many years he refused to take producer's talkback, and when reluctantly he gave way about a year ago he did so with very bad grace. He now in fact has dirty talkback, but there were repeated instances in the last Test Match when he wore his earphones so far from his ears that it was quite impossible for him to hear instructions given to him. It is true to say that he is clearly not able to listen to the producer's instructions to the cameras – and to the commentator, at the same time carrying on a coherent commentary – one of the first essentials of a good television sports commentator.

Apart from his technical inefficiencies, he has over the past years been a very difficult colleague. He has never got on well with Roy Webber the scorer, and even less so with Denis Compton. There have been rows at Lord's with the authorities and the famous contretemps over the feeding arrangements at the Oval.

I think you have known for a long time my view that we should drop Swanton out of the commentary team, and I am delighted that this view is now held by senior members of the Corporation. I felt that in the forthcoming season we might have offered him one Test Match as against three for West and one for Robert Hudson, but as you say, it might be kinder to make a complete break and not employ him at all. This, I think, is a policy decision which I leave to yourself and C.P.Tel. [*Controller, Programmes, Television*]

As you know, I have had a preliminary talk with Robert Hudson and sounded him out on his feelings on doing television commentary. He is very keen to try his hand at it, and I personally feel he will be an excellent substitute.

Denis Compton has, in my view, improved out of all knowledge since I first tried him out a year or two ago. No-one will doubt his great cricketing knowledge as a player, and this is most apparent from his comments. He is not, and never should be considered, an authority on the game as Swanton is, but Compton is still a great name in the game and will always remain a legendary figure as one of the greatest batsmen this country has ever produced. I would like to think that we could retain his services for at least the next series of Tests. I have approached Colin Cowdrey to find out whether he would be interested in doing the kind of thing Compton does. He has expressed very great interest in this, and although he may not be available to us for a few years he would be able to give the time to it and I think would do it with exceptional skill. He is, of course, a far more intelligent person than Compton, with a far stronger personality.

I would not propose to use more than one summariser until the Australians come here again in 1964, when I hope we would again get Jack Fingleton.

Finally a word about Peter West in the general context of cricket commentary. It has been a sad thing not to be able to use him more because of Swanton. He is, as you know, a complete professional as regards television, and on top of this he has over the years gained immeasurably in his authoritativeness on the game. I would regard him as my No. 1 cricket commentaro [sic] with Johnston, for different reasons, running his close second.

Following this reasoned and responsible missive, action at last was taken and there was an agreement to send a letter on behalf of television and radio to Swanton at the end of the season saying that the BBC did not propose to renew his contract and that any future engagements would be on an ad hoc basis. In doing this it was realised that the undoubted result would be that Swanton would protest to everyone he knew at the BBC including the Director of Television and the Director-General. Nevertheless, in the words of Peter Dimmock:

Everyone is unanimous in feeling that we can no longer tolerate Swanton's inability to adapt himself to the technicalities of television commentary. In spite of repeated warnings he refuses to listen to the producer's instructions and has been a constantly difficult colleague. Next year we propose to use Peter West, Brian Johnston, Robert Hudson and, I hope, Alan Gibson on commentaries, with Denis

Compton as our main summariser. Although Swanton's summaries were good he was not prepossessing in vision. There is no doubt that Denis Compton looks better and certainly means more to the marginal and younger viewers.

As was expected Jim soon was writing to the mandarins in the upper corridors of the Corporation, such as Kenneth Adam, Director of Television:

> Dear Kenneth,
>   I think you may have heard of the different TV Test arrangements regarding my services which are proposed for this summer. I should much like to see you on the matter and would be free almost whenever you chose to say. I hope you will be kind enough to find a time, and leave it to you, of course, whether or not Peter Dimmock should be there. I am anxious not to do anything behind his back, but feel that at this stage I want a word at the top level.
>   Yours ever,
>   Jim

Adam, no doubt, would have smoothly passed the ball back down the line to Dimmock who, equally no doubt, and with a touch of reluctance, would have finally met up with Swanton. At the meeting, after initial platitudes, there would have been murmurs from both parties expressing regret that it should have come to such a sorry pass, followed by a certain degree of firmness and self-justification from each as they outlined at length their conflicting positions.

Dimmock, then, possibly sensing an opportunity, perhaps would have utilised an arbitration ploy by claiming that while wearing his administrator's hat he was one or two stages removed from the front line troops and he could only go on what he was being told and that to an extent his hands were tied, and that it had been good to hear face to face what Jim had to say and that certainly he would bear all that in mind when he had another word with Antony once he had returned from his visit to the States and that you have to understand things are not the same as they once were in the BBC, we're moving on – goodness known where it's all going to end – and new ideas and policies are being tried all the time – got to give the youngsters their head, you know – with all this modern technology, of course I'm very sympathetic to your views and all that, but, well – there it is, really . . . Can't say any more. A drink, more conciliatory noises, flattery of Jim's unique contribution to the game, how much still they valued his work – and . . . must dash, I've got another meeting, never stops – see you very soon, old chap . . . what!

My dear Peter,
    It is good to think one can talk with complete frankness, and not to incur any resentment. I had that feeling this afternoon, and respect very much the attitude you took. I appreciate your position, and I believe you understood mine. As you say, let us meet – at lunch or wherever – on Antony's return, and get the thing finalised. I suppose he will not have committed himself to the Tests and the three or four other games (e.g. Canterbury) until then. Do not bother to acknowledge this.
    Yours ever,
        Jim

Now that imaginary reconstruction of Dimmock's approach might be completely wide of the mark, but the covering of mutual embarrassment almost certainly would have incorporated many elements of such managerial non-speak. *Toujours la politesse*, much saving of face and with dignity left intact. Important to do so but, essentially, a charade to deal with unpleasant matters in a civilised way.

The net result of all this was that the BBC – in those days still a rather benevolent employer – made a token compromise. Jim was to be offered one Test on television each summer. This duly happened and continued until 1966. As for radio, his summaries were to continue uninterrupted until his retirement from the *Telegraph* and full-time broadcast media work in 1975 when he was receiving £125 plus expenses per five-day Test match.

The aforementioned Robert Hudson, eventually himself to become Head of Outside Broadcasts and who worked with Jim in the commentary box many times, makes an interesting observation: 'Swanton had a pompous manner, but I don't think he was a pompous man.' It is an astute and subtle distinction, which would be lost amidst the casual camaraderie of a television crew for whom Swanton's old-world pontificating would have caused a mental double-declutch every time he opened his mouth. But however much they might resent his lordly dictatorial air, none would dispute his command of summary. Conceivably that had been part of the trouble: Jim's love and nourishment of the English language left no room in his mind for the subsidiary technical aspects of the craft.

Hudson continues:

> Jim was a master of the art of summarising a day's play, but even masters find life difficult when they don't know how much time they will be allowed.
>
> Very often – and at Lord's in particular – the clocks on the ground were in disagreement, both with each other and with GMT. Also, if an over could be started even fractionally before 6.30, it would be bowled and Jim's five minutes' time allocation would suffer a further setback. For all these reasons one would sympathise with his exasperation, as his carefully prepared and very important points about the day's activities had to be jettisoned one by one. Fortunately he usually had a further five minutes on the air, later that evening, from a local studio, so all was not entirely lost.
>
> Jim had the enviable ability, born out of long experience, to put his finger on the key moments of the day's play. The ball-by-ball commentator can become bogged down in detail and lose sight of the bigger picture; Jim would restore the balance for his late-night audience, which would often include the commentators themselves, anxious to find out what they had been talking about! I suppose as a commentator he was perhaps less at ease – particularly as on one occasion, when his allocation of twenty minutes consisted entirely of maiden overs!

I have always enjoyed giving a summarized picture of the day at the close, whether in vision or sound [*wrote Jim in* Sort of a Cricket Person], but it is a fairly concentrated exercise done off the cuff with a minimum of notes, and in this particular thing I can be easily put off by adjacent movement or conversation. The TV producer and his team of technicians (some 30 all told) do an excellent job presenting Test cricket, but often one used to feel that the last person they ever thought about was the commentator. I was doing a TV close-of-play summary one evening at Headingley when, immediately behind the camera I was looking into and only a few yards away, a fool of a stage-manager started waving his arms about like a lunatic. I stood this for a few seconds, then paused, pointed, and told him sternly to keep still. This must have looked strange to a million viewers, but I couldn't otherwise have continued to make sense. Anyway, one lady wrote in to say that my gesture had put her crying baby to sleep. The reason for the SM getting excited, it turned out, was nothing more serious than a man behind me, and therefore 'in shot', stacking chairs. A natural scene, surely!

When Peter Baxter, as a young producer, took over *Test Match Special*, he was very aware of the ritual surrounding Jim's summaries:

> As the close of a day's Test cricket approached, a presence would arrive in the radio commentary box. The passage of this day's events was about to receive the Royal Assent which would set it properly in its place in history. Jim Swanton would give his summary of play.
>
> He would come armed with a thermos flask which he would set down on the commentary desk with his notes, after a courteous, 'Do you want me here?' to the young producer. He would probably have to endure an irreverent comment or two from Brian Johnston, either on the air or off it. 'Always fourth form, Johnston,' he might protest, with a long suffering and almost avuncular smile. The jacket would come off and be arranged on the back of the chair, revealing braces that would in themselves be far too tempting a target for the commentary-box prankster.
>
> While the commentator, entrusted with the last twenty minute session, aware of the preparations for the end of his day's work, was describing the final overs, Jim would be reaching across to receive Bill Frindall's scorecard and make sure that it was understood that he would be reading it out at close of play.
>
> Two more things were required of the young producer: stopwatch set on the precise clock time and a card inscribed in large figures with the time he must finish, would be set down in front of him. There was an instruction for the young producer, to be repeated every evening until the great man was sure of him. 'No signals!' This was delivered in a tone that brooked no discussion. Not for Jim the indifferently manicured finger raised before his eyes to indicate that he had a minute to go.
>
> 'Now, with his summary of the day's play, here's E.W. Swanton of the *Daily Telegraph*.' And he was away. Until that hand-over he would not be sure of how long he would have to do. In those days play finished at 6.30, but if a fast bowler began an over thirty seconds before that, the nominal nine-and-a-half minutes could be greatly cut. Hence the insistence on his prop: 'I shall begin by reading the scorecard,' he would intone. This could be read through, with or without comment, setting the pace of his summary with consummate skill.
>
> Sir Jack Hobbs, seen leaving Lord's early on a Test match day, explained that he would be all right if he could hear Jim Swanton's summary. It was a brilliant factual summary of events. Nothing left out and opinions delivered only in passing if relevant – and, of course, if the

unforgiving stopwatch permitted. It was delivered with no more than the odd note to prompt him. And his final great gift to the young producer – he always finished bang on time.

For collectors of Swantoniana there was a much recounted occasion during the August Bank Holiday in 1963 when Jim was commentating on the match between Kent and Hampshire at Canterbury. England left-hander Peter Richardson opening for Kent and Colin Ingleby-McKenzie the exuberant captain of Hampshire decided to try and prick his self-importance by 'setting him up'. 'The open-air broadcasting place was on some scaffolding at the far end of the ground,' remembers Richardson with a laugh. 'We knew that he was due to start broadcasting at a certain time and Ingleby and I had had a word and we agreed that if I lasted that long I would make a complaint to the umpire about the noise from that area being too distracting to carry on batting.

'We had also spoken to Bill Copson who was one of the umpires – he was wary about being involved at first because he was a bit worried about the reaction if Lord's heard about it. Anyway, he agreed to do it and Peter West in the commentary position was in on it too and when Jim came on Peter waved a white handkerchief. Shack's bowling [Derek Shackleton] and so I stop the game and go up to Bill and say I can't concentrate, there's a booming noise coming from up there (pointing to where Swanton's in full flow). Bill then starts to walk over to the commentary position and Jim's on air saying, "There appears to be something going on down on the pitch. I can't quite make out what's happening." By this time Copson's quite close and he calls out, "The batsman's complaining about a booming noise, can you please stop." Mystified, Swanton turns and whispers to West, "What booming noise? I don't know what they mean." "It's you they're complaining about, Jim," replies West, "it's the sound of your voice."'

Apparently, on this occasion Jim's somewhat channelled sense of humour deserted him and Richardson was the recipient of a sharp note pointing out that if he were to spend less time playing silly jokes and more time practising his batting he would be a better cricketer. As Richardson had just scored 172 that was a trifle hard.

'You couldn't help but be fond of Jim though,' says Peter Richardson with a chuckle. 'He had the good of the game at heart.'

The apparently thick skin of Swanton was not immune to being punctured on another occasion. In a speech at an MCC dinner late in 1968, Colin Cowdrey made a few jokes at his expense.

Dear Colin,

Well done on a good speech, but I would like you to know that your cheap laugh at my expense on such an occasion was not appreciated. I think you should realize that we both hold positions of respect in cricket and that mine has been built by the work of a life-time. If you had accompanied what you said at Lord's – and at the Board dinner in Barbados – by some word of regard it would have been acceptable enough but you did not, in either case. I dare say our philosophies of cricket may be a longish way apart in certain aspects. You have, however, always had the best support I could give you when you most needed it, and I don't think this sort of thing is a very generous return.

Yours, Jim

Jim's support was particularly noticeable as a counsellor during the breakdown of Colin Cowdrey's first marriage, to Penny Chieseman.

Dear Jim,

If I have offended you then I am sad, and I hasten to apologise. I thought we knew each other well enough – still, if I exceeded the bounds of fair humour, I am sorry.

Colin

Speeches made by himself, and those of others at dinners at which he was in attendance, were a permanent ingredient of Jim's life. At one such in 1964, both he and his correspondent Lord Cobham had enjoyed a laugh at the expense of the Toastmaster:

Dear Jim,

Yes, I think the Toastmaster scored one out of ten on a good day!

Whilst listening to his excoria upon our Cricketers, I was reminded of a quotation by Robert Louis Stevenson in which he wrote to the Reverend H.B. Gage – or was it the Reverend Dr. Hyde? 'the blue ribbon which adorns your portly bosom forbids me to allow you the extenuating plea that you were drunk when it was done'.

I thought the pronunciation of Graveney was deplorable: it wouldn't have mattered had it been Gaukrodger, or even Tarbox.

Yours ever,
Charles

It would be wrong to imply that Jim was devoid of humour, or that he appreciated only *schadenfreude*. There were many occasions in which he seemed to enjoy an empalement of the stoked-up grandeur.

THE DAILY TELEGRAPH

Nov 21, 1963

Memorandum to Mr E.W. Swanton
    from News Telephones
    We have respectfully dedicated the enclosed to you and hope it will cause you amusement,
        With best wishes,
            Old Uncle Tom Cobley

In response to many requests from devotees of cricket we give below an 'Order of Cricket' being a solemn act of dedication to the game, fitting and proper to be observed at all county matches and especially suitable for Test Matches.

ORDER OF CRICKET

To the accompaniment of Sir Walford Davies's 'Solemn Melody', the assembly will rise as the procession enters the ground. First shall appear a small boy clad in green, bearing on an emerald cushion a first edition of Wisden. Then shall follow an Archofficial of MCC in full regalia flanked by two small boys each carrying a lighted stump. With dignity and in their customary white attire will follow the two umpires (but unencumbered by surplus sweaters). Taking up the rear will be the two captains, badged, blazered and beducked. For special occasions such as Test Matches an esoteric incense may be burned producing an aroma of linseed oil, willow and seamed leather. Banners and insignia are considered decent for 'high' matches.

Turning towards the scribes of the Press Box the Archofficial will say:

Do ye, O scribes and historians of our ancient game, swear to testify to the flight of the ball, angle of the bat, flick of the wrist and all manner of fielding acrobatics?

Then shall the reigning Chief Scribe, E.W. Swanton, arise in all his magnificence and opine:

Verily, what is performed shall be written with just embellishment, metaphor, simile, oxymoron, litotes, hyperbole, epigram and alliteration as is consistent with good commentary in couched terms and pensive style.

Through a microphone the Archofficial will then address those assembled:

All ye today, being gathered together to witness the rites of this most noble of all games are called upon to show cause or just impediment why these two Umpires (M and N) should not arbitrate, interpret and give irrevocable decision according to rules laid down and authorised in this realm. We do further declare that all decisions they make carry with them ex-cricket-cathedral quality and are under the seal of Umpire Infallibility. That shall be so.

We, therefore, now call upon you all to testify in the words of the Cricket Affirmation: (the assembly will then recite)

By two bats, six stumps, four bails and one leather ball we earnestly affirm our zeal, objectivity, discernment and innocence of mind to witness any pattern of proceedings which may come to pass in these next hours. With humility and sincerity of heart we pay homage to the chosen one score and two, and give utterance to our faith in the heritage and survival of this noble sport. Let justice be in our eyes, cheers in our throats, applause (but not barracking) in the meeting of our hands. May the joy, sorrow, anxiety and tumult of this occasion give rise to the serenity of memory in the aftermath of wholesome, goodly and liquid refreshment. May the game be played.

The assembly will then rise and sing the following two verses of the Cricket Anthem:

> Cricket, cricket through the ages
> Our true sport and way of life;
> By thy great and lustrous pages
> For thee we leave our home and wife.
> Thou, the Pennine Chain of England:
> Thou the willow of our right.
> Cricket, cricket through the ages
> Our companion – our delight.
> In the meadow of our counties –
> Survivor of the changing scene,
> With thy trophies and thy bounties
> Vanquisher of motives mean.
> Score the six o'er time's crude boundaries,
> Bowl along thy ageless seam.
> Cricket, cricket through the ages.
> This be our eternal theme.

A bugler will then sound the 'Last Stump' and with decorum the procession will make its exit to allow play to commence.

> Delf House, Sandwich,
> Kent
> 28th November 1963

Dear Mr. Cobley,

I am quite unable to do justice to your superb rolling prose. No wonder my halting sentences are occasionally greeted with a repetition which is an unspoken rebuke. I think the 'Order of Cricket' ought to be published, and I am trying to think where. What about the *Church Times*? A little lightness of touch would do them good.

In much appreciation . . .

> News Telephones Dept.
> December 2, 1963

Mr. E.W. Swanton,
Dear Mr Swanton,

Many thanks for your compliments and appreciation of 'Order of Cricket'. Your sentences, on the contrary, are by no means halting (litotes!) and if any among us here should repeat a word it is usually to make sure of hearing and interpreting you correctly.

'Order of Cricket' was No. 4 in a series. No. 1 was 'Much Blinding on the Phones' (dedicated to foreign correspondents). No. 2 'Rave Notice' (music critics); No. 3 'Hems Ancient and Modern' (Woman's Page). Yours has the distinction (?) of being the only prose effort so far.

Finally I would like to add that among all the acknowledgements I have received none has been addressed to 'Tom Cobley'. You are the first to show that degree of imagination. As for 'T. Cobley Esq.', that is a synthesis of a deft order, welding, as it does, the enduring and the aspiring.

Your praise gave me great satisfaction.

> Yours sincerely,
> Tom Cobley

When it came to fanciful asides from employees of the *Telegraph*, the bristly ginger-haired Leonard Crawley could not be repressed:

My dear Lord Sockem,

I have yours of the 10th inst., regarding your forthcoming Sporting Column in the S.T. [*Sunday Telegraph*] 'about to be'. In view of your multifarious duties, in re private organiser of international cricket tours, journalist, spokesman, broadcaster, and world's number one cricket authority, it is respectfully pointed out that your number 2, John Thicknesse, will have to do most of the work.

He, it appears, will be assisted by your admirable secretary, the beautiful Miss Surfleet, whom I suggest should be known as your number three as from the launching of the S.T. It would give her greater confidence in herself and also the authority to speak for you in your absence. This is important.

I see the policy of your office, 13 C on the third floor of the main building, will be looking forward rather than backwards and that the aim will be to find subjects of broad rather than of local interest. Might I therefore suggest that in your dummy run of January 29th you take Fougasse's simple cartoon of the pig looking forward and the pig looking backward as being illustrative of your policy.

A pig is broad and of universal interest.

To illustrate your policy by word I suggest two paragraphs:–

The first, looking forward. 'Colonel Barry Armstrong, late of the Royal Engineers, has been appointed to succeed Mr Cyril Grey as Secretary of the Golf Foundation. He is himself a fine golfer and was educated at Dublin University and the Royal Military Academy, Woolwich. Since his retirement from the Army he has from time to time done good work for *The Times* and the *Daily Telegraph*. Grey, a golfing cricketer of the front rank, has suffered considerably from a diseased bone in his right arm for several years and all will regret his retirement.'

The second, looking back. 'Overheard at Rye from one of the younger brigade during the President's Putter Meeting. "E.W. Swanton has now reached the very top, and in cricketing circles is generally regarded as the only link between Gubby and God."'

Four guineas please!

Best wishes,

Yours ever . . .

My dear Leonard,

Many thanks for your letter in respect of my diary feature in the new S.T., and it is a great comfort to a diffident journalist like myself, of limited scope and experience, that you are prepared to give your powerful assistance. Obviously the piffling figure of two guineas will have to be amended in your case, and I will see Mr Stevens personally to agree a more adequate scale of payment.

Your reference to the attractions of my secretary I take as a

compliment to my taste, and in view of your high opinion she shall be
referred to in future as my No. 2A.

The very promising drawings after Fougasse interested me greatly
because as it happens we (Nos. 1, 2, and 2A) are trying to find a
cartoonist. Miss Surfleet suggests that if you wish to be considered for
this important post you might care to submit a third picture, of a
bewhiskered brute looking not backwards or forwards but sideways (or,
if you like, sidelong).

Apart from the note of blasphemy your letter was much relished.
May I point out, incidentally, that the well-known Harrow names you
referred to should have been, respectively, Gray and Thicknesse. Many
great writers have been curiously fallible in the matter of spelling.

There had been an air of eleventh-hour improvisation about the
launch of 'the *S.T.* about to be' as Crawley had put it. Jim had been
involved in many of the discussions leading up to the first issue of the
Sunday Telegraph in February 1961:

Two diarists – Kenneth Rose and I – at first shared a room in 'the
Sunday' segment of the *Telegraph* building. But not for long. Whereas
he has been at large tickling our palates with his unique brand of social
commentary for 30 years, my editorship of the sporting diary lasted
little more than three weeks.

True, Michael Berry kindly insisted on my taking my own cricket
side in March on a long-arranged tour against the West Indian
Territories. Yet I suspect editor Donald McLachlan may have realised
this ageing dog was scarcely up to new tricks, at any rate on so wide a
stage. He wanted plenty of short, pithy paras – two adjectives seldom
applied to me.

But I had greatly enjoyed being in on the gestatory months in
conference with McLachlan and the sports editor Roger Wright. We
aimed, and surely with success, to be fast with Saturday's sporting
news, sound in critical comment, and, not least, different from big
brother.

With the *Daily Telegraph*'s sports editor, Kingsley Wright, Jim had a
good working relationship. But shortly after Wright's appointment
they had a strident disagreement:

Let me now make a few observations which I hope will clear the way to
a friendly and profitable relationship between us. I was not happy

Very Cosa Nostra. Presenting to the world a face unscarred by either the excoriant
lavas of ambition or the slow leprosies of indulgence?

The Arabs departing from Heston, 1936: apparently the first cricket team to travel by air. (*l. to r.*) J.D. Eggar; R.C. Robertson-Glasgow; R.G. Tindall; J.C. Bune; A.J. Wreford-Brown; E.W.S.; N.S. Hotchkin; J.M. Brocklebank; J.S.O. Haslewood; A.A. Muir; Umpire Hicks. Absent, H.T. Bartlett.

Two leg-spinners at Adelaide during MCC's tour 1950/51. E.W.S. with Clarrie Grimmett.
John Woodcock

Cartoon by Ronnie Carr during the Arabs' tour of Barbados, 1966/67. Oswald Gibbons, Jim's faithful driver and friend over many years, was apt to be led astray by the team. "Gibbons, you've been on the rum!" "Oh no sir! By the omnipotent one, I've only had a drink!!"

E.W. SWANTON'S XI IN WEST INDIES 1956.

Mending the fences: Jim's side in the West Indies, 195?
(*back*) M.J. Stewart; R.G. Marlar; D.E. Blake; Swaranjit Singh; A.S.M. Oakman; A.C.D. Ingleby-Mackenzie; R.C.M. Kimpton; G. Goonesena.
(*front*) E.W.S.; F.M. Tyson; G.M.G. Doggart; M.C. Cowdrey (cpt.); J.J. Warr; T.W. Graveney.

A central figure in the Press Box at Adelaide, 1958/59 tour.

John Woodcock

Giving fielding practice at Berbice. E.W.S.'s International Team's tour of the West Indies, 1961.

Press posse for the 1958/59 tour of Ceylon, Australia and New Zealand:
(*back row, l. to r.*) Johnny Wardle (*Daily Mail*); John Woodcock (*The Times*); Charles Fortune (seconded to ABC); Brian Chapman (*Daily Mirror*); Ian Peebles (*Sunday Times*); Charles Bray (*Daily Herald*); Alex Bannister (*Daily Mail*); John Clarke (*Evening Standard*); Frank Rostron (*Daily Express*).
(*seated*) Bill Bowes (*Yorkshire Evening News*); Crawford White (*News Chronicle*); John Kay (*Manchester Evening News*); Bill Bailey (*Star*); E.W.S. (*Daily Telegraph*); Alec Bedser (*Star, broadcasting ABC*).
(*ground*) Ron Roberts (*freelance*); Denys Rowbotham (*Manchester Guardian*); Harry Gee (*Reuters*).

John Woodcock

A party at Half Moon Bay, Jamaica, during the MCC tour 1959/60.
(*facing camera, from left*) Mrs Rostron; Frank Rostron; Ian Peebles; Ron Roberts; E.W.S.; Ann Swanton.
(*turning to the camera, from left*) John Woodcock; Ramon Subba Row and his fiancée Anne Harrison; John Goddard; Gerry Gomez; Mrs Rex Alston.

Jim looking slightly bemused,
having just got married.

An ecclesiastical conversation with
David Sheppard, shortly to become
Bishop of Woolwich.

At the marriage of Jim's niece
Jane Nelson to David Biggins,
St Mary's Church, Harrow on
the Hill, 8 August 1964.
(*l. to r.*) Jim's father, 'Billy';
his stepmother, Helen;
another niece, Judy
Langdon; E.W.S.

Hands on with the boys in rolling
the pitch. The Arabs match at
Horris Hill in Berkshire took place
annually for over 50 years.

The induction of Canon David Naumann as Rector of St Clement's, Sandwich in 1982. Robert Runcie, Archbishop of Canterbury, officiating. Jim was the churchwarden.

The book launch for *The World of Cricket* in Melbourne, January 1966. With Sir Robert Menzies and Doug Walters.

Making a point when speaking at a Cricket Society dinner. Roy Hattersley and Hubert Doggart either side.

'A word in your ear!' Lord's Bi-Centenary Auction, 1987. (*front row*) Colin Cowdrey and Marcus Williams of *The Times*; (*row behind*) Michael Sissons, literary agent and Tim Rice listening in.

A tender moment on the beach in Barbados.

Pondering his next move at Crystal Springs Cottage,
St James, 1977.

Ann in the garden at 'Coralita'.

Having a quick net!

Shrimping!

'Now, look heah!' Differing views over cricket with South Africa.
(*l. to r.*) The Duke of Norfolk; E.W.S.; Arthur Gilligan.

With the Rt. Hon. John Major, Canterbury Week, 1993.
Major was there to support Surrey in their match against Kent.
Kent CCC

Admiring his
wife's horticultural
skills in the garden
at Delf House.

At his 90th birthday celebration, with Ann in front of Andrew Festing's portrait in the Old Library at Lord's.

about our exchanges on Sunday, and probably on reflection you were not either. If I had thought the Devon game was of prime importance I would have gone down myself. If by chance Sussex had won it would perhaps have justified the lead as one of the miracles of the season. No Southern county has ever won a quarter final tie, and the result was virtually inevitable. Further there were only three men from Sussex clubs in the side and there is correspondingly scant local interest. The game of much more general appeal was that in the Midlands where the Champions, Warwickshire, were knocked out. I would have gone there had I not seen the Midland Counties play at Birmingham a week or two before. As it was, the Wasps game, with ten Internationals performing and everyone wanting to know the form of Sharp who had been excluded, as you know, from the team against Wales, was in my view the event with the widest interest – quite apart from the principle of the No. 1 man being given the lead.

I have gone into this incident again because you are inclined, if I may say so, to jump in and pronounce judgement without much apparent regard for the expert's point of view. (As a Yorkshireman you won't, I hope, mind my writing bluntly.) When I wished you well in the new job I did it with all sincerity, and in the knowledge that you are a top-class inside man – none better. I said as much to Michael Berry the last time I saw him (which was on the subject of Marlar leaving, and the problems made by that), and I repeated it more recently to the Editor.

Fine. That's one side of the job. But there is also the business of selection, knowing what pulls best and is of first importance from the point of view both of our readers and of the game itself. Here I would say: when there is a decision to be made and it is practicable to do so, ask the No. 1 man's opinion. You're not bound to take it! But if it's not worth seeking the chap can't be up to his job!

As you know I've been knocking around among games-players of all sorts and kinds for thirty-five years and been in Fleet Street all that time apart from the war. And I've got stacked away here many thousand readers' letters – all of which, I might say, have been acknowledged formally or answered in detail. Therefore I flatter myself I know pretty well what our public wants.

I'm sure you've picked up a pretty good idea yourself from contacts in golf clubs and so on, and I expect you're hoping to get around more now outside as soon as you can palm off some of the detail work. I won't play the point further except to say I'm sure the best results must come from a partnership, with the ultimate responsibilities of course taken by the man on the spot.

I will, of course, come on Monday (though in fact as I'm always working on Saturday and Sunday I reckon often to give myself Monday free), and will bring various idea notes I have. Particularly I think we could get a much better balance as between straight news and newsy features, and hope to enlist your support for a scheme in that direction.

One of the things to tackle pretty quickly is the question of my No. 2 both for cricket and Rugby football, Melford and Marlar having virtually deserted, and I, of course, having to devote a good deal of time to the S.T. That, of course, must be talked over outside a Sports Conference, and I suggest we could tackle it, if you have time, tomorrow afternoon. I am due to have a session with Pawley and we might discuss it together.

I feel we have the chance now of making a better sports section than Fleet St. has yet seen, if we co-operate as we should, and as I am sure we will. You are just a little quick-tempered, if I may say so, and I am afraid I am too. But it is bad for discipline and morale if we disagree forcibly in front of junior people on the staff, and I will certainly do my best to avoid it . . . on the terms I've mentioned you can rely on all possible co-operation from me.

Jim's involvement with the internal politics of the *Telegraph* meant that he was acting as a kind of deputy editor regardless of the fact that he had not been given that post. And the paper seemed to indulge his commitment and indeed benefited from it as he gave advice on all sorts of appointments in the sporting field (angling, athletics, tennis, golf, football, rugby) as well as formulating schemes for structuring the management pyramid and presenting ideas for the editors.

I, for instance, have various notions which I would like to raise. But I would want to do so at a different level. Indeed I feel after 14 years in a senior position and having introduced to the paper most of the principal sporting writers, that I am entitled to ask for this.

The demands of cricket in the summer and now winter led Jim to relinquish the job of rugby correspondent in 1964. But it was not just the workload that hastened the decision. He was also falling a little out of love with the way the game often was being played. After an encounter between Ireland and Wales in Dublin, which former international fly-half Cliff James described as 'quite the worst forward brawl I have ever seen. This match was a disgrace to the name of rugby', the *Telegraph* and its correspondent were threatened with libel by Brian Thomas, the Welsh forward. Jim first heard the news when on a cricket tour of the Far East and when contacting the *Telegraph* suggested, in support of his opinion, other possible witnesses including H.A. Toft of the *Observer*, A.A. Mulligan, Tony O'Reilly and Windsor Lewis. Criticism of the game had been widespread. The relevant section of Jim's report read:

> Before going further into analysis and detail, one must refer with regret to a more important aspect of the play.
>
> There was a good deal of time-out obstruction, frequently penalised. There was also much wilful holding and some striking of men not in possession which the referee presumably missed because, unlike several of the participants, he was giving his attention to the ball.
>
> Thomas of Wales, though by no means the only offender, was the man particularly involved, often with Leahy, the new Irish lock and Thomas's opposite number.
>
> To an impartial eye, Wales generally looked the aggressors, with Thomas in the thick. When the latter was an undergraduate at Cambridge, his impetuosity was bad enough. Now, in his fourth season, it can no longer be put down to youthful exuberance, and is accordingly the less excusable.
>
> The physical exchanges at forward were not only plainly seen by the crowd, but also on Irish Television, and although the presence of the cameras is incidental to the offence, the effect on viewers and especially on aspiring young players, is not at all incidental.
>
> Nor is it enough to say that blows in the heat of the moment are quickly forgotten afterwards over a drink.
>
> No doubt they are, but the damage to the reputation of a magnificent game remains, and the time has come, I believe, when because of the failings of a few of their foremost players, the national Unions should face their problem together.
>
> If they look at the situation honestly, they have to recognise that since the New Zealander, C.J. Brownlie, was sent off the field at Twickenham 40 years ago, no referee in the home counties has taken extreme action in an international match.
>
> This despite the law which says that for a second offence of foul play or misconduct the referee must order the player off.
>
> The hullaballoo over Brownlie was such that the player in an international match can feel he is completely safe, whatever infamies he gets up to. This being so, is there not a special onus on selectors not to consider persistent offenders for international teams?

> Either the referees must be fortified to face a highly unpleasant duty, or moved from the scene by those who choose the teams.

Subsequent enquiry revealed a 'Biters' Club', with evidence of teeth-marks as victims' qualification for membership. The *Telegraph* were prepared to justify Swanton's comments in court; however the plaintiff hastily withdrew.

It had only been fourteen months since Jim had threatened litigation himself. During the England tour of Australia in 1962–63, captained by Ted Dexter, the *Evening News*'s E.M. Wellings, self-styled as cricket's most controversial writer, had disturbed the Swanton equilibrium:

> The touring party have been cosseted. The presence of the Duke of Norfolk as manager has caused them to be regarded as something special.
>
> Their fibre has been sapped by the presence of a sycophantic following of English writers who think none should criticise the Duke's followers and deeply resent any [criticism] that others may make.
>
> One of their number, indeed, has been unwilling to speak to me since I uttered criticism in Adelaide. This week, when the local Press accused Dexter of following a negative policy in the field, this English contingent were disturbed to the point of writing letters of protest to the Sydney papers.
>
> It seems that the players are to be regarded as being not so much under the management of the Duke as under his patronage. This is a thoroughly unhealthy state of affairs, the team members obviously weakened temperamentally by favoured treatment.
>
> The team's propaganda has caused this to be seen as a goodwill tour and the players have been persuaded that the important thing is to be good losers.
>
> They are, in fact, here to play cricket seriously for the Ashes, and to do so in such a spirit of enterprise that England's tarnished cricketing reputation in Australia shall be restored.
>
> They will not gain the respect of people here in any other way.

Various Australian newspapers syndicated the *Evening News* report and a large wodge of legal correspondence testifies to the fact that Jim was a long way down the path towards instigating proceedings. Incensed by what Wellings had written, he wrote a letter of protest to the *Sydney Herald* and did an interview on the subject for the ATN

Channel 7 'Comment'. An apology was then drawn up for the offending journals to print. None of them did.

APOLOGY

In your issue of November 21 an article appeared under the heading 'ENGLISH SIDE IS TOO SOFT, SAYS CRITIC'. This article contains an inference that Mr E.W. Swanton in his capacity as a cricket correspondent has sapped the fibre of the English cricketers by his failure to fulfil his proper function as a critic. The word sycophantic was used in this connection. This newspaper regrets that the article in question which was written and supplied by Mr E.M. Wellings should have seemed to make any attack on the character or reputation of Mr Swanton and accordingly withdraws any implication against his character or reputation which may arise out of the publication of the article in question and apologises for any embarrassment which may have been caused to him.

From London, the Editor of the *Telegraph*, Sir Colin Coote, sent a supportive note:

My dear Swanton,

I am sorry you are having trouble with Wellings and will await any further information you feel to be necessary.

I am always ready, as you know, to defend the people who work for us, and it is intolerable that dog should try to eat dog in this way. Do let me know how you get on.

Yours sincerely,

Colin R. Coote

Dear Sir Colin

Thank you for your sympathetic note of November 30th about my slight trouble with Wellings.

I find that although I am advised by Minter, Simpson & Co, one of the leading solicitors in Sydney, that I have a case against him, and probably also against the *Melbourne Herald, Sydney DT*, and *Sydney Morning Herald*, who reprinted the *Evening News* piece of November 20th, the practical difficulties of getting anything done before I am due to leave for home are formidable. It's not worth all the time and trouble and cost.

Therefore Minter, Simpson are merely writing warning letters to the papers in friendly terms – they no doubt reprinting the stuff without realising any implication as far as I was concerned – and a stiff warning letter to Wellings. He will be told that if I do not proceed here that is without prejudice to any action that may be taken in England.

As regards an approach to the *Evening News* I will of course be guided completely by you. They could be asked to print an apology, or merely warned that the article in question contained a damaging imputation against me, which if repeated would involve proceedings.

It is hard for me to do anything at this range, and if you approve of this line I hope you may be good enough to get the office solicitors to send something.

It is a small matter really, and I hate troubling you with it. The fact is, though, that Wellings' vituperative stuff does more harm to Anglo-Australian cricket relation, and to the reputation of English journalists in Australia, than anything else. In this case any or all of the English press in the box would witness to the fact that in this piece he was referring specifically to me, and inferring that I was not doing my job for fear of offending the Duke. The latter and I are very good friends, and have been long before this tour; but you will have seen enough of my stuff from Australia on this tour to know that it has been critical where the need has been there . . .

In an interview with the one-time *Newsnight* reporter James Hogg in 1992, the acerbic Wellings revealed his true self. Of Swanton he said:

He was an appalling snob and he did appalling things on the field. Once in a game against Hampstead he was caught in the gully early. He said 'Good God!' and they almost had to carry him off the field.

I caught him for five at Beckenham. It was the only time I've heard a side cheer the dismissal of one of their own players.

He was a good, but stodgy bat. No good as a bowler. As a writer he was a very good judge of a batsman, though not of bowlers.

I didn't care for his manner on or off the field. He didn't have many friends at Lord's. He asked Bertie Henley of the *Mail*, 'Why am I so disliked?' Bertie replied, 'Well, old man, you do **bound**.'

These spats with which Jim seemed to be irresistibly embroiled at one time even embraced his 'very good friend' the Duke of Norfolk:

Dear Swanton,

My attention has been brought to the articles which you have written in *The Cricketer* in what would appear to be a private feud between yourself and Dexter. After the first one I took certain action and informed the MCC. At the same time I told the Secretary of the MCC that I proposed to have a word with you when next we met as it would be a more friendly gesture than writing. The MCC were fully prepared for me to take this action. However, only yesterday another article, written by you, was shown to me and I do not feel that I can wait, in the hope of meeting you, hence this letter.

As President of the Sussex County Cricket Club I resent very much the remarks which you have made concerning what I assume to be the m members of the County Committee, which presumably are also meant by the words: Men at Hove. I would have thought that anyone in your position would at least have written to the Committee concerned before writing such articles which, in my own humble opinion, were entirely unnecessary, and I should be glad if in the future you feel it necessary to make any comments that we should be informed prior to having to read it ourselves.

I am sending a copy of this letter to the Secretary of the MCC and the Secretary of the Sussex County Cricket Club.

Yours truly,
Norfolk
President, Sussex County Cricket Club

In a series of articles in *The Cricketer* in 1965 Jim had criticised Ted Dexter for some comments in his *Observer* column. Dexter was reacting to a further furore over the legality of the action of West Indian fast bowler Charlie Griffith. This had arisen during the first Test match of a series between West Indies and Australia in Kingston, Jamaica. Everyone, it seemed, had an opinion.

In the English press, comment has varied from the full and lucid analysis by the cricket correspondent of *The Times* entitled 'Griffith both victim and culprit' to several lurid quotes from other quarters and, in particular, a remark which has given much offence in the West Indies by E.R. Dexter . . .

Griffith is obviously making a great effort to bowl fairly. Whether he is succeeding is a matter of opinion . . . No . . . justification can be made regarding Dexter's comment in the *Observer* to the effect that to the English players who took part the result of the 1963 series against the West Indies was 'meaningless'. Anything more calculated to injure the proud feelings of a friendly cricket power, most of whom still like to look up to English cricketers, and are inclined to take their example from them, would be hard to imagine. To my mind it is disgraceful that a defeated Test captain should hazard his country's sporting good name by a comment of this kind.

Indeed under the heading Disciplined Decisions, the Rules of County Cricket specify that it is the responsibility of each County club to ensure that none of its registered players makes any public pronouncement that is 'detrimental to cricket'. The committee of the club must give 'prior consent' to all articles, books, and material for broadcasting and TV. . . . Sussex gave no such permission, their captain presumably faces disciplinary action: if they did they surely must have a strange idea of what can be said without, in the International sense, detriment to cricket.

In the May issue of *The Cricketer,* Jim wrote:

I had hoped in these Notes to comment on a remark in the *Observer* by E.R. Dexter prompted, I gather, by some words of mine in the April issue of *The Cricketer*. Did he call me 'a tetchy schoolmaster'? Unfortunately the cutting has not yet arrived, so meanwhile I can only metaphorically pull on my gown and take a few preparatory swishes with the nearest bamboo cane. As an admirer of the profession I feel rather flattered.

And then, one month further on:

Talking, incidentally, of Dexter I have now seen the *Observer* piece wherein I am referred to as a 'tetchy history master complaining of an impertinent pupil'. This remark follows his reprinting of some words of mine in the *Daily Telegraph* saying that there will be little respect left in the West Indies for English sportsmanship if a defeated captain (E.R.D.) is allowed to write that the victory of his Test opponents has been 'meaningless' on the grounds that a bowler's action was unfair. (Bowler Griffith, Test series England v. West Indies, 1963).

'I always understood sportsmanship to be a matter of playing the game, and to quote the dictionary, being fair and considerate in the process. Of course, the gracious winner and the good loser are part and parcel of the sporting idea, *but surely only on the assumption that the contest has been fair in the first place.*'

So writes Dexter in justification of his remarks, the bold italics being mine. But who said the England v. West Indies series was unfair? This remark illustrates the essential difficulty of the player commenting on current events wherein he has taken part, for here is the prejudiced competitor judging his own cause. Dexter, disregarding the umpires, himself decides and therefore apparently absolves himself from obeying the normal dictates of good sportsmanship. That is the only inference to be drawn from the comment I have quoted.

To any Englishman in the West Indies sensitive to the reputation of English cricket, and having furthermore no small admiration for Dexter himself, it has been mortifying to see a headline across a whole page reading:

DEXTER ADDS TO THE DISGRACE

– to hear the hurt comments of old players and administrators, and to read disparaging letters on the subject . . .

Dexter . . . was in the best possible position to pass on his opinion about Griffith to the highest authorities either through his county committee, or the England Selection Committee of which he was a co-opted member, or the MCC Cricket Committee.

It was precisely to guard against this sort of spicy disclosure that MCC and the counties recently made their stringent regulations as regards player-writing. Did Sussex pass his article, or was it not submitted to them? I gather from them that after several meetings the matter has now been resolved and MCC have been informed. It sounds as though there may have been some more tiresomely tetchy people down at Hove.

Eventually, Ted put pen to paper:

My disagreements with you over the years, mild as they have been, invariably stem from your patronising manner towards England cricketers, not to speak of your *penchant* for championing even the worst causes on behalf of any cricketing body other than that of your mother country . . . Similarly, I can fault some of my friends who see the replacement of your good self, as doing nothing but good to the world at large and cricket in particular.

Dear Ted,

Thank you for your spirited letter which I enjoyed . . . Now let's get it straight. What I am concerned about is the good reporting of cricket in the eyes of the public, because this is vital to the character of the game itself. Spice and off-field 'revelations' – guff about bitterness in the field – are saleable in a certain market for big money. I think that if a player has a loyalty to the game that has made him, then he ought to be proof against this sort of temptation . . .

My writing! Patronising? I have written a good many thousand words about you, and they are all in my cuttings books. Next time you come down show me something that could fairly be termed patronising. I'd have thought more of it was pretty appreciative.

Championing the other side? Well, I dare say it may seem so sometimes as compared with the jingoistic style of the populars in many cases. All one tries to do is to see people and things dispassionately and to give the other point of view equal insight . . .

'We often were at daggers drawn,' remarked Ted Dexter over the phone from his French home recently, 'but during those run-ins with Jim, I used to lead him on and try to tease him. I liked to pinprick that old school attitude who thought that a house match at Eton was as important as a Test Match in Australia. You know, something was wrong with the world if you weren't paying lip-service to the clubby traditions. But really, I admired him enormously in many ways. To carry on caring for cricket as much as he did and for as long as he did was quite remarkable.'

Equally remarkable was E.W.S.'s editorship – with the invaluable assistance of several eminent hands – of a monumental tome entitled *The World of Cricket* which gave comprehensive coverage of practically every branch of the game on the library shelves. Produced in 1966, the massive undertaking involved 117 writers contributing 600,000 words in over 1000 entries. It demanded much of his time and concentration. Still Swanton always found a few hours to escape on to the field to play himself, where it was noted in Press reports that 'E.W. (Lucky Jim) Swanton's dignified episcopal gait made his pads look like gaiters' and that his 'finest stroke was less a drive than excommunication.' On one occasion 'a further disaster occurred when Swanton ambled amiably along for an easy single to find that a brilliant shy by Silk at one stump hit the wicket well in advance of his arrival.'

A.A. Thomson reporting for the *Trade News*:

As has frequently happened, this was a triangular tournament between the National Book League, the Authors and the weather. We had been optimistic, because after all, this had been a mild winter and indeed, the real severity did not set in till the first week in June. The game, however, began under disappointingly cheerless skies, which ought to have been ashamed of looking down discouragingly on such eager cricketers and such fascinatingly garbed spectators.

The cricket writers' best-worn cliché is: Play began quietly. But the main thing about truisms is that they are true. E.W. Swanton, the Authors' captain, was accompanied to the wicket by H.C. Blofeld, of Cambridge and Norfolk, who could not make an unattractive stroke if he tried. When he had the bowling he would score an elegant two or a single; Swanton, though equally elegant, started less productively, frequently removing his bat from the orbit of rising deliveries, in such a manner as to draw from the pavilion the approving cry: 'Oh, well left alone, sir!'

There was in his reception of a maiden over an archiepiscopal dignity which was a lesson to us all. It was sad that he left at 16.

In that game Richie Benaud top-scored with 42 for the Authors who declared at 160 for 9. Benaud then took four of the five National Book League wickets to fall, before they passed that total with heavy rain threatening to bring the game to an untimely close.

The match which had taken place at Vincent Square in Westminster was immortalised in the published correspondence between the pastoral poet and eminent academic Edmund Blunden and his Christ's Hospital schoolmate, Archibald Hector Buck, affectionately known as 'Buckie', who became a house master at Oakham before returning to teach at his alma mater. 'Buckie' re-enacts an amusing episode in the game:

A.H.B. (umpiring after the lunch interval, to the not-out R. Benaud): 'D'you want guard?'

R.B.   'Naow, the other umpire [no less a figure than I.A.R. Peebles] gave it me before lunch.'
And again:

E.W.S. (puffing and blowing and looking majestic at mid-off, puts about 8 or 9 men into position, but nevertheless says to Benaud) 'Now, Richie, what about these chaps – put 'em where you want, you know, have the field just as you want –'

R.B.   (dead-pan face) 'Aow, that's all right, Jim.'

E.W.S. 'Oh yes, but you have the field just how you want –'

R.N.   'But I never do, Jim.'

E.W.S. 'What? What? What d'you mean – ?'

R.B.   'I never do put 'em when you're captain, Jim.'

E.W.S. 'What? Why? What? –'

R.B.   'I just want to see where you put 'em and bowl to it.'
        And if you can extract the urine from anyone, and especially from Jim Swanton, more prettily than that, I'll be proud to hear from you.

Soon fun on the cricket field was to seem a rare event. A riot in a Test match in Jamaica and the dark clouds of Powellism and apartheid were looming on the horizon. Jim's regard for the Caribbean and its people was reciprocated with an invitation to give the address at a Memorial Service for Sir Frank Worrell at Westminster Abbey in April 1967.

WORRELL MEMORIAL ADDRESS
WESTMINSTER ABBEY
April 7, 1967

In this ancient Abbey church, which enshrines so much of the history of England and of the British Empire and Commonwealth, we, gathered here today, are taking part in a unique service.

Here, where the most famous have been buried, and the lives of the greatest commemorated, we are assembled to mourn for, and to pray for the soul of Sir Frank Mortimer Maglinne Worrell, a cricketer.

It is making history to open the doors of the Abbey for the passing of a sportsman. My privilege and responsibility now is to try and give you such a picture of the man as will explain why in their wisdom the Dean and Chapter of Westminster have allowed us, his friends and admirers, from so many parts of the world, to pay our last respect in this glorious, awesome setting.

Frank Worrell was born at Bank Hall on the outskirts of Bridgetown, Barbados, on August 1st, 1924. His father was a sailor, and so it came that when his mother emigrated to America he was brought up by his grandmother. It was from the roof of her small wooden house, adjoining the ground of the Empire club, which has produced so many of the best Barbadian players, that he watched his first cricket. It was this environment no doubt that fired his ambition and gave him models of excellence to follow.

While he was learning to be a cricketer he was also growing up as a Christian. There is perhaps scarcely a firmer stronghold of Anglicanism in the whole communion of Canterbury than Barbados – a fact that perhaps adds a little more to the appropriateness of this service. Frank sang as a boy in the choir of St Michael's Cathedral, and ever after had a great love of church music. A pleasant story is told by his brother-in-law of how some years ago in Lancashire they both attended the three hours service of devotion on Good Friday. After the service, Frank complained there had not been enough hymns, and so they went home and played some more on the piano and sang.

The foundations of the Christian philosophy that governed his life were laid then as a boy. As a cricketer he grew up fast. At the age of only 19 he scored 308 not out against the great rivals across the water, Trinidad.

Here in fact was a prodigy, whose succession to the West Indies team when war ended, and Test Matches were played again, seemed an automatic thing. He was soon being hailed, in company with two other young Bajans, Everton Weekes and Clyde Walcott – all three born close to one another and in the space of 18 months – as a great player.

This is not the occasion to speak either of his technique or of his achievements on the field, except perhaps to say this – that cricket, like any other art, is an expression of character, and there was always about Frank's play a grace, a dignity, and an unruffleable serenity that reflected the man.

But Frank had set his eyes on horizons beyond the cricket field. He came to Lancashire to earn his living as a professional in the league, and at the same time to take his degree at Manchester University. He warmed to Lancashire (and in particular to Radcliffe where he played), and Lancashire warmed to him. His twelve years there made him the most fervent of Anglophiles, and so he remained.

It was a Lancastrian, George Duckworth – that shrewd, humorous, lovable man – who, I think, first saw in Frank the special qualities of leadership. At the early age of 26 (ten years before being honoured by his Country) he was captaining with much promise a mixed Commonwealth team, mostly of men a good deal older than he, managed by Duckworth in India.

When at last he was named as captain of the West Indies, on the tour to Australia in 1960, the appointment was accepted by the rest of his team, if not by him, as a challenge to his race.

Under the subtle knack of his personality differences of colour, island prejudices, seemed to melt away. The tour of Australia was a triumph both on the field and off it, ending, as everyone will remember, with a motorcade through the streets of Melbourne lined with half a million cheering people.

Three summers later he brought the West Indies team to England for a tour that enthused the sporting world no less than the one in Australia. He retired from playing after this, and in the New Year of 1964 received the honour of Knighthood.

For the last three years of his life he was, of course, a national hero, but in bearing that difficult mantle he lost none of his modesty, none of his warmth.

It is, of course, a deep sorrow that by the workings of Providence he has been taken away with such suddenness when it seemed that he had so much more to contribute in areas outside sport: in social fields, and in particular in the life of the University of the West Indies.

He had made a deep mark already in Jamaica as University Warden (with a seat also in the Jamaican Senate). Since last year he had been Dean of Students in Trinidad. In both these islands the civic authorities had utilized his influence with young people and his readiness to identify himself with them.

He had not worked in Trinidad for long but it was a measure of the affection he attracted that four chartered aeroplanes were needed to fly mourners to the funeral in Barbados.

No doubt, in course of time, he might have served in one or other of the Caribbean territories in the very highest office. He was a Federalist, nearest whose heart was the unity of the West Indian peoples in all their diversity.

Myself, I believe he harboured a special ambition to help bring on that branch of the University in his native Barbados which is now building, and on the site on which he is buried. He had a warm, understanding heart and a sort of sleepy charm that endeared [him to] old and young alike. He was essentially a bringer-together by the sincerity and friendliness of his personality; a sporting catalyst in an era where International rivalries too often grew sour and ugly.

In the television age men famous in the world of games have a formidable influence, and strange figures are sometimes magnified into heroes. Frank Worrell was the absolute antithesis of the strident and the bumptious, or, so to speak, the great-sportsman-who-is-not.

It is his example – and that of many of his West Indian cricket contemporaries – that has helped so much towards an appreciation and an admiration for his countrymen, in England and throughout the Commonwealth.

One of his opposing captains in an appreciation of him wrote that however the game ended 'he made you feel a little better'. (Which isn't a bad epitaph.) No doubt he made many of us feel a little better, from the youngsters in Boys' Town at Kingston to Sydney hoboes on the Hill.

Have I pictured a paragon? Well, he certainly didn't look the part and would have been horrified at the very thought of a tribute such as this. He was gay and convivial, and though his convictions were deep and sincere they were never paraded. Yet, just as England brought cricket to the West Indies, the West Indies in return, I believe, has given us the ideal cricketer.

When His Excellency the High Commissioner was reading those . . .

Beatitudes just now the thought came: whom do I know who has fulfilled them better? May God rest his soul and give consolation to his widow and daughter. And may his example live with us.

From canonisation to vilification is but a short step. One year and two weeks later, a speech by the Rt Hon J. Enoch Powell, MP to the Annual General Meeting of the West Midlands Area Conservative Political Centre at the Midland Hotel in Birmingham triggered a chorus of execration. Shortly afterwards, Jim was drawn to write a condemnatory letter to the *Spectator*:

Sir: In a recent letter to the *Daily Telegraph*, Mr Patrick Wall, MP, seemed to applaud Mr Enoch Powell's infamous speech as a clarion call to Britons who have pride in their country.

Within the last few days an Indian student at Highbury has been set upon, kicked and slashed, by four sixteen year olds chanting 'blackman, blackman, Enoch, Enoch'. A respectable West Indian citizen at Wolverhampton celebrating a family christening has been attacked without provocation and injured by people also invoking the name of Enoch, the prophet. 'Enoch dockers' at Westminster have been putting their boots into students off the ground.

Are we to explain this sort of behaviour as some sort of twisted expression of national pride?

Many will echo Mr Wall's cry for leadership of a kind that will kindle 'those principles that made us great', but what has this aspiration to do with a bloodthirsty, hateful speech, lacking a single compassionate phrase towards fellow-members of our Commonwealth, which has so fanned the flames of ignorance and prejudice as to bring about such episodes as these?

If Enoch knew what passions he was about to unleash, he was guilty of an act that was the complete negation of patriotism. It is possibly more charitable to suppose that his frothy speech was a bid for future political power which, pray God, he may never achieve.

If 'Enochism' were ever to win through there would surely be a migration from this once great land of white as well as black.

E. W. Swanton

Delf House, Sandwich, Kent.

Towards the end of that 1968 season came perhaps the most tumultous time in the history of cricket. Forever after, it was to be known as the D'Oliveira affair.

Jim's diary:

England halved the rubber with Australia, Basil D'Oliveira, the South African-born Cape-coloured resident in England, having played a memorable innings of 158 which should surely have clinched his place for the forthcoming tour to South Africa.

But it did not. After D'Oliveira's crucial contribution to England's victory at that final Oval Test a bombshell lay in wait. When the selectors emerged at 1.50 am on August 28th from a meeting which had lasted nearly six hours, there was widespread astonishment at learning that D'Oliveira's apparently secure place had gone to Tom Cartwright.

I have scarcely met anyone, nor have I had a single letter, that has attempted to make a case for the selectors. One reader seems to sum up a general feeling when he writes of 'The grotesque casuistry of the attempt to explain the omission of D'Oliveira on cricketing grounds'.

It was this attempt on the part of the chairman to justify what had been done that was for many about the last straw.

To say that there were 'several better batsmen' after a Test innings of such a calibre; to assert on the one hand that the South African pitches are expected to be grassy enough to suit Cartwright and on the other that D'Oliveira's bowling did not come into consideration; this in the language of ordinary followers was merely adding insult to injury.

This setback in esteem comes at a time when the control of cricket is just being established on a constitutional basis for the first time, and has been put in the hands of an MCC Council on which the committee of the Club has a considerable representation.

As a cricket historian I believe that the game has generally been wisely and selflessly guided from Lord's, and that its collective judgment comes well from scrutiny over the span of a century or more. There are, however, moments that call for reform in all institutions, and such a one must surely have arrived for MCC. 4 September 1968.

The public reaction had been immediate. MPs and many others voiced protests. There were the first resignations of MCC members. The general feeling was more against the Committee than the selectors who, it was felt, had been acting under duress. A dissident movement sought a Special Meeting. And then, on 14 September, Tom Cartwright dropped out, injured. Two days later the MCC Selection Committee met and announced that 'Basil D'Oliveira is being invited to join the touring party'.

When on Tom Cartwright falling out, D'Oliveira was named in his place the South African Prime Minister John Vorster declared it was a political decision and denied him entry. Thereupon MCC cancelled the tour. It was an unhappy note on which the Club handed over authority to the Cricket Council which later became controlled by the counties. *Daily Telegraph*, 4 September 1968.

The volcano had been waiting to erupt for a long time. A dozen years earlier during the 1956–57 tour of South Africa Jim had seen at first hand the change in attitude in that country. At first, after coming to power in 1948, the ruling Nationalist Party had trodden carefully, but now it was certain of its position. Jim abhorred apartheid, and therefore had opted out of the subsequent 1964–65 tour of South Africa. By early 1968 the increasingly political policies in the Republic had made a potential confrontation much more likely when it came to external ties. Assurances of no pre-conditions on the selection of an MCC team (requested by Secretary Billy Griffith in a letter to the South African Cricket Association) had received no response. The advice to the MCC Committee from former Prime Minister Sir Alec Douglas-Home after talks with both South African Government officials and members of SACA was that there should be no insistence on a definite answer. Hypothetical questions might produce a premature reply detrimental to prospects of the tour taking place and could appear 'politically inspired', he said. When Lord Cobham (a former MCC president, who had a South African mother and extensive business interests in the Republic) visited there in February/March 1968, he found that even hypothetical questions received an unequivocal rejoinder. In a letter to Swanton in 1972, he related what had happened:

When the telephone message came through that the PM would like to see me for a few moments before I left for England, there was, in fact, no reluctance on my part. I had expressed to a friend that I would like to meet the PM at some time and had presumed that this could not be arranged since, when the message came, we were actually packing to go on board the ship which was due to sail in two hours. What is true is that I had no wish to become involved and merely passed on *informally* what I had gathered from an informal discussion.

PS: To this day I am not quite sure who fixed up the meeting with Vorster. Certain it is that when I left for Parliament House I had no idea that our meeting was to be in any way an 'official' one. After a few generalities, the subject of the coming Tour was broached, probably by

me, and at once V. made it absolutely clear that a team which included
D'O. would not be welcome.

The MCC has been bitterly criticized – I think unfairly. Two factors
tended to obscure the issue:

(1) V.'s previous conversation with Sir Alec, which quite clearly left
the door ajar, if not open, and

(2) the fact that D'O. was *at that time* by no means an automatic
choice for the S.A. Tour.

What could MCC have done, even had they got Alec and me
together before this committee? Our stories would have been wholly
conflicting. Presumably their only course of action would have been to
have *insisted* on a reply to Billy's previous telegram to the SACA. Their
answer *must* have been a discouraging one; and then V. would have
been able to say 'I *told* Sir Alec to wait: now MCC have gone off at
half-cock, and *they* are responsible for the cancellation of the tour!'

Initially Cobham's 'informal meeting' with Vorster was known
'unofficially' to only a few members of MCC's Committee, the *raison
d'être* being that any official response from the main body would have
soon led to termination.

In his recent book, *Basil D'Oliveira: Cricket and Conspiracy*, Peter
Oborne tells of an approach made by MCC Secretary Billy Griffith at
a dinner on the eve of the Lord's Test against Australia in 1968. The
astounding proposition to D'Oliveira was that he should declare himself
unavailable for England and instead announce his availability for South
Africa. Apparently, D'Oliveira angrily rejected the proposal and then,
on the next day, received an identical suggestion from Swanton. Oborne
conjectures that a plan by the South African cricket authorities to save
the tour with a special dispensation for D'Oliveira had snowballed,
and that the approach had been recommended by, among others, Arthur
Coy (the Secretary of the South African Cricket Association) who was
being entertained by Cobham in his private box for the full five days of
the Lord's Test. Coy had been sent specifically to look for a solution to
the D'Oliveira problem. 'The most elegant solution involved persuading
D'Oliveira to make himself unavailable', writes Oborne.

It can be surmised that amid all the friendliness and chatter at Lord's
Coy suggested that D'Oliveira should turn down England and declare
himself for South Africa. This was by no means a new idea. D'Oliveira
was periodically put up by ingenious commentators, normally in the
non-white South African press, for selection in the Springbok team.

Crucially, it was also an idea close to Swanton's heart. His general view, perhaps not always as well thought through as it might have been, was that cricket broke down barriers. The following year he unsuccessfully urged Wilfred Isaacs to include a scattering of black cricketers in the all-white touring side he took to England in 1969.

Neither Swanton nor Billy Griffith was racist, and Swanton was one of D'Oliveira's most eloquent champions in print . . . [and] it is easy to see how [both], in their well-meaning quest for a solution, might have got caught up in a scene which on an exceptionally shallow reading would have done more good than harm.

It is extraordinary that in Jim's voluminous correspondence and thirteen-page précis of the sequence of the D'Oliveira affair, there is no reference to these proposals. Given his obsession for detailed note-keeping on every aspect of his life, one would have expected to find some mention of the conversations. If the episode was as described, it does seem like a response to a desperate desire to seize any solution to the problem. But was it as described? Jim is recorded in print saying, 'those who thought the tour should be forced through at all costs, it seemed to me, were pursuing a political principle at the expense of the game'. Doubly naïve he would have been if he thought that the South African authorities would have actually honoured to the letter a commitment to make a special dispensation for D'Oliveira to be in their team or, more to the point, that the man himself would even consider such a proposal in the first place. Assuming they even countenanced such a situation, there would have to be yet another special dispensation and a long interregnum before there was any chance of swapping sides.

Bob Moore, onetime Honorary Secretary to the Cricketers' Association, who ghost-wrote The D'Oliveira Affair under Basil's name in 1969 and who was extraordinarily close to the personal and professional sides of Basil's life at that time, has written, 'Never, with any shade of inference, did I hear such an incredible suggestion ever being made, either to Basil or to anyone else. Indeed, not only is it incredible today, but it would have been ludicrous then . . . there is no hard evidence that this suggestion was ever made.' Even if it was, in the convivial atmosphere of a box at Lord's, could it have been in semi-jocular fashion or as a kind of sop to Coy by demonstrating that literally every avenue was being explored, and that this was picked up by Swanton shortly afterwards? Who can say? Memory can be unreliable at such a distance, particularly when probed by a searching interlocutor, and it is not helped by the onset of Parkinson's disease.

One thing, however, is incontrovertible. Shortly after D'Oliveira's original omission from the touring party, Jim had received a grateful letter from the man who had been at the eye of the storm:

> Dear Jim,
>
> During the past week when I have had to try and understand many things, it has been very reassuring to read what you have had to say, particularly about my cricket. May I say a very sincere thank you.
>
> Yours, Basil

When Jim had been calling for a reform of the MCC after they sought compromise and avoidance of what seemed to many a matter of fundamental humanity, there were those who felt his advocacy had been governed by a concern not for the latter but solely for the game's future health. Whatever the fairness of that view, in a letter to David Sheppard, for whom it was a most bitter and difficult time and who had proposed a vote of censure, Jim made his concerns clear.

> As to my personal position, unless things come out of which I have no knowledge, I would not vote against the Committee in Resolution I (in effect, a vote of no confidence) though I might abstain. As you know, I criticized their handling, but there are degrees of guilt, and I would not be party to humiliating a body many of which put in very hard voluntary work on behalf of cricket, on the whole with fair success.

Swanton went on to criticize Lord's committee for being too in-bred and admitted he was 'a very pale pink revolutionary' as 'in my case, friendship comes into this with most of those concerned'. Sheppard, however, felt that 'Jim stood his ground firmly and with a lot of courage.' Certainly – as has been obvious – he was never shown to tilt at windmills regardless of their position on the campus although his reaction had surprised many who saw him only as an archetypal Establishment figure.

In 1970 the South Africans were scheduled to tour Britain. Mayhem was predicted. The previous winter's Springbok rugby tour had been accompanied by scenes of perpetual disorder and violence. And then in January, twelve country cricket grounds were attacked on the same night in a concerted anti-apartheid action.

> When the season began the Cricket Council were still determined to proceed with the arrangements, despite the most widespread opposition. The TUC advised its members to boycott the tour. The

Prime Minister appealed for cancellation. A Commons motion was signed by 51 MPs of all parties. On 14 May an emergency debate on the tour issue took place in the House of Commons. I had been coming gradually to the conclusion that in the heat of conflicting political pressures the chief loser would be cricket. I therefore wrote, following the parliamentary debate, that I thought the tour should be called off.

Edward Heath won the election. As I was showing pleasure at the results at the Election Night party at the Savoy, the then Deputy Editor of the *Daily Telegraph* expressed surprise saying: 'Oh, I thought you had gone over to the enemy.' *Daily Telegraph*, 15 May 1970.

Jim's stance had not been popular with his masters at the *Telegraph*. Editor Maurice Green felt that Home Secretary James Callaghan's decision (just before Labour vacated office) to cancel the tour had been taken partly for party political reasons and partly in surrender to the threats of violence. 'I cannot say that I "almost wept" at the views you yourself expressed,' he wrote to Jim, 'but as we are about it, I might as well register my profound disagreement. You are, however, always at liberty to express your personal views on the paper on a matter of this kind.' Jim's reply mentioned the sense of relief at the cancellation felt by 'almost everyone closely concerned' and described the whole affair as a Greek tragedy. 'I've had a letter from Don Bradman, seeking information and advice, the South Africans being due there in 1971–2. I'm afraid you may think he's gone to the wrong man.'

After many misgivings, I felt before the situation had reached its present pass that perhaps the risks were not worth taking. I believe now they are not, and that the consequences might well do irrevocable harm to cricket. Most of the players likely to be concerned, and many responsible administrators, are now of this opinion. There would be no joy in the tour for them, and certainly not for the South Africans. Nor could the game be a conclusive test. Note the cricket considerations again, as distinct from the political.

If I be accused of vacillation, I would say that the person who sees this agonising issue in absolutely clear-cut 100 per cent terms is surely either extremely clever or very stupid. And I would presume to remind readers that for the last year and more, in the *Daily Telegraph* and also in the South African press and in *The Cricketer*, I have pressed for a multi-racial tour party, sufficient to make two sides, to come over together.

There would certainly have been non-Europeans good enough for inclusion in a party of, say, 30, fulfilling First XI and 'A' fixtures simultaneously. On the analogy of the South African Olympic decision in 1967, such a project would have been within the law, and it would have been irrefutable evidence of white goodwill.

What an infinitely melancholy thought that if such an initiative had been taken we might have been looking forward to the tour with pleasure and in comparative peace of mind! 15 May 1970.

And so began two decades of South African sporting isolation. Contention over whether the maintenance or severance of cricketing links as the best was to defeat apartheid went on endlessly. The issue broke many friendships or at the very least threatened to:

Dear Jim,

Before we came to your match in August this year against the Sussex Martlets, of which I am Patron, could you tell me where you stand in the world of cricket?

I read your article and heard about your appearance on Television. It made it abundantly clear that you were against the South African tour – I am now wondering really where you stand. If people cannot support the game, I cannot support them.

Yours ever,

Bernard [*Duke of Norfolk*]

Dear Bernard,

I was cut to have a letter from you, saying 'If people cannot support the game, I cannot support them.' Me not support cricket? It has given me my livelihood, and I have given it most of my life. As to 'support' for the last five years I've given something like half of my time to keep *The Cricketer* going almost for nothing – I get a few hundred a year – because I believe the game should continue to have an independent paper.

As to the South African tour I said in my article on May 15 that on 'a balance of evils' I thought the Council should call it off. I hated having to do it, but I couldn't bear the thought of cricket, which has done more for the Commonwealth than any game, being remembered for ever as the cause of the collapse of the Commonwealth Games – which was certain in that only the whites would have opted: for the probable division of Test cricket into black and white camps: for the racial trouble at home that the experts feared: all for a series of Tests behind barbed wire which no one would have enjoyed and which from the cricket point of view would have meant little.

I wrote to Gubby on May 15 and said I thought the Council could extricate themselves with honour saying (1) that the present atmosphere was largely due to the incitement given by the Prime Minister and other members of the Government, (2) that cricket was acting to help other sports, notably athletics, and to free other cricket governing bodies from the threat of political interference, and (3) that they were unwilling to subject the South African cricketers to a tour in such an atmosphere, which had been fomented by various elements since the invitation had been confirmed.

Gubby was down here that weekend, and he said 'Your views and mine are not very far apart.'

I appeared twice on TV and once in *The World at One*, each time at their invitation and not sought by me. I'm sorry you didn't see me because I would have fixed you, as well as several million others, with my eye, and you would have heard me talk about the ministers who had by their remarks made the tour such a threat to law and order, adding 'I can't think that the cricket world will ever forgive Mr Wilson for his speech urging people to "demonstrate against".'

It has been a terrible time for everyone, and the hardest thing has been that friends have been honestly divided as to what was the best thing to do. Personally I'm relieved greatly that it is off, and so are 95 per cent of the people who would have been most closely involved – the players, the umpires, the administrators, and not least the police. I haven't had the chance of talking recently to Colin, but Penny told me when I was sitting with her at Canterbury on Saturday that he had decided about the same time as I did that it just was not on.

You write about the Arab visit to Arundel. Please don't identify me too closely. Peter Hill-Wood and a committee run the club – I'm only the founder. I shall miss my usual visit.

Dear Jim,

Thank you for your letter. I did not mean you to go so fully into the explanations which you have taken the trouble to give.

I cannot, of course, accept your suggestion that 95% of the people who would have been most closely involved were relieved when it was off. I have not yet met any of them. The anger all round here is enormous.

Yours ever,
Bernard

Following the cancellation of the South African visit to England in the summer of 1970, a series was arranged against a Rest of the World Team. Illingworth led the English side in place of Cowdrey, who had been injured. During the 1970 season the Press, when not occupied with the South African 'Ban the Tour' news, concerned itself about the prospective captaincy of MCC for the winter tour of Australia. Lobbies were divided between Cowdrey as captain and Illingworth as his number two, or vice versa.

There was, of course, no doubt about Swanton's preference. After the tour was over and with the Ashes regained, the victorious captain Ray Illingworth appeared on BBC Radio 4's *It's Your Line*:

> **Robin Day:** Good evening, this is Robin Day and *It's Your Line* tonight to a sportsman who will be honoured next Monday at a celebration banquet at Lord's – Ray Illingworth, England's Captain on last winter's victorious, dramatic and sometimes stormy tour of Australia, the tour which won back the Ashes for England after twelve years, but a tour also which stirred some heated controversy about the way the game was played and about Ray Illingworth's captaincy. The gloomy verdict of one pundit was that this was a tour which damned international cricket. After the angry incident during the Final Sydney Test one of our veteran cricket correspondents wrote, 'By openly questioning an Umpire's verdict, Illingworth showed a singularly bad example to cricketers everywhere.' On the other hand, according to one Australian columnist, Illingworth showed more guts and common sense than has been shown by anyone in this entire series. But what is your opinion, because *It's Your Line* tonight to Ray Illingworth, whether you think of him primarily as a Captain who led his team to victory in this series or as the Captain who led his team off the field at Sydney after those beer cans began to fly.

Jim chanced to be listening and rang in, rather to Illingworth's discomfort after he made the following comments:

> **Illingworth:** Some of the press you do see quite a bit of, but in actual fact it was perfectly true what I said that from the start of the tour until the finish of the tour, I don't think I saw Jim Swanton at all; in fact, I think the only time I saw him was when I pulled up at the traffic lights and he was in the car next to me.
>
> Jim Swanton doesn't stay in the same hotel as the rest of the press boys, he stays on his own somewhere and this is probably the reason we never saw him. Most of the press did stay in the same hotel as us but

Jim didn't.

[*Later in the programme*]

Day: . . .and now Mr E.W. Swanton. And that I expect is the Mr E.W. Swanton whom we were talking about earlier, the distinguished and veteran cricket correspondent of the *Daily Telegraph*, known widely as Jim Swanton. Is that the Mr Swanton?

Swanton: Good evening Robin Day.

Day: Good evening.

Swanton: I'm answering your invitation.

Day: Oh how fine of you to call in, and I'm sure that Ray would like to talk to you as he appears to have not talked to you very often in Australia if his report be accurate. You're calling from Sandwich, go ahead with your question or comment Jim Swanton, please?

Swanton: Well, my comment is this. Ray said that he didn't see me on tour. Now there's an implication in that. I see something of all players on tour. I didn't see a great deal of him, but I'm just going to ask him about one or two times when he certainly met me. I'd like to say first though, that I'm an old 'un now, on my seventh tour in Australia, and I never think that young or youngish cricketers like to be bothered too much with the older generation. I'm generally there if they want to listen to me, if my experience and reminiscence is of any interest, but I rather wait for them to come to me. But I was, in fact, with the team in four of the Test matches in the same hotel. He said that I wasn't in the hotel with them in any of the Tests – I was there in four – but if he is listening, as I take it he is, I'd like just to ask him three questions. In the first place, Ray, do you remember that when the team was chosen, I said to you . . . I'm sorry, when the Captain was chosen, I said to you, 'Well, Ray, I hoped myself that Colin Cowdrey would be chosen. I thought that he did a wonderful job in the West Indies when he returned, having won the rubber, and I thought it was his prerogative to be chosen, but now you've been chosen, I'll do the best I can and I wish you well' – do you remember that?

Illingworth: Yes, that's correct – at Headingley.

Swanton: That's right it was at Headingley, yes it was. Now do you remember that on our arrival at Brisbane, we had quite a long talk and you were kind and told me a little bit about what had been happening on the tour up till that point, because I didn't get there until just before the First Test?

Illingworth: That was the first day you arrived in Brisbane, yes.

Swanton: That's right. Do you remember that I congratulated you as warmly as I possibly could on the excellent performance in winning the

Fourth Test at Sydney and I did so in the Hotel Windsor at Melbourne where we were both staying?

Illingworth: I can't remember that particular occasion, Jim, no. But I'm not saying you didn't stay at the Windsor. It's probably one hotel you did stay in.

Day: Jim Swanton, Robin Day here. I think the main point being made by Ray in his earlier answers was not any personal point against you, but the fact that you were a cricket-writer who, on the whole, remained a bit remote from the players and therefore perhaps didn't take the trouble to find out about what the cricketers were doing and why in their games. I'm summarising it badly, but I think that's what he was getting at. Is that right, Ray?

Illingworth: Yes.

Day: Now what about that, Jim? That was the general point. However often you talked to each other.

Swanton: Well, I think that the critic has got a difficult job, just as the player has got a difficult job in his relations with the critics. What I think is that I try to make as close a touch as will give me an idea of what they're thinking, what lies behind what they're doing, and although I didn't see very much of Ray, I did see something of him, including the questions I put to him at the last Press Conference which I'm sure he hasn't forgotten. But there were sixteen other members of the team, or fifteen and the manager, and I regard myself as being the best judge of how much to see of them all.

Day: Well thank you for calling, Jim, but just before you go, I'd like to know whether Ray would like to ask you a question, because it's rare that we get a critic of your standing and a cricketer of his standing.

Illingworth: Well, there is one piece I would like to . . . you wrote a summing up on the tour, Jim, and you did write that there'd been a lowering of standards on and off the field, and I wasn't very impressed with that for the amount I did see you on the tour.

Swanton: I said there was a lowering of standards. Yes, I did say that, Ray, with very great reluctance. It's no pleasure to anybody like myself who loves to see England win and nothing else, to see certain of the things that went on. I thought I'd never hope to see an England Captain threatening or seeming to threaten by wagging his finger at an Australian umpire with twenty or thirty thousand Australians looking on. If the game is going to come to this sort of pass where the umpire is going to be openly challenged on the field, I think that the end of cricket in the Test Match sense is really pretty near. If, for instance, you'd done that sort of thing in the West Indies, such provocation would almost certainly – you've been talking about the West Indies – it would almost certainly have literally brought the house down.

Day: Now Ray Illingworth, do you want to add to your explanation of why you did that?

Illingworth: Well now, Jim knows why. Does he think the umpire was right on that occasion?

Swanton: Did I think the umpire was right? Well, I think that the umpire must always be right, and he must always be respected by the players. I know all about tensions and that sort of thing, but I've been watching Test Matches for longer than I care to remember. I've seen some two hundred odd of them, and I've never before seen a captain resort to that.

Illingworth: No, it's probably very true, that you've never heard a captain speak his mind before.

Swanton: We've had a great many captains who've spoken their mind very well, Ray. Don't imagine that because you're a Yorkshireman and tough, you're the only person who can speak your mind.

Illingworth: Oh no, I don't imagine that at all.

Swanton: I think that there were a great many of them before that.

Illingworth: Well, we shall see.

Swanton: Douglas Jardine for a start.

Illingworth: Ah, well, I don't go back that far, Jim.

Swanton: No, well there you are – I have the advantage of you.

Illingworth: Yes, you're quite right there.

Day: Well, E.W. Swanton, thank you very much indeed for responding to our invitation to call in and to have it out a bit with Ray. You haven't convinced one another, but it's been nice hearing from you and perhaps the matter will come up again. I only just go back to Jardine, but I'd better not admit that.

Illingworth, of course, had picked up the joke most frequently told at Jim's expense: 'Jim Swanton isn't a snob: he's perfectly happy to travel in the same car as his chauffeur.'

Two years on and Illingworth declined to lead the England tour to India, Pakistan and Sri Lanka. After M.J.K. Smith also found a reason not to go, the captaincy was offered to Tony Lewis, who told me:

'I was very honoured when Jim came out. India was not on his normal itinerary. Mind you, he came for just two Tests and stayed with a very big English industrialist in Calcutta. There was that joke, wasn't there: Jim's been in India for two weeks and so far he's not spoken to anybody beneath a Maharajah! But I had breakfast with him several times – he was a great letter writer – and at breakfast he would read out the letters and say, "I've had a very good letter from J.J. Warr" – or from Gubby, or whoever it was. He would be meticulous about keeping careful notes on everything about organisational matters. He had these standards, you see, standards of behaviour, of turning up on time and so on. And because of the rather stringent way he ordered his life he expected the same of other people. It sort of sharpened everybody up. As a working journalist he was damn good.

'I remember once we were in Gibbs Bay in Barbados, where Jim and Ann were staying with two American ladies. One night they gave dinner for the great E.W. Swanton and invited both Michael Melford and myself along. I am not sure they knew exactly what he did, but he was quite big in St James's. I tried to explain to this lady that Michael was going to the *Daily Telegraph* and I was going to the *Sunday Telegraph*, and so in a way we were all pursuing Jim, and she looked puzzled and then said, "You both one day hope to be like the great Jim?" I said, "Well yes, that's the general idea." And then she said, "Gee, what moccasins to fill!"'

Both John Snow and Geoffrey Boycott had declined an invitation to go on that tour of the sub-continent with Tony Lewis's side in 1972–3. And by 1974 the affairs of Yorkshire County Cricket Club and their maverick son were making unwanted headlines. Jim was sent 'the Boycott file' by the latter's ally, solicitor Donald Mutch, and asked for his thoughts:

My first comment must be to commend you for all the labour of friendship which has gone into this strange and in some ways sad saga. I only hope Geoff is grateful, and feel he probably is, for there is a side of his nature that clearly craves affection and respect.

If only he realised that he could have these things in good measure from the cricket world if only he sometimes put other people before himself. Especially, of course, his team.

The only way now he could convince people of a change of heart is to throw his wicket away now and then, when the time was opportune, to give others an innings, and in other ways go out of his way to amend the image of a difficult, selfish, self-centred person.

There is a likeable Boycott whom in many ways I admire, but I'm old-fashioned enough to believe that a man who has been made by cricket has a duty to it, and that this involves him playing for England when required. It was foolish, for instance, to plead that he was out of form last June when only a week or two he had made two hundreds in the Trial Match. People aren't taken in by that sort of thing. In the circumstances I thought the press reaction was generous – though, naturally, I don't in any way condone two of the cuttings you included, the *Evening Standard* one (disgraceful), and that in the *Mail*.

Incidentally, I didn't think he'd stepped out of line – apart from one phrase, possibly – in the Dexter interview, and in view of this Yorkshire C'tee reaction, can believe that the faults in the relationship are (or hopefully were) far from one-sided.

I've looked up the Roses Match at Headingley, and confirmed my impression that Stevenson's criticism in the *DT* was no less and no more than was his duty as a critic. On a good pitch and in normal conditions it seems to me there is a moral obligation on a side to at least attempt initially to get 244 in three and a half hours. It is the death of cricket if a reasonable challenge is ignored, especially – as seems to be the case – in the personal interests of the captain himself.

As you will probably realise I think you have gone a long way astray in your summary of the position vis-à-vis both Denness and the press in the memo of September 10. I'm sorry to read that he may have abandoned hopes of leading England, for I can conceive a situation wherein he might be thought the best candidate, but this could only happen if he were to 'restore his professionality' by playing when he is invited, and generally toeing the line like everyone else.

What I suppose must be got across to him is that he is not different from anyone else – nor, for that matter, better than anyone else, if one sees him in the context of, say, the last fifteen or twenty years.

I've run on longer than I intended, and I'm afraid you may think a somewhat harsh letter that you may not want to show him – though I would have no objection if you did. I write in this way because I believe that the change has to come in him, and not in his critics and detractors (some of whom are not worth worrying about, anyway), and that a friend does him the best service in the long run by saying so.

In a phrase has he not to defeat his pride, accept the risks of failure, and put complete trust in his talent?

The 1974–75 tour of Australia, during which he championed the oft-maligned captaincy of Mike Denness, was Jim's last outing as the cricket correspondent of the *Daily Telegraph*. The fire-eating, ferocious little Sports Editor of the paper, Kingsley Wright – another Yorkshireman to boot – told him to 'go on as long as you like – pick your own time for retirement.' As Jim had been nominated for the MCC Committee in 1974 with election likely the following year, he felt at sixty-eight years young that that time had arrived.

In fact, he had made an unsuccessful bid for membership some years previously when a fully starred system (MCC advising of their preferred candidates) had been in operation, and had even cleared conflict of interest matters with the *Telegraph* proprietor, Lord Hartwell. But on that occasion he had come bottom of the poll.

The Final Test at Melbourne was won by England by an innings, but it was only a consolation prize because the Ashes had been lost. Jim was now bowing out after no less than 270 Tests. Twenty years later he told me that his lasting memory of the occasion was of Colin Cowdrey in a sun hat, leaning on a barrier, signing autographs. There could have been few more appropriate recollections.

> My dear Jim,
>
> I watched you having a pre-lunch drink with the MCC [*Melbourne Cricket Club*] and then afterwards surveying things through your glasses. It is, of course, a special day and my thoughts were with you.
>
> It was nice for you that your last official Test Match day with the pen should be recording an England win over Australia.
>
> I know you will be writing again from time to time so it is no time for solemn farewells – suffice it to say that I noted the end of the official E.W.S. era – a sad occasion – but we thank you, Sir!
>
> Yours, very humbly,
> Colin

Of course, it was not the end, more a new beginning. But all that comes later.

Chapter 10

Teams of his own choosing

The trail along the clear tracks and through the undergrowth of Jim's life has so far deliberately avoided the on and off-field activities of his own side, the Arabs, and the international tours under his managership. That should not be thought to reflect any lack of importance to him of these extramural activities. Far from it, for both gave him a stage on which to demonstrate his own distinctive values.

The Arabs – no political or racial connotation, simply a name suitable for a nomadic side suggested by Jim's friend and fellow writer R.C. Robertson-Glasgow (who himself was called 'Crusoe') – were born in 1935. In later years a few of those who were to be half willing victims of Jim's generally benevolent totalitarian rule – a smile and/or a grimace from the teller of the tale decides the degree of willingness – would claim that he had to form his own side, because no other team would put up with his dictatorial ways. Even if that is not quite true (and he was admittedly not the most popular figure on the club circuit in the 1930s), the E.W.S. personality was such that he could only really be fulfilled if he could convince himself that he was in control. Jim, of course, saw it slightly differently:

Like any other touring club we came into being for no deeper purpose than to enjoy ourselves. If we succeeded in that, our opponents would naturally become our friends, irrespective of how hard we played the game. It mattered a great deal to win while one was on the field, afterwards not at all. That was our subconscious philosophy and has remained so.

Sometimes, of course, the philosophy emerged from the subconscious, but we will come to that in due course. As has been mentioned in Chapter 3, the Arabs' first outing was not to Bermuda as had been expected, but instead to Jersey in the Channel Isles – by air. The fragile craft taking off from Heston contained a number of apprehensive passengers:

> For most of us, if not all, it was a novel experience. It was also a nervous one, not least because at the other end in those days one landed on the beach. If the wind was off the sea the plane skimmed low over the cliff and fetched up just short of the water. That was preferable to the reverse procedure when, if the wind was off the land, one humped one's luggage over the sandy beach to the water's edge preparatory to a take-off straight towards the cliff-face, narrowly clearing it . . .

The experience was sufficiently unnerving to persuade the umpire accompanying the team, a sturdy fellow with 'a countenance not unlike either Wilson or Keppel but definitely not Betty', to give himself out. No amount of spurious courage drawn from cordials – Crusoe's phrase in his report of the tour for *The Cricketer* – could persuade Hicks, for that was his name, to board the plane for the return journey. Instead he went by sea together with eleven cricket bags. Apparently at Waterloo he was spotted fast asleep on top of the pile. On one of the bags was a chalked notice: ARABS C.C., BEWARE!

On that first tour were a heady mix of talented ex-Public school and Oxbridge players, the two sources which were to provide a continual conveyor belt for future Arab teams. Neil Hotchkin, who was the honorary secretary, had met Jim when he was playing for Cambridge against India at Fenner's. Until his recent death in early 2004, Hotchkin was the last survivor of the original team: 'We were a very unruly lot in those days. On that first visit to Jersey I think we trashed the hotel which was quite an imposing one called the Palace. They wouldn't have us back after that – quite rightly – and so on other trips we stayed at the St Brelade's Bay Hotel. I remember Johnny Brocklebank drank a lot of highballs. Jim was a bit upset – very disapproving.

'But Jim was a great disciplinarian as captain – inspected everybody's boots and equipment before a game. "I'm not having people playing for me turned out like that," he would say. People would wear the wrong shoes just to wind him up. After the war we called him the Führer.'

Not untopical, as the Arabs made two trips to Germany to play the Army and Air Force of the Rhine just after the war. At Bentheim, just over the German frontier, the 2CV taking the team to their destination came to a spluttering halt through a block in the petrol feed. Immediately, Jim ordered everybody out of the vehicle for fielding practice in a stubble field beside the road.

> The sight of Jim, in a smart brown cloth cap and a long grey coat, giving catching instructions to a young German farm lad called Etwulf or Egfirth or something, can never be forgotten [*wrote Alan Young in his account of the trip*]. Little perhaps did he then realise how many of his team needed it as much! Etwulf showed less promise than his younger brother Odburth (?) who was at length called away by Dad and disappeared at the rate of knots round a beanfield in true Wagnerian style, riding a horse at least 8 times larger than himself.

During one of the tours of Germany, there was an unfortunate accident. 'One of our players got his leg smashed up pretty badly in a car crash,' continued Hotchkin. 'I had two hours' sleep after taking him to hospital. I always used to open the batting with Jim. When I complained about feeling tired and suggested I should bat lower down the order, he said, "Nonsense, if you're any good you can bat after no sleep at all. You're just frightened of their fast bowlers."

'I once ran him out on the fourth run and I was in disgrace for days. Later he laughed about it. "You need to watch him, he's a terror between the wickets."'

Although approaching ninety years of age, Hotchkin's fund of stories showed no signs of drying up 'Coming back from one tour we smuggled all our cigarettes through customs in his golf bag – Jim didn't smoke and he didn't know about it. Anyway, on that flight back we hit very bad weather and the captain came over the Tannoy and said he was very sorry but we might have to turn back. Immediately Jim got up and walked down the aisle: "There is no way can the captain turn round. I have a very important engagement. I leave tomorrow for Australia with the England cricket team!"'

On the SS *Stratheden* for the five-week sea journey to Australia for the 1950–51 tour were a bevy of Press correspondents including Beau Vincent, Robertson-Glasgow and Neville Cardus and there was also a lanky medium-fast bowler called John Warr. Known universally as J.J., he remembers how E.W.S. had been responsible for getting him his chance to play in first-class cricket. 'Swanton really kick-started my career. In 1949 the Arabs came up to Cambridge to play a game against the Crusaders and they were short of an opening bowler, so I played for Swanton against the Crusaders and got a few wickets and then I got picked for the Crusaders and from there I got into the University side. A season later I was playing for Middlesex and then England.

'I became quite friendly with Jim – we lived close to one another in St John's Wood – though I was never invited to be an Arab, even though I'd played in that one match. In order to do so I think you had to have pretty good credentials on the public school or university side – I don't think there were many state school people in the club. In that sense I think Jim was a bit of a snob, because he cherry-picked his friends. He was not a great mixer with the lower classes, put it that way. He had this reputation for being pompous and all the rest of it, but the great thing about Jim was that he could take a joke against himself. I used to rib him and he would sometimes say, "You old fool" or something like that, but his rebukes were never that strong. I got on well with him.'

The Arabs' fixture list cultivated some of the most attractive cricket grounds in the country: Arundel, for a game against Lavinia, Duchess of Norfolk's XI; Highclere, against Lord Porchester XI; Warnford, versus Hampshire Hogs; Torry Hill, Sittingbourne, courtesy of Lord Kingsdown, to take on Band of Brothers; and Horris Hill near Newbury in Berkshire for games against R.M. Stow's XI. There were many other equally appealing grounds.

It was a match at Horris Hill, the preparatory school run by Monty Stow, that Dennis Silk, who in his time played for Cambridge, Somerset and MCC, remembers because of an extraordinary day's cricket: 'I was playing for Monty's team and the Arabs batted first and went on and on and on – Jim hated losing – and left us an impossible total to get, something like 300 after tea and we thought, bugger it, we'll go for it. And so we did and Jim rather lost control of the match. Walter Robins was in the Arabs' side, you know, the old Middlesex and England leg-spinner, and we were smashing it around and got to about 90 for no wicket and I was in at one end and John Thompson, J.R. Thompson, was my partner.

'John, who was a wonderful player, went and tried to hook a chap called David Foskett who was a Wellingtonian and Oxford Blue and he got a big heavy top edge, and it went up and up and up and Jim was circling under it [giggles] and when the ball was dropping and it was about thirty feet above his head the voice of Walter Robins sounded all round the ground "eight to one on the ball" [laughs] and

Jim just had time to say, "For God's sake shut up, Walter!" and as it fell he never laid a finger on it. It went just straight through and virtually landed on his foot. Jim was absolutely incandescent, and he pretended that this ball had hit his finger and hurt it and he went off the field steaming with rage to get this untouched finger put right and his last words on leaving the field were to Simon Kimmins. He said, "Simon, take over the Captaincy." Well, the obvious person was Walter Robins. "Simon, take over the Captaincy and whatever else you do, do NOT put Walter Robins on to bowl."

'Well, their fate was sealed from that moment and we got this amazing total losing very few wickets with about ten minutes to spare. I think I got 90-something and John Thompson got a lot and the rest piled in afterwards and smashed it around. And at the end of the match Robins, who had not bowled at all, announced to the world, "This is the first time I've ever been played for my looks." And he then summoned the umpire and said, "Put those three stumps back, will you please, and put the bails on." And as we all stood round he bowled a leg-break which pitched on leg-stump and hit the off. He bowled a top spinner which hit the middle having pitched middle and then he bowled his googly and it pitched off and hit leg and those were the only three balls that he bowled all day. The match was over and he was making a point that perhaps he should've bowled a bit. Jim was in a towering rage. And after that there was a terrific spat with Walter, and the "no speaks" for some months.'

Colin Ingleby-Mackenzie first encountered the Swanton determination to come out ahead when he was still a schoolboy. 'Jim always loved blue-eyed old Etonians and I was a blue-eyed young Etonian, so it was a double whammy. I don't mean that in any suspicious way at all, it was just that he was very interested in young cricketers and he was very helpful and quite delightful.

'I think he'd come down there for either MCC or the Forty Club and they were playing against the College. I was not a great fielder to be honest, but I managed to catch him in the gully – it was a very good catch as it happened, because he'd hit it very hard. He was horrified when he was out and sort of grunted, as he always did, and he couldn't believe that I had caught it. That sort of got us chatting and we became very friendly. Then he asked me to be an Arab which, of course, was a great accolade.'

I put it to Colin that Jim was never a good loser. 'It wasn't a question of being a good loser, he was an outrageous loser. I remember a long time later at Medstead in Hampshire, he hit the cover off the ball and was caught at second slip. And he went up the wicket – I was wicket-keeping – and he went up the wicket and patted a spot and came back to me. And the umpire having moved, he said, "I nearly got very close to that one." And in Bermuda once, when we had a tour out there to the West Indies, he was caught then. He opened the batting, and played very well, really. Eventually he was caught, I think at first slip, and he couldn't believe it. He waited for a moment, hoping that if the umpire had had courage he could have given him not out, but unfortunately for him the umpire suddenly realised he couldn't ignore it and he was given out. He was a terrible walker – he never ever walked . . . But to be fair, he, I think, thought that you shouldn't necessarily walk. I remember talking to him – he said you have two expert umpires, and they're there to give a decision. But these reactions were only because of his extreme passion for the game.'

Colin then enlarged on Jim's style of captaincy: 'I think there are three forms of captaincy. One is to do it by example – you're a clever operator in the field and get your results by tactical genius or you are so good a player that you're able to win a match with your batting or bowling. Number two is that you are a nice chap – people play for you and by perhaps being not quite as good as them, you get more from the other ten players and that makes up for the shortfall in your expertise. And the third is to captain by terror and Jim did that and was quite frightening at times.

'Not, of course, frightening in a serious way, but he was very severe. If you dropped a catch or didn't field very well he would give you a fiendish glare – and you would shrivel within yourself. And, of course, the other members of the side would be saying, "My God, Jim's giving him some stick down there," and they'd send you up, humorously, of course.'

And if the captain himself dropped a catch?

'Oh, you didn't dare say anything. There was a lot of grunting and in a jocular way he would be "mobbed-up", to use the old school phrase. But you didn't say too much. You looked away. But he had a tremendous following. He was, without doubt, the leader, the absolute icon, that we all looked up to.'

Another member of the Arabs is former Glamorgan and England captain, Tony Lewis. 'I think Jim would purposely run with the winners, not the losers. I don't detect many failures in Jim's backyard, so to speak. He chose his allies carefully. The Arabs is a classic case of it and yet I was a Neath Grammar School boy, so maybe there were other things going for me. I enjoyed the cricket, it was competitive and cricket can't be enjoyed unless it's played seriously.

'But if you were captain of an Arabs side, he'd be waving his arms about off the field telling you to declare or put the Earl of Cottenham on, who was a good quick bowler, or to do something else. I remember a match at Canterbury, it was a cracking pitch and we batted on a bit. Jim was at the boundary edge waving his golf umbrella and shouting, "Declare, declare, declare." I must admit it did have the effect of making me delay the declaration by a couple of overs. Eventually I declared and then he said, "You've got no earthly idea how you're going to bowl them out." I said, "Well, if it comes off I'll say: well, I told you so." Anyway, we bowled the seamers and then we put a little leg-spinner on. I got him to bowl a foot wide of the off stump. There's a bit of a slope at Canterbury too and it would turn a bit for the leg-spinner. And we actually won the match with a combination of leg spin and seam and we had ten minutes to spare. All he said afterwards was "Humph. You were jolly lucky."

'Basically though, Jim was meticulous about planning, organisation, behaviour, standards. I don't think there were many unthought-out moments, whether he was collecting the cards after a round played by the Arabs at St George's on the Saturday morning – "I see you've crossed out hole 3," or "I see you've made an alteration. Alterations aren't very good, you know," or whether he was appointing a new match manager. All that sort of stuff. I think there were people who were in awe of him. It was intimidating and I suppose everyone along the way was slightly intimidated, but once you found that you could make fun of that and that he would laugh, then it was better.'

Leaving aside Arab activities, Jim himself wrote that the greatest enjoyment he derived from cricket came from the three 'private' tours under his own name, naturally, which he arranged and managed, and on the Duke of Norfolk's tour to the West Indies in 1970, for which he acted as Treasurer.

Obviously the choosing of the players is one of the most important items, and it was not always easy. One had to keep within a budget, which put a limit on the number of professionals, and it was important to find a side strong enough for the purpose. One tried to avoid difficult or temperamental fellows if only because there was no sanction that could be applied to any such, in case of trouble, apart from the extreme step of sending a bad boy home. Naturally the ideal was a good cricketer and an easy mixer rolled into one, and these were plentiful enough. I find that we had forty-six players altogether on these four tours, and there is not one I would not be delighted to invite again, if the chance arose. A heterogeneous bunch they were, made up of thirty-four Englishmen, four Australians, three West Indians, three Indians, and two Ceylonese, Several, Colin Cowdrey, the Nawab of Pataudi, Mike Griffith, and Ian McLachlan came twice, and Colin Ingleby-Mackenzie three times. Every county has subscribed one or more, and I'm glad to say all were returned to them fit and well. Of the forty-six exactly half were Test cricketers when they toured: several others became so, most of them being, I think, helped towards their caps by the experience.

The 1955–56 tour to Barbados, Trinidad and Bermuda was undertaken, in the words of J.L. Manning, 'to bind the Commonwealth together with Swantonian cement'. The England tour of the previous year had caused a great deal of upset in the Caribbean through the attitude taken by some players to umpiring decisions and this excursion was hoped to be a salve for hurt feelings. Despite banner headlines in the English press calling it, 'The Tour with the Tact of a Cactus' and a 'piffling expedition', the tour was a great success socially and politically. The side was a formidable outfit: M.C. Cowdrey (captain), G.H.G. Doggart (vice-captain), T.W. Graveney, F.H. Tyson, J.J. Warr, D.E. Blake, G. Goonesena, A.C.D. Ingleby-Mackenzie, R.C.M. Kimpton, R.G. Marlar, A.S.M. Oakman, M.J. Stewart and Swaranjit Singh.

'Jim gave to each match on this tour, as to any match in which the Arabs were involved, the importance that any game of cricket deserved,' reflected Hubert Doggart. 'He would also show consideration for each member of the party. I recall vividly his indignation when one hostess invited all the side to her house – except Gamini Goonesena and Swaranjit Singh, who incidentally sported wonderful turbans of a different hue for every day of the week.

'I remember when we were in transit in Puerto Rico, Colin Cowdrey and I had been resting and we came down to find that Jim had been displeased with the service at supper. He had summoned the poor fellow whom he considered responsible and in ringing tones, described him as "the worst bell-captain in the whole of the Caribbean".'

J.J. Warr also recalls moments on the tour which had a greater

degree of levity. 'We played a match against a West Indian XI, and
Everton Weekes was in their side. Now, of all the three W's, I think
Everton, at the time, was the best and he was impossible to contain on
those wickets. Anyway, after lunch we'd only got one wicket and
Everton was coming in at three and I thought, "Oh God, we're going
to get hammered all around the ground." But luckily, I'd been with
him the night before and we'd been having a few bevvies and I said,
"When you come out, Everton, don't hit me all round the ground, just
take it steady." He said, "J.J., I'll do better than that. When I come
out, if you keep the ball somewhere outside the off stump I'll play and
miss a few times." So he did it quite deliberately, he played inside and
the crowd were going "Aaah" and I bowled three overs, three maiden
overs in the height of the afternoon on a good West Indian wicket and
Everton was playing and missing. After that he said, "I think we've
had enough, don't you, J.J.?" I said, "I think so, Everton." He said,
"I'll show you how easy it is," and the last ball I bowled he turned
round and hit me with the edge of his bat, not the middle, just to show
he could do it.

'I said, "Oh my God." And then after that he started . . . well, thank
goodness, I was taken off and he hit the other bowling all over the
park and when I came in old Jim didn't know what had gone on and
he greeted me at teatime and he said, "J.J., I have to tell you that
you've just bowled this afternoon some of the finest spells of bowling
I have ever seen in my life". And he didn't know it was all a conspiracy
between myself and Everton. I never revealed it at any stage, because
he was enraptured at me getting Everton Weekes to play and miss that
number of times. "You must have been moving about a lot," he said.
I said, "Jim, I was inspired."'

The last game of the tour was a one-day affair in Bermuda. Owing
to problems with the aircraft, the team did not arrive until 3.00 a.m.
on the morning of the match. Play started at 10.30 a.m. and Jim
opened the batting with Alan Oakman. Having been hit on the pads
with what looked like a plumb lbw, he could have been accused of
trying to intimidate the umpire when he bawled out a stentorian, 'No.'
He then lasted practically until the first interval when he was caught
at short-leg for 13. At the airport buffet afterwards, he could be heard
calling out once more: 'Hands up for hamburgers.'

With many of the players having found some difficulty in adapting
to Caribbean conditions in such a short time-span, only one out of the
four first-class matches in an itinerary of seven games was won.
Nevertheless, the desired favourable impression had been gained.

The Trinidad Government guided by Prime Minister Dr Eric Williams helped financially support the visit of Jim's international side in 1961 – *international* being the operative word as Everton Weekes, the Nawab of Pataudi, A.A. Baig and Ray Lindwall were among the team. The remainder of the side comprised Colin Ingleby-Mackenzie (captain); R.W. Barber, H.J. Rhodes, D.M. Walker, R.A. Gale, I.M. McLachlan, A.C. Smith, B.D. Wells and Ossie Wheatley.

> In a month's tour nine matches were played and the only defeat was against British Guiana. In the other three first-class matches the Windward Islands and Trinidad were beaten and the game against Berbice was drawn. Overall five matches were won. The Lancashire captain Bob Barber epitomised the attractive cricket that was played by topping the batting averages in the first-class games and notching nineteen wickets with his leg-breaks. Incidentally, the match against St Kitts was the first in the island involving a touring team for over sixty years.

The last major cricketing tourists had been Hawke's side in 1896 and according to Jim 'the whole island went *en fête*'. When in Trinidad the Swantons had been the guests of the Governor, Sir Solomon Hochoy and his wife. By doing so, he had again perhaps unwittingly given spurious credence to the stories of the more irreverent members of his party who delighted in telling how Jim, marooned on a remote desert island and coming across another shipwrecked survivor, enquired the way to Government House.

The Far East tour of 1964 came about as the result of a suggestion by a neighbour of Jim's in Sandwich called Alex Hill: 'If you want to do a bit of good politically why don't you take a side to Malaysia?' Never slow to accept a challenge, E.W.S. soon was getting finance put in place with subscriptions from the 'Rubber Growers Association, the Chamber of Mines, British Banks, Shipping Companies, the Oil Industry, Manufacturing Interests and Merchant Houses' with close Malaysian connections as well as twenty-two other sources. There were also guarantees advanced by the Indian Board of Control and the Hong Kong Cricket Association covering their parts of the tour. With the invaluable help of his secretary at the time, Daphne Surfleet (later Benaud), Jim's industry was little short of incredible. He even organised the printing of a booklet giving the team, itinerary and fixtures:

TEAM
A.C.D. Ingleby-Mackenzie, Captain (Hampshire)
T.B.L. Coghlan (Cambridge)
M.G. Griffith (Cambridge and Sussex)
R.A. Hutton (Cambridge and Yorkshire)
I.M. McLachlan (Cambridge and South Australia)
S. Nurse (West Indies)
Nawab of Pataudi (Oxford, Sussex and India)
J.D. Piachaud (Oxford, Hampshire and Ceylon)
N.C. Pretzlik (Public Schools 1963)
S. Ramadhin (Lancashire and West Indies)
K. Taylor (Yorkshire and England)

Joining at Singapore
G. Sobers (South Australia and West Indies)

Joining at Hong Kong
R. Benaud (New South Wales and Australia)

Hon. Manager   E.W. Swanton
Hon. Treasurer   J.S.O. Haslewood, MC

ITINERARY AND FIXTURES
March
Sunday   15   Leave London 1045 (Air India 112)
Monday   16   Arrive Bombay 0500
                    Leave Bombay 0655 (BOAC 788)
                    Arrive Kuala Lumpur 1545
                    Leave Kuala Lumpur 1655
                    (Malayan Airways 052)
                    Arrive Penang 1820
                    Stay: E. & O. Hotel, Penang
Tuesday   17   Nets
Wednesday   18   v. PENANG
Thursday   19   M.C.A. PRESIDENT'S INVITATION XI
Friday   20   Leave Penang 1656 (Malayan Airways 049)
                    Arrive Singapore 1935
                    Stay privately
Saturday   21   v. M.C.A. XI (1st day)
Sunday   22   (2nd day)
Monday   23   Rest

Tuesday   24   v. SINGAPORE
Wednesday 25   Leave Singapore 1830 (Malayan Airways 010)
                         Arrive Kuala Lumpur 1935
                         Stay privately
Thursday   26   v. SELANGOR
Good Friday   27 Rest
Saturday   28   v. ALL MALAYA (1st day)
Easter Day 29   v. ALL MALAYA (2nd day)
Monday   30   v. M.C.A. PRESIDENT'S XI
Tuesday   31   Leave Kuala Lumpur 0855 (Malayan Airways 512)
                         Arrive Bangkok 1020
                         Leave Bangkok 1105 (Cathay Pacific 224)
                         Arrive Hong Kong 1430
                         Stay privately

April
Wednesday 1   v. ISLAND XI, Hong Kong C.C. Ground
Thursday   2   v. MAINLAND XI. Kowloon C.C. Ground
Friday   3   Rest
Saturday   4   v. COLONY XI. Hong Kong C.C. Ground
                          (1st day)
Sunday   5   v. COLONY XI. Hong Kong C.C. Ground
                          (2nd day)
Monday   6   Rest
Tuesday   7   Leave Hong Kong 1640 (Air India 105/A)
                          Arrive Bangkok 1815
                          Stay privately
Wednesday 8   Rest
Thursday   9   v. ROYAL BANGKOK SPORTS CLUB
                          Leave Bangkok 2050 (Jap. Airways 453)
                          Arrive Calcutta 2140
                          Stay Great Eastern Hotel
Friday   10   Rest
Saturday   11   v. THE INDIAN BOARD OF CONTROL XI
                          (4 days)
Sunday   12   v. THE INDIAN BOARD OF CONTROL XI
Monday   13   Rest
Tuesday   14   v. THE INDIAN BOARD OF CONTROL XI
Wednesday 15   v. THE INDIAN BOARD OF CONTROL XI
Thursday   16   Leave Calcutta 0005 (Qantas 735)
                          Arrive London 1100

In his 'Malaysian Memories', Jim wrote:

After a first stop at Penang we descended on Singapore on a Friday evening (March 20th), and after having the honour of being introduced on the field to His Excellency the Yang di-Pertuan Negara next morning we embarked on the first of three days' cricket. The Nawab of Pataudi and Seymour Nurse in the first innings of the two-day match, Ken Taylor in the second, ensured that we had enough runs and to spare, while the spin of Dan Piachaud and Sonny Ramadhin posed great problems on a wicket which made batting very difficult. Still, Alex Delilkan put up an excellent all-round performance for the M.C.A. XI, while in the one-day match that followed against Singapore the home team were able – with some help from the weather – to achieve the only draw of the tour. This was the one game of 12 we could not win.

The only disappointment about our visit to Singapore was that owing to a late aircraft from Adelaide to Sydney Garry Sobers missed his connection and so could not play against Singapore.

However, he soon made his presence felt at Kuala Lumpur, and I suppose that the crowds there over Eastertide will have equally lively memories of his batting 76, 0 and 1 (!), 102 (in 73 minutes), and of his bowling, especially the five wickets in five balls that so cruelly crushed the All-Malaysian first innings after the bowling of Christie Shepherdson, Felix Perera and Delilkan had put us out for the relatively modest score of 211. Mike Shepherdson's 70 in the second innings of this game was one of the best knocks played against us on the tour, and while I am reminiscing about K.L. I must not forget the extraordinary hitting in the first match of Don Leong, or, for that matter, the patient effort of Steve Houghton who carried his bat for 58 in the last game against the President's XI.

Mention of the President reminds me of the debt my side owed to Dr Ong Swee Law, and to all who looked after us so kindly – which was everyone with whom we came in contact, from the British and Indian High Commissioners right down the scale.

From Malaysia the team went to Hong Kong where, on the Chater Road ground in the middle of the commercial district, Nick Pretzlik smacked the Communist Bank of China with a mighty six. Then a brief stop-off in Thailand for a match against the Royal Bangkok Sports Club where 'the evening entertainment was prodigal, to say the least'. Jim noted that 'future tour managers calling in may like to know in respect of so-called massage parlours that the phrase is an understatement'.

In more sombre mood, he could not resist the opportunity to make a pilgrimage to some of the old POW trouble-spots and the site of the so-called hospital at Nakhon Pathom where he found endless rows of beautifully tended graves. And then back in Bangkok he managed to locate the saviour of so many prisoners, the trader Boon Pong, now the proprietor of a Bus Company. These looks into the past brought feelings that were impossible to express in words.

Once they were in Calcutta, there was serious cricket against virtually an Indian Test side. The match was one Colin Ingleby-Mackenzie will not forget, if only for Jim's reaction to his captaincy. In temperatures exceeding 100 degrees the Indians had led on the first innings by 348 to 321. When they batted for a second time E.W. Swanton's Commonwealth XI effervescent captain put on Sobers to bowl.

'I did perhaps over-bowl Sobers a bit. But he was bowling so well and the ball was moving about a bit, and they'd led on first innings, and we had to make around 250 to win. But Sobers did bowl an enormous number of times, with his agreement. And of course I kept on coming up and saying, "Now Garry, are you sure you're all right? We want to get these boys out and then we'll knock them off." And there were a hundred thousand in the ground. Anyway we walked off, and I thought to myself: well look, it's infernally hot, I can't ask Sobers – who'd made a hundred in the first innings and normally went in number four – to go in at that position in the batting order, because if there's a couple of quick wickets it's such a waste. Not that we were likely to lose a couple of good wickets, of course, because there was Seymour Nurse, who also made a century in the first knock as an opener – he was solid as a rock – and then there was Richard Hutton and so on.

'So I said to Garry, "Now why don't you go in number six?" "Colin, that's a great idea, absolutely a great idea, and really kind of you," he said, "I'd like that, because I'd really want a massage," and so he lay on the table. So I put up the order on the scoreboard, and suddenly the door opens and there's a bellow from Swanton: "Ingleby, what on earth is going on here?" So I said, "Well hello, Jim, are you pleased with us?" And he shouts back, "I am pleased with you not . . . I'm pleased with everybody but you." So I said, "Well, what on earth, why are you so worried?" "I've seen on the noticeboard Sobers is going in number six. I've never heard of anything like it. You are an absolute buffoon. You cannot put our finest player in six." And I said, "Well look, I've replaced him with Benaud, who's not a bad batsman –

maybe not as good as Garry – but I've insisted on Garry having a bit of a rest." "Well, this is the worst thing I've ever known," he replied, "I'm going off and I can't think of anybody who could make such a ridiculous decision." And so he went off in a storm. Anyway as it happened it worked out very well, thank goodness. We won by seven wickets at about five runs an over. But he in no uncertain terms let me know his views on that particular change of plan.'

In the heat of the moment Jim somehow forgot to mention that he had a bet on the result with his pal, the Maharajah of Cooch Behar. The amiable 'Cooch' had laid 1000 rupees to 100 against the visitors winning . . .

'Jim was a frustrated captain,' laughed Richie Benaud, 'and not even leading the Arabs to many victories could ease the pain of defeat with someone else captaining.

'I'd joined his Commonwealth side in Hong Kong after the end of a series in Australia. On the last afternoon of that game in Calcutta, Colin listened so diligently to Jim's instructions on leadership that we won the match with ten minutes to spare.' (A finely controlled assault on the Indian bowling by R. Benaud himself had been of no small help.)

'A year or so later Colin was also captaining the Arabs on a short tour around Kent. It involved both cricket and golf and, at the evening function following the golf, Ingleby had apparently been given a bad ice cube. At any rate, he declared himself unfit for the match at Torry Hill and I was dragooned into the captaincy, something I regarded with a certain amount of unease, remembering the explicit off-the-field, non-playing captaincy of Calcutta.

'We set the opposition 250 and they looked like winning with an hour to spare. All the bowlers were taking a hammering. I had 0–70 from not many overs and was wishing I had found the ice cube. Jim, with an eye to tactics, had stationed himself by the sightscreen with the wind at his back so there was no chance of his voice being carried away.

'When I brought John MacKinnon (occasional left-arm medium) on to bowl, there was quite a clamour from the sightscreen to the general effect that this was the most stupid bowling change he had ever seen. I instructed MacKinnon to bowl left-arm over-the-wrist spin and he bowled them out. Jim was generous in his praise, "It remains one of the more incomprehensible captaincy decisions I have ever seen . . .!"

'He was a tough competitor on the golf course. Playing at Sandy Lane in 1965, on the first green I sank a forty-footer which left Jim with a twenty-foot putt for a half. "Makes yours look a bit longer, Jim," I said, as I picked my ball out of the hole. "I claim the putt, under 2–21!" he replied happily – and suddenly we were all square.

'When we were having a gin and tonic with Ann at the nineteenth later, having finished the match all square, I said to her to ask Jim what happened on the first. Jim had the good grace to splutter but then said, "Nothing at all, nothing at all, Ann. Pay no attention to Benaud." Ann though knew something was up and I described the happening. The look she gave Jim would have made up for any lack of ice in his G and T – "You didn't, Swanton!" she said, and then repeated it three more times for good measure.'

With the Duke of Norfolk's tour of the West Indies in February and March 1970, Jim had acted as team-gatherer as well as treasurer. A star-studded side included Colin Cowdrey as captain, Mike Denness, Tony Greig, Chris Old, Phil Sharpe, Derek Underwood, Mike Edwards and the Earl of Cottenham. The twenty-one-year-old Earl who, according to William Hickey in his *Daily Express* column, was better known as 'Charlie' to the late-night set at the Club Dell' Aretusa in Chelsea's King's Road, was enticed to go on the tour by the irrefusable Jim.

> Let me tell you why I think it would be a good thing for you to come from the cricket point of view, if by chance it would be feasible from yours. It would help the tour greatly from the aspect of general fun and the social side if you and another amateur were with us. Bernard is determined to pick a side of good chaps, but you and I both know the average county cricketer of today: he's all the better for a bit of stimulus from outside his own ranks.
>
> Also in general cricket terms it would be all to the good if you and a few more of the Faber-Cazalet vintage made good. They're both going up to Oxford, so have a that much better chance. My belief is that if you were prepared to put enough into it you could certainly make the Sussex side if you wanted to, in a year or two. I mean playing perhaps for a fortnight at a time, or something of that kind. You might go higher – one couldn't do more than guess at this stage.
>
> As to what it would demand of you, I have an idea that you would enjoy the challenge of playing in a class above yourself, so long as you arrived as hard as you could make yourself. Bernard is a marvellous person in my view, and anything that he runs goes with a swing. These tours are the best fun in the world, and I'm sure you'd have a month you'd never forget.

Cottenham was a more than useful medium-fast seam bowler who had opened the bowling for Eton against Harrow in three successive seasons and had also played for Northamptonshire second eleven. Jim was concerned that with such a high profile professional outfit and the absence of the originally selected Mark Faber who had been forced to drop out because of Prelims at Balliol College, Oxford, Charlie might feel that he did not fit in.

> One point that arose when we lunched yesterday. The Governor-General of Trinidad – Sir Solomon Hochoy, no less – has asked Bernard and Colin as well as Ann and me to stay. Colin feels he ought to be with the team, and the duke thought you might be a useful liaison if you were with us. Hochoy (Chinese) is one of the best chaps I've ever come across, and it wouldn't mean you couldn't go out on the tiles occasionally if you wanted to – we're there five nights. Also the comfort is high class, a cut above the Queen's Park Hotel. But if you really feel you'd rather be avec les garcons write by return and I'll accept for three. I'll hold back my reply to the G-G until after the weekend.

'It was a good tour,' said Mike Edwards, Surrey opener and excellent close catcher and who had first met Jim when up at Cambridge. 'We had three games in St Lucia with two drawn and one victory. Then we beat Dominica and St Vincent – they were both limited over games. Trinidad got the better of us – a guy called Inshan Ali captured a lot of wickets. We beat Tobago – I managed to get a fifty in that game and then we lost the last two games pretty heavily to Barbados. Jim had everything so well organised throughout and although Duke was with us, he was manager in all but name.'

Jim's love affair with the ruling classes was a constant source of amusement to his fellow scribes. That doyen of the pack, Alex Bannister, remembers how at a cocktail party a group of players and press were standing on an upper balcony. Looking down they could see the Duke of Kent at one end of the floor below and at the other end, E.W.S. 'We took bets on how long it would take Jim to reach the Duke,' laughed Alex. 'And as we watched he stepped this way and that and slipped neatly past dozens of people. As he finally got to the Duke we sent up a great cheer.'

And so Jim did continue in his own inimitable way. On the cricket field with the Arabs, the Hon. Jeremy Deedes, until recently Managing Director of the Telegraph Group and now Deputy Chairman, recalls with relish Swanton's treatment of his old housemaster at Eton who had provided many moments that were too painful to forget easily. 'Bend, you idle bugger,' shouted Jim, when the erstwhile tutor failed to get down in sufficient time to stop a drive slipping through his fingers at mid-off. 'Bend.'

Jeremy's father, the illustrious W.F. 'Bill' Deedes (Baron Deedes of Aldington), formerly Editor of the *Daily Telegraph* and who held many parliamentary offices, perhaps did not relish the Swanton way on the golf course quite so much. 'He needed watching,' he chuckled. 'A dangerous opponent. It would be an understatement to say that he played to win. He was a great gamesman and knew when to be silent. When you'd got a short putt and might expect him to concede a hole, his silence could be deafening. And he could make his disapproval very heavily felt. It could make a difference of several shots.'

There were many others who experienced Jim's questionable behaviour on the golf course. The brothers John and Peter MacKinnon, distantly related to the MacKinnon of MacKinnon, who played Test cricket for England in the nineteenth century, remember an occasion at the Royal Sydney Club in Australia where there was an argument over the rules on the final hole.

Peter MacKinnon: 'I was playing with Johnny Woodcock against Sandy Gregory, who was captain of the club, and Jim, and there was a stake involving Woodcock and Swanton. Sandy's second shot – it's a dog-leg – was hit against a tree which was about fifteen to twenty feet high. And Jim marched up to his ball, picked it up and moved it quite a long way, and of course Woodcock, seeing this, said: "Hey, Jim, what are you doing, you were in an unplayable position and we have won the hole by virtue of you conceding the stroke." And Jim said, "No no no, I'm playing this ball!" And Woodcock said, "You can't play it from where you've put it. Play it from the spot where Sandy Gregory hit it." And Jim said, "No, that's a staked tree." Now quite clearly it was not a staked tree – I don't know if you're familiar with this, but when playing golf a staked tree, a young tree, is staked until it's grown to about six foot, just to make sure it doesn't bend over and break in the wind or whatever. And you are allowed to move your ball away from a staked tree, but this wasn't one, and Jim had moved it because he said the first time he played the course, in 1946, which was about thirty years earlier, it had been a staked tree. That was a typical contentious moment when you were on a golf course with Jim.'

Changing the size of the ball, John MacKinnon remembers an incident at the beautiful cricket ground at Wormsley when the Arabs were playing John Paul Getty's side.

John MacKinnon: 'What happened was that one of the opening batsmen for the Arabs came down the steps from the pavilion onto the field to start his innings, and he was wearing a helmet just like every opening batsman in the land does now. And Jim rushed up and said that under no circumstances was any Arab going out to bat in a helmet. "You go back into the pavilion and put on a cap, or don't wear anything at all on your head." And so he turned round, took his helmet off, and went back. Fortunately the Wormsley wicket is very placid and the only reason to wear a helmet there was because you were comfortable doing so, not because you needed it. Mind you, if it had been two weeks earlier with Sid Lawrence bowling flat out, trying to prove a point to the County that he was fit enough and still able to bowl with a bit of the old fire, there would have been some pretty black looks from any batsman who had been denied the opportunity of wearing a helmet.'

Two decades before, helmets had not even been manufactured. On a Kent tour in the early 1960s the Arabs were playing the Band of Brothers at the spacious King's School, Canterbury ground. With the Arabs fielding and Jim in command, a slow bowler sent a delivery down the leg side and the batsman, in his eagerness to hit the ball, swung round and hit the wicket-keeper, David McCarthy, who was standing up, a fierce blow above the eye with his bat. The keeper, not unnaturally, slumped to the ground in a pool of blood. Charles Fry, grandson of C.B. and present President of MCC, was playing in the game. 'It was extraordinary, really. No sooner had it happened than Jim waved to his wife Ann, who was sitting in the family Jaguar on the boundary, motioning that she should "come forward".

'Ann drove the Jag directly onto the square and got out to help. Jim, conscious that the prostrate, dazed and bleeding wicket-keeper didn't know Ann, proceeded to introduce them. "David, I don't think you've met my wife Ann." Only Jim would have seen such an introduction as a necessity in the circumstances!' [laughs]

In more recent years with the turnover of generations, Jim became something of a revered grandfatherly figure. James Martin-Jenkins, son of Test Match Special's 'C. M-J' and present secretary of the Arabs, feels that by surrounding himself with young people Jim himself kept young. It was in a warm glow of nostalgia that the Founder's long years at the helm were acknowledged on 11 February 1997 in the Long Room at Lord's with a celebration of his ninetieth birthday.

Anthony Fincham (Secretary): My lords, ladies and gentlemen, Jim has issued a whole series of directions in relation to this evening, as you might imagine, and they included an injunction not to give him a present. Now I'm pleased to say that Henry Hely-Hutchinson thought of a way around this injunction, and a large number of Arabs have contributed to a fund which will be used to plant trees at grounds with which the Arabs are particularly associated, to commemorate Jim's ninetieth birthday.

Jim has asked me to deal with correspondence, rather I suppose in the manner of a best man at a wedding. (laughter) I received a host of letters. The standard apology has been 'I'll be here for the 100th.' I won't mention many of the letters but I will just speak of a few. There have been personal letters of congratulations and good wishes from our Prime Minister, also from the Prime Minister of Australia, John Howard, and from all those Arabs with the English touring party in New Zealand, who include the President of MCC, Colin Ingleby-Mackenzie, the Secretary, Roger Knight, the Treasurer, Michael Melluish, and the team manager Johnny Barclay. Jim's ninetieth birthday will have already come and gone in New Zealand, and I know they toasted his health.

I thought I would read just one letter, which is from Her Royal Highness the Duchess of Kent: 'I remember with great fondness the happy cricket days with the Arabs at Hovingham, and these memories will always remain close with me. It seems incredible that Jim is celebrating his ninetieth birthday tonight, and it is heartwarming to know that so many of you are present to join him on this special occasion. I wish that I too could be with you for dinner in the company of so many friends. We all owe a deep gratitude to Jim as founder of the Arabs, and I wish you all a good celebration of Jim's ninetieth birthday.' Signed Katherine.

(applause)

Secretary: Right, that's all from me. Tony Lewis will now propose the health of the founder.

(applause)

Tony Lewis: Some toast without a glass! My lords, ladies and gentlemen, our founder is about to address us, and I have been asked to roll the pitch. (laughter) I will repair a few footholes, repaint the creases, but whatever I do I can promise you has to take twelve minutes. (laughter) Whatever you do, the founder said, keep it moving. (laughter) If you captain the Arabs as I have you don't get all fazed by that sort of command. (laughter) In my day Jim used to say: 'Give Cottenham the new ball, and the wind, Hutton can come upwind, and then at 11.53 I suggest Peebles downwind . . .' (laughter) 'and at 12.19 an early show of wrist spin perhaps. On no account bowl Daniels before lunch.' (laughter and applause) 'Or tea.' (laughter) Well, we all know now that Jim really is a David Lloyd at heart. (laughter and cheers) Jim Swanton was probably the first off-the-field manager, and all he lacked was a tracksuit. (laughter) I know you will agree that the Long Room here at Lord's is truly spectacular and a most appropriate place to fête someone who has done so much for cricket, and indeed for MCC.

All: Hear, hear! (applause)

Tony Lewis: I did think it was a little over the top for Dickie Bird, though. He walked through here, the corridor of Test players, standing ovation everywhere, all tears and handkerchiefs. It was a show of populism I thought reserved perhaps for Eva Peron in Buenos Aires, (laughter) or Geoffrey Boycott in his own imagination! (laughter) Arabs don't go in for a lot of fuss, and in any case tonight is very much family. And I'd really and truly want Jim to feel the warmth of the affection which we have for him, for having selected us in the first place as Arabs, for offering us excellent cricket, but perhaps, and more importantly than we all thought, when we played our first games for the club, we owe Jim our gratitude for bringing many cricketers together who by playing cricket or golf for the Arabs, often with families in tow, themselves have become lasting friends. And I think we are all grateful, Jim, for what you've done in that respect, that regardless of the man with the umbrella on the boundary we have become your great friends, and between us we have a terrific Arab camaraderie. Thank you for that. (applause) We have coped happily with your many strictures. The key to it all is to see them coming! (laughter) Let me give you a clue. 'Look here, dear boy,' – with a frown – is one to be avoided. (laughter) 'Look here, Macleay, you don't mean to tell me that you intend wearing a helmet?' (laughter) 'To bat for the Arabs at Wormsley?' I remember that well and my advice to Rory would have been, agree with Jim at that early stage, then it's only a yellow card affair. (laughter) Alas, poor Rory Macleay, press on. 'Well yes, Mr Swanton, I do intend to bat in a helmet, I'm much more comfortable wearing a helmet, even against spin.' Jim then gave him one of his thundering 'I am the founder' looks . . . (laughter) as if to say, I haven't got where I am today, Macleay, by wearing a helmet at Wormsley. (laughter) And then came the red card speech, which usually begins: 'Look here, I have to tell you . . .', and usually ends:

'You may never play for the Arabs again.' (laughter and applause) I remember poor Rory Macleay that day retreating into the pavilion. I expected to hear a great scream as he fell on his own Arabs umbrella, but instead, helmetless, he went out to bat, and continued his glorious career as one of the Arabs' leading run-getters. Of course what Jim had in mind was the Arabs' batting spirit as exemplified in my day by Stanley Metcalfe in Barbados in 1974. Our top batting had been routed in the first innings by some pretty quick bowling by Gregory Armstrong and someone called Selman, who kept fizzing the ball past our noses. We were thirty-five for five at one stage. And so the second time around I asked the forty-one-year-old Stanley to move up the order. He'd only come on a holiday to watch us. (laughter) At one stage all nine runs had come off Stanley's head. (laughter) The first was a four down the leg side, off the Oxford cap – plunged forward, hit the head, umpire . . . four . . . The second off his head to third man. Plunged forward, umpire . . . It was then that I walked down the pitch to Stanley and suggested that he try to play the fast bowling, which was very short, off the back foot not the front foot. Great players, Don Bradman, back foot – you can duck, you can weave. 'I'll have you know that I've played the new ball off the front foot all my life – I'm not about to change now.' (laughter) Next ball. (laughter) And the Arabs' score raced on to thirteen. (laughter) Well, Jim on the subject of helmets, on the subject of ping-pong in Peter Carroll's garage in Sandwich, Jim getting warmed up about anything, is all about standards. And I've seen professional cricket drawn into semi-showbusiness, these days the England players tend to throw their briefcases into the dressing room first, followed by the mobile phone, before the cricket bat. The Arabs have always played proper cricket matches according to the laws, highly competitively, and attending at all times to the smallest detail of sporting behaviour, and for this again our thanks to Jim.

All: Hear, hear! (applause)

Tony Lewis: I've never been so honoured as to propose a toast to a nonagenarian, ninety years old. I've been close – well, by that I mean I have made a couple of memorial addresses . . . (laughter). I've telephoned Sandwich for the past few weeks, seeking pieces of information, until one day Jim said, 'Look here, dear boy, let's agree, if I don't feel well I'll ring you.' (laughter) Jim Swanton I think you'll agree is just not the dying sort! (laughter) But I must say how we are thankful too for the peaceful and persuasive presence of Ann, who has done so much to make the Arabs such fun for us.

All: Hear, hear! (cheers and applause)

Tony Lewis: I can't imagine what you'd have done without Ann, to be honest, Jim. I think she's been absolutely terrific. Today is not only your birthday but your wedding anniversary – thirty-nine years of marriage. Terrific day for you. (applause and cheers) Now I'm still not certain how I myself became an Arab. Neath Grammar School is not exactly a pillar of the Headmasters' Conference, and the founder's homeland appeared to be very much Kent and MCC, a little Oxbridge – no one's actually sure about Oxbridge and Neath. (laughter) And I've often told a story of retreating home after playing full back in the university match in 1959, parading conspicuously down a main road with a light blue scarf round my neck, feeling chipper, when towards me came the old barracker from the rugger ground at Neath – flat hat, few teeth – Meg Downey was his name – and he said, 'I hear you've got your blue then, Tone.' I said, 'Yeah, I was very lucky, Meg, very lucky.' He said, 'Yes, funny you know, I never saw you in the boat.' (laughter) . . . My pleasure to lead the Arabs to Barbados in '74 . We had a talented crew, like Cottenham with Fry, with city interests, obsessed with the crash of secondary banking, while Kinkead-Weekes, Faber, Hooper, Priestley and Daniels, as far as I could tell as their captain, were obsessed with Charlie Fry's nanny. (laughter) It was on that tour that the great merits of J.S.O. Haslewood were truly understood. In his younger days an original Arab from the very first match, and then emeritus, a friend, an expert on nannies, (laughter) officer in charge of nets transport, and most importantly in charge of complaints against the Founder . . .

After a couple of lost matches the Founder took to advising us rather loudly from the boundary. He's never given up the captaincy, of course, from day one. And I received a letter from Richie Benaud, with whom I work in the summer for television, and he first of all records warmest wishes from Mrs Benaud, who as Daphne Surfleet was once a dedicated porter of the Swanton typewriter. But she sends her love, Jim, from Australia. Richie writes: 'We shall raise a glass to Jim at the appropriate time on the night and we wish all Arabs a delightful evening. My own memory was of Ingleby-Mackenzie being taken ill overnight. A bad ice cube, I believe.' (laughter) 'And I was instructed . . . – this is Richie Benaud – 'I was instructed by Jim to captain the Arabs, but at the same to, "Pay attention, I'll be standing at the sightscreen".' (laughter) And Richie concludes: 'Enclosed is a cheque for the equivalent of two tickets – do as you wish with the money. A cold bottle or two, or a small forest of trees perhaps. Yours, Richie.' There were no complaints against the Founder really, it was just that we couldn't beat anyone. And he sent Gibbons, his driver, to me one morning as we were preparing for nets at the ground in Barbados. Jim's letter reads exactly as follows: 'Tony, here is a twenty-six yard length of cord, which you may think a help in guiding the bowler's line. If you mark out a narrow rectangle . . .' – are you with this? (laughter) – 'outside the off stump, I'll answer Hutton's snorts by betting him five dollars he can land it six out of six. If you just stretch it wicket to wicket it would at least indicate where they must pitch a good length ball to hit the off stump. Only a tentative suggestion. I'd like the cord back.' (laughter) And later when Jim enquired about the experiment, I said, 'Well, do you know, Jim, cord worked well. Ian and Emma Balding, newly wed, have been in single beds all the trip, so we used the cord to lash the beds together.' (laughter) Red card! 'I have to tell you, you may never play for the Arabs again.' (laughter)

And a last story, because you will understand how my relationship with Jim has extended beyond the Arabs' world in many ways, and he was I suppose, with his good cricket sense and civilised style of writing, the one writer all cricketers of my playing days with Glamorgan always chose to read every day. He made cricket writing a profession that so many of us wanted to follow, and throughout the whole wide journalistic world he was a stickler for press box protocol. There were no free-loaders in any press box where Jim was working. It was his office, and should be treated as such. He did fail once, however, and I was there. I was ill, flying into Calcutta where I was to lead England into the second Test of the series. A special car took me from the airport ahead of the team to the Grand Hotel. Thousands were in the streets outside waiting to greet us, but the driver had been briefed to take me to the rear and allow me to climb up the stairs at the back of the hotel into my room. I couldn't get rid of the security man – he was standing at my bedside while I was already in bed. 'Just one more thing, sir,' he said. 'What is that?' 'Please sign autograph. Anything.' I scrawled 'Tony Lewis'. 'Please sign "MCC captain".' So I signed 'MCC Captain'. It was two days later in the hotel after play that Mr E.W. Swanton of the *Daily Telegraph* greeted me with the words, 'I have to tell you dear boy,' – with a frown – 'that being the captain of England does not entitle you to issue passes for hangers-on into the press box.' (laughter and applause) The hotel tried to compensate for the trickery of their security man. They cosseted Jim. Even the pageboys were lectured that they should meticulously look after each of Mr Swanton's requests. Indeed at breakfast next morning a small liveried lad advanced on Jim with a blackboard and a bell, with number 232 chalked up on the board. 'Are you Swanton, sahib, room 232?' 'Yes.' 'Good morning sahib, this is your wake-up call.' (laughter)

I personally owe a great deal to Jim Swanton, but not least to the Arabs. I ask you to think of cricket without the Arabs. We've always been a club which others have wanted to defeat with undisguised relish. So be it. That is merely the burden of propagating the standards which are the pillars of the club and of the game itself, and therefore it's my pleasure to give you the health of the Founder.
The Founder!

All: The Founder!

(applause)

All: (sing 'Happy Birthday to You')

(applause)

Jim Swanton: Thank you.

(applause)

Jim Swanton: I don't think there's much chance of my being able to live up to the affectionate caricature that you've just heard from Tony. (laughter) We are very proud, Ann and I, of this turn-out, to celebrate our thirty-ninth wedding anniversary. (laughter) After all, you wouldn't all be here if it were not for her. I'd have gone to the dogs long ago! (laughter) I welcome you all. And I wonder when such beauty, talent, virtue, in all its forms, has decorated this Long Room. And I think perhaps not since the Arabs had their eightieth party here ten years ago. (laughter and applause) 11 February is a day which naturally I remember, but it has other connotations, and one of them is that Mike Griffith's father, Billy Griffith, a great friend of a great many of us, made his one and only hundred on 11 February at Port of Spain in the Test match for England against the West Indies. And I remember that for the only time in my life I saw the heat was such that the sweat came through the front of his pads, and I never remember that before. 11 February 1948. It's also by the way the birthday of Mr Dennis Skinner, the MP for Bolsover. (laughter) I do very much hope you like this arrangement. I was very keen to be near this door. This door has many memories of course for everyone who's ever played cricket, and it has a memory for me which goes back to 1921 when, as a member of Surrey – my father had made me one – I somehow got into here for the Middlesex and Surrey match, captained Middlesex by James Mann's grandfather, the famous Frank. And I'd been to the Test match at the Oval, and I'd lost my father's binoculars. And I got hold somehow of another pair, and I was sitting out there just in front and in due course

I wanted to go away for something or other, and there was an old fellow next to me, and I said, 'Excuse me sir, I wonder whether you would mind just keeping an eye on these things.' And right away, he said, 'My boy, you're at Lord's, not at the Oval'. (laughter) Through this door every great cricketer of every country has passed. It's a historic place, as I need not tell you, and I should think probably at least half the people in this room have been through this door to play an innings out there. To take the sublime to the fairly ridiculous, I went out there myself in 1937 as a member, (laughter) at 11.30, against the Lords and Commons – you generally reckoned to get one or two off the edge against them – and I was back at 11.31, (laughter) caught by one Lord off another. All I will say is that the bowler became Prime Minister – it was Alec Dunglass.

Now we've got, as you've heard, a few of the old and bold here, and in particular John Haslewood, the only man who has driven with a buggy over the bridge on the fourteenth at St George's, the diameter of the buggy being considerable larger than the bridge. (laughter) And Peter Carroll will bear witness because he jumped off the thing in absolute terror. However, there's John and he's still with us, which is good. (applause) And then we have a chap called Hotchkin – Neil by name – and the most extraordinary thing about him is that as a cricketer he got worse and worse. (laughter) In the Eton and Harrow match he made 153 in the first year, 109 and 96 in the second year, and 88 and 12 in the third year. So he obviously left school thinking he'd get a pair in the next year if he played on. 458 he made, I think that comes to, and that's the most that have ever been made in the Eton and Harrow match. But, however, it wasn't really quite what he was up to, and he decided that he'd play golf instead. And he's a man of tremendous importance in the golf world, Neil, and I think it's probably true to say he was President of the European Golf Union, and probably, if you like to mention his name anywhere on the Continent, you can probably get it courtesy of the course, I wouldn't wonder. Do you think that's possible, Neil? Anyway he and I went in first in the first match, and he was run out fourteen. A good throw by Nobes – I've looked it up. (laughter)

And then we had a young chap – we thought we'd better have a bit of young blood, and so we got a young undergraduate from Trinity by the name of Woodcock. (laughter) And on our tour to Germany we thought we'd better have him along, and so he came, and I remember him giving most tremendous lip to some air-marshal or person of very great consequence. (laughter) And who could tell then that this brazen boy really would become the Editor of *Wisden*, Trustee of MCC, and to have watched more Test matches and reported more Test matches than anyone else has ever done in history?

(applause)

The President of MCC, as you've heard, is in New Zealand, but he is represented here by his quieter half. Her name is Storms Ingleby-Mackenzie, she's representing the President here, and it's lovely to see her. She is the quieter half. Thank you. (laughter and applause) You know, looking round I think I can see . . . almost every face recalls some sort of memory or other. For instance Henry Blofeld. A most remarkable thing about Henry was that he was the absolute toast of Sydney for quite some while. He was a sort of Bertie Wooster of Bondi Beach really. (laughter) And he was there in the Monty Noble stand, you see, and a chap came along with a piece of paper in his hand, and so Henry put on the famous smile. 'My dear old thing,' he said. And the chap said, 'I don't want your autograph, this is a writ!' (laughter) Probably from that awful Packer I dare say. But anyway, Henry, he never got you, he never got you into court did he? (laughter) Talking of which, as far as I know, unless people have been very quiet about it, we've been going for sixty-one and a half years, and as far as I know there are no Arabs who've been asked to help the police with their enquiries. (laughter) But it's time to make a long jump now to the present, and especially to acknowledge our deep gratitude to our hosts here tonight, who allow us to play on their lovely grounds. Hubert Doggart is the Chairman of Arundel Castle Cricket Club, where we love to play. Robin Kingdown, the chief of the Band of Brothers, that great club, allows us to play twice at Torry Hill against BB and against the Foresters. Henry Carnarvon allows us to play at Highclere, which we love to do, and Paul Getty allows us to play at Wormsley, and allowed us to have our diamond jubilee there. There they are, and very benign they look. But I tell you this, (laughter) I don't know which is the keener to win – it's a very very nice point. (laughter) As Wodehouse says, 'verging on the moot'. (laughter)

You've heard about trees, a rather clandestine affair altogether. I was at something of a loss, but I wondered whether whoever thought of the idea remembered that I had quoted a critic, who in the days when I used to write an awful lot on Monday mornings because there was nothing much else going on, and the critic said that the characteristic sound of a Monday morning was Jim Swanton barking up the wrong tree. (laughter) . . .

Now I've been here a little bit too long, I think, but let me leave you with this thought for young Arabs, wherever they are. It's quite easy to be a good Arab, quite easy – you only have to get there at eleven o'clock. (laughter) You keep out of sight not only helmets, but also those ghastly jockey caps. Watch the ball in the field, keep your head still when you're batting, and remember, we must always laugh at ourselves as well as at and with one another. Thank you so much for making this for me a memorable night.

(applause)

Chapter 11

Retired but not retiring

When Jim retired from the *Telegraph*, nobody seriously supposed that was the last they would hear of him. For retirement is but a word and Jim never did discover quite what it meant. He was not a man to be attracted by what Dr Johnson referred to as its 'soft obscurities'.

So the new beginning after the old ending was really doing more of what he did best and with greater freedom to do so. He continued to write for his paper – obviously not with such a great regularity, but there were not too many days that would pass without his name appearing either at the head of a sports feature or in an editorial column. He still opined with distinction and remained an authoritative voice in his role as prep school headmaster, displaying for the most part approbation with some reservations or occasionally controlled testiness when faced with often unruly pupils skipping around the playgrounds in uniform white or rebellious colours. The academic analogy is not inappropriate, as before the war he once considered a career as a schoolmaster.

As we have seen in these pages, not everyone smitten by the high-and-mightiness liked it. Jim has, at various times, been described as 'over-bearing', 'pompous', even 'papal', although the latter perhaps is a sort of compliment. In 1963, at the time of the Lord's Test, there was a conclave of cardinals at the Vatican to select Pope John XXIII's successor. During the cricket commentary, white smoke was seen billowing from a distant chimney that had caught fire. Brian Johnston turned to fellow colleagues in the box: 'Ah, I see that Jim has been elected Pope!'

But the days when, during stormy exchanges, 'Jim's fingers flicked with the noise of a Bren gun', in John Woodcock's words, were now mostly in the past. The taper on the fuse was much slower burning and the explosion longer in coming – that is, assuming it arrived at all. The recently retired MCC Curator Stephen Green remembers an occasion when there was no actual detonation but rather a drawn-out personal vendetta: 'There was a fairly young but highly competent promotions girl on the staff who apparently had given permission for a book to be published which did not meet with the full approval of E.W.S. As you know, Jim was no shrinking violet and he did rather keep getting at her in a somewhat bullying manner – he could be overpowering.

'On the other hand, he did work extraordinarily hard – he was very industrious and you always got a prompt, courteous reply to any queries you put his way. I think he was lucky that he had the sort of personality that compelled people to do quite a lot of work for him.'

Jim was no rantipole bully – the thought would have dismayed him – but his expectancy that people would unquestioningly do his bidding was, at times, an imposition they could well have done without. 'The trouble with Jim is two things, one is that he always exceeds his brief, and the other is, he asks you to do something and when, in a rather overcrowded day, you do it, you discover he's already done it himself.' The words of former MCC Secretary, Jack Bailey. The current Chief Executive of MCC enlarges on the theme: 'I think Jim could get away with a lot of things and he used that position pretty well whether it was with the newspaper or whether it was just as the grand old man of cricket. I think he pushed what he believed very hard and, in many ways, that helped all sorts of other people who perhaps hadn't quite got the same amount of clout to drive things forward.

'Jim was a forceful personality and, although you could accuse him of being domineeringly confident, I don't think he needed any official position within the Club to persuade people to do anything. He cared much about the Arts and Library aspect, the publications and what we did in the Museum, and he would always have his viewpoint and he made people argue their case and I think that's always helpful. I didn't often see him beaten in an argument. Although there was one occasion when I had to put a different view and I thought he handled it brilliantly, because first he tried his normal approach and said, "Well, this is what I think," and I said, "Well, this is what I think," and, in the end, he said, "Well, I still don't agree, but I accept it." I felt that was fair enough.'

Jim had been elected on to the MCC Committee in 1975. When touting for support he had enquired of his old friend, J.J. Warr, whether he might count on his backing: 'My dear Jim,' replied Warr, 'that's rather like asking Satan to put forward the Pope to be Chief Rabbi.'

Jim's official time on MCC bodies – as opposed to the long time having an influence on its affairs unofficially – was hugely productive. Chairman of the Working Party before the building and of the Indoor Cricket School, 1977–82; Chairman of the Arts and Library Sub-Committee, 1982–85; and remaining a member of its committee until his death, and then in 1989, being elected life Vice-President of MCC, only the twelfth to be so honoured. There are many who thought he deserved the Presidency itself. Colin Ingleby-Mackenzie, himself a President, says, 'My greatest regret was that Jim was never made President of MCC or knighted. This was one of cricket's great oversights.' As far as the former was concerned, Jim probably arrived at the starting gate too late. He was not even on the Committee until not far short of the age of seventy and the fact that, until that moment, he was a full-time working journalist impeded rather than propelled any chance he may have had of gaining the position. And as for the latter, when he was awarded a CBE in 1995, as always, the final decision fell to the Honours Committee. The Prime Minister at the time, John Major, told me: 'Many people have the mistaken belief that the Prime Minister can decide the level of an award. That is not the case. It is not in the PM's gift. He or she can support a recommendation for an honour, but that is as far as it goes. The Scrutiny Committee alone judge what each individual should get. You can say I privately hoped that Jim would receive a knighthood, but it was not to be.

'I much enjoyed watching cricket in his company and the stimulating conversations we had together. And I much miss his reporting of cricket. Jim was a national icon.'

Cricket has rarely been without some kind of controversy though that term would be an understatement to describe the effect on the game of what Jim called 'the Packer intrusion'. The shock waves could be likened to an earthquake. Jim was vociferous in opposition to the commercial strike by the Australian tycoon whom he memorably dubbed the Antichrist (later modified to anti-hero). At an early stage of the saga, it seemed as if cricket faced an irreparable schism. In an attempt to save the game he loved, Jim was moved to write to a leader in the breakaway pack, England captain Tony Greig:

Dear Tony,

When you said at the Lawrence Trophy dinner that cricket was entering the phase of really big money and would I come to Hove and hear about it I never imagined you would have lent yourself to something which – if what I read is true – looks like blowing the whole fabric of Test cricket sky high.

Let me try and picture your position as I see it today, and as it is likely to be if this project goes forward. You are on top of the English cricket world with all the prestige of the Indian tour behind you, and the England captaincy yours probably for five years to come at least, if you maintain your form.

If the estimates are only fairly near the mark you're asking more money than any of your predecessors, with the certainty of a continuation plus a very large tax-free benefit. Your PR value is such that any number of openings must be open to you when you retire: in other words no fear of a drop in your standard of living.

You've worked hard for the position you've won for yourself. But I don't need to say that you owe it to the present English first-class system, which has grown up over the century of Test cricket. You've taken a lot – and indeed you've given a lot, and I don't criticize you or any other of the top players trying to get more cash out of the game in these more prosperous days, provided they can do so without detriment to it.

But this circus, if it goes forward in the way suggested this winter, will ruin four Test series and put Australian cricket especially into the greatest disorder and danger. Your top players will be seen by the cricket world as having kicked in the teeth the game and those within it who have made you what you are.

And the greatest opprobrium would surely descend personally on you, because of your position and the responsibility it gives you. Your notion would be seen as essentially selfish and a threat to the well-being of all your fellow county players, since of course Test cricket is the backbone of the English game.

If you say that commercial sponsorship would still keep county cricket afloat my answer would be that they have identified with the game because of its special place in the world of sport – a place that has been made for it by all the great cricketers and great sportsmen of the past. Whether they would support a game that has suffered the sort of injuries that look like being inflicted on it is far from certain.

Could you really live happily with the situation that would have been created by the personal greed of a few? As I see it, you are the key to the thing as the captain and the dominant personality concerned.

One of the things that I've always admired about you is your capacity to see where you've gone wrong and to acknowledge it frankly. That's a great virtue, and not a common one, and it gives me hope that you may see this miserable business in perspective and pull out in time to save your own reputation – and that of others who would probably follow your lead.

I don't need to apologise for having been so completely frank because I always have been so with you, and you've never seemed to resent it: rather the contrary. As you must know you have never had a warmer supporter – you're the only cricketer I've ever written to the selectors to consider. It was in June 1970, and it so happened you were picked for England for the first time that month. That may have been a coincidence but at least it did your cause no harm. Just previously you had come with us to the West Indies where you took the chance of showing your full potential and made it clear, to me at any rate, that you should have gone to Australia in '70/'71.

As Alec Bedser is a very old friend of mine as well as the man who has put you where you are I'm sending him (but no-one else) a copy of this letter. That it comes from the heart I won't need to say. See things straight, Tony, before it's too late.

An extraordinarily persuasive letter it would seem, but its resonances were not loud enough to stifle the sound of the cash register. Very soon it became clear that Packer was using cricket as a tool in a struggle for television rights. Eventually after a court battle over restraint of trade, rebel tours and a million words in print, the game adapted to the changed circumstances and the issue faded into the history books, though not without leaving marks that were not easily erased.

When it came to writing to England captains, Jim much preferred a welcoming tone:

Dear Michael,

I can't remember when I last said it, if ever, but I thought I must add to all the messages of goodwill and encouragement you will be receiving as England's new captain. Whatever happens I'm sure you will bring dignity and dedication to the job, and I believe that if the luck runs reasonably kindly you will enjoy it – and be able to convey a sense of that to the followers of English cricket. They deserve it.

Did you know that apart from Nigel Howard in India and Ken Cranston (once) in West Indies you are the first Lancashire man to captain England since Archie MacLaren in 1902 and 1909? He, incidentally, was a fine player but poor leader – reputed to have said in the dressing-room: 'Look what they've given me.'

Enough of the history lesson – I'm so pleased to see you live in Didsbury, a lovely club which made me a life member (or v-p) because I used to bring cricket writers' sides there for years in aid of Lancashire Beneficiaries.

You'll be overwhelmed with good wishes – so I don't expect an acknowledgement.

Yours sincerely,
Jim Swanton

In an interview with Robert McCrum in 1998, Jim added to the warmth of that letter by saying that 'Michael Atherton has all the guts in the world. I admire him very much.' There had, of course, to be a rider: 'I do wish he would have a closer affinity with his razor.' Atherton's lengthy tenure as captain, at fifty-four Test Matches the most by any English skipper to date, was followed by the second longest, that of Nasser Hussain. 'I hope I never live to see the day when somebody called Nasser Hussain captains England,' Jim once said to me when we were preparing a book together. When I berated him for what appeared to be a racist remark, he smiled ruefully and remained silent. A year or so later, when Hussain was the new skipper, I reminded him that in fact he had lived to see the day. His response was: 'Did you read what he said about getting a bit of nastiness into our game . . . and that we should apply the Australian fashion for abuse, rucking and making it very clear they want you back in the pavilion pretty quick?'

I realised then that the original comment had been impersonal, not so much against the man himself as the trends in modern cricket he so much disliked. His beau idéal was a blending of golden youth and athletic distinction, a John Crawley, a Matthew Fleming, or a player in the classic mould from the old amateur traditions rather than the modern proletarian and pragmatic alternative. Nevertheless I took the opportunity to point out that I thought Nasser was a splendid, passionately committed captain and that he displayed very much the right spirit of cricket when, for instance, running nearly to the pavilion to congratulate his opposite number who was on his way back having made a hundred. Would, I wondered, Jim have thought the same way had he realised Nasser Hussain was distantly related to Nawab Abdul Ali, the Prince of Arcot?

England's charismatic leader from a previous generation, Mike Brearley, remembered an occasion early in his career with Middlesex, when Jim called him down to one of the Secretary's rooms at Lord's. 'He invited me in an orotund way to become a member of the Free Foresters and I said I didn't think I wanted to, I was playing enough cricket. And he said, "Well, you don't have to play very much, just once, you know." Eventually, having been pushed rather, I said to him, well, I wasn't sure I wanted to play that sort of cricket. And then he sort of looked at me and I repeated, "I'm not sure I want to play that kind of cricket, with ex-colonels and so forth" – which, I suppose, was a bit harsh of me. And he drew himself up and said, "Michael" – he always called me Michael, which I rather liked actually – "there is such a thing as inverted snobbery." When I told the Middlesex players, one of them said, "It's not the kind of snobbery he knows very much about."'

Brearley went on to say that, at the time, there was probably an element of truth in Swanton's assessment of his reply, and that they always got on rather well. 'He seemed to be someone who was nicer than his image and the image he had of himself would allow. Besides the pomposity and snobbishness he had a lot of good qualities. I found that when you stood up to him and didn't let him be a sort of puffing bully, he was much more human. There was a warmth to him and a humour, even a somewhat self-deprecating humour at times. And it was quite fun ribbing him. After I got beyond the point, as a youngish man, of feeling a bit nervous about him, I started to enjoy his company.'

I asked: 'If, mirroring patterns of the past, E.W. had tried to tell you, as England captain, how to run the ship, what would have been your reaction?'

'I might easily have lost my cool with him. Presumably, he would have chosen his own way of doing it and said in a very surreptitious manner, "A word in your ear," and you'd probably just let it go in and out again. Or not stay in very long. But I could imagine a way in which he could have said it to me where I would have got furious with him. It wouldn't have taken much, especially if he had written a letter about it or started haranguing me.'

I then tapped Michael's psychoanalytical expertise by putting to him the difficulty in understanding Jim's mind-set. Surely Jim was not thick-skinned enough to fail to realise that, many times, he upset people?

'Well, I'm not actually making a comment about Swanton. I didn't know him well enough. But free-associating to your interesting comment, I would be inclined to think there's something that this sort of person has to defend himself against in a kind of massive way. There's some sort of insecurity or some feeling of inferiority, or some feeling that he was put down by his father or his school or some humiliation he felt he suffered. Or perhaps some feeling of ineptitude and he has to pump himself up and thicken his psychological armoury in order not to be affected by people's upset, hurt, anger. He becomes self-righteous. And the skin is a kind of narcissistic skin. If people actually disagree with him, he's so sure he's right. I'm not saying that that's what I think about Jim because I just don't know, but I would think along those lines.'

Which is a fascinating analysis. Graeme Wright, who twice had periods as editor of *Wisden Cricketers' Almanack*, reckoned that 'Swanton created a persona for himself in much the same way as does the art expert Brian Sewell. But he was comfortable with himself in the process, because he was becoming something he never was or had started out as. He was becoming a sort of grandee. That didn't stop him being an incredibly useful reporter. When you look back at some of his books to see what happened, he explains things in extraordinary depth, which is very valuable for future generations, but whether people needed to know all that detail at the time is debatable, because they probably knew most of the background anyway.'

When Jim vacated his seat at the *Telegraph* in 1975, his friend and colleague Robin Marlar wrote a compelling encomium under the heading, 'Passing of the Emperor'.

> The cricket Press-box is a lovely place. Its purposes are clear, its confines narrow. If outsiders consider it a dangerously closed community, those inside can if they choose feel as warm and safe as if they had never left the womb.
>
> Tomorrow that small and happy world is to lose a continent.
>
> Like many another I shall feel a personal loss, because it was thanks to him that I was given an introduction to what has been a long and satisfying experience.
>
> His readers will surely feel the greatest deprivation. Swanton has done a superb job for the *Daily Telegraph*. His style and his standards are uniquely and unmistakenly suited to the needs of his public. Like another much-loved big man and clear communicator, Richard Dimbleby, Swanton summarises and conveys the scene – whether writing or speaking – in words, and at a pace which signifies authority and promotes comprehension.
>
> In marketing terms it would be hard to find a writer who has

consistently done more to sustain a newspaper's attack on the upper frontiers of its readership, while deepening that paper's hold on its natural supporters. His colleagues will miss him. He has done things his way, and that is the way to win respect.

But that is not the whole story. Cricket is not in as healthy a state now as many of those Jim Swanton has left behind in the Press-box would like. Swanton's standards are agelessly in need of support. But there are other factors equally relevant to the age in which we live: success, for instance, and the quality of stardom.

Nor can he claim that his appeal has been nationally balanced. Years ago Johnny Wardle comforted a colleague who had fallen foul of the 'Emperor' in print. 'Never mind, lad, folks read different kinds of *Telegraph* in Sheffield and Bradford.' Not long ago I was sent a clipping from the *Yorkshire Post* which showed how quick Swanton had been to call for Illingworth's replacement, and to attack those who criticised Denness. Take that in conjunction with his condemnation of Boycott's behaviour, his support for Cowdrey against Close and try and mount a Swantonian defence against a Yorkshireman who knows that Swanton is a member of the Kent Committee. It isn't easy. Especially when, 25 years ago, after he had reached his 100th Test, he attributed Australian superiority over the years to their advantage in 'the fields of selection and captaincy.'

Thus I make no bones about it. It is the man and his writing I shall miss rather than some of his opinions and judgments on cricket and cricketers. Deeply miss, at best. For me the cricket Press-box can never be the same. Alan Gibson found the definitive verdict on Jim Swanton in some lines of Addison:

> In all thy humours whether grave or mellow,
> Thou'rt such a touchy, testy, pleasant fellow,
> Hast so much wit, and mirth and spleen about thee.
> There is no living with thee or without thee.

Can such a man ever really retire? I hope not.

And, of course, nor did he. The perennial themes which exercised him throughout his career continued to occupy his typewriter: intimidation, sledging, behaviour on the field, raising standards of sportsmanship, a divided County Championship, the pyjama game, orthodox principles and so on – this custodian was not about to capitulate. For, as Matthew Engel, editor of *Wisden Cricketers' Almanack* and then a staff writer on the *Guardian*, rightly pointed out in a ninetieth-birthday salute, he was 'still sharp-eyed, still trenchant, and sometimes he is even right. He has more energy than men half his age. I know this: I am half his age.'

Engel subscribed to the view that though Jim liked to think of himself as a dinosaur he always adapted.

> He has never been so obsessed with the past that he could not appreciate the present. Yet his literary style has not adapted. He wrote as a 19-year-old in 1926 (for a journalist to whom yesterday is old hat – this is not so much Jurassic as Palaeozoic) as he does as a near-90-year-old. It is impossible not to mention John Warr's delicious description of Swanton's writing: 'halfway between the Ten Commandments and Enid Blyton'. Yet it might be more accurate to quote Matthew Arnold: 'People think I can teach them style. What stuff it all is! Have something to say, and say it as clearly as you can. That is the only secret of style.' Swanton has always said it clearly, indeed sonorously. This may not explain his longevity as a human; it explains his extreme longevity as a journalist.

As a journalist Jim was always inquiring; a trait that was part of him throughout his life. Even as late as 1998, soon after Tony Blair had come to power, he was making contact with the Prime Minister's ex-house master at Fettes through an intermediary who had been a contemporary of Blair's at the college. It transpired 'he had been a promising cricketer in the Junior Colts, if not captain of that XI', but that later on 'cricket was not regarded as a fitting pastime by the Blair mafia'. The intermediary remembered A.C.L. Blair as bumptious but amusing, and that his main claim to fame was acting: 'he is a skilful showman, loves the limelight and is a shrewd stage manager'. Armed with this knowledge ahead of most of the populace, Jim knew now where to place his vote at the next election.

Another aspect of Jim's journalistic life was that he had rarely been without hired help. John Kitchen, tragically for thirty-four years a quadriplegic, but once a hugely talented golfer who got a blue at Oxford before playing internationally, met Jim in 1948.

> I felt I knew him already, because I'd heard about him pre-war – '*Evening Standard* Swanton' they used to call him and I'd heard that he was a bit of a pusher who was once removed from Vincents, you know, the club in Oxford which personifies the ideal of '*Mens sana in corpore sano*' [a healthy mind in a healthy body] because he was not a member. Anyway, I was watching Australia play the University when I was

passed a note asking if I would like to play golf. Two days later I found myself playing golf with Swanton against Sam Loxton and Lindsay Hassett [who were in the Aussie touring side].

Now, Jim's swing was unbelievable. It's not fair to criticise him, because he was damaged physically as a prisoner – I think it must have been his left shoulder, which prevented him swinging a club properly, but we had a lovely game and as a result of that he invited me to start working for him. He obviously thought I was quite nice looking – he liked good-looking young men, you know, and because I had blue eyes and fair hair, I almost began to describe myself as one of Swanton's blue-eyed boys. It was just admiration for their physique and that, rather in the Corinthian way, no question of being approached or interfered with – with me anyway – and I had first-hand evidence of that because we shared the same bedroom for a few months. Anyway, he knew I could play cricket and obviously I could play golf. Well, very soon I was introduced to very august company – in fact, he was pretty grand himself to a young man like me – Denis Compton and his first wife and Don Bradman.

At first, I didn't like him much – he was aloof and I think he had a sense of inferiority because he hadn't been to University, nor was he quite a member of the Establishment – but I grew to like him more as I got to know him. My job was to select the correspondence that I thought he needed to see, get the papers in the morning, of course, and then deal with the correspondence. Well, I didn't have a typewriter. He was always very efficient at the typewriter, and I'd probably put a few letters on his bed or something and he'd knock off answers straight away. He was always very punctilious in answering things people asked. Very good like that. And then the most important part was to take detailed notes on the day's play, which he would use for his piece. And then when his piece was done, I had to phone it through to Frank Coles, the Sports Editor at the *Telegraph*. And Jim was terrified of Frank Coles – you see, it was a plum job and he didn't want to lose it. And Coles was snappy in the way that Editors are and, at the end of the day, Swanton was prolific. As Len Hutton said, he wrote a toilet roll of stuff every day.

On one occasion Jim got very angry with me. It was during the [19]48 Test match at Headingley and I'd phoned through the copy. The next day Jim had put the papers down in front of him and he read through his own piece first. 'What's this, Kitchen? What the devil do you think you're doing here?' And I said, 'What do you mean, Jim?' 'What came as a joke was when Hutton played the sweep four times running.' He said, 'I wrote "jolt", and you've phoned through "joke".' I said, 'It's not true, I did phone through "jolt"' – the line was always bad in those days, in the background old typewriters clacking away. But he was absolutely livid. Anyhow, actually we formed a most enjoyable partnership.

The termination of Kitchen's partnership with Swanton came after he turned down an offer to join him on the 1950–51 tour of Australia. Kitchen's health was not good, he suffered from periodic bouts of depression and he was afraid of the onset of what he – and Winston Churchill – called 'the black dog'. Importantly also, he was 'in love with a pretty girl' and so instead he took up a job at the preparatory school, West Downs, in Winchester. As Kitchen entered the teaching world, his replacement, his great friend John Woodcock, left it. At that time he had been working in a secondary modern school in Hampshire, but the thought of a trip to Australia with the mighty Jim was far too attractive to be put aside.

'I had met Jim initially in the first post-war cricket season at Oxford,' said John Woodcock.

Club sides would come down to play against the colleges and I was playing for Trinity and he was playing for the Cryptics. And when I went to Australia with him I took a camera and did that *Elusive Victory* picture for BBC Television News. I'd had a week's instruction at the old Alexandra Palace studios, because before I'd just about managed a box Brownie. The camera was pretty cumbersome – it was, if I remember, a Newman and Sinclair 35mm – and we had about 20,000 feet of film. And Jim sorted out the contract about the 'rushes'.

I did a bit of secretarial work for him and we became great friends – he was incredibly kind to me. I owe him an enormous amount. There is no doubt he could be demanding, but one learned so much because he was so efficient and you didn't get away with anything that was shoddy. He set himself very high standards and he could be impatient and he didn't have the longest of fuses, but I'm absolutely certain that everyone who worked for him would have benefited from it.

In *The Cricketer* magazine, April 1987, Woodcock listed his successors:

I was pretty nearly the first of his 'acolytes' or 'dogs-bodies' – or whatever else we were called. After me came Brian Moore, now of TV fame, then Christopher Ford, who was to ghost Jim Laker's controversial 'autobiography', *Over to Me*, and is now assistant arts editor of *The Times*; then Tony Winlow, cricket-writer and now a Jockey Club handicapper, and Irving Rosenwater, cricket historian, and Daphne Surfleet, who was soon to become Mrs Richie Benaud, and C.M.J. as Jim's assistant editor on *The Cricketer*, and very briefly, Scyld Berry, now cricket correspondent of the *Observer*. The job was unique as a training ground and marriage bureau – and however great the temptation, it never did to answer the great man back.

Daphne Surfleet had been working as a television production assistant for the BBC in Manchester when first she met Jim in 1959.

I began working for Jim in October 1960 having resigned from the BBC in August. He had asked me what I was going to do and I told him I was most interested in working on something to do with cricket. I was at the Scarborough Cricket Festival when Jim called to say that he might be able to offer me something on the *Sunday Telegraph*, commencing publication in February 1961 but, in the meantime, if I was prepared to move to London, I would be able to do some secretarial work for him.

I had no idea what the work would involve except that I had hopes of seeing much more cricket, but it could also have meant I stayed in one spot in Fleet Street. It was the Rugby season when I started and I saw some games and telephoned Jim's match reports through to the *Telegraph*. As it happened, I then went to every cricket match Jim covered for the *Daily Telegraph* and the BBC during the summer months, starting with the Australian tour in 1961. The first of those matches at Worcester meant breaking new ground by being a woman in what was traditionally a male preserve. The friendly voice I heard as I walked behind Jim to our seats in the press box was that of the late John Bromley, who was working for Charles Bray. 'Hello Daphers, welcome,' calmed some of my nerves.

Jim had so many different interests that no two days were ever the same. There was a lot of correspondence to do with his team, The Arabs, and he always replied to every reader's letter, radio listener or TV watcher. There were always one or two books on the go, either being written or edited. At the matches I was in the press boxes dealing with correspondence and phoning Jim's articles through to the *Telegraph*'s copytakers.

His attention to detail was extraordinary and it taught me a great deal about organisation and efficiency. He dictated all his letters to me and they were so well thought out that he never had to change a word. He was happy with what he'd said the first time, which was good for me. There were no computers, word processors, e-mails or anything like that

43 years ago – just a lot of carbon copies. Jim was definitely a perfectionist and I would have been very unpopular had I ever been a couple of seconds late.

12.23 pm at the bottom of the press box steps with a double gin and tonic and a pork pie meant exactly that.

Daphne stayed at the helm until 1965 and then during the summer of 1966, before becoming an assistant to a succession of Australian managers. She married Richie Benaud in 1967. Jim always spoke of her work for him in glowing terms. Others who took over the mantle were Fiona MacKinnon, briefly, and Robin Whitcomb, who had been working in the music business in the USA, and who again was a schoolmaster and who had played fly-half for Richmond. When it was Christopher Martin-Jenkins's turn to pick up the baton, he found Jim a stern taskmaster.

He would almost be like a schoolmaster who would look at what had been produced and mark it with red ink here and there. I can remember him writing clash, C.L.I.S.H., on anything of which he didn't approve. He taught me quite a lot really, to avoid clichés, to brush up on my history and read about the game in greater depth than I had. He also taught me to think about news angles – he always knew exactly what was going on and he had wonderful contacts.

There was a certain amusement and stories swapped by those who did work for him. It was Robin Whitcomb who had been sent to get Jim a gin and tonic and came back and said there was no ice. 'No ice?' expostulated Jim. 'Did you tell them who it was for?'

I remember one incident which showed his not-so-nice side. We were having lunch at the Bath Club discussing cricket business or something and a very obviously nervous waitress came in and plonked the soup in front of him from his right side. And he said, 'Now look here, you serve on the left-hand side. Pick up the plate, go through to the kitchen, come back in and come round and serve me on the other side.' And, of course, she did and she was very upset and I bet she never forgot it. He was unbelievable, really. I was very embarrassed for her.

But that was sort of the five per cent that was bad and the rest was honourable and good. You know, Jim's career was in Victorian graft and professionalism. And his encouragement and loyalty to aspiring young people was exemplary.

The point that all these servants of the sultan seem to be underlining is his continual search for perfection. An enneagram of the type would set out the dilemma:

Ones were good little girls and boys. They learned to behave properly, to take on responsibility and, most of all, to be correct in the eyes of others. They remember being painfully criticized, and as a result they learned to monitor themselves severely in order to avoid making mistakes that would come to other people's attention. They quite naturally assume that everyone shares their desire for self-betterment and are often disappointed by what they see as a lapse of moral character in others.

The Perfectionist outlook is encapsulated in the image of our Puritan ancestors. They were hard working, righteous, fiercely independent, and convinced that plain thinking and goodness would prevail over the shadow side of human nature. Ones are convinced that life is hard and ease must be earned, that virtue is its own reward, and that pleasure should be postponed until everything else gets one.

Perfectionists are usually not aware that they deny themselves pleasure. They are so preoccupied with what they 'should' do and 'what must be done' that they rarely ask themselves what they want to get out of life. Their natural wishes were forbidden when they were young, and so they learned to block out their desires by focusing attention on the correct thing to do.

One suspects there may have been something teutonically '*korrekt*' in Jim's make-up that had been inherited, not directly from his parents, but from previous generations. While all of us, in a sense, are prisoners of our own personality he appeared more trapped than most. Doreen Waite, his last secretary at Sandwich, felt that there was a behavioural barrier positioned across a very soft underbelly, which could not be lifted: 'Underneath that formidable exterior, I think he was a very kind man. Probably when he'd been clambering up the pyramid he felt he had to adopt certain airs and graces and it was a protection against a certain shyness.'

Dennis Silk: I think the great thing about Jim is that the rich pickings fell into his hands; I don't mean money or anything like that, but the things that he would've loved, which were basically the love of his fellow men. And he was sensitive enough to know that he hadn't got that in middle age, but through the kind offices of Ann and other friends he became a well-loved highly respected scribe. And bigger than that, he became a sort of depository for world cricket. He'd seen more Test Matches than anyone except Johnny Woodcock and one thing I admired enormously about him was the discipline of his work. He didn't let bad writing go through the mill, from his pen anyway. He had standards. He didn't like sensationalism of any sort and he told the story of the game as it should be told, and by degrees this sank in with the general public and they revered him for it.

'And, of course, he'd seen everything and done everything and suddenly he found himself on a pedestal and he actually played the part extremely very well. He was a battered old tramp steamer coming into harbour and finding himself welcomed on the shore.

Sir Donald Bradman, A.C.: Yes, he was pompous, but less so as he got older. His workload was horrendous and I think he was our greatest ever cricket writer. Cardus has a special turn of phrase, but I think Swanton got to the heart of the game better.

In 1996, Jim was given a standing ovation in the Long Room at Lord's at the Jubilee Dinner of the Cricket Writers' Club of which he was one of the founders. His recollections, delivered with urbanity and humour, of times before many of the company present were born, had hard-to-impress fellow luminaries listening intently. There was no doubt that sheer longevity was bringing its own rewards.

Five years previously, in 1991, he had gone to South Africa and in a broadcast speech welcomed them back into the cricket community after the years of isolation. There were meant to be 730 people present at the dinner but, as Jim told them, one could not make it, so reminding him of the 1930 Test Match at Lord's where the Australians accumulated the same total. 'Unfortunately, nobody could find a figure 7 to put on the Tavern scoreboard . . .'

A year later, in 1992, a letter arrived from Cliff Morgan, a seminal figure in Welsh rugby and BBC Sport:

Dear Ann & Jim,
   I telephoned Sandwich this morning – but should have known that this is BARBADOS TIME. But I simply wanted to say to Ann that last Sunday night as I was driving to London from Cardiff, there were the old songs: 'Laura, She's Funny that Way', 'What is There to Say', 'You Make Me Feel so Young', 'He's My Guy', 'There will never be another You' . . . and so on and on. The M4, on Sunday, must have only been about 20 miles Ann for your music sped me on my journey. Thank you. Your tape is a constant companion and I only wish I could play like you.

So today, I simply had to contact you both. We tend to neglect keeping in touch with the people we should. The only real comfort is that true friends pick up exactly where they left off – even if the time span is years and years. You are, in sport – at its best – enriched. You Jim – 'Napoleon of the talking and commenting Trade' – have given so many of us so much for so long. Thank you.

The reference in Morgan's letter to Jim and Ann's annual holiday in Barbados demonstrates that it was a fixed point in their calendar year. Those holidays continued to take place even after they had been forced to sell their house 'Coralita'. Jeremy Deedes explains what happened:

> Jim and Ann had built the house, and it was not long before he was going to retire and Jim was always worried that he was never going to have enough money.
>
> Someone told Jim and Ann that this chap was going to do a development in St James's just down the road, not far from the church where they used to go, lovely church in St James's – I remember going to Matins with them. And this chap was going to do a development which was going to be a huge success, Barbados the up and coming place. And why didn't they invest some money in it, he was looking to raise some money . . . and Jim thought this would be a good way of increasing his nest egg for his coming retirement. So they put some money in – I think not a huge amount but a decent chunk of money – into this development with this guy who turned out to be a wrong 'un, eventually. And things started going wrong. I can't remember what held things up, anyway there was a need for an injection of some more money, because things hadn't gone according to plan or things had been held up or whatever. I think they extended themselves quite badly then, to put some more money in. And it was a real case afterwards of good money after bad. To make a long story short they lost a lot, and in order to cover it they had to sell the house.
>
> I remember playing a round of golf at Sandy Lane and Coralita was just the other side of the old 8th on the nine-hole Sandy Lane course, and there was this hollow by the green they called 'Swanton's bottom'. And it must have been very sensitive, because every time he played golf he must have had this horrible experience of being reminded of his folly, you know, investing the money in the first place which cost him his beloved house, and he got reminded of that every time he went to play golf because he'd have to go past the house.

After the house had gone, for their holidays Jim and Ann would stay with friends on the island and then latterly at Sandy Lane itself, where they would be the guests of former international Irish rugby star and later newspaper proprietor, Tony, now Sir Anthony O'Reilly.

> I loved Jim. He had such a perceptive eye for people and was so unabashed and optimistic about everything. I looked forward to his oblique phone calls, 'We might just consider venturing to the island in February – would you yet be in a position to be able to say whether or not you will be in the vicinity . . .?' [laughs] He had more than his fair share of marbles and I regarded him as one of the most remarkable men of my time.
>
> And as a public speaker I loved his declamatory delivery. I remember an autumn dinner at the big city hall of the Royal and Ancient at St Andrews – they are, of course, the governing body of golf. And it's a very dressed-up prestigious occasion with world-famous speakers. And at this particular dinner Alastair Cooke was the main speaker. And as he was about to speak he froze on the spot. He opened his mouth and nothing came out. It's a very daunting assembly of distinguished people and even for someone of his calibre it was too much – stage fright, almost like a seizure. And the secretary, Michael Bonallack, desperately started looking round the room to see if he could spot anybody who could fill in and save the situation. And his eye landed on Jim and he beckoned to him frantically and Jim rose magisterially, walked to the front and, entirely ad lib, delivered a most charming and amusing speech. At the end he was a hero, and as he walked back to his seat he was positively gloating.

Reverting back to the West Indies: for Jim, and indeed Ann, the fact that they were on holiday did not mean there was any relaxation of their routine. Jeremy Deedes again:

> Jim played golf in those days every other day. When you met for lunch, Jim and Ann used to come midday to the bar and if it was a golf day he'd have one rum punch before lunch and if it was a non-golf day he and Ann used to share a second one. And it was an absolute ritual, everything that Jim did was exactly to ritual, never a deviation . . . and he would go in and swim for five minutes at midday, then come to the bar and then they'd go through this ritual.

Jeremy's father Bill Deedes, the former editor of the *Telegraph* and nonagenarian war correspondent, who has long been suspected of being the inspiration for 'Boot', the hapless central figure in Evelyn Waugh's

1937 novel *Scoop* – a mantle he firmly rejects – also played golf with Jim at his own club near Sandwich, the Royal St George's.

> When I got there our opponent was Ian Fleming of James Bond fame and somebody else. Anyway, Jim and I played against Fleming and as we walked down the first hole at St George's, Fleming's partner said rather casually, anything on the match? And Fleming said, 'Oh, usual, I suppose.' And before we got to the first green it emerged that the usual to Fleming, and I think it was 1962 or 3, the usual was £100. I don't know what that would be today but it was quite a large sum in those days . . . and Jim said without turning a hair, 'Why don't we play for a golf ball?' And Fleming, who'd never heard of anything like that before, said, 'Mmm, good idea, yes.' So we played for a golf ball and Jim and I won 3 and 2. If we'd had £100 at stake, and mind you this was £100 a corner – each partner paid the other one £100 – we wouldn't have won. Fleming didn't do anything by halves and I can't tell you how rich he was. It was the time of the Great Train Robbery, and I was going down one of the fairways with Fleming and he said (we were talking about the robbery), '*Time/Life* want me to do a piece, they've offered me £5000, but,' he said, 'it takes a lot of research and I've turned it down.' So I said, 'but you could get a guy to do the research for £1000 and keep the £4000.' 'Oh yes, but it wouldn't be worth it,' he replied. You see, it didn't mean anything to him.

As Jim approached his ninetieth birthday, he and I worked together on what he was convinced would be his final book, *Last Over*. The publisher Richard Cohen suggested to him that for an 'Envoi', he should take a prophetic look to the future of cricket, almost as a last will and testament.

> My concluding note must be of deep thankfulness for my life in cricket, for all that it has brought me in so many ways. Old men forget, Duff Cooper thought, and of much this is mercifully true. But so deeply happy are many cricket recollections that for me they remain wonderfully clear. The luckiest thing I ever did was to found the Arabs. We celebrated our Diamond Jubilee, courtesy of Mr J. P. Getty, on his lovely ground at Wormsley, and I am deeply grateful for friendships in every generation.

The idyllic pastoral setting of Wormsley in the Chilterns and its beautiful ground makes a lasting impact on all who go there.

John Paul Getty's devotion to the game was very much in tune with

Jim's. He too deplored some of the aspects of modern cricket which to him threatened to make it 'halfway to baseball'. What first had attracted him about a game that essentially was so English? 'Its complexity and endless variety. There is an inner excitement about it, even when it is superficially boring. There are so many different skills, such a diversity of tactics. As an American I had supposed that baseball was the more strenuous and demanding game, cricket by comparison a pastime of softies. Not so, I discovered. Baseball, on the contrary, is simplistic, draughts as compared with chess.'

After his sad death in 2003, the cricket environs of Wormsley are under the custodianship of Victoria, Getty's delightful widow. 'Paul used to enjoy Jim's company immensely. They would talk for hours about what to me seemed complex cricketing matters, and swap stories in which there was much laughter. When I first met Jim I was very much in awe of him, because he came from a previous generation, but I loved the fact that he was so gentlemanly, gallant, and I suppose what you might call courtly. He reminded me very much of my father. They don't make men like Jim any more – they've thrown away the prototype.'

> Fond memories too of so many grounds and places. Barbados and Adelaide, the Oxford Parks, Fenner's at Cambridge, the Saffrons at Eastbourne pre-war, Beckenham on either side of it, Trent Bridge, much-lamented Bramall Lane and the Oval, each with an atmosphere all its own; St Lawrence, Canterbury, most gracious and beautiful of county grounds.
>
> Lord's, however, is for me a place apart, a home from home, hallowed as only the richest of histories can make it, both a symbol of the past and, surely, a pledge for the future.

As far as Jim's future with his 'darling Ann' was concerned, it came to an end in November 1998. With no warning she died from a stroke. His sense of loss was, needless to say, profound. The arrangements he had made for her funeral were, as everyone expected, detailed and immaculate. At the service at St Clement's, Sandwich, he even managed to read a text from the scriptures, unfalteringly. Afterwards he murmured quietly to me, 'the saddest thing in life is knowing that never again will you see someone you love.' Though Jim continued to occupy himself with his various commitments, one sensed that for him now there was not much need to carry on living. But carry on he did, in his own way that had been fashioned over a lifetime.

If, at this stage, a personal memory may be allowed: ten days before he died – not that the imminence of death was evident, because he was in such sparkling form – Jim and I recorded an interview for a BBC Radio 'Late Tackle' programme at Broadcasting House. After the recording we adjourned to the top floor of the adjacent St George's Hotel, the site of the old Queen's Hall, for afternoon tea with scones. I remember feeling that Jim seemed unusually subdued. His final words of the recording had been along the lines of: 'There was a wonderful fellowship in cricket of previous eras, which I fear can never be recaptured.' And he started to muse on that point. 'There are too many people writing about cricket today, who have no love of the game.' He shook his head sadly. And then, mysteriously, 'I don't care what they say about me now. They can say what they like.' It brought back to me a moment on the steps leading to the Long Room at Lord's some years before, when in a moment of ennui he admitted, 'You know, David, you'll be surprised to hear me say this, but I've seen too much cricket in my life.'

Soon, however, he brightened up and laughed about the time in the not too distant past, when he had been stopped by the police for speeding in his car on his way to play golf at the Royal St George's – this, when he was in his late eighties. There was a reminiscence about a journey on a train from Canterbury to London. 'I was sitting quietly in a first-class compartment waiting for the train to depart when a bunch of lads got in and I thought they might be unruly so I said, "I suppose you realise that this is a first-class compartment, don't you?" And one of them replied, "Yes, we do, mate. We've got first-class tickets. Can I look at yours?"' After shared laughter the conversation moved on. He began telling me how he proposed shortly to proceed a few streets away to All Saints, Margaret Street, the church where he had married his beloved Ann, for High Mass. Unbeknown to me at that time, Anthony Fincham, Secretary of the Arabs, was scheduled to meet Jim there to celebrate the Mass in his company. Too soon I had to depart to return to the studio to complete the requirements of programme editing. Jim did not want me to go, nor did I, but the financial constraints of broadcasting left little option. Much later I found out that Anthony too, because of business commitments, had been unable to meet up with Jim. Today, both of us regret such a truncated farewell. The final image I have is of him reclining in a large armchair, looking over the roofs of London, in the general direction of Lord's. The light was fading, and he could not have seen very far.

Back in Sandwich, Jim was being looked after by his devoted housekeeper, Valerie Hillier, and what could be termed a Man Friday,

Peter Knight. Over the years they had given wonderful care and support, and lived in a cottage adjoining Delf House.

I'm not a cricket man. I used to spend an hour with him every night, and I'd read a bit about the cricket on the back of the paper, so I'd know something if he started talking about it, but apart from that, he liked reading, and he liked reading aloud. And, of course, in the later years Mrs Swanton had cataracts, and she couldn't see very well, so he used to read to her in bed at night. When she died, I used to go into his room, and if he was reading, he would say, 'Peter, I shall read you a passage out of this.' And the last book he was reading was John Major's autobiography, and he was a great admirer of John Major as well. But apart from that he used to tell me all sorts of stories about when he was a Japanese prisoner-of-war, and he used to roll a cigarette, and I mean he didn't smoke but they used to roll these cigarettes and he thought this was being really close to the mark. He would say, 'And do you know what they used to call this, Peter?' I said, 'No, sir' – sir – I never called him Mr Swanton, I don't know why but I could never bring myself to do so. 'Well,' he said, 'they used to call it nag's bush.' And then he told me that the bed he laid on in the camp was split bamboo. I spent twenty-odd years in the army, and in the way I felt about him I was kind of his batman – because I used to bath him and help him dress, you know. And he would be laying in bed reading the paper and I would go up there and he would say, 'Go and pour the bath, Peter.' And at the very end, this was a couple of days before he died, we went to visit him in the Chaucer Hospital and the nurse in there said they wanted to give him a shower, and he wouldn't let them. 'No,' he said, 'my man'll be in tomorrow' – that was me. Anyhow, I got him ready, and we were singing ditties together – all those old army songs like 'Mademoiselle from Armentières', with the dirty words. When I got him in the shower, I was fully clothed. By the time I came out I was wetter than what he was, wasn't I!

The cause of Jim's passing on the death certificate read: 'Myocardial infarction, left ventricular failure, diabetes mellitus', all of which really meant that the heart had stopped beating. It was the first time in Jim's life that it had even got close to doing so. The gross value of his estate amounted to £1,114,531. That and his effects were dispersed liberally among his relatives and friends.

His earthly departure was a tripartite affair. On the evening before the funeral at St Clement's there was a Requiem Mass celebrated by Father

Aelred, a member of the Community of the Resurrection, an Anglican order based at Mirfield in Yorkshire. 'We talked of this priest of the Resurrection as the opium dealer with his waspish beard,' remarked Anthony Fincham, solicitor and secretary of the Arabs who played a great part in the arrangements of the three services. 'The service that evening was not exactly a private affair, but it was primarily intended for the people of Sandwich although quite a few Arabs went to it actually. And then, of course, next day for the funeral itself the Church was absolutely packed with a loudspeaker broadcasting outside.'

ADDRESS AT FUNERAL OF E.W. SWANTON
ON TUESDAY, 1 FEBRUARY 2000 AT
ST CLEMENT'S CHURCH, SANDWICH
THE RT. REVD LORD RUNCIE

Jim Swanton died as he lived: with dignity and with style.

His masterly summaries of the cricketers who made the twentieth century had been published. Impeccably bound, infallibly indexed. He had circulated his sixty-sixth New Year letter for the beloved Arabs – packed with detail of games played, courtesies exchanged and wry humour on the evil effect of late-night eightsome reels [laughter].

The Rt. Revd. Lord Runcie, former Archbishop of Canterbury, had already engaged the congregation. His voice was firm and clear although, bent under the weight of his bishop's regalia, he looked drawn and tired. His final illness was upon him and the effort he had made to make the journey, let alone speak, was a measure of the man and reflected his love for Jim.

He celebrated a last Christmas party of the Millennium with family and friends and just over a fortnight ago was taken into hospital close by the St Lawrence Cricket Ground. There, perfectly conscious, but weak, he received absolution, took Communion for the last time and died the following day.

You could write over those final moments the words of St Paul: 'Godliness with contentment is great gain'.

Of course there is sorrow. It is a sin not to grieve. It's part of love's price, but we are never meant to hug our grief and allow it to overwhelm us; rather to keep sacred a memory and get on with life.

It isn't difficult for anyone in this church to keep a memory of Jim. Others can, and will, pay more comprehensive tributes but it is for me to insert a personal word into the Prayer Book Liturgy which Jim loved so that our prayers may be warmed by his humanity.

We shared together the exhilaration of the immediate post-war years in Oxford. Jim arrived so emaciated from his years in captivity that his father could pass him on a railway station without recognising him. That the cricketer, journalist and commentator who had established himself in the [19]30s could so quickly revive was little short of miraculous.

There was his innate character – Jim was not a man plagued by self-doubt. [prolonged laughter from the congregation] Someone who served with him closely during the war described him as 'arrogant, yes, but the bravest officer I ever knew'.

For the rest of his life he bore the mark of the polio he suffered in captivity but hardly ever mentioned.

In the camps he had also embraced the Catholic faith in its Anglican form through the friendship of the Oxford MP, Lawrence Turner. That brought him his lodging at Pusey House, a centre for Anglo-Catholic undergraduates – immortalised in the poems of John Betjeman. Jim, to the end of his days, loved the order, dignity and colour of Anglo-Catholic worship. The sight of him at High Mass amid the candles land incense of Pusey or Margaret Street was unforgettable, lustily singing to his Creator 'Pavilioned in splendour and girded with praise'. But that of course was top-dressing which the superficial may take to be the whole story. Jim had his rule of life and it was methodical, strict, unparaded but for every day. It embraced the hard bits too like penitence and forgiveness, and church on saints' days which sometimes kept his rector up to the mark.

Above all in those Oxford days he picked up where he had left off as an increasingly recognised authority in the world of sport generally and cricket in particular. He loved the company of the young and encouraged cricketers and writers. He enjoyed the University but never pretended to belong to it like a pretentious bore. It was the same in his religion. Jim recognised and respected holiness and the religious orders – he wanted Ampleforth to be here at his funeral; but he didn't pretend that he was himself an ascetic.

In 1946 he embarked on his long career with the *Daily Telegraph*. To their eternal credit they took him up but never took him over. He exacted an undertaking that no copy would be tampered with.

Nor did he flinch from taking a line which was not always supported in other parts of the paper, either about the behaviour of Archbishops or contact with cricket in South Africa in the apartheid years. There was moral courage there and to be rewarded in 1991 at the inaugural meeting of the Non Racial Cricket Board of South Africa. The two guests they wanted for their banquet were Jim Swanton and Garry Sobers. He spoke words of welcome to 700 cricketers of every age and colour.

Jim's style as a writer, commentator and summariser were inseparable from his character – and that was his strength. Arnold Bennett once said, 'You have said sometimes to yourself, "If only I could write." You were wrong. You ought to have said, "If only I could think and feel." When you have thought clearly and felt intensely you never had any difficulty in saying what you thought and when you cannot express yourself, depend upon it that you have nothing precise to express and that what incommodes you is not the vain desire to express yourself better but the vain desire to think more clearly and to feel more deeply.'

Jim's clarity of mind and commitment of the heart to cricket was, in my view, unrivalled.

That well-stocked mind was endlessly surprising. His natural habitat seemed obviously the great cricket grounds of the world – hard to beat Colombo – or Canterbury Cricket Week or traditional fixtures Eton & Harrow or Oxford & Cambridge. A short time ago we had an absorbing conversation about Liverpool in 1941 where I was in my last year at school and Jim, a young officer, turned out to play for Bootle in the Blitz. He described how one day they turned up and found a bomb crater on the ground and he had to rearrange the rules. Characteristically he remembered that this rather grey, and in those days slummy, district of Liverpool had its streets named after Oxford colleges and that Liverpool bus conductors would bang the bell and shout out 'Balliol Road'.

Jim also took very seriously his association with the Libraries and the Art Collection of Cricket, for many years chairman of the Library Committee at Lord's and presiding with great care over anything put into the pavilion at Canterbury.

The Kent curator, David Robertson, was in New Zealand, otherwise he would have been among the many county representatives in the congregation. Jim had been Honorary Curator from 1981 and then President of Kent in 1985. 'He always was particularly enthusiastic about any donations to the club of pictures,' David Robertson told me. 'He was very involved.'

Music and art were part of the family that Ann brought when they were married at All Saints, Margaret Street in 1958. It was Ann, the golfer, who brought him to Sandwich. Here they made their home and as I have said before from this pulpit, it was a dream ticket. Jim loved the golf club and the game which he was able to play into his nineties. I am told he was a poor golfer and a bad loser but here, as everywhere else, Jim was the first to enjoy such legends about himself.

He was a big man who loved the grand occasion and there were those who said that when he passed the throne of St Augustine in Canterbury Cathedral he cast a wistful glance towards it. But in Sandwich we learn the truth of Chesterton's 'Nothing is real unless it is local.'

Some of Jim's most revealing articles are to be found in the parish magazine. A series on the Anglican Church was bound together into a small book. When I was archbishop and he churchwarden, I can testify that he took more trouble over choosing a new rector than he would for the selection of an English cricket side.

He and Ann were generous in hospitality, befrienders of the young, reconcilers of those at variance. If he believed in something he would back it with enthusiasm and if it required financial support he would give it. Infinitely courteous except to the small-minded, mean-spirited and rude. His glare could always freeze the opposition.

Wintering with Ann at their house in Barbados, membership of the Church of St James there was hugely influential. The rector was given the same deference and loyalty as he gave to his rector in Sandwich.

When I paid an official visit to Barbados I found in my hotel bedroom greetings from Jim and two tickets for the Barbados Oval with the words, 'If you don't use these you will be a disgrace to Kent.' An unusually forthright word to his Archbishop.

But there are many misconceptions of Jim. That he had no sense of humour was one. He was not jokey, nor could he produce a string of smart stories for a slick after-dinner speech, but he had the sort of humour and wit that put life in proportion. I remember on one of my first nervous visits to Canterbury Cricket Week I knocked a bottle of wine over at lunch and it spilled on the dresses of two lady guests. We all jumped up; only Jim quietly murmured, 'This is a moment to think of eternity.' We all know people without a sense of humour. They should never be put in charge of anything. Jim was not of such a character.

Jim also enjoyed the quite mistaken idea that he was a dinosaur who outlived his age. I owe to Matthew Engel the rebuttal of that. His genius was that while many developments in cricket and many changes in the Church gave him pain he adapted to their existence, understood them and commented sensibly on them though he never surrendered his own convictions.

Nothing to my mind is more remarkable than the way in which the solemnity, prickliness and, yes, arrogance that were part of the serious perfectionist gave place gradually to the gentle self-mockery and kindly wisdom which never seemed to fail us.

He kept his high standards, but they were combined with compassion at failure among his friends – public disgrace or personal follies did not mean the end of friendship – might indeed be heard as the cry for help to stand by them.

Sitting in a pew, Jonathan Aitkin acknowledged this comment with a wry smile. The former MP for the Isle of Thanet (including Deal) once had told me that 'at the depth of my much-publicised troubles Jim would invite me to lunch and dinners with some of his grandest and greatest friends . . . and right through my prison sentence he wrote to me.'

I tried to think how to hold together this character to whom I owe so much and whom I both loved and admired. I am haunted by a memory and a quotation. The memory was not so long ago. It was in Jim's home. He told me conspiratorially that he had received a letter from the Don – Don Bradman. He went to a drawer, opened the letter with trembling hands and spread it out for me. 'I don't think it's improper for me to show it to you,' eagerly waiting for my reaction as a schoolboy might show me an autograph.

The quotation? It was scrawled in the Christmas card sent to me by a distinguished scientist – 'The enlightened person thinks they can no longer enjoy the stories which so delighted their childhood years, but this is a false notion. We should rather ask whether childhood has not its own particular virtues – a happy trustfulness, a particular candour, an eager expectation of good things to come, which the grown person must retain at all costs if he is not to end up in sterile dogmatism or corrosive cynicism.'

Jim was not childish. He had long since left behind the tantrums and the sulks; but he never lost that childlike quality which Our Lord assures us will be needed for heaven. It explains his faith, his enthusiasm, the loyalties and energy that lay behind the authority, lucidity and measured words and it gives us the assurance we need for the prayers we shall offer commending him to the Lord in whom he put his trust so staunchly.

Anthony Fincham: Several of Jim's relatives took part in the service. His stepson Billy Carbutt read from the Gospel of St John; his nephew Martin Nelson sang 'Welcome Death' by John Stanley; and his brother-in-law, Canon Bill Langdon, led the prayers. And then his other nephew, David Langdon, was one of the organists. As the coffin was sprinkled with holy water and incensed and Dom Felix Stephens from Ampleforth sang a plain chant – I think Jim would have been pleased about that – I well remember the poignant moment when we Arabs were charged with the task of carrying the coffin. There were six of us: Colin Ingleby-Mackenzie, Tony Lewis, Matthew Fleming, Charles Fry, James Mann and myself – we were all very nervous because it really is a professional task and although we had been drilled by the undertaker, we were afraid we would drop the coffin.

With the task safely accomplished, and buoyed by the Recessional hymn, the congregation filed out of the church in the way that every congregation files out of funeral services, wrapped in thought and once outside not knowing quite what to say.

Some six weeks later there was a Solemn Eucharist of Thanksgiving for Jim's life at Canterbury Cathedral. In the last months of his life and with the knowledge of his growing physical incapacity, Jim had made plans to move into a flat in the Cathedral Close. There had not been time for that to happen.

Again there was a large congregation, around 1200 people with the then Dean, the Very Revd Dr John Simpson, and the celebrants, Father Mark Roberts of St Clement's, Sandwich, and Canon Andrew Hatch, formerly Rector of St James's, Barbados, presiding.

> **Anthony Fincham:** Jim had left suggestions as to who might be considered to give the address. Bill Deedes was one and so the executors invited him. When he arrived the Dean made clear that he should enter as part of the solemn procession as if he were an ecclesiastical dignitary, but Bill was very much against that. So as a compromise he agreed to sit in something approaching an Episcopal throne up in the sanctuary.

The Eucharist of Thanksgiving (also known as the Holy Communion, Lord's Supper or Mass), began most appropriately with the preparatory hymn, 'The Church's One Foundation'. There followed the Kyrie from Mozart's Coronation Mass, sung in Greek, the Collect, the Ministry of the Word, an Old Testament Reading read by John Woodcock, Psalm 139, a New Testament reading from Anthony Fincham, the hymn 'Lord Enthroned in Heavenly Splendour', the Gospel, and then the Address by Lord Deedes of Aldington.

> **Anthony Fincham:** Bill had been sitting immediately behind the Thurifer who was operating the incense. And all through the Service the Thurifer – and I could see this – was ladling on more charcoal and incense, creating

an ever greater fog and after about fifteen or twenty minutes Bill Deedes disappeared from view. And nobody quite knew if he was still there – there was a very anxious moment when it came to his address. Suddenly he appeared from this cloud, spluttering and coughing into his handkerchief and he staggered up to the pulpit and when he got up there, there was a long pause while he consumed the entire litre of water before embarking upon his address.

LORD DEEDES OF ALDINGTON, MC, FC, DL
Memorial service address, Canterbury Cathedral
Wednesday, 29 March 2000

It does occur to me, looking round, how greatly pleased Jim would have been to see so many in this great cathedral today. Himself a most loyal attender of memorial services for his friends, he would have expected a good turn-out. 'I thought it was satisfactory!' I hear him saying. And I start there, because we are today giving thanks for a life that, all talent apart, fairly shone with human qualities.

There was a great cricket writer, said to have written some eight million words about the game, who certainly brought the game closer to every man than anyone of his time. There was the author of twenty-five books – not to mention the editor of that monumental *World of Cricket*. But this was also someone who stamped his personality on almost everything he did. We greatly admired his professionalism; we enjoyed his small idiosyncrasies even more.

Each one of you here will have some portrait of Jim in the mind's eye. Arabs, old and young, will see him on some sunlit cricket field and will remember him as their founder in 1935 – who took the field with them until he was sixty. Others will forever see him in the Long Room at Lord's.

You have to be of my generation to recall that confident voice, bringing the Test match, ball-by-ball, into the home. And there will be a fair number here today with reason to be infinitely thankful for Jim's gift of encouraging young promise. It was there he bridged the years so well. In Jim, youth always found a friend.

Myself, I shall see him always somewhere on the St Lawrence ground, grey-suited, IZ or BB ribbon round the panama, in early days a millboard in hand, imparting cricket gossip from Lord's or Canterbury with the utmost gravity. 'You know, of course, that the Committee decided last night to dispense with the captain's services . . .!' How could you possibly know? and from whom other than Jim would you expect to hear it?

I think of him too at Delf House one Sunday morning, shortly before he died. We sat drinking pink gin, beautifully put together by his housekeeper Valerie, who took such care of him. And Jim showed me the last picture of Ann, his wife, taken in some television show we were in. When she went, and their lives together ended, the sun went down in a cloudless sky.

And then, as his colleagues knew, there was willingness always to give sensible professional advice. He knew where everything was in that well-ordered study of his. And until the day he died, he knew where everything was in his head.

We leader writers at the *Telegraph* would ring him on a Sunday afternoon, after some cricketing disaster overseas. 'Jim, we're doing a leader on the death of English cricket . . .' Rather a cagey – 'Oh, I see . . .' 'Have you any thoughts on the subject?' 'Well, yes, I might have . . . you realise, of course, that things were a great deal worse after Warwick Armstrong's Australians toured here in 1921.' After ten minutes of that, you could write quite a decent leader. And every homily decorated with an anecdote.

As his friends knew, the war and captivity in Japanese hands had profound consequences for him. It was during a post-war retreat at Pusey House that he found comfort in the Anglo-Catholic faith which from then on deeply informed his life. You cannot seriously discuss Jim and his ways without reference to his deep and abiding faith. Never golf on Sunday morning; always in St Clement's. He might well have joined the Church – what a marvellous bishop we lost there! (laughter)

It was his religion, furthermore, that gave him some deep-rooted principles. His anger, for example, over the D'Oliveira affair in South Africa. Anger and distress. At some point, I remember, South African Breweries asked me to go out and look at what they were trying to do for black sport. Jim was very shocked, and tried to dissuade me.

But there was a positive side to this. Some of you will remember the cricket side he took to the West Indies in the 1950s after some disastrous MCC experience there. It helped to make the peace.

And with it all, what fun he was. Whether playing cricket or golf, there was always a little bird perched on Jim's shoulder, piping, 'You gotta win.'

Jim never made the mistake of confusing sportsmanship with being a joyous loser. Nor did winning draw extravagant praise from him. Only a few months back, he drove me round Royal St George's in a buggy, acting as my caddy. It was the B of B match. Goodness, how hard I tried. We won by a short head. And what did he say, as we drove back to the club house in the buggy? 'I thought that was satisfactory!' (laughter) He would have made a good bishop, but an even better magistrate. The magisterial style. How enjoyable it was . . .

But best of all, Jim Swanton so well conveyed the spirit of games played long ago. Games like the Arthur Dunn Cup, the Varsity match at Twickers – heyday of the amateur – much of it enshrined in the Arabs.

He never repined against modern sport, with its aspects of the Roman circus. But you couldn't keep his company for long without a feeling that he had known another and different world. And, in that sense, he did awaken an echo of those lines of G.K. Chesterton's that I have used before. He was:

'The last and lingering troubadour to whom the bird has sung,
That once went singing southward when all the world was
young.'

The Service continued with the Nicene Creed, Intercessions in which prayers were read respectively by a member of the family, Kent CCC, the MCC, the Cricket Writers' Club, the Arabs and Sandwich Parish Church. After that there were prayers of Penitence, the Peace, the Preparation of the Bread and Wine during which a collection was taken in aid of the Kent Cricket 2000 Appeal for the development of Youth Cricket in Kent, an Offertory Prayer, the Prayer of Consecration, another movement from Mozart's Coronation Mass, sung in Latin, the Lord's Prayer, the Communion, the Agnus Dei and the choral anthem 'God is Hope', Schubert's 'Ave Maria' sung by Jim's nephew Martin Nelson, the hymn, 'Thine be the glory', a Benediction, Post Communion and the final Blessing. After which the choir and clergy departed to St Andrew's Chapel and the congregation were invited to refreshments at the Kent County Cricket Club, St Lawrence's Ground, by the Old Dover Road. They needed them.

Anthony Fincham: At the end of the Service I went up to Bill to thank him. 'You'll have to excuse me,' he gasped, as he shot out of a side door, 'I'm desperate for some fresh air!'

In wanting that he was not alone. As the numbed congregation mingled together outside on the concourse like exhausted survivors from a marathon run around the Elysian Fields, a shaft of sunlight fell on Doug Insole, who was among the throng. He looked round, smiled and then said: 'Swanton's revenge!'

Envoi

For once the last word does not lie with Jim. With his voice finally stilled, there was a feeling among his followers of a vacuum waiting to be filled. But, of course, it never could be, because there was only one Jim.

At the beginning of this journey we sought to answer questions surrounding the factors that made and governed Swanton. Hopefully that task is now thought to be complete. But if any feel that there are answers still to be found, there should, at least, be an understanding of why the questions were asked and a realisation that there are complexities of human behaviour which defy rational explanation.

To everything in which he was involved, Jim brought as much care, preparation, and indeed passion, as any Managing Director of a large Corporation and by doing so was able to treat the future as if it was as certain as the past. In a match at Canterbury in 1996, batsman Matthew Walker was approaching the highest individual Kent score on the ground of Frank Woolley – 270 against Middlesex in 1923. Woolley, as we know, was Jim's lifelong hero. Without a second thought, Jim went into the Kent dressing room and tried to persuade the captain Steve Marsh to declare before the record was passed. Ever the controller, Jim too, at that moment, was not only trying to preserve the past, but juggle with the future.

With his death there was a sense that a treasured part of old England had passed away – totally irrecoverable – gone for ever. And that feeling surely would not be denied even by those who, fairly or unfairly, saw him only as the arch-symbol of what they would term cricket's stuffiness and elitism. For one thing was incontrovertible, the Archbishop of Lord's would not be forgotten.

In 1989 a surgeon in Harley Street wrote him a letter. He finished with words assuredly true: 'Allow me to take this opportunity of saying that to me, as to millions of other Englishmen, you epitomised all that was best in cricket, which is to say, all that was best in the England of days gone by – fair play – generosity of spirit, and the placid and gentlemanly nature of things. Ah, well . . .'

Acknowledgements

It is not often that one approaches the acknowledgements of a book with a heavy heart. In this instance, though, as with any biography of length, one has been living with the subject in a quasi love/hate relationship for so long that the stage of letting go is not dissimilar to signing a decree nisi.

Swanton strode with such majestic certainty around so many corners of the cricketing campus – as well as, of course, occupying his own special place in the centre ground – that it would be possible to write three different biographies of the great man with very little replication.

Before attempting to list those who have helped during the birth pains of this biography, I would like to express my deep gratitude to Jim's executors, John Woodcock and the Hon. George Plumptre, who gave me access to the E.W.S. correspondence files and diaries. Without such a resource the main thread and a valuable insight into his thinking would have been lost. The same is true of Jim's file kept by the *Daily Telegraph*. The paper's Managing Director (now Deputy Chairman and Chief Executive Officer) the Hon. Jeremy Deedes, and his father, the distinguished politician and reporter Bill Deedes (Lord Deedes of Aldington) were hugely hospitable and answered every question with candour and kindness.

Enlightenment into Jim Swanton's religious convictions came from pilgrimages to Warrington, the Wirral and Oxford where three wise men, Dom Felix Stephens OSB, Lord Sheppard and Father Davage respectively, kindly took time out to record their valuable thoughts. In London, at the Travellers Club in the Mall, Field-Marshal The Lord Bramall gave a masterly overview of the military situation at the time of the fall of Singapore, and on the 'phone and by letter the Rt. Hon. John Major CH answered my queries promptly and knowledgeably. To all five, mere thanks are not enough.

I also would like to record special thanks to literary agent John Pawsey for his role as overseer, and to editor Graham Coster for his unswerving support and sagacious guidance – he was always 'hands on' and helpful. A very special thanks, too, to Sibylla Jane Flower, official historian of the War in the Far East, who, in the midst of preparing her own book, was wonderfully generous with her knowledge and advice. Another vote of thanks to those comrades of Jim in the dark days of the War, particularly Derek Gilbert, Ken Holland, Eric Samuel and Jack Wragg, who put up with my constant enquiries with equanimity and who were always forthcoming. Each and every one of the survivors has my unstinting admiration for his great fortitude.

To Tony Lewis enormous thanks for his major contribution to this opus, and to James Hogg for making available the nuggets of his own tour around Swanton. Again, to Gideon Haigh in Australia my grateful thanks for his lobbying of POW organisations and various individuals on my behalf. Jim's nephew, the highly regarded singer, Martin Nelson, lent valuable family albums without which the illustrations herein would be much the poorer – I am in his debt. Others too, notably Irene Janes and former members of the Bedfordshire and Hertfordshire Yeomanry, were extremely accommodating with their photographs.

My gratitude to Roger Packham for his industrious seeking of data in the Public Record Office; to Janet Reeve for her weekly miracle with copy in a competition against the clock; to Lindsay Allen, Samantha Hunt and Judith Wells for transcribing taped interviews; to Briony Allen for her wizardry with modern technology and to my wife for keeping the vacuum cleaner in the cupboard when the carpet was strewn with Jim's correspondence.

And now to give due acknowledgement to many others who have been tremendously generous with their time and recollection. Space forbids the separate billing and by-line which each deserves. They will know of their contribution and also, I hope, of my gratitude. Sadly some have passed on since being involved in the early stages of this book.

Jonathan Aitken; the late Major R. J. Archdale; Alex Bannister; Peter Baxter; Daphne Benaud; Richie Benaud; the late Sir Donald Bradman; Michael Brearley; Margaret Brookes and staff at the Imperial War Museum; Milton 'Blue' Butterworth; Billy Carbutt; Peter Carroll; Adam Chadwick; Phoebe Clapham; the late Viscount Cobham; John Cook; the late Antony Craxton; the late Lord Cowdrey of Tonbridge; Vivian Cox; the late Leonard Crawley; Ken Daldry; Timothy D'Arch Smith; Dr Peter Davies; Ted Dexter; Henry Dixon; Hubert Doggart; Basil D'Oliveira; Dr Michael Down; the late Geoffrey Edrich; Bill Edwards; Mike Edwards; Stephen Eley; Jim Elliott; Matthew Engel; David Faber; Anthony Fincham; Charles Fry; Maureen Garrett; the late

Sir John Paul Getty; Lady Getty; the late H.M. Garland-Wells; the late Gerry Gomez; Stephen Green; the late Hubert Gregg; the late S.C. Griffith; Gideon Haigh; Jeff Hancock; Trish Hayes and staff at BBC Archives, Caversham; Henry Hely-Hutchinson; Canon John Hester; Valerie Hillier; Mary E. Horsley; Michael Horsley; the late Neil Hotchkin; the late Geoffrey Howard; Dr Gerald Howat; Robert Hudson; John Hoskins; Richard Hutton; Colin Ingleby-Mackenzie; Doug Insole; Desmond H. Jackson; the late Vivian Jenkins; Dr Eric Kemp; John Kitchen; Peter Knight; Roger Knight; David Kynaston; David Langdon; Tina Langdon; Joan Lewis; Giles Lyon; John MacKinnon; Peter MacKinnon; the late George Mann; Jill Marlar; Robin Marlar; Christopher Martin-Jenkins; James Martin-Jenkins; Colin Maynard; J. W. McKenzie; Henry McCreath; Lawrence Moody; Val Morgan; Edmund Nelson; Martin Nelson; Bill Nicholson; James D. C. Noble; Sir Anthony O'Reilly; Maddy Pickard; Liz Pook; the late Jim Porter; William Powell; Fred Ransome Smith; Raman Subba Row; Rev. Mark Roberts; David Robertson; the late Rt. Rev'd Lord Runcie; Christopher Saunders; Jim Shuttleworth; Dennis Silk; George Smith; Roderick Suddaby; Philip A. Truett; Bill Turner; Ronald Vearncombe; J. J. Warr; Doreen Waite; Glenys Williams; Iain Wilton; Wendy Wimbush; the late Michael Wolton; John Woodcock; Enid Wooller; Graeme Wright; Dr Neil Young.

Staff at Cranleigh School; Pusey House; the *Evening Standard;* the *Daily Telegraph;* the Army Personnel Centre, HQ Secretariat, Historical Disclosures; F.E.A. POW; Barbed Wire and Bamboo (Australia); Colindale Newspaper Library; Chorleywood Public Library; Hertfordshire Libraries.

If there have been any inadvertent corporate or individual omissions, please accept my apologies. Notification of such will ensure inclusion in future editions.

Bibliography

The bulk of source material has come from recorded conversations with Jim and Ann Swanton and those who knew him. The names of the latter are to be found in the Acknowledgements section and within the body of the book. Jim's vast collection of personal correspondence has also been an invaluable source, as has his published writings for various newspapers (primarily the *Daily Telegraph*) and unpublished typescripts and cuttings, all of which were kept in immaculate fashion in folders and stiff-backed covers in his study at his home. Files held under his name at both the *Daily Telegraph* and BBC Archives have also contained useful material. The Imperial War Museum in London and Army Historical Disclosures Centre in Glasgow were extremely co-operative, although the full details of E.W.S.'s career in the Services cannot be divulged until the statutory 75-year period has been reached following his discharge at the end of World War II.

Other main sources are to be found in the text or below.

Brightlands Chronicle 1920
Forest Hill, Sydenham and Penge Examiner (various issues)
A History of Cranleigh School by Alan J. Megahy, Collins, 1983
Cranleigh School Magazine, 1924
Illustrated Sporting and Dramatic News
The Field
The Cricketer (various issues)
My Life and Soft Times by Henry Longhurst, Cassell, 1971
Various South African *Argus* newspapers, 1938/39
3½ Years of Hell, by Jim Porter, privately printed
The Spectator, 1992
Railway of Hell, by Reginald Burton., Leo Cooper: Pen and Sword, 2002
Radio Newsreel, POW Style, by Desmond H. Jackson, The Nat West Boundary Book. A Lord's Taverners Australia Miscellany of Cricket, 1988
The War Diaries of 'Weary' Dunlop, Dunlop, Leonard Publishing, 1987
I am Well, Who Are You? by David Piper, Delian Gower Publishing, 1998
Piety and Learning: The Principals of Pusey House 1884–2002, edited by Barry A. Orford and William Davage (limited edition of 300), Pusey House, 2002

The Complete History of Cricket Tours at Home and Abroad by Peter Wynne-Thomas, The Hamlyn Publishing Group Ltd, 1989

More Than a Brother: Correspondence between Edmund Blunden and Hector Buck, 1917–1967, edited by Carol Z. Rothkopf and Barry Webb (limited edition of 250 copies), Sexton Press, 1996

Arabs in Aspic, 1935–1993 by The Founder, E. W. Swanton, Boundary Books, 1993

Enneagram (*Understanding Yourself and the Others in your Life*) by Helen Palmer, Harper San Francisco, 1988

Sort of a Cricket Person by E. W. Swanton, The Pavilion Library, 1972

Follow On by E. W. Swanton, Collins, 1977

Last Over by E. W. Swanton with David Rayvern Allen, Richard Cohen Books, 1996

E. W. Swanton: A Celebration of his Life and Work by David Rayvern Allen, Richard Cohen Books, 2000

E. W. S. Publications

A History of Cricket (with Harry Surtees Altham), Allen & Unwin, 1926. 391pp illus. ports. bibliog. (previously serialised in *The Cricketer*)
— 2nd ed. 1938. 450pp [bibliog. omitted].
— 3rd ed. (with a new postscript) 1947. 476pp [bibliog. omitted].
— 4th ed. 1948. 480pp [bibliog. omitted].
— 5th ed. 2 vols. 1962.
    Vol. 1: From the beginnings to the First World War, by H. S. Altham. 323pp illus. ports. stats. bibliog.
    Vol 2: From the First World War to the present day, by E. W. Swanton. 334pp illus. ports. bibliog.
Denis Compton: A cricket sketch, Sporting Handbooks, 1948. 79pp. illus. ports. stats.
— 2nd ed. Playfair Books, 1949. 95pp.
Elusive Victory: With F. R. Brown's MCC team, 1950–51: An eyewitness account, Hodder & Stoughton, 1951. 256pp illus. ports. scores, stats.
Cricket and the Clock, Hodder & Stoughton, 1952. 256pp illus. scores. A post-war commentary covering 1946–51.
Best Cricket Stories (compiler), Faber, 1953. 318pp
— another ed. Sportsman's Book Club, 1963.
West Indian Adventure: With Hutton's MCC team, 1953–54 (edited by Michael Melford), Museum P., 1954. 205pp illus. port. scores, stats.
— another ed. Sportsman's Book Club, 1955.
An edited account of contributions to the *Daily Telegraph*. Test Matches of 1953. *Daily Telegraph*, 1953 [iv]. 172pp illus. scores, stats. An account of the 1953 Australian tour of England.

Test Matches of 1953

Daily Telegraph, 1953 [iv], 172pp, illus. scores, stats. An account of the 1953 Australian tour of England.

Test Matches of 1954/55

Daily Telegraph, 1955. xxiii, 172pp illus. scores, stats. An account of the victorious 1954/55 MCC tour of Australia.

Test Matches of 1956

Daily Telegraph 1956. xix, 164pp illus. scores, stats. An account of the 1956 Australian tour of England.

Report from South Africa: with P. B. H. May's MCC team 1956/57, Hale, 1957. 253pp illus. port. diagrs. scores, stats. An account of the 1956/57 MCC tour of South Africa.

West Indies Revisited: The MCC tour of 1959/60, Heinemann, 1960. 288pp illus. scores, stats. An account of the 1959/60 MCC tour of West Indies.

The Compleat Cricketer: A short sketch of H. S. Altham, [Southampton, Hampshire C.C.C.], 1960. 8pp port. A limited edition of 25 copies only. First published in Hampshire C.C.C. Handbook, 1960.

The Ashes in Suspense 1962/3: Test matches of 1962/6 . . . the series in figures by Arthur Wrigley. *Daily Telegraph*, 1963. 176pp illus. stats. An account of the 1962/63 MCC tour of Australia.

The World of Cricket (general editor E. W. Swanton, associate editor Michael Melford. assistant editors Irving Rosenwater and A. S. R. Winlaw), Michael Joseph, 1966. 1165pp illus. (some col.) ports. diagrs. stats. bibliog.

Revised as:

Barclays World of Cricket: The game from A to Z (general editor E. W. Swanton, associate editor John Woodcock, assistant editors George Plumptre and A. S. R. Winlaw, statistician G. A. Copinger), Collins in association with Barclays Bank, 1980. x, 662pp col. frontis., illus. stats. index.

New and revised edition: Willow Books in association with Barclays Bank 1986.

Cricket from All Angles, Michael Joseph, 1968. 328pp illus. ports. scores. Selections from his writings for the *Daily Telegraph* from 1946.

Sort of a Cricket Person, Collins, 1972. 318pp illus. ports.

— another ed. Sportsman's Book Club, 1974.

— paperback ed. Fontana/Collins, 1974. 301pp

— reprinted ed. Pavilion Books, 1989 [v]. 318pp illus. index.

Swanton in Australia with MCC, 1946 to 1975, Collins, 1975. xix, 252pp illus. ports. scores, stats.

— paperback ed. Fontana, 1977.

Follow On, Collins, 1977. 288pp illus. ports. This is a sequel to *Sort of a Cricket Person.*

— another ed. Sportsman's Book Club, 1978.

As I Said at the Time: A lifetime of cricket (edited by George Plumptre), Willow Books, 1983. xvii, 542pp illus. scores, index.

— paperback ed. Unwin, 1986.

Gubby Allen: Man of cricket, Hutchinson/Stanley Paul, 1985. xiii, 311pp illus. scores, index.

Kent Cricket: A photographic history 1744–1984 (with Christopher H. Taylor), Ashford (Kent), Birlings, 1985. 44pp illus. (some col.) scores.

— 2nd ed. Geerings, 1988.

The Anglican Church, from its origins to the present: A layman's sketch, with foreword by His Grace the Archbishop of Canterbury, Canterbury Diocesan Board of Finance, Communications department, Diocesan House, 1988. 29pp illus.

Back Page Cricket: A century of newspaper coverage, Queen Anne Press, 1987. 208pp illus. facsims, scores, index.

The Essential E. W. Swanton: The 1980s observed (edited by George Plumptre), Collins Willow, 1990, 318pp index.

Arabs in Aspic, 1935–1993, Boundary Books, 1993. 158pp illus. stats. ports. index. Introduction by Tony Lewis.

— limited edition of 50. Signed by E.W.S. & T.L.

Last Over (with David Rayvern Allen), Richard Cohen Books, 1996. 285pp illus. ports. index. An anthology of Swanton's writings interspersed with biographical outlines and new comment.

— limited edition of 90, Boundary Books, 1996. Signed by both authors. Foreword by Tim Rice.

— paperback ed. 1997.

Cricketers of My Time: Heroes to remember (the *Daily Telegraph*), André Deutsch, 1999. 240pp illus. port. index. A celebration of a century of cricketers.

— limited edition of 100, Boundary Books, 1999. Signed by E.W.S.

— paperback ed. 2000. Foreword by Lord Deedes. Two printings with different covers.

E. W. Swanton: A celebration of his life and work, by David Rayvern Allen, Richard Cohen Books, an imprint of Metro Publishing, 2000. 446pp illus. ports. index. An amalgamation of *Last Over* with remembrances of his friends and associates. Foreword Rt. Hon. John Major CH.

— Paperback ed. Metro Publishing, 2002. New foreword by 'Dickie' Bird.

Jim's various tours to the West Indies inspired some souvenir programmes cum booklets at different centres. The tour to the Far East undertaken by him with a team under his name also attracted booklets:

E. W. Swanton's Commonwealth XI in the Far East, 1964, Holywell Press, Alfred Street, Oxford. 12pp. Pre-tour. Outlining team, itinerary and fixtures, postal addresses, tour guarantors.

Penang Cricket Association, E. W. Swanton's Commonwealth XI cricket tour, 18–19 March, 1964, at Penang Sports Club ground. Penang, the Association. [1964] 28pp adverts. illus. ports. Pre-tour.

Malayan Cricket Association, E. W. Swanton's Commonwealth XI visit to Singapore, March 20–25, 1964. Souvenir programme. Singapore, the Association. [1964] 56pp adverts. illus. ports. Pre-tour.

Selangor Cricket Association welcomes on behalf of the Malaysian Cricket Association, E.W. Swanton's Commonwealth XI, 26–30 March '64. 72pp booklet, adverts. illus. ports.

Royal Bangkok Sports Club, E. W. Swanton's Commonwealth XI v. R.B.S.C., the R. B. S. C. ground, Bangkok. 8th April, 1964: Souvenir programme. Bangkok, the Club, 1964. 32pp adverts. ports.

There was also a booklet produced on the occasion of Jim's 80th birthday in 1987:

Eighty – Not Out, An interview broadcast by the BBC between Cliff Morgan and E. W. Swanton, OBE, recording his eightieth birthday on 12th (sic) February 1987. Esher, Penmiel Press, 1987. 16pp frontis. A limited edition of 110 numbered copies signed by Edward Burrett, designer and printer of the booklet.

E. W.S. (1907–2000): The Last Interview, David Rayvern Allen. Christopher Saunders, 2000. 16pp. Edition limited to 93 copies, numbered and signed, of which 90 copies (numbers 4–93) were for sale. Interview recorded, 6 January 2000.

Index